BUDDHA in Central Asia

Sunita Dwivedi is a keen photographer, an avid traveller and a journalist by profession, having worked in several dailies including *The Times of India*, *Hindustan Times*, *The Pioneer* and *Northern India Patrika*. She left a full-time job in 1997 to pursue her passion for travelling and photography on the Silk Road through Asia and Europe.

A post-graduate in English Literature from Lucknow University, she completed her schooling from St Mary's Convent, Allahabad, and Bachelor's and Master's in Education from Allahabad University.

She has authored two travelogues—*Buddhist Heritage Sites of India* and *In Quest of the Buddha: A Journey on the Silk Road*. This is her third historiographical travelogue on the Buddhist sites in Central Asia from Afghanistan to Kazakhstan.

BUDDHA in Central Asia

~A Travelogue~

SUNITA DWIVEDI

RUPA

First published by
Rupa Publications India Pvt. Ltd 2014
7/16, Ansari Road, Daryaganj
New Delhi 110002

Sales Centres:
Allahabad Bengaluru Chennai
Hyderabad Jaipur Kathmandu
Kolkata Mumbai

Copyright © Sunita Dwivedi 2014

Map copyright © Arrt Creations 2014

Photos courtesy: Author archives (unless mentioned otherwise)

All rights reserved.
No part of this publication may be reproduced, transmitted,
or stored in a retrieval system, in any form or by any means,
electronic, mechanical, photocopying, recording or otherwise,
without the prior permission of the publisher.

ISBN: 978-81-291-3467-7

First impression 2014

10 9 8 7 6 5 4 3 2 1

The moral right of the author has been asserted.

Printed by Gopsons Papers Ltd, Noida

This book is sold subject to the condition that it shall not,
by way of trade or otherwise, be lent, resold, hired out, or otherwise
circulated, without the publisher's prior consent, in any form of binding or
cover other than that in which it is published.

*In memory of
Devi Saraswati,
my mother,
who instilled in me hope
and courage
to mark my own journey in life*

Contents

Foreword	ix
Author's Note	xi
Prologue	xvii

Section One: Afghanistan

Afghanistan: Gateway to Central Asia	3
Travels in Kabul	6
At the National Museum of Afghanistan	18
Giant Buddhas of Bamyan	30
In Search of Naubahar Monastery	47

Section Two: Tajikistan

Routes into Tajikistan	63
The Great Reclining Buddha at Dushanbe	66
Buddha along the Kafirnihon and Vakhsh Rivers	76
Monastery of Ushtur Mullo	92
To the Monastery of Ajina Tepe	103
Penjikent: The City of Divastich	113

Section Three: Turkmenistan

Routes into Turkmenistan	127
In the Desert City of Ashgabat	130
The Dragon Mosque at Bagabat	142
Parthian City of Nisa	150
Monastic Site of Ancient Merv	165

Section Four: Uzbekistan

Routes into Uzbekistan	183
A Spring in Tashkent	185
Samarkand: Heart of the Silk Road	203
To the Oasis of Bukhara	217
To the City of Khiva	232
The Stupas of Termez	246
In the Valley of Ferghana	262

Section Five: Kyrgyzstan

Routes into Kyrgyzstan	279
Gods of the Osh Caves	282
The Mountain Road to Bishkek	290
Chuy: The Valley of the Buddha	294
To Ak-Beshim and Balasaghun	306
On the Banks of Lake Issyk Kul	317

Section Six: Kazakhstan

Routes into Kazakhstan	333
Buddhist Rock Art on Almaty Highway	336
Ivory Buddha of Talgar	351
To Kayalik in the Footsteps of Rubruk	363
Journey to Sauran, Turkistan and Otrar	377
Epilogue	397
Acknowledgements	399

Foreword

The journey of Buddhism from India into Central Asia along the Silk Routes is a fascinating story. The Indians have been in concourse with the Central Asians for several millennia. They have been the closest and the oldest neighbours with whom Indians had historical relations for generations. This book recapitulates the threads of old linkages with Central Asia—an extended neighbourhood of India.

During the first half of the first millennium AD, Central Asia had grown into an important centre of Buddhist culture; and besides being a halting place for Indian and Chinese monks, it served as a transmitting centre for new ideas and technology. The routes starting from north-west India in those days passed by Hadda and Nangarhar (Jalalabad) and reached Bamyan before crossing the Hindukush into the Amu and the Syr Darya regions. We need to revive these routes between India and Central Asia to enhance regional cooperation.

Sunita Dwivedi has researched almost all Buddhist sites and produced a volume which combines historical narratives with a contemporary travelogue. She gives graphic details of the varied Buddhist sites in Central Asia and Afghanistan.

In an age torn with conflict, war and tension, the message of Buddha remains a source of inspiration.

I commend Mrs Dwivedi for her scholarship. I am sure this book will be of interest to scholars, policy-makers, diplomats and decision-makers in India, Central Asia and Afghanistan as well as students of Buddhism and Central Asia around the world.

(Padma Bhushan) K. Santhanam
President, India–Central Asia Foundation

Author's Note

Travelling with the Buddha

My journey along the ancient routes through India, China and Central Asia in essence has been a journey with the Buddha. A long, long time ago, I had left 'Kusinara', my home in a remote village of eastern Uttar Pradesh, to follow the fragrance of the Buddha. I was a lay traveller who nurtured the dream of tracing the routes that carried the wisdom of the Buddha...of seeking the hidden layers of the Buddhist past of many modern cities. And of photographing the ruins of Buddha Viharas and the objects that were dug out by archaeologists and displayed in the museums around the world.

It was to the neighbouring land of Nepal that I first turned. Apart from the metalled roads that ran through the borders at Bhairahawa and Birdpur, there were river and mud tracks that led from the villages of Kakrahawa and Koilabasa along the Buddhamarg into Lumbini—where, on a Vaisakha Purnima, the Great Buddha was born over 2500 years ago.

Surprisingly, the mud tracks and pebbled pathways between India and Nepal still exist and trading of grains and vegetables still flourishes along these border villages. The ancient routes from India to its north-western regions (now Pakistan), which ran towards Afghanistan and other countries of Central Asia is, however, shut to common travellers; roads leading to the northern and north-eastern regions of Xinjiang and Tibet (both in China) are also not in use or have withered away. There was a time when village markets were held in these border regions and inhabitants freely walked into neighbouring lands.

These were the strands of the Silk Road that bound together diverse cultural regions. They formed the conduit along which ideas and faith travelled. The intoxicating fragrance of the Dhamma that rose from the land of India spread far and wide along these very routes. It was along the southern Silk Road dropping from China and passing through the north-eastern regions of India that the Mauryan emperor Asoka is believed to have travelled to the Yunnan capital Talifu/Tali/Dali in the 3rd century BC. Here he is believed to have married a Chinese princess Chien-meng-Kui, whose descendants ruled over Yunnan.[1]

Royal princes abdicated their throne to follow the 'Noble Precepts' of the Buddha. Great scholars thronged monastic centres of India and Central Asia to study Buddhist texts. They became the dhammadutas and mahamatras of the Buddhist ideology. Even great emperors bowed before the Buddhist monks and scholars from the 'Western Regions'. It is said that whenever Kumarjiva, the great Central Asian scholar of Indian descent, delivered a religious discourse, kings kneeled down beside his seat, so that he could step on their knees to reach his seat.[2]

Lokottama or An Shih Kao, a Parthian prince, abdicated the Arsacid royal throne and the luxuries of palace life to don the orange robes of a monk. The famous scholar Ghosaka, born in Tokharistan, played a prominent part at the fourth Buddhist Council at Purushapura. Likewise there were many Parthian, Tokharian and Sogdian monks who preached the message of the Buddha.[3]

The geographical spread of Buddhism was far, far beyond the borders of India. It spread against the wind, the mountains, over the seas and across the horizon. It went along the craggy Uttarapath and followed the gigantic network of the Silk Routes, reaching the desert and oases settlements of Central Asia and to the faraway land of China. It travelled across the giant Himalayas, to the heights of the Pamir and the Tien Shan. As far as the valleys of the Ili, Lepsi, Karatal, Talas, Talgar and Sumbe rivers in Kazakhstan and the Chuy river valley and around Lake Issyk Kul in Kyrgyzstan.

Renowned Buddhist centres arose not only in the green valleys of Ferghana along the Syr Darya (Jaxartes) in Uzbekistan and along the banks of the Oxus and its tributaries in Tajikistan, but also in the hot deserts of the Karakum and the Taklamakan.

Central Asia showed the way to the world. It provided the first disciples of the Buddha who, on returning to their lands, built the first stupas on the Buddha's relics. Many of the first missionaries carrying the message of the Buddha were 'unrivalled' native scholars of Central Asia. Great kings like Devmitra (Demetrius), Milind (Menander) and Kanishka, who favoured Buddhism, belonged to Central Asia.

The Dhamma of the Buddha changed the hearts of kings and conquerors like the mighty Macedonian conqueror Alexander the Great and the Mongol leader Genghis Khan. When Alexander the Great, in the 3rd century BC, halted on the borders of India, he is said to have taken away a great treasure from the land of the Indus—a *sramana*—the meditating monk Kalanos who preached Nirvana.[4] Genghis Khan is said to have halted in the land of the Indus where he had reached in pursuit of Jaladdin, son of the Khoresmian ruler Sultan Mohammmad in the 13th century. After seeing a 'Bodhi deer', Genghis Khan was convinced that India was a sacred land and could not be conquered. He retraced his steps after taking with him two Buddhist monks to his capital Karakoram.[5]

Some of the biggest institutions of Buddhist learning existed in Central Asia. There was a time when pilgrims, instead of coming straight into India, halted at the Central Asian monastic centres for special studies in Buddhism. At the monastic centre of Naubahar in Balkh, the Chinese pilgrim Hiuen Tsang stayed for a month. Other renowned Buddhist centres lay in the deserts of the Karakum at Merv, in the lap of the Hindukush at Bamyan, on the road to India at Kapisa, and Gandhara.

Most Buddhist centres of Central Asia were made of rammed earth and unbaked bricks. Being exposed to the elements of nature, they are crumbling. The site of Dalverzin Tepe near Termez was several feet underwater following rains, when I reached there. The Buddhist site of Arytam near Termez is now a levelled ground. When I arrived at the Friendship Bridge at Termez in 2007, I was shown a completely furrowed land in place of the Buddhist temple.

At Merv, the Gyaur Kala monastery has not been seen by anyone in recent times. Some believe that the hill on which the monastery was built may have been levelled. Neither has the giant Buddha head, a part of a colossal statue, been seen in the museums of Ashgabat or Mary. The famed Ajina Tepe and the Kafirnigan monastic centres, built of clay, are braving the fury of nature in the valleys of the Vakhsh and the Kafirnihon. Nearly all signs of a monastery are missing at Ushtur Mullo. I had to cancel my trip to the grand monastic centre of Khisht Tepe in Tajikistan whose outlines (according to reports in Dushanbe) could barely be traced over the ground. The Buddhist centres of Bukhara (whose name itself is believed to have been derived from Vihara) and Samarkand exist only in the pages of al-Narshakhi's *History of Bukhara* and Hiuen Tsang's memoirs *Si Yu Ki—Records of the Western Regions*.

The monastic sites that once reverberated with chants of the monks are gradually merging into dust. Soon they will become a thing of the past. In the *Buddha in Central Asia* I have recorded the last leg of my journeys into the past that lingers on in these crumbling ruins.

References

1. Sobhan, Rehman. *Rediscovering the Southern Silk Route: Integrating Asia's Transport Infrastructure* (Dhaka: The University Press Ltd., 2000), p. 2
2. Chaudhuri, Saroj Kumar. *Lives of Early Buddhist Monks: The Oldest*

Extant Biographies of Indian and Central Asian Monks (New Delhi: Abha Prakashan, 2008), p. 100
3. Puri, B.N. *Buddhist Tradition Series: Buddhism in Central Asia* (Delhi: Motilal Banarsidass Publishers Pvt. Ltd., 2000), p. 94, 100
4. Manfredi, V.M. and Halliday, Iian (trans.). *Alexander: The Ends of the Earth*, Volume 3 (London: Pan Books, 2002), p. 459, 475
5. Warikoo, K. (ed.) and Soni, Sharad K. (ed.). 'India and Mongolia'. *Mongolia in the 21st Century: Society, Culture and International Relations* (New Delhi: Pentagon Press, 2010), p. 107

Prologue

This book is reminiscent of the dream-space of Emperor A'soka, whose global vision is unique in the annals of India. As viceroy at Taxila, the cultural heart of the Gandhara region, he was close to trans-Gandhara (Uttarapatha) or the Central Asian kingdoms where his dharma-vijaya found a brilliant efflorescence in later years. Mrs Sunita Dwivedi as a daughter of Kushinagar—the capital of the Mallas where Lord Buddha transited from this world into the dharmakaya—finds her mind roaming in the trans-Gandharan regions, once highlighted by Buddhism as a way of values, dotted with great monastic centres and stupas, richly endowed libraries of sacred texts and profound philosophical treatises, as their literati created the immensity of the East Asian diction.

The acculturation of the ferocious tribes of Central Asia was commenced by A'soka when he sent his ministers to Khotan to establish a kingdom. The Chinese nidana of the blinding of A'soka's son, which was translated in AD 391 by Dharmanandin, says that his empire comprised Kucha (Watters 1904: 1.59). Imperial pennants of A'soka flew over Gandhara, and it is natural that Sunitaji should begin her travelogue from Afghanistan.

The Afghans are mentioned by Varahamihira (early 6th century) as 'Avagana', and repeated by Hiuen Tsang in Chinese transcription (*Ap'o-kien*). Gandhara is the only region which gives name to one of the seven notes of Indian music as GA (*sa re ga...*). This travelogue is fascinating in its evocative description of contemporary life in the six countries traversed by the author. She begins her odyssey in quest of the footprints of Lord Buddha by a flight to Kabul. The most ancient reference to Kabul is in the hymns of the Rig Veda. Kabul as her first destination is true to her name 'Dwivedi' which refers to the two Vedas: Rig Veda and Sama Veda. This journey of an Indian to Central Asian countries—the Serindia or 'India of the Silk' of the Roman historian Procopius—kindles new sensitivities of the phylogeny of time.

The cool of Kabul, the mountain pass of Paghman, its orange ice-lolly, roaring gush of the river, the tombs of the mother, sister, wife, favoured begums of Babur, and finally, of Emperor Babur himself, recall the glories of this historic capital where he finally based his kingdom. The remains of the Buddhist city of Mes Aynak belonging to nine centuries (1st–9th century AD)—with two monastic centres with richly ornamented shrines, hundreds of statuettes, and coins of Kushan kings—bring up the glories of classical Afghanistan. Sanskrit manuscripts on palm leaf, use of the Gupta script, Lord Siva as the tutelary deity of Kujula Kadphises, the founder of the Kushan Empire—are thrilling experiences written in the simple flow of Sunitaji's narrative.

She describes her visit to the National Museum, its reconstruction, the alms bowl of the Buddha, statue of Kanishka from Surkh Kotal, murals from Kakrak, Bamyan, Nangarhar, Dalverzin Tepe, ivory statuettes and other amazing antiquities. It is a reassuring thought that the contributions of the forefathers of the Afghans are treasured for understanding the cultural outflow that gave rise to the glories of distant China, Korea and Japan.

The preservation of Bamyan by experts from France, Italy, Germany and Japan; the setting up of a site museum, a database of all the objects in the National Museum of Kabul; and a Japanese artist recreating the Bamyan colossi using laser beams—all read like a travel in the wonderlands of the mind. In the vast void of 'sunyata', the author celebrates small fragments of a lost immensity. In the words of Yogini Ekavajra:

In the volume of sky-like emptiness
Write with letters of pure awareness and wisdom.

The book gives a bird's-eye view of the important Buddhist sites of Afghanistan, beginning with Bamyan, its cave shrines, the efforts to find the 1000-feet Buddha in Nirvana, the colossal statue of Lord Buddha at Kakrak, the original home of the Kakkars. Balkh or Bactra—'the armoured city' from Persian *bakhtar* 'armour'—where Alexander married Roxana, the charming daughter of a nobleman; where Trapusa and Bhallika put up the world's first Buddhist stupa with the hair and nail pairings of Lord Buddha, which had 100 convents with 3000 monks during the visit of Hiuen Tsang, and other such treasures are a dazzling sweep of time in the words of Sunitaji, which will tempt any reader to visit these hallowed spots by the first flight. The massive stupas at Top-e-Rustam and Takht-e-Rustam in the Samangan province; are they the ancient Navbahar? Navbahar is the new (Nav) bahar (Vihara, monastery) of Vajrayana with the concupiscent charm of the images of Buddhist goddesses. The blue-tiled Blue Mosque is the most sacred shrine of Afghanistan as the mausoleum of Ali, the cousin and son-in-law of the Prophet. Blue is the colour of meditation in Buddhism; layers of time owned in the amnesia of centuries.

The scene shifts to Tajikistan known in Sanskrit through the astrological work *Tajika-nilakanthi* which is used in our days for horoscopic calculations. In the capital Dushanbe, she describes the largest 12-metre-long reclining Buddha whose feet she touched in reverence. When I saw it in 1967, it was whole; later it was cut into parts for transmission to the Hermitage Museum, and is now back in Dushanbe. It represents the Nirvana School based on the *Mahaparinirvana-sutra*. This sutra maintains that the dharmakaya is eternal and Buddha's nature is inherent in all beings. These teachings were expounded by Lord Buddha immediately before his Nirvana. The reclining Buddhas represent the state of Nirvana endowed with four virtues of eternity, happiness, the true self and purity. The author continues with her walk along the Rudaki Street, visit to the Gissar Fortress and to a caravanserai, and then heads to the museum to photograph the Hindu–Buddhist antiquities. It is a rich repository of seals with dharani-mantras, votive stupas, Buddha heads from different monastic centres: Ajina Tepe, Kafir Kala, Kalai-Kafirnigan, and Penjikent. A four-armed goddess astride a lion is Simha-vahini Durga, the palladium or guardian of the State. Uma and Maheshvara (not Siva and Parvati) and Narayana and his consort are from the Buddhist Mantrayana.

The author recalls the busy life of the monks of the monastic town of Kafirnihon whose many rooms with their corridors and niches in ruins have been victims of Arab forces. She speaks of the Sacred Temple to the Oxus river where a bronze figure of a Greek god playing a double-barrel flute was discovered. Antiquities found here are on view at the museum in Dushanbe. More than 2000 gold and silver coins of the 4th–3rd century BC were discovered in 1887 and are well preserved in the British Museum. Ancient cultural treasures belong to humankind and their conservation and study are more important than possessive instincts of nations. The Greek name Oxus is from the Sanskrit Vakshu from the root vah 'to flow', meaning the 'fast-flowing river'. As the Greek alphabet does not have a letter for 'va' it was substituted by 'o'. So vakshu is derived from oxu plus the final s for the nominative case forms Oxus. It is mentioned in the *Brahmanda* and *Matsya-puranas*, as well as in the *Mahabharata*. The king of Vakshu came to the sacrifice of Yudhishthira on donkeys that were sturdy like horses. On a visit to the Oxus, I made it a point to see these donkeys that are really strong riding and draught animals.

A salient feature of this work is a delightful and engrossing reading of difficult trips to the classical Buddhist sites after crossing bureaucratic hurdles. The congregation halls, stupas, fragments of icons, architectural elements of monasteries at Ushtur Mullo, Kafir Kala, Kurgantube and Khisht Tepe, remind one of centuries when these lands were blessed by philosophy, sacred sutras, exquisite hieratic architecture, sculptures, both colossal and votive, mural paintings and scrolls on silk and other fabrics. These lands were vectors of the highest intellectual attainment of India to the celestial empire of China. The colossal reclining Buddha hallowed the Ajina Tepe monastery as a symbol of saving beings from undulations that surge violently and silently against the shores of the illusion-clad human continent.

The author has a detailed description of Penjikent whose last ruler Divastich made a strong resistance to the Arabs in the 8th century. His archive of Sogdian documents was discovered on Mount Mugh. Penjikent was conceived on a pentad plan ('penj' five) like the five Tathagatas of Mantrayana. The ruins form a pattern of four clearly demarcated areas: the ruler's citadel, town proper (shahristan), suburban settlement and necropolis. The fifth should have been the sacred monastic area. It is an exceptionally preserved archaeological site to study the plan of the town, its architecture, advanced construction techniques and has yielded the greatest quantity of pottery of different types, including kitchen and tableware. The Mugh archives have official documents, diplomatic reports, marriage contracts, financial records, besides fragments of astrological, medical and mineralogical texts. It is the richest site in monumental art of wall paintings, woodcarvings and clay sculptures. An attractive little scene illustrates a fable of the *Pancatantra:* a hare frees the animals from the tyranny of the lion by his persuasive eloquence that induced the lion to jump into a deep lake. In a sense it refers to the hope of freeing the kingdom from the tyranny of lion, a stark metaphor for the tyranny of the Arabs.

The art of Penjikent emerged from the temple and the palace and took an important step to relate it to the general body of citizens. Bussagli speaks of the infusion of Gupta art in natural development of traditions inherited from Kushan art. A four-armed goddess discovered in the second temple in 1964 relates to Nanaia whose name has been found on coins minted locally. The Indian name Nanaka means a son born by the blessings of this goddess.

The last ruler of Penjikent, Divastich, fled the city pursued by the Arabs and sought refuge on Mount Mugh but was slaughtered in AD 722, and that was the end of Sogdian culture. By a happy coincidence, in the 1930s, Soviet archaeologists discovered that the Sogdian language was spoken by the residents of the Yagnob Valley. The Tajiks are their descendants, who have lost all memory of the cultural excellence of the Sogdians, their paintings, their metalwork, their textiles, their sculptures, and their flamboyant expressions of prosperity and power. A small ivory head of Alexander found at Dushanbe attests to a settlement as far back as the 3rd century BC.

An 8th century mural from Penjikent XXII has been named Vesparak in Sogdian letters. It is equal to Is'varaka, attested by the Copper Ladle Inscription from Taxila datable to the first century AD. The hand sketch of the mural illustrated below (from Guitty Azarpayl, ed: *Sogdian Paintings*, Berkeley, 1981, p.29, fig. 5). He is clad in armour, holds a trident, and has three heads and six arms. All the three heads have the third eye on the forehead. The leonine head on the left is the Narasimha face of Harihara, while the boar face on the right is Varahamukha. The pelts with heads covering the shoulders are the Vyaghra-carma 'tiger skin' of Harihara. The identification is confirmed by a Sogdian fragment of the end of the dharani: Aryavalokitesvara Nilakantha, found by Sir Aurel Stein from Tun-huang Ch0092. It is in Sogdian and Brahmi scripts. Nilakantha Siva at Penjikent was a guardian of the State. It is clear in the version of Amoghavajra who hailed from Sogdiana and invokes him to bring the small princedoms under the control of the State (Shigrahm vasham me rashtram sarajakam kuru).

Turkmenistan came into being in 1990 when its Parliament passed a resolution of sovereignty and it gained full independence from the Soviet Union in 1991 under the present name. It has yielded the earliest traces of human settlement in Central Asia in Palaeolithic times, but the Turkmen entered the area in the 11th century. About nine-tenths of the land is desert. Its Karakum sand desert is one of the world's largest. The main rivers are Oxus (Amu Darya), Tedjen, Murgab and Atrek. Oxus is the westernmost river to have a Sanskrit name Vakshu (as discussed earlier). It is

Sketch of Is'varaka from Penjikent XXII.1-dharani

mentioned in the *Sabhaparva* and *Bhishmaparva* of the *Mahabharata*. Murgab, the 'river of Merv', retains the ancient Sanskrit name of Mriga, which occurs in Avesta as Maurva, and as Margu in the Achaemenian inscriptions. Murg was the medieval name of Merv. The eleventh chapter of the *Bhismaparva* of the *Mahabharata*, describes the Sakadvipa in which it says that the Brahmanas were present in large numbers among the Mrigas (brahmana-bhuyisthah mrgah).

The capital Alexandria Margiana was founded by Alexander the Great on the Margus river and rebuilt by Antiochus Soter (ruled 280–261 BC) when it was destroyed by the barbarians. It was ruled by the Achaemenians, Parthians, Sassanians, Arabians and others in its ever-changing fortunes. Buddhism was its major cultural expression and the present narrative goes into details to trace this heritage, unfortunately under constant destruction. She speaks of the capital Ashgabat with its forests, orchards, flower gardens, as a hill station in the sprawling surrounds of the sandy desert. Monumental institutions are being built in this glittering oasis city by Indians, with the most beautiful marble from India.

Dragon Mosque at Bagabat (modern Anau), built in 1456, has dragons from the non-Islamic past. The dragons are shown with flowers in their mouth to indicate that the evil of paganism has been reduced to submission.

She also describes Nisa, the ancient capital of Parthia, a place of prime importance among Hellenistic sites in western Central Asia. It has yielded 2500 inscribed sherds in the Parthian language written in the Aramaic alphabet. They are records of wine from various districts to the royal wine cellar dated to the 2nd–1st century BC. It was built by Mithridates and was known as Mithridatkert or 'the city of Mithridates'. The Arsacid dynasty gained power in Parthia about 247 BC and ruled until its overthrow by Ardashir in AD 224. Their beginnings correspond to the reign of Emperor A'soka who ruled about 268–232 BC. The Parthian prince An Shih Kao gave up the throne, donned the Buddhist robes, and became the first master to translate the Sanskrit texts into Chinese. The Chinese remembered him as the Parthia(An) Lokottara(Shih Kao) master. The Lokottaravadins consider the Buddha as a supramundane being. He must have brought a large collection of Sanskrit sutras from his native land of Parthia. The author speaks of other monks from Pallavabhoga 'Pallava country' (compare Pahlavi) who participated in the consecration ceremony of the great stupa under King Duttagamini (108–77 BC). Buddhism could have been introduced in Parthia by the monks of the A'sokan period.

It is a delight to read through the glorious episodes of Parthian victories, their sanctuary for guarding the eternal fire (akhanda jyoti) in the Round Hall, colossal towers imposing even in ruins, and the goddess of Nisa of white marble—clad in a long dress and a sash across the breast in the National Museum, ivory objects as elephantine links with India, and the 'Madustan' winery found in a building adjacent to the ancient royal treasury. Huge wine jars from this winery are treasured in the National Museum. The Chinese General Chang Ch'ien who travelled to Ferghana and Sogdiana in 128 BC says that the Parthians have wine made from grapes. He took its seeds, and the Son of Heaven or the Emperor of China was the first to plant the vine in fertile soil.

Sunitaji's prose becomes the vibrating awareness of the silence of time when she speaks of the magnificent city of Merv, the Mrigah of the *Mahabharata*, the Margiana of the Greeks, and the Murg of the Iranians. Sanskrit mriga (pronounced mruga in Maharashtra to this day) becomes 'murg' or cock in modern Persian. Vessels from Gonur citadels to analogues of Harappan objects, residues of ephedra reminding of soma in the Rig Veda, but above all the plenitude of Buddhist monasteries as at Gyaur Kala, stupas, statues, manuscripts of Buddhist sutras in Sanskrit inscribed on birch bark reveal the widespread of Buddhism in this land. This book is a stunning aesthetics of tranquil and serene karuna and prajna—compassion and wisdom—of the Prince of Peace, Lord Buddha. The evocative words of Sunitaji in the hushed agony of ruins are stepping stones of the path to the mind-house. Her words recall an ancient poem: 'What a wonderful lotus it is that blooms in the calyx of the heart'. From the fall of Merv to the Arabs in AD 651 to the discovery of a Buddhist monastery in 1890, it is a long journey to renew our memories of a time when the Parthians discussed philosophical texts in Sanskrit, their hearts being the very eloquence of the Buddha. The author dropped coins in the deep waters of the sardoba to make a wish. The Turkmen believe that those who throw these coins are blessed by saints: an ancient Buddhist practice still prevalent among the Buryats of Transbaikalian Siberia who drop coins in Lake Baikal to earn 'punya'.

The details of Buddhist antiquities at Erk Kala, Gyaur Kala, Sultan Kala, the rich holdings of the museum at Mary, a painted vase for storing a text of the *Vinaya* dating to the 5th century and much more has been narrated for the first time. She is beyond words in the dream to see the head of the Giant Buddha, alas gone in the utter silence of dogma.

Here we are with the author in Tashkent, the glamorous capital of Uzbekistan. Tashkent has the suffix 'kent' for city, which is mentioned by Panini 4.2.142 for the ending of the names of the cities in Usinara. The Ka'sika commentary on Panini mentions Tashkent as Daksikantha. Tash means stone in Turkish, and Buddhist monks from Tashkent bear the ethnicon Chih or 'stone' in the Chinese Tripitaka. Kalpana-manditika of Kumaralata (of 2nd century AD) tells of the piety of a painter from Puskalavati who went to As'maka ('stony') or Tashkent to decorate a Buddhist monastery. The people of Tashkent are mentioned in the *Mahabharata* as Kanka, which means stone (compare Hindi 'kankar'), and also in the *Bhagavata-Purana* 2.4.18. Al Beruni's *Ta'rikh al-Hind* is the second work in which the name Tashkent occurs, after the Ka'sika commentary. At one point of time, Tashkent must have been a famous centre of Buddhism and an important seat of political power and economic prosperity. Modern Tashkent with its parks, ornate hotels, and the History Museum come alive in the words of the author. She saw a Buddhist statuette from minguruk at the museum, but it was no longer there on her second visit. Destruction is an ongoing process. Hiuen Tsang speaks of Buddhism in this country.

She refers to Tashkent being in the Chirchik oasis, watered by a tributary of Syr Darya. The Kalacakra-tantra was promulgated on its banks where it is named the Sita river. His Holiness the Dalai Lama has been giving it empowerment over the years. The author spent the evenings in Tashkent sitting on a bench in front of the statue of Timur who took a wife from the clan of Genghis Khan and wanted to restore his empire. He had a strong reverence for Sunni Islam and has been remembered as a supremely charismatic figure for centuries.

Khiva, with its 10th century minaret of the Juma Mosque, has carved wooden pillars from India with svastikas and elephant-head (representing lord Ganesa). The great grandfather of Prime Minister Rajiv Gandhi studied here. Feroze Gandhi was of Persian descent and Persians studied in the madrassas at Khiva. In the museum of Avesto at Ichon Kala she saw a fragment of the Avesta written in gold letters on bull skin. Alexander the Great saw 12,000 such bull skins in golden letters.

The author's quest of Buddhism in Khorezm led her to a terracotta Buddhist statuette of the 1st century AD found in the Kazakliyatkan site in 1999.

The author heads to Bukhara in search of Buddhist monasteries whose sacred icons might be in the museums and in the quest to see the ruins of Viharas. Sitting in Paris, George Roerich was overjoyed to discover that Bukhara is the word Vihara. It was confirmed by Paul Pelliot, the great savant of Central Asian history. She saw the mausoleum of the founder of the Samanid dynasty, the 1718 Bolo Hauz mosque of the Bukhara emirs, and the execution square where British officers were murdered by the emir: a story narrated in *The Great Game*. Buddhism was dominant in Bukhara according to Narshakhi's history. Buddhist icons were sold here as one of the Samanids had become a Buddhist after marrying a Chinese princess.

Samarkand was the second important metropolis in the 6th century BC. King Vishtaspa had the copy of the Avesta written in letters of gold and preserved in the Stronghold of Records at Persepolis. Another copy containing all the 1200 chapters in 2,000,000 verses, inscribed on golden tablets, was kept in the treasury of the fire-temple at Samarkand. These archetype copies, preserved with zealous care, were destroyed in the invasion of Alexander when he burned the palace at Persepolis and conquered Samarkand. The excavations of Macedonian tombs have brought to light rich caches of gold which were sought for in vengeance by Alexander's hordes.

Samarkand became the heart of the Silk Route. Archaeological evidence at Tepe Afrasiab confirms Hellenistic presence. According to the Annals of the Wei Dynasty compiled in AD 437, a dynasty of the Yueh Chih had been reigning here before the Christian era. Hiuen Tsang visited Sa-mo-kian in AD 630 and he found two abandoned Buddhist monasteries. From the Han period onwards, it was called K'ang-ku. A number of monks from Samarkand translated Sanskrit sutras into Chinese:

- K'ang Chu in AD 187
- K'ang Meng Hsiang worked at Loyang in AD 194-199
- K'ang Seng-k'ai alias Sanghavarman in AD 252
- K'ang Seng-hui, worked from AD 247-280
- K'ang Tao-hu, translated a sutra in AD 396
- I-tsing gives the biography of Sanghavarman of K'ang who went to China on foot during the Tang dynasty, came on a pilgrimage to Mahabodhi where he carved the images of Buddha and Avalokitesvara under an A'soka tree.

The last Buddhist pilgrim to India, Hyech'o (born AD 704) from Korea, says that there was one monastery in Samarkand, with one monk who did not know how to revere the Triratna.

The author mentions the visit of Hiuen Tsang, whose discourses on Buddhism so impressed the king that he requested to be ordained as a monk. In the 10th century, the western gate of Samarkand was Naubahar, a nostalgic memory of the glories of the Navavihara of Balkh. There were many Navbahars or Vajrayana monasteries in Iranian lands. As late as the 13th century, the Naubahar was celebrated in Persian poetic themes. Poets like Gorgani, Ayyuqi, Onsori, Manucehri, Farroqi Seystani and others employ similies pertaining to the moon faces of the images and to the grandeur of the buildings of Naubahar. Yakut evokes the Vihara in describing the royal palace, and compares the beauty of human faces to the moon-faces (mahruy) of the concupiscent images of the Vajrayana goddesses in Naubahar.

The grace and charm of Buddhist images, particularly of the enchanting Tantric goddesses in all their concupiscence gave the equation 'ideal beauty=Buddhist image', which was an established fact in the East Iranian world. Even when Buddhism had faded away, early Persian poetry continued to cultivate abstract mental forms poignantly recalling the grace of Buddhist statues. Ayyuqi, in his novel *Varqe va Golshah* (Tehran 1956: 6), writes of his beautiful heroine that: 'she was...a Buddha in a temple full of offerings'. Further, we find the crescendo in stanzas 2138–2142, where she is addressed as *Bot* (Buddha), then *lo'bat* (statuette), and finally as *nowbahar*, the Buddhist monastery which was well known for its graceful statues in Iranian literature (both in Persian and Arabic languages) up to the time of Yaqut in the 13th century. In early Persian poetry, young beauty whether masculine or feminine, is constantly referred to by the poet or addressed by various characters in their romance as *Bot* (Buddha). Early Persian literature, as we know it, is a creation of the Eastern Iranians and till the 11th century, Persian poetry was exclusively written in Khorasan, Sogdiana, and adjacent lands—areas once steeped in the Buddha. The Buddhist overtones of Persian poetical vocabulary were memories of a time when the images were loaded with their full emotional and aesthetic import. No wonder that the metaphor of the *Bot* is the term that the description of beauty spontaneously calls for.

The author writes about a votive terracotta plaque with a Buddhist image discovered at Sattepa, Brahmi and Kharosthi inscriptions on monastic wares, the graffiti at Shatial Bridge on the Indus in Sogdian. Today, Samarkand is the city of Timur. In 1967, I saw a small relief of Durga riding on a lion at the top of the gateway of the Bibi Khanum Mosque constructed by Timur. Samarkand fascinates the author and every page is a temptation to feel with her the landscape and mindscape of this metropolis of history.

The author travels to the village of Ayrtam, famous for the frieze of male and female musicians. It is 20 inches high and 23 feet long. Its Bactrian inscription dates back to the Kushan King Huviska (around AD 164–174). Her narrative is a journey into Kushan history. She finally reaches the sites of Kara Tepe and Fayaz Tepe in Old Termez. Hiuen Tsang says that there were twelve monasteries and about 1000 monks in Ta-mi or Termez. A Buddhist monk from Tar-mi-ta is mentioned in the Tibetan Kangjur. In AD 689–90 Termez was conquered by the Arab Musa.

In the archaeological remains, we can have the feel of the stupa, the beautiful paintings and sacred sculptures of Fayaz Tepe 'the mound of liberality', where people could go to get their wishes fulfilled long after it lay in ruins. The Kara Tepe 'Dark Mound' of the 2nd century has caves which constituted the monastic complexes from the 2nd to the 4th century. There are Indian inscriptions on pottery. An inscription gives the name of this monastery: Khadevaka Vihara or 'Sovereign's Monastery'. Kha-deva means the Son of Heaven (kha). Kushan, post-Kushan and a large hoard of Hepthalite silver coins have been found. There are inscriptions on ceramic vessels and graffiti scratched on the walls of the rooms in different languages. Inscriptions on ceramics are in Brahmi and Kharosthi. For example, an inscription on the southern wall of the southern corridor in Complex B reads: Mahe'svaradharmasya. An interesting inscription on a jar reticulated with glass reads: *ayam' pa(ni)-'yo-kumdika buddha'si[-] da(jh/l)aka-mahadharmakatha*. It means: 'this water jar (belongs to) Buddha'sira, the great exponent of the daljh/laka (school)'. Buddhasira is Buddha-*misira*=Buddha*mihira*. The Mishra jati of the Brahmans is this *misira* (*mihira* from mitra 'sun'). It is the most ancient occurrence of the word Mishra. The doubtful reading of the second syllable as 'jh' or 'l' has to be corrected from Pali vedalha/vedalla that were mahasunyatavadins, also known as uttarapathakas or the School of the Trans-Gandhara region. This inscription is the earliest reference to them. Termez played a major role in Buddhism and it needs a detailed study.

The great academic traditions of Termez continued even under Islam. In the 9th century, Abu Isa Mohammad (AD 825–892) authored a great collection of 'hadith' for which he travelled widely in Khorasan. The episodes begin like Buddhist sutras: 'Thus I have heard'. There are other stylistic resemblances to show how deeper cultural layers lived on. The mausoleum of the Sufi philosopher

Al Hakim al-Termezi of the 9th century composed over 400 works including the life episodes of the Holy Prophet. Sunitaji went inside his mausoleum to pay homage. While Buddhism no more sanctified the place, it became the sanctum of another faith and bore a rich harvest in its new incarnation.

The author takes us to Ferghana's horses, wines and sweet melons in its picturesque setting. In ancient India it was known as Kamboja, celebrated for its horses in the *Mahabharata* and also mentioned in the Girnar and Dhauli edicts of A'soka. Emperor Wu-ti (140–87 BC) sent Chang Ch'ien in 138 BC who saw divine horses of Dayuan or Ferghana. An anonymous poem of the Han dynasty speaks of the superb courage and marvellous spirit of these horses prancing through floating clouds. The horse of Lord Buddha is named Kanthaka, from kantha (modern kent) referring to its Central Asian origin.

The author speaks of the image of the goddess of Kuva (a nagara devi) and Sridevi to whom a whole chapter is devoted in the *Suvarnabhasottama-sutra*. As a flourishing trade centre, Kuva should certainly have paid homage to the goddess of wealth. It was discovered from the Buddhist temple. Likewise we find a number of votive plaques of Lakshmi in Nalanda for the monastic centres are patronized by rich merchants for blessings. A twice life-size image was recovered from the depths of the temple. This massive clay bust with the third eye represents the Buddhist Nilakantha Avalokitesvara worshipped to this day in all the monasteries of East Asia. Images of ferocious deities of Vajrayana and ceramic bowls for offerings speak of the vogue of the compassion of the Tathagata. Few fragments of its wall paintings that have survived show that the *Vinaya* injunction of decorating monasteries was adhered to.

She takes us to the silk city of Margilan, which Babur praises for its excellent apricots and pomegranates. It dates back to the 2nd century BC. Thereafter, we are in the great religious centre of Kokand 'City of Winds' where stands the palace of the last Khudayar Khan (AD 1845–76) and the Jam-e Masjid built in 1814. It had 300 mosques in medieval times. She evokes the splendour and intense love of Babur for his birth town of Andijan. In her words, we behold the soul of these towns, once Buddhist and now Islamic, wonderful in their modern life and radiant in their hearts in silent in-dwelling piety and tranquillity.

The sacred mountains of Osh in Kyrgyzstan, rock paintings in a cave deep in the belly of the a mountain, a trek to Babur's cave refuge where he worked out the strategy to win back his kingdom and the Chuy Valley speak of times that created history. Archaeological diggings recall the Dharma of the Western Turks. As the Arts Centre of Novopokrovka began to sink, archaeological excavations were carried out. They yielded the head of the Buddha, Buddhist bronze figurines, and the structures could have been a monastery. At Krasnaya Rechka were discovered two Buddhist temples with a monumental Reclining Buddha of the late 7th century, and fragments of birch bark manuscripts in Sanskrit. Clay fragments of the limbs of a Buddha point to a six-metre high statue. The monastic centre of Navekat yielded a gilded bronze sculpture of a Buddhist monk.

Hiuen Tsang reached Suyab in AD 629 and expounded the Buddhist doctrines to the Khan, who became a devotee. The Buddhist shrine of Suyab belongs to the 7th to 8th centuries. An image of an eleven-headed Avalokitesvara from the Chuy Valley is prized at the State Historical Museum at Bishkek. Mother earth treasures the way-faring of the Tathagata, and this is touchingly expressed in the book: 'time can never obliterate Buddha from history, or from the mind of believers'.

Finally, the author takes the reader to Kazakhstan to see the Tamgaly of the Bronze Age through paintings on the rocks, and the 8th-century Buddhist petroglyphs on the mountains. Buddhist deities were carved on treeless cliffs with the mantras 'Om Mani Padme Hum' written under them in Tibetan. In a gorge near Taygak village, again the same mantra in the Tibetan script has been written by passing travellers. She has found ruins of a monastery on the right banks of the Sumbe river with inscriptions on stone, which was functioning in the 19th century. In May 1859, Golubev stayed in this monastery which had 30 monks. An ivory image of the Buddha was found in the Talgar village. Excavations in Kayalik had remnants of a Buddhist temple. Gulnara, who accompanied Sunitaji, chanted what she believed to be a Sanskrit mantra, as the smoke of the fire touched the stupa in the Kora Valley. Gulnara explained the mantra: we are one with the sky and earth. Altai people worshipped the sky as a god and the deities of towns for protection from evil forces.

Haunting descriptions of the pilgrimage, rather than a travelogue to the six republics of western Central Asia are an invitation to their enchanting landscape, friendly people, where Indian monks and merchants once spread the message of compassion as well as enriched the lives of the people with material goods. All those cultural strands have been erased, monasteries destroyed, and local languages replaced during the second millennium.

This book is a far journey to the inner regions of ourselves, a feat uniquely rare as very few Indians have written or will write about these lands. Reading through the book, I was reminded of the travels of the Chinese envoy Chang Ch'ien in the 3rd century BC, of Hiuen Tsang and I-tsing, and many Indian acharyas who have left no record of their dreams. This recount is deep in history, flowering in the wrappings of life, as the dynamic and divine resonate in the onrush of the future. Today it rests on their historic evolution: No flowers can forget the spring.

Professor Lokesh Chandra
Director, International Academy of Indian Culture

Section One

AFGHANISTAN

Afghanistan: Gateway to Central Asia

On the world map, Afghanistan might seem like a tiny blob, but take a step back into time and the nation suddenly acquires gigantic historical importance. Standing at the crossroads of world civilizations since the days of the Persian Empire, Afghanistan has been one of the most significant stretches along the Silk Road, with crucial trade routes converging and passing through here to every direction of the world. Not surprisingly, it served as a conduit between India and Central Asia, China and Russia.

Afghanistan was the hub where a hundred flowers bloomed and a hundred routes congregated and a million trades happened. The tiny nation absorbed ideas and art forms from various quarters and transformed and disseminated them in all directions. In history, Afghanistan was both significant and magnificent. Without it, the history of the Silk Road would be incomplete.

Older routes came across the Oxus river from the Caspian region and from the territory that is now Uzbekistan into Balkh and also from Tajikistan into Kunduz; from India across the Indus into Gandhara; from Persia into Herat; and from China into the Wakhan. West of Peshawar (now Pakistan) in the foothills of the Sulaiman Range of the mighty Hindukush begins the famous 50-kilometre-long Khyber Pass that once nurtured the caravan route from north-western India into Afghanistan.

During the reign of Sher Shah Suri (1540-1545), the ancient Uttarapath, or the Mauryan Highway from Taxila to Pataliputra and Tamluk, was developed into the Grand Trunk Road. This new road ran from Kabul, crossed the Khyber Pass, and through Peshawar ran up to Chittagong (now in Bangladesh) on the Bay of Bengal. Today, the Grand Trunk Road remains the main link between Kabul and Peshawar. The modern crossing point from Pakistan into Afghanistan is at Torkham, from where the road passes through Jalalabad, once the site of numerous Buddhist shrines.[1]

The Taxila-Bamyan-Balkh road was in ancient times the main route from India into Central Asia. For centuries, the trade to and from India flowed along this route and then dispersed globally. The principal trade route from India passed through Taxila and then through the Khyber Pass to Bamyan and finally across the Hindukush to Balkh. From Balkh, the highway led east along the Wakhan Corridor and through the Pamirs and the Tarim Basin along the Kashgar, Yarkand or Khotan routes into China. Another route from Balkh ran northwards into Termez, in modern Uzbekistan; or eastwards through Kunduz into Shahrituz in modern Tajikistan, and onwards into all parts of Central Asia. Westwards, the route from Balkh ran through the Karakum desert into the land of Merv, in modern Turkmenistan.

It was through this network of trade routes that the message of the Buddha reached the territory of Afghanistan, where it was assimilated and where it flourished in huge monastic establishments in Kabul, Bamyan and Balkh, to name only a few. Buddhism was depicted and glorified in art forms and thence carried into the lands across the Oxus and the Pamirs, taking those areas by storm and evoking a movement of temple building and monastic constructions. It is believed by scholars that Buddhist art originated in Gandhara (eastern Afghanistan) in the second or the first century BC under Hellenistic influence and lasted until the 5th or the 6th century AD. It is from here that it spread northwards into Central Asia and eastwards into China.[2]

References

For routes into Afghanistan see: Tucker, Jonathan. *The Silk Road: Art and History;* Puri, B.N. *Buddhist Tradition Series: Buddhism in Central Asia;* Thapar, Romila. *The Penguin History of Early India: From the Origins to AD 1300*

1. Tucker, Jonathan. *The Silk Road: Art and History* (New Delhi: Timeless Books, 2003), p. 55. Also see, map: p. 55
   Thapar, Romila. *The Penguin History of Early India: From the Origins to AD 1300* (New Delhi: Penguin Books India, 2003), p. 183
2. Puri, B.N. *Buddhist Tradition Series: Buddhism in Central Asia* (Delhi: Motilal Banarsidass Publishers Pvt. Ltd., 2000), p. 297-298

Travels in Kabul

Romance of the Khyber Pass, which I happened to pick up at a seminar at the Jamia Millia Islamia, a central university in Delhi, filled me with hope and imagination. I dreamt of taking a slow train across the high mountains of the Sulaiman Range through the Khyber Pass into Afghanistan. The esteemed Pakistani historian and author, Professor Ahmad Hasan Dani, gives a picturesque account of the historic pass through the centuries, a pass that ushered in many an invader into the Indian subcontinent. The narrative takes the traveller on a journey from the caravanserais and the *Qissa-Khwani* bazaar (the market of story-tellers) of Peshawar to *Serai Hindian* (the Hindu Serai) in Bukhara across the Khyber.[1]

Before I could put a foot into Afghanistan, I was in a quandary; caught between an adventure on a bumpy road and growing wings to fly into Kabul. I could have opted for the direct Taxila-Torkham-Jalalabad route—an exciting, low-cost, overland journey into Afghanistan, but I was advised against this short but daring entry into the land of my dreams. The endless wait, entailed by the journey along this route due to visa problems, also threw a spanner on my romance with the Khyber.

Wisdom prevailed. I grew wings and took a flight into Kabul. Not just into Kabul, but also to other sites on the main Kabul-Bamyan-Balkh route that touches the Friendship Bridge near Hairatam (a counterpart of which lies on the other side of the Oxus near Termez in the village of Arytam).

As I slumped back into the aircraft seat, I remembered the rounds I had made of the Afghanistan Embassy in New Delhi before I could actually meet M. Jalili, the consular head. I wanted to walk through the Buddha Route in Afghanistan and enquired if I could get a visa. Jalili kindly consented. And lo! As if in a blink, he granted me a 30-day visa. I was elated and grateful to Jalili for his kindness. Another moment spills out of my memory. At Arytam, a few years ago, I had waited long for permission to cross the Oxus, but in vain. I had to return after a few shots of the village where a Buddhist shrine had been discovered. But this time, I was lucky.

A Picnic on the Kargha

As the aircraft hovered near Kabul, the glaciers on the high ranges of the Hindukush soared into view, beautiful and majestic. The thick layers of blinding white snow paradoxically promised secure and safe travel, since the melting snow (according to my friends in India) brings down the slopes not only rivulets which lend an emerald hue to the land, but also the much-dreaded Taliban out of their mountain hideouts. Thankfully, I was in Afghanistan when summer was still a few weeks away.

I breezed through immigration. No forms to be filled, no questions asked. I almost walked through the counters. At the waiting lounge, Fauzia and Ahsanullah, my hosts, were waiting. My trepidation melted with Fauzia's warm embrace as if we were long-lost sisters, though it was my first meeting with her. We headed straight to the Karte Parwan area of Kabul city where she lives with her husband, the renowned Dr General Mussa Wardak, Afghan Ministry of Defense Surgeon General.

Kabul seemed to be reeling at 21 degrees Celsius; for me, it was a pleasant respite from the sweltering heat of Delhi. People here thronged the streets and drove bumper to bumper throughout the day, culminating in major traffic snarls everywhere by the evening. It was a bustle of humanity, and in the busy restaurants and hotels, multi-cuisine buffets were laid out to the live music of the rabaab.

I landed in Kabul on a Thursday evening. The following day, all government and private establishments were closed for Juma, when all of Kabul seemed to be on a picnic, rushing to the recreational spots on the outskirts of the Afghan capital.

Fauzia, Doctor Sahib and I set out for the Kargha Lake. Taking the road through Karte Parwan towards the snow-covered Paghman hills, we drove through the famous Baharistan, the watering hole of Bollywood lovers, and the Bagh-e-bala and Afshor localities. I mistook the hills for the Hindukush but Fauzia corrected me. These were merely the foothills; the majestic mountains lay further beyond. The city seemed to be sitting in a big bowl cut into the hills. The air was refreshing but the road was cluttered. Cars, buses, three-wheelers, carts and mini trucks—all laden with countless men, women, children heading towards the leisure spots of Kabul.

The leisurely, devil-may-care mood in Kabul took me by complete surprise. All of Kabul was on a picnic. Several gun-toting youths with blue eyes and black/brown/golden hair, dressed in salwar-kameez, were guarding large establishments and hotels on the Kargha Road, which is flanked by rows of malls, hotels, wedding halls, multi-storey apartments and residential colonies. Massive buildings and huge compounds of the Afghan Civil Services Institute, the Red Cross Hospital and, further down the road, the imposing building of the Afghanistan Military Academy, lie near the Kargha block. Many private and technical universities and training centres have mushroomed to provide education to the Afghan youth. Kite-fliers and footballers littered the open-air compounds, street corners, markets and by the malls. At the Pul-e-Sangin gateway, people were busy playing cricket in the terraced fields.

The Kargha Lake is a pool of blue in the midst of beautiful gardens—apricot trees with white blossoms, kikor bursting with purple bloom, and the naked grapevine erupting into bunches of green leaves over long wooden trellises covering the verandah of every restaurant, hotel and roadside choykhana (tea house). Cartloads of turnips, carrots and radishes were being washed in narrow streams that overflew from the Kargha Lake. In spring, Kabul basks in its abundant waters.

We arrived at the multi-storeyed four-star Kargha Palace Hotel, much of which is an open air boulevard restaurant hemmed by circular gardens with vines. Within a week or two, the small bunches on the bare vines would become emerald branches of efflorescent climbers, turning the hotel into a large grape garden with bunches of the succulent fruit hanging over the heads of the visitors.

As we sank into the luxuries of the Kargha Palace Hotel overlooking the lake, a huge black storm began to brew outside. The blue lake started turning a dark violet, reflecting the darkening skies. The vacationers left the lake and took shelter in small yurts or camps in the surrounding gardens. Meanwhile, inside the large dining hall of the hotel, lunch was being served. Three young waiters walked in with large white metal platters loaded with delicious Kabuli dishes—Kabuli pilaf, aubergine with tomatoes, lentils, shashlik on long iron skewers, naan and bottles of Coke. As the storm blew outside and a sharp drizzle hit the lake, we dug into the steaming pilaf and melt-in-the-mouth aubergine.

The Kargha Lake was a cherished project of the late president of Afghanistan, Daoud Khan. The Paghman river, gushing out of the mountains, was dammed at Kargha, some 20–30 kilometres away, creating this beautiful site on the outskirts of Kabul. Its crystal-clear waters lend the lake its shimmering blue hue and the neighbouring golf course adds a stroke of green. Many restaurants, choykhanas and hotels have now come up along the shores of the lake and it has become the favourite picnic spot for the Afghanis who converge on the lake every Friday.

At the Zahir Shah garden, the holiday scene was a frame out of a miniature painting. Afghan families had pitched their tents under blossoming apricot trees. While the men indulged in a game of football or cricket, children played hide and seek among the ruins of the Shah's palace grounds. The enormous structure of the king's palace with surrounding gardens and streams is under renovation and will soon be opened to the public.

To the Paghman Darrah

Our final destination was the Paghman Darrah. On the way, we stopped at the high portals of bright yellow painted Aman Takhi mosque, which was built in 1919 by the first president of Afghanistan, King Amanullah Khan. History tells that us that he also built a cinema on the low hills in the gardens around the mosque but it was reportedly burnt down by the mullahs. Adjacent to the mosque is the memorial for the heroes of the War of Independence.

We were soon in Paghman Bazaar where despite the cold, people were guzzling Paghman 'lassi' which was full of cream and flavoured with saffron, sold in bottles that had been cooled in the icy waters of the Paghman river. Young boys holding trays of lassi were running to every car that slowed down at the bazaar. As we approached the Darrah (a pass between the mountains), we bumped into more lassi and ice cream sellers. Orange 'chuski', or a traditional ice-lolly, was a bestseller. So were strawberries and apricot jelly.

In the gardens surrounding the Yellow Mosque was a children's park where a toy train was doing the rounds. The garden was full of picnickers. We failed to find any parking place so we drove ahead to the bazaar.

After taking a round of the Paghman Bazaar, we headed straight to the Darrah. But not before taking shots of the massive Arch of Victory, the Paghman Gate or Taq-e-Zafar, the famous arch built after the Afghan victory of 1919 over the British then ruled by King George V. Near the mosque was another favourite spot on the bridge over the river, where Bollywood actor Feroze Khan danced while shooting for his film *Dharmatma*. On the other side of the bridge lay the impressive Salamkhana School.

On both sides of the Paghman–Darrah Road lie farmhouses which are built around bungalows. The farmhouses are surrounded by orchards and dairy farms that supply Paghman Bazaar with the fresh dairy products out of which the famous lassi is made.

The Paghman hills still had a hint of snow but the lower slopes were covered with apricot, plum and walnut trees. Soon, the loud, roaring gush of the Paghman river drowned all noise from the heavy traffic. It was like a great roar of nature as the river rushed through the pass and flowed down the mountains into the narrow valley below. The view of the river escaping like a white sheet of water from the mountains is stunning. Large divans or takhts had been placed over boulders along the river banks to enable visitors to dip their hands in the water and enjoy the great scenic beauty of the snowy peaks, the roaring river and the dense forest.

Dozens of shops had been set up here. The choykhanas had large samovars to heat water for tea, tandoors were set up for baking fresh naan, and huge fires had been lit for making the favourite Afghani 'boloni' (stuffed parantha). The locals were filling plastic containers with river water for drinking. Much of the water from the Paghman goes to a laboratory for bottling to be sold as mineral water.

We crossed the wooden bridge over the river and went through a hilly tract to the other bank where we occupied a divan whose legs were dipped into the river. From our perch, we could dip our hands and touch the icy waters. Soon, a choykhana sent some piping hot black and green tea with boloni and kebabs and also some sheer fera (similar to Indian barfi). Some divans had been set up under willow trees which had been decorated with cages holding fancy forest birds like the 'kaok'. At several points over the river, wooden planks had been set up as bridges.

Several gypsies were roaming the hills of Paghman. Their dress was different from the Afghanis—they wore what looked like a skirt that reached just above the ankles and a dupatta that did not cover the head. They went from one divan to another, mixing freely with the people, asking for money, joking and laughing.

They had collected quite a lot of food from the shopkeepers and money from the visitors and were gesticulating wildly and dancing over the bridge.

Bagh-e-Babur

It was difficult to trace the numerous gardens on the Kabul hills mentioned by Gul-Badan Begum in the *Humayun Nama*.[2] Their names could have changed over the centuries. Their landscape could have altered. The gardens mentioned by the daughter of the first Mughal Emperor Babur teemed with orchards, shady trees, flowers, running streams, and fountains. These were sometimes turned into residences for the begums, or love nests for the princes who went there accompanied by their harem. They could also be used as royal reception and audience chambers and points from where caravans started for their long journey on the trade routes. Caravanserais were occasionally built near the base of a hilly garden where the travellers could drink from flowing streams and rest for a while before departing to the next halt.

Some of the famous gardens of Kabul mentioned by Gul-badan Begum are the *Bagh-i-khilawat*, the *Bagh-i-nau-rozi*, and the *Bagh-i-orta*, where Humayun sometimes set up camp; the orange gardens in the mountain passes near Kabul visited by the princes with their harem; and the Bagh-i-wafa somewhere on the outskirts of Kabul. Many gardens were gifted by Babur himself to favoured begums. The Bagh-i-khilawat was gifted to Sultan Begum Bayqra, Babur's elder sister, for her residence in Kabul. Many gardens became memorials for the Mughal prince and princesses, like the Bagh-i-nau-rozi where Kutlugh Nigar Khanum, the mother of Babur, was laid to rest. The tomb of Gulrukh Begum, Babur's wife, also stands here.

It was in these luxurious surroundings that the Emperor Babur (AD 1483–1530) wished to be buried. It was the tradition of Mughal princes to develop pleasure gardens during their lifetime and choose one of them as their last resting place. Having initially been buried in Agra, where he died in 1530 at the age of only 48, Babur's body was moved to Kabul in the beautiful hill gardens of Bagh-e-Babur a decade later.[3] It is said that during his rule in Kabul, Babur used the Bagh as a guesthouse for special occasions, especially during the summer season, when the cooling spray from the streams and the fountains, perfumed by the numerous flowers growing on the hills, brought much relief from the heat and dust of Kabul.

Babur's great-grandson Jehangir is said to have erected a marble headstone that still stands today alongside the graves of Babur's son Hindal Mirza and one of his grandsons. Babur's tomb is surrounded by a marble lattice enclosure, outside which grow shrubs that gently bestow confetti of purple flowers on the tombs. A gateman at the mausoleum holds a thick picture book which he opens to show you for a small remuneration. In it are photos and hand-drawn pictures of the Babur mausoleum through the ages, a record of the repairs done, and the names of famous visitors to the site. Just below the mausoleum is the Shahjehani Mosque, where even today, thousands gather to offer prayers. Set a bit apart from this area is a viewpoint building from where visitors can gaze at the vast gardens and the streams flowing into numerous pools along the avenue.

Today, the hills and gardens of Bagh-e-Babur are incredibly beautiful. In spring, the garden is full of flowers. As you walk up the terraced hills of Bagh-e-Babur, you see the variety of aromatic shrubs that spread their fragrance along the avenues, the cascading waters of some hilly stream channelled from the hilltop to the base, children playing in the green manicured lawns and old and young couples enjoying a peaceful evening.

Water flows down the length of the garden, as it did in Babur's time. A new caravanserai has been built on the pattern of an old one at the base of the garden. Remains of the ancient gateway built by Shah Jehan have also been preserved. A notice in the park and wall illustrations at the viewpoint, detail the excavations and restoration of the park.

It seems Babur had a special liking for the river of Ferghana—

the Syr Darya. His love for nature remained with him even while he was in exile and dreamt of ruling Samarkand. So much so that when he planned to set up a kingdom elsewhere in Afghanistan or in Hindustan, he desired a place by the side of a river and a kingdom like Samarkand with gardens and fountains, tall trees and various kinds of flowers.

When he finally laid out his kingdom in Kabul, he created the Charbagh on the hills by planting trees. Nature to him was like poetry. In the *Baburnama* we read about the extreme beauty of the Gulbahar hills, the plains of Baran and the plateau of Chash Topa—all areas known for their lush greenery and a great variety of tulips, rendering Kabul a paradise in spring.[4] Babur loved springtime excursions into the Gulbahar and Baran. He also writes about four lovely meadows around Kabul. It was one such beautiful hill, full of fruit and shady and flowering trees and natural streams, which Babur developed into a park for recreation. The elevation of the garden and flowing streams probably prompted Babur to go for an avenue garden, shaded on both sides by flowering and shady trees and where water was channelled into a narrow canal running from the terraced hills into pools at intervals.

To the beautiful homeland of Babur at Andijan in the Ferghana Valley and his favourite resort in the cave mountains of Osh was thus added another chapter of a garden memorial at Kabul. Kabul was to compete with Andijan in both beauty and authenticity. While Kabul saw the actual remains of Babur being brought home and buried, Andijan got only a few handfuls of the earth from Agra. Kabul fulfilled the wishes of Babur in giving him a kingdom that he so desired, by the side of a river with an unmatched beauty like Samarkand. The Ferghana Valley could only give him exile.

References

More on Babur: Begum, Gulbadan. *The History of Humayun: Humayun-Nama*; Also see: Lamb, Harold. *Babur the Tiger: First of the Great Mughals;* Thackston, W.M. *The Baburnama: Memoirs of Babur, Prince and Emperor*; Lane-Poole, Stanley. *Rulers of India*

1. Dani, Ahmad Hasan. *Romance of the Khyber Pass* (Lahore: Sang-e-Meel Publications, 1997), p. 10-11
2. Begum, Gulbadan and Beveridge, Annnette S. (trans.). *The History of Humayun: Humayun-Nama* (Delhi: Low Price Publications, 2003), p. 8, 21-27, 103
   Also see: Lamb, Harold. *Babur the Tiger: First of the Great Mughals* (Dehra Dun: Natraj Publishers, 2003)
3. Lane-Poole, Stanley and Hunter, W.W. (ed.). *Rulers of India* (New Delhi: Low Price Publications, 2005), p. 200
4. Thackston, W.M. *The Baburnama: Memoirs of Babur, Prince and Emperor* (New York: Modern Library, 2002), p. 243

A Buddhist City near Kabul

Historians and archaeologists from the Afghan Institute of Archaeology and the Délégation Archéologique Française en Afghanistan (DAFA) are currently excavating the massive Buddhist city of Mes Aynak, 38 kilometres south-east of Kabul and spread over a vast area of a thousand hectares around the Baba Wali mountains where copper mines are located.

Since 1963, the site has being continuously studied and explored by the Afghan Institute of Archaeology in collaboration with DAFA and UNESCO's team of archaeologists and historians. Emergency excavations and documentation at the site are currently in progress on a war footing—the Chinese Mining Company, MCC, has a contract to extract the world's largest copper reserves in large open-cast mines, which pose a greater and more imminent danger to the historical and religious treasures buried in these hills.

It is believed that two millennia ago, the city of Mes Aynak was part of the flourishing kingdom of Gandhara, ruled by a Buddhist king. Large-scale construction of monasteries and shrines at Mes Aynak began, according to Afghan scholars, as early as the 1st century, when the site was ruled by the Kushans whose kingdom extended up to the Ganga basin. This was the time when the territory of Afghanistan was the melting pot of various cultures, Greek, Persian and Indian. From this churning arose the glorious art of Gandhara taking the Buddhist world by storm.

The Afghan Institute of Archaeology has identified the remains of the Buddhist city as belonging to the Kushan period up to the late Shahi period (1st–9th century AD). The site lay on the main trade route to India and the great wealth derived from its silver and copper mines and international trade on the Silk Road financed the wealthy decorations of the monastery. The huge quantity of artefacts excavated from the site also shed light on the Buddhist art of the Kabul region.

Archaeologists have discovered two large monastic centres, namely the Gol Hamid and Kafiriat Tepe. Within the centres are monk cells with domed ceilings and richly ornamented shrines in courtyards. Hundreds of painted clay statues of the Buddha, bodhisattvas and donors have been discovered. Painted representations of the Buddha and bodhisattvas have also been found on the walls.

According to the National Museum (*Mes Aynak: New Excavations in Afghanistan*), several clay images of the Buddha seated on rectangular podiums were discovered in the courtyard. There are stone reliefs portraying scenes from the Buddha's life. In one chapel were found a three-metre-long Reclining Buddha and a seven-metre-high Standing

Buddha. From a second chapel was recovered a five-metre-high Standing Buddha. A wooden sculpture of a seated Buddha has also been unearthed here.

The archaeologists are working to preserve, catalogue and scan three-dimensional images of hundreds of statues of the Buddha and his worshippers, stupas, paintings, coins and ceramics which have already been found there.

Nicolos Engel, vice-president of the DAFA, whom I met at the National Museum at Kabul, said that only a small area of the Buddhist city has as yet been uncovered. Engel said it may take several years to excavate the city. The Red Zone, demarcated by the Afghan authorities for early completion of excavations, itself may take another year. The efforts by the archaeologists may, however, save at least two monasteries out of the several that are believed to lie beneath the surface of the earth.

(Based on the author's interviews with Dr Omarakhan Massoudi, director of the National Museum of Afghanistan at Kabul; Dr Nicolos Engel, vice-president of the DAFA; exhibition publication of the National Museum of Afghanistan, *Mes Aynak: New Excavations in Afghanistan,* asmuth druck + crossmedia gmbh & co. kg, Germany, US embassy in Kabul, Serindia Publications Inc., Kabul, 2011.)

At the National Museum of Afghanistan

I had long wished to see the National Museum of Afghanistan, considered to be the most important museum in Central Asia, housing over a 10,00,000 artefacts found during excavations carried out in various parts of the country since 1923 by Afghan, Russian, Japanese and French archaeologists.

However, the stories that I had heard aroused my enthusiasm. I was told the National Museum of Afghanistan was in ruins. That everything had been destroyed. That there was nothing to see there. The reason given was that the museum, which has the largest collection of Buddhist artefacts in Central Asia, had suffered tremendously during the three decades of war.

Deep in my heart, however, I held on to the desire to visit the museum. I expected to see it in an 'utterly devastated' condition, as reported by most books on Afghanistan. But the moment I stepped into the National Museum, my jaw fell. It was not in ruins. It was not devastated. What stood before me was a grand double-storey building in the Darul-Aman area, which also houses the palace of the late King Amanullah Khan. The location was calm, peaceful and beautiful. Rows of flower beds bordered the museum building.

Before I entered the building, I was led into a security cubicle, where a female guard frisked me gently. I was then led inside to meet the director, Dr Omarakhan Massoudi.

Dr Massoudi is a kind man and has a great love for India. He spoke fluent English and answered my questions about Buddhist antiquities. After a short interview, I walked around the museum with Mr Fahim Rahimi, the chief curator. I came to know that since 2002, approximately 15,000 works of art, including 8,500 from outside the country, have been returned to the National Museum. This was good news for me.

I had no other engagements for the day and decided to spend all of Saturday at the museum. More than anything else, I wanted to linger in the divine halls of the Buddha: to gaze at the Gandhara statuary art decorating the alcoves in the corridors and the mural paintings of Buddhist deities from the Bamyan and Kakrak Valleys hanging along the stairways.

I stood at the double door entrance of the museum, on the marble stairs, and was transported into a bygone era—the era of pre-Islamic Afghanistan. The first sight to greet my eyes was a huge replica of the cave of the Bamyan Buddha, donated by a Swiss company. The colossal Buddhas of Bamyan, made of stone and clay, are believed to have represented the glory of classical Afghanistan. Tragically, this heritage was destroyed by the Taliban regime in 2001. The replicas in the museum are indeed impressive but that's just what they are, replicas.

The huge alms bowl of the Buddha has the pride of place. It stands in the front gallery facing the entrance, as if welcoming the visitors. The massive black marble bowl was found in 1925 at the shrine of Mirwais Baba in the city of Kandahar. It is known as the Buddha's Begging Bowl because of the lotus flowers carved on its underside. Two Persian inscriptions in Arabic script were etched on it later. The inner inscription, dated 1490, lists rules and regulations of the Kandahar madrassa (religious school). We also find mention of the Buddha's Begging Bowl at a monastery in Kashgar while reading about the life of monk Kumarjiva who tried to lift the bowl but could not. The Archaeological Survey of India has procured impressions of the six-line Persian inscriptions on the Buddha's Begging Bowl, the 'Bhiksha Patra', claimed to have been used by the Buddha at Vaishali.

Dr Phani Kant Misra, Regional Director, Archaeological Survey of India (ASI), Kolkata, along with Dr G.S. Khwaja, Director-Incharge Epigraphy (Arabic and Persian), ASI, Nagpur, had gone to Kabul to inspect the bowl. He revealed to me that the bowl came quite close to the Begging Bowl of the Buddha. This was supported not only by circumstantial evidence but also matched well with the description given by the Chinese pilgrims in their memoirs. The bowl is believed to have been carried away by the Kushan ruler, Kanishka, to Peshawar and later to Kandahar in the 2nd century AD.

It has 24 delicately carved petals of the lotus flower. Of these, six are untouched and in their original shape, pointing to the antiquity of the vessel. The Persian inscriptions had been superimposed on it at a later date, said Dr Misra.

We learn from the narratives of the Chinese pilgrims, Fa Hsien and Hiuen Tsang, that after the Nirvana of Buddha, his *Bhikshapatra* (Alms Bowl) came to a monastery in Peshawar where it was in the care of the Buddhist sangha and worshipped for many centuries. It was predominantly black in colour with a bright and glossy lustre, its thickness being about a fifth of an inch. The bowl is believed to have moved about from place to place, passing mysteriously through the air and working miracles for the good of the people. After traversing many countries it reached Persia.[1]

Such bowls made of single, huge pieces of limestone or marble were generally kept at the gate of monasteries and khanaqas of saints to symbolize the renunciation of life.

Back in the museum, the statue of a Kushan grandee, a royal personage, perhaps Kanishka, the great Kushan emperor, stands against the pillars of the hallway. The statue was found at Surkh Kotal. Kanishka (AD 127–151) was an ardent follower of Buddhism and had convened the Fourth Buddhist Council in Kashmir. Near the statue hangs the famous Rebatak Inscription written on a stone slab. Discovered in 1993 by the governor of Baghlan, the stone inscription dates back to the 2nd century AD and was translated by Nicolos Sims William. The historic inscription on limestone, in the Bactrian language written in the Greek alphabet, mentions that 'Kanishka the righteous' obtained his kingship from 'Nana and other gods'. It also mentions the name of Kanishka's grandfather as Vima Takto. Two other Zoroastrian gods—Narasa and Oshasina—are also mentioned in the inscription.

The beautiful Gandharan Buddhas in clay and stone stand in tall alcoves in the walls along the staircase that takes me to the first floor of the museum. They portray the 'Miracle of Sravasti'—flames erupting from the body of the Buddhas while their feet touch the water. One is speechless by the artistry of the huge life-size images and the amazing portraiture of the Buddha—a marvel of Gandharan art.

Also hanging on the walls and in showcases are brightly coloured paintings from the Kakrak Valley, Bamyan, Dilberjin Tepe, and Nangrahar—they all depict the Buddha, his worshippers, and the Buddhist king of Bamyan. Huge khums (clay jars) stand like sentinels in the galleries of the museum. More Buddhas from Gandhara adorn the Pre-Islamic section of the museum.

The most awe-inspiring is the bust of Mother Goddess Durga, recovered from Tepe Sardar in Ghazni. The size of the original image can be guessed from the huge head of the goddess preserved in a glass case. The head of the Mother Goddess is seen as evidence that female divinities were worshipped in Afghanistan.

On entering the 'Buddhist Heritage of Afghanistan' hall, my eyes first fell upon a huge banner depicting the Guldara Stupa, found 22 kilometres south of Kabul, not far from the village of Guldara (Gol Darreh) on a high hill. It has been dated to the 2nd century AD. Gold coins date to the Kushan period, that is, Vima Kadphises (r. AD 113–127) and Huvishka (AD 150–190). I am told these were recovered along with some gold ornaments when the British explorer Charles Masson opened the stupa chamber in the 19th century and stole the antiquities, much like the theft at the Dunhuang Cave 17 in China by British and French explorers. Or for that matter the Rawak stupa inside the Taklamakan desert near Khotan, which was stealthily opened by Aurel Stein and depleted of precious antiquities. The crumbling Rawak stupa even today bears the stamp of Stein's theft in the form of a large gaping hole, big enough for a person to creep in.

A seated Buddha is often seen surrounded by apsaras, as in a schist stone painted stele portraying the *Dipankar Jataka*, preserved in the Mes Aynak hall. Coins discovered at Mes Aynak relating to the Kushan king Kanishka II have the image of an enthroned goddess, Ardoksho, on the reverse. The unique painting from Dilberjin Tepe portrays both male and female divinities (perhaps Siva and Parvati) in splendid decorations and wearing elaborately designed crowns on their head. Two large halls in the upper floor are devoted to the Buddhist heritage of Afghanistan and ongoing excavations at the Buddhist city of Mes Aynak.

The Mes Aynak halls are an eye-opener to the enormous wealth of Afghanistan obtained not only from the caravan trade of its Silk Road cities but also from the world's largest mineral riches in the form of silver and copper and precious gems like lapis lazuli and turquoise.

The amazing antiquities now find a place in the museum halls. Poster-size photographs of the on-going excavations at Mes Aynak are on display. The site is located 38 kilometres south-east of Kabul on the trade route to India. First surveyed in 1963, the official salvage excavations led by the Afghan National Institute of Archaeology started in 2009 after an agreement was signed between the Afghan government and the Chinese Mining Company, the MCC, for the extraction of copper at the site. Excavations are going on and archaeological deposits stretch over a 1000 hectares. So far, three areas of the site have been explored through excavation, namely, Gol Hamid where a Buddhist monastery was first discovered, Kafiriat Tepe with a second monastic complex, and Baba Wali which is close to the ancient mine's gallery.

The artefacts discovered here date from the Kushan and Kushano-Sassanian periods from the 1st century AD to the emergence of Islam in the 9th century. The best sculptors, painters and architects were hired and the best materials obtained to decorate monastic establishments. The vast quantity and the high quality of the coloured ceramics, wall paintings, unbaked clay sculptures and stupa reliefs, according to scholars, make Mes Aynak comparable to such historical sites as Hadda and Bamyan.[2]

The amazing statuary art from Mes Aynak on display include numerous painted clay heads of the Buddha decorated with black peppercorn curls of hair, pink pigment on the serene face, embossed 'urna' between the artistically curved eyebrows and dreamy, half-closed eyes, as if in deep meditation. Parallels can be drawn with the numerous Buddha heads excavated from the monastery of Ajina Tepe in Tajikistan.

An outstanding painted clay image is that of a female donor wearing orange robes designed with golden polka dots over which is draped a brown shawl. Her kohl-filled eyes and thinly drawn eyebrows turn up to focus on the central image in the shrine, perhaps that of the Buddha. Her hands appear close to her chest as if bearing some gift for the central deity. The gentle smile on her face depicts her blissful state.

A relief depicts the Standing Buddha in the 'abhay mudra', with the right hand raised in a gesture of blessing. The central figure of the Buddha is surrounded by bodhisattvas. Another relief depicts 'amorini' (cupids) carrying garlands of flowers, just like the relief found at Arytam village near Termez of musicians and garlanders.

A photograph of a rare painting, discovered on the walls of the Kafiriat Tepe monastery depicts the Buddha with donors. Bright pigments have been used to portray the Buddha's robes, the pillared hall and the halo surrounding his face and body.

The close intimacy shared with India is depicted on the ancient coins found at Mes Aynak. Dated from the 2nd to the 6th century AD, the coins show the image of the ruling kings (Kushan, Kushano-Sassanian or the Hephthalite) on the obverse, while the reverse has the images of divinities like the Buddha and Siva with Nandi bull and the trident. It is said that Kujula Kadphises, the founder of the Kushan Empire, favoured the cult of the Hindu god Siva. According to scholars, preference to Indian religious worship and use of Indian scripts had become a historical necessity in the context of the growing importance of Indian trade along the Oxus river.[3]

The Museum Library has some of the most precious manuscripts from the ancient sites of Afghanistan. Here, in rows of wood and glass cupboards are stocked several volumes of the Schoyen Collection of Mahayana Sutra palm leaf manuscripts dating back to the 5th century AD. There are a host of other publications on archaeology, history and culture.

Fragments of manuscript have recently been found during excavations at Mes Aynak. Nicolas Engel, in charge of the excavation site, mentions fragments of a manuscript which on first glance appeared to have been written in Brahmi.[4]

There was much, much more to see. The most famous treasures of the international Silk Road that were excavated from the ancient cities of Afghanistan are the 'Begram Ivories' and ancient Bactria's 'Gold Hoard'. These were, unfortunately, not on display in the museum halls. I learnt later from curator Rahimi that a part of the gold treasure was on international display at an exhibition in Melbourne, Australia. I was, however, fortunate to obtain a copy of *Afghanistan—Crossroads of the Ancient World* (British Museum Press, 2011) from Dr Omarakhan Massoudi. The superb photographs of the carved ivories of Begram[5] and the gold ornaments of Tillya Tepe[6] conveyed the unparalleled beauty of the artefacts and artistic excellence of the craftsmen.

The museum publication displays carved ivories found in Begram Room No. 13 that expose the craftsmanship of a superb ivory chaser. The French archaeological missions led by Joseph Hackin discovered the magnificent Begram treasure in 1939, revealing the exquisitely carved ivories from India, and the fact that Afghanistan was at the centre of the Silk Road trade.

It would not be far-fetched to assume the possibility of their being actually rolled out in workshops at Sanchi in India. Consider the theme of the 'decorative arched gateway' under which stand full-figured Indian beauties in nritya mudra (dancing pose) with exposed breasts and lower garments resembling the Indian 'dhoti'. The carved piece formed the decorative part of some wooden pieces of furniture. There is a marked similarity with the stone carvings on the torana (gateway) of the Sanchi stupa No. 1 and stupa No. 2.

The ivory statuettes found in Begram Room No. 10 of women clad in the Indian 'dhoti', wearing heavy jewellery on their bare upper bodies and standing in 'nritya mudra' on their 'vahan' (carriage) of 'makara' (crocodile) have been likened by scholars to the Indian river goddess Ganga, whose animal mount is the makara.[7] The posture of their head shows that they might be carrying water pots.

I missed the above masterpieces of Indo-Afghan (amalgamation) statuary art. Some other day, some other time, I would have waited to see the treasures with my own eyes but sadly, most have been reportedly lost in bombings over a period of time during the civil war from the 1990s.

References

Information based on: The author's personal visit to the National Museum of Afghanistan in Kabul; Information obtained from [a] The National Museum of Afghanistan publication, *Mes Aynak: New Excavations in Afghanistan*; [b] Interview with Dr Omarakhan Massoudi, director general of the National Museum of Afghanistan; [c] Hiebert, Fredrik (ed.) and Cambon, Pierre (ed.). *Afghanistan: Crossroads of the Ancient World*; and [d] Chief Curator Fahim Rahimi, National Museum of Afghanistan

1. Watters, Thomas. *On Yuan Chwang's Travels in India: 629-645 AD* (New Delhi: Munshiram Manoharlal Publisher Pvt. Ltd., 2012), p. 202-203
   Also see: Fa-Hsien, Faxian and Legge, James (trans.). *A Record of Buddhistic Kingdoms* (New Delhi: Munshiram Manoharlal Publishers Pvt. Ltd., 1998), p. 33-34

Hwui Li, Shaman and Beal, Samuel (trans.). *The Life of Hieun-Tsiang* (Delhi: D.K. Publishers Distributors Pvt. Ltd., 2001), p. 63

Tsiang, Hiuen and Beal, Samuel (trans.). *Si Yu Ki: Buddhist Records of the Western Country*, Book II (Delhi: D.K. Publisher Distributors Pvt. Ltd., 1995), p. 98-99

2. The National Museum of Afghanistan. *Mes Aynak: New Excavations in Afghanistan* (Kabul: asmuth druck + crossmedia gmbh & co. Kg, US Embassy in Kabul and Serindia Publications Inc., 2011), p. 23
3. Harmatta, J. (ed.). 'Religions in the Kushan Empire'. *History of Civilizations of Central Asia: The Development of Sedentary and Nomadic Civilizations (700 BC to AD 250)*, Volume II (Delhi: Motilal Banarsidass Publishers Pvt. Ltd., 1999), p. 318
4. Engel, Nicolas. 'The Buddhist Monasteries and Settlements at Mes Aynak Copper Mine, Logar Province'. The National Museum of Afghanistan. *Mes Aynak: New Excavations in Afghanistan* (Kabul: asmuth druck + crossmedia gmbh & co. Kg and Serindia Publications Inc., 2011), p. 4, 20
5. Hiebert, Fredrik (ed.) and Cambon, Pierre (ed.). *Afghanistan: Crossroads of the Ancient World* (London: The British Museum Press, 2011), p. 162, 188,189
6. *Ibid.*, p. 218, 243, 247
7. *Ibid.*, p. 162

Interview
Status of the Buddhist Antiquities

Dr Omarakhan Massoudi is the director of the National Museum of Afghanistan at Kabul. In this interview, he discusses the current status of the Buddhist sites in Afghanistan.

SD: What is the present status of the world's biggest Buddhist site at Mes Aynak?

Massoudi: Many, many objects have been excavated by the current teams at the Mes Aynak site. Massive stupas and big statues of the Buddha have been uncovered. However, the biggest problem is of transportation and storage. It is not easy to bring all the objects to the National Museum. They are mostly made of clay and are fragile, hence their excavation and restoration is a difficult task that can be done best at the site itself.

The government plans a site museum at Mohammad Agha district where the ancient site is located and to where it will be easy to transport the objects. Already, 60,000 square metres of land have been acquired and possible donor countries are being contacted for its construction. The door is open to any country that takes an interest in the setting up of the museum at the mentioned site. The engineering plan for the surrounding wall is in progress.

The foremost need in the excavation and storage of the Big Stupa and Giant Buddhas is the site museum and a specially equipped laboratory for post-treatment and restoring. We are also inviting global expertise, including UNESCO, to aid in the difficult process of restoration of statues and paintings found at the site. Since 2009, excavations at Mes Aynak are continuing in the Red Zone. As soon as it is completed, copper mining will begin by the Chinese MCC company.

SD: What about the preservation of the Bamyan caves and the paintings there?

Massoudi: Bamyan is a huge ancient site but it was blasted in 2001. Since 2003, Japan has evinced an interest in the preservation of the site and has also given funds through the UNESCO. The funds are specially meant for the preservation of the caves and niches of the Small Buddha. Experts from Italy and Germany, with the cooperation of the International

Council on Monuments and Sites (ICOMOS), have brought all the demolished pieces under one roof. Japanese experts are also working hard for the preservation of the Buddhist caves. Since 2003, Japan has been collaborating in cleaning the caves which have wall paintings. They are also planning to make a small centre for the preservation of the cultural heritage of Afghanistan.

UNESCO is working closely with the Afghanistan Institute of Archaeology and the Ministry of Culture. Since 2003, the Afghan–French archaeological team under Dr Zemaryalai Tarzi has been excavating the area lying between the two Giant Buddhas in search of the largest Reclining Buddha, as mentioned by the Chinese pilgrim Hiuen Tsang during his visit to Bamyan in the 7th century AD, and have already found many important objects and Buddhist complexes. The Afghan and the French archaeological teams are working together on the Bamyan site for two months every year since 2003. We are also working on the setting up of a provincial museum in Bamyan. We have already acquired land in Bamyan and have sent proposals to Japan for funds.

SD: What are you doing to get back the lost objects from the National Museum of Afghanistan?

Massoudi: About 70 per cent of the museum's objects were lost and looted during the civil war. In 2002, the Ministry of Information and Culture in cooperation with UNESCO held an international seminar in the rubble of the National Museum, where the future challenges of the museum, including recovery of looted pieces and reconstruction of the museum buildings, were discussed. About a hundred people attended this seminar. That was the time when the museum had no roof, no doors and no windows. Many countries like Greece, Italy and the US came forward to help. Now, the museum has been repaired and rebuilt.

It is now important for us that the lost pieces of Buddhist art from the ancient sites of Afghanistan are brought back. The lost objects are rare pieces belonging to different excavated sites.

UNESCO has been requested to help in getting back the lost objects. In 2005, Afghanistan became a member of two UN Conventions of 1970 and 1995 by which we were able to get back 9,000 lost objects from the UK, the US, Norway, Denmark, Switzerland and Germany in 2007.

In 2005, we made a Red List of all the lost objects and submitted it to the Interpol, UNESCO and ICOMOS. Now, the National Museum of Afghanistan has good relations with different countries and museums around the world and other cultural institutions. The UK, in cooperation with the British Museum alone, returned about 3,000 objects. We call upon all countries to help us in getting back our lost antiques and artefacts.

A MOU was signed in May 2012 with the Oriental Institute of Chicago University for a partnership programme running for three years to building a computerized database of all objects belonging to the museum. By 2015, this work should be completed in two languages—Dari and English.

Giant Buddhas of Bamyan

To the west of Kabul at a distance of about 200 kilometres is the Valley of Bamyan—a natural corridor formed between the Hindukush and the Koh-i-Baba mountain ranges. This was the ancient 'Corridor of Migration' that linked trade from the Ganga and Indus regions with that of the Oxus and the Caspian regions.

Due to its strategic position on the Silk Road, midway between Balkh and Taxila, trade is said to have flourished in this valley. Caravans passed through the valley with immense riches from the great empires of India, Persia and China. Bamyan also became a great resting place for travellers, with its lovely weather amidst an enchanting landscape of beautiful mountains, gurgling rivers and dense forests. There was an abundance of grain for humans and the best alfalfa for their cattle. Traders, scholars, artistes, painters, stone carvers, missionaries and monks, all travelled through Bamyan making it a place of trade, scholarship, religion and art.

Even today, we can see the remains of numerous caravanserais and ancient bazaars lining the road running in front of the Bamyan caves. The road passes through a rich agricultural region irrigated by canals carrying water from mountain streams. Many of the once dilapidated serais have now been turned into beautiful guesthouses or modern serais that open onto the caves. Instead of harbouring ancient traders and travellers, these serais are now occupied by modern adventurers—researchers and restorers from all over the world.

Buddhist monks are believed to have settled in the Bamyan Valley during the Kushan period or even earlier, turning it into a major monastic centre. Itinerant monks from the Buddhist centres of India perhaps settled there during the time of the Mauryan emperor Asoka's Dhamma missions to the Greek kingdoms of Central Asia. Two immense rock statues of the Buddha, believed to represent 'Lokottara' and the 'Lord of the World',[1] once dominated the Buddhist complex. Thousands of cave shrines, assembly halls and residences for monks were carved out of cliffs between the two Giant Buddhas and were decorated with paintings. The Buddha colossi were dated between the 3rd and the 4th centuries.[2] Today these are represented by dark empty niches standing like tall shadows in the face of the beautiful Bamyan mountains, thanks to their desecration by the Taliban.

When the Chinese pilgrim Fa Hien visited the territory of Afghanistan in AD 400, he did not mention having seen the two colossal figures of the Buddha although he did mention the flourishing state of Buddhism. Another Chinese pilgrim, Hiuen Tsang, visited the area in AD 630, and his writings include the two colossi. He also mentions ten religious foundations with several thousand priests belonging to the Hinayana sect of Buddhism.[3] According to the traveller, one statue was 150 feet high while the other was 100 feet high, both standing figures of stone on the declivity of the hill. Hiuen Tsang also spoke of a Reclining Buddha of about 1000 feet in length within the monastic settlement.

The Giant Buddhas stood guard over the valley for over a millennium and a half before being blown up in March 2001 by the Taliban. This was the second major assault on Bamyan after 1221, when the city was razed by the armies of Genghis Khan turning it into a 'City of Lamentations' or 'Shahr-i-Gholghola'.[4]

Since 2002, world organizations have left no stone unturned in their efforts to restore the World Heritage Site to its former glory. Immense store houses, sealed and enclosed within wire meshing, have come up near the archaeological site for preserving the shattered pieces of the Buddha colossi. Scaffoldings have been set up at the giant caves to prevent loose rock from falling and to enable restorers to reach the upper caves. The area is being beautified at a fast pace. The remains of stupas, cave paintings and carvings are being preserved, some under lock and key to prevent theft. A proper motorable road now passes in front of the caves and also through the numerous villages of the Bamyan and the adjacent Kakrak and Foladi Valleys to facilitate tourist inflow and restoration efforts.

The Afghanistan Institute of Archaeology, the Japanese research team from the National Research Institute for Cultural Properties and the Delegation Archeologique Francaise en Afghanistan (DAFA) are at the site to take special care of the cave paintings and for further research and explorations. There is continuing research towards restoring the giant images through the process of anastylasis—reassembling the blasted rock pieces from the original to rebuild the image with the aid of little new material.

Interestingly, the local populace of Bamyan is excited by the news of the discovery of a 19-metre Reclining Buddha by renowned Afghan-French archaeologist Dr Zemaryalai Tarzi. Dr Tarzi and his team of French archaeologists from DAFA have been searching for the 1000-feet-long Reclining Buddha at Bamyan, mentioned by Hiuen Tsang. There is also news about a Japanese project by artiste Hiro Yamagate to recreate the Buddhas using laser beams. UNESCO also plans to build a museum at Bamyan to spread worldwide awareness about the cultural heritage of Afghanistan.

Journey to the Feet of the Buddha

Nestled 8000 feet within the high cliffs of the Hindukush mountains, Bamyan can be reached from Kabul by two routes—one passing through the Shibar Pass, the other through the Hajigak Pass. The 250-kilometre road journey, I learnt, was long and tiring. Seats were available on the domestic KAM Air flight but it returned to Kabul after a gap of four days. Instead, I chose a seat in the UNHAS (UN Humanitarian Air Service) aircraft to return to Kabul after two days.

After being checked and re-checked at the entry gates of Kabul airport, and also sniffed by a huge Alsatian dog for potential weapons, I gained entry into the departure terminal and headed for the UNHAS lounge. After waiting for an hour to board, I was told that the flight was cancelled. The weather had turned inclement with incessant rain and lightning.

The following morning, I was at the Kabul airport again to take the UNHAS flight. This time the weather was fine both at Kabul and Bamyan and, after hovering over the Koh-i-Baba range and the Hindukush mountains amidst dense clouds and mist, the aircraft landed directly in the Valley of the Buddha. Abbas, the translator and guide was waiting for me outside the airport and the Bamyan Silk Road Hotel had sent their car to pick me up.

It was only 12.30 p.m. and I had two days to explore Bamyan and the Kakrak and Foladi Valleys. The way to the hotel ran near the caves and I could photograph them from a distance. The road then turned towards the Lantern Crossing (where a huge lantern hung, perhaps as a protest against the relentless shortage of electricity!) and drove straight to the Silk Road Hotel—the impressive five-star hotel in Bamyan.

Little did I know that the Buddha would be there too. Just outside my first floor Room No. 6, I was in for a joyful surprise—my room directly faced the Buddha caves and the three giant hollows. I could step onto the verandah and be with the Buddhas any time. I could have spent a million moments standing there, gazing toward them, but that journey was awaited. Abbas had suggested I first visit Kakrak and the Foladi Valleys asnd then return to the Bamyan caves. I had no idea that the other valleys of the Kakrak and Foladi rivers were so close. I hopped into a red car at Lantern Crossing and sped off on an exciting journey.

To the Kakrak Valley

We turned towards Sayeedabad village and drove down a hill slope through a narrow alley and along the courtyards of old mud houses. The gravelled road ran along apricot orchards and large alfalfa farms. Villagers had set up their own dairy units and also cultivated summer fruits like plums, peaches and apricots. Little school girls and female teachers were walking back to their homes from the village school.

As we left the village, the road ran down a steep slope several feet below into the valley of the Kakrak river. Here, the wide path was laid between two mountains along the river formed by the melting glaciers on the Koh-i-Baba ranges. On the foothills, farmers were hand-ploughing their fields, preparing furrows for sowing potatoes. Wheat is also grown in the valley, but Bamyan is famous for its potatoes. I even noticed a small potato storage house. However, it falls far short of capacity for the enormous potato production here and often farmers are compelled to undersell their crop due to lack of storage facilities.

Alfalfa appeared to have covered an entire hill slope. Abbas was unsure whether it was grown entirely for cattle or also used as an oil crop. It is said that the best horses are bred in the Ferghana Valley amid the alfalfa fields; however, we saw very few horses in Kakrak. All we could see were milch cows and mules serving as transport animals.

Shortly, I noticed a group of women and children clearing their field of rocks and weeds just on the banks of the river next to a thick forest of oak. The scene was so beautiful that Sher Hasan, the driver, stopped the vehicle and I lowered the window of the back seat to take a photograph. As I aimed at the scenic beauty of the mountains and forest in the backdrop of the happy family, the children stared throwing stones in my direction. Abbas urged me to shut my camera as people did not like being photographed, especially women. We quickly drove off deeper into the valley.

Having left the alfalfa fields, we started driving past rows and rows of tapak—round cow dung cakes used as fuel for cooking and for warming the house during winter. Some paths along the valley were near impassable, with cow dung cakes packed along the walls of the houses. In some fields, high dung walls separated one farm from another. Some houses were located higher up the mountains, but I was told they were mainly used for keeping cattle or storing farm goods.

Suddenly, the farms vanished and the river entered a small oak forest. The mountains were now in front of me. Sher Hasan stopped the car near a cliff by the side of the river. From my perch I could see a huge niche in the mountains which had once held the famous image of the Kakrak Buddha, much revered and worshipped by the monastic community. Further up, there was a broken structure which appeared to be the remains of a stupa. There were thousands of caves in the surrounding hills. The Kakrak Valley must have been a chosen residence for the monks as the river and rich cultivable fields were close by and the dense natural forest of oak, apricots and peaches provided sustenance.

Kakrak Valley is renowned for its pictorial art. The paintings here are said to be the earliest known examples of the 'mystic mandala of esoteric Buddhism',[5] some of which are displayed on the corridor walls along the right staircase of the National Museum at Kabul. The mandalas depict the central image of the Buddha believed to be 'Vairochna', surrounded by a galaxy of smaller Buddhas.

An outstanding painting from the Kakrak Valley, now displayed at the museum, portrays a royal personage, presumably the Buddhist king of Bamyan, sitting cross-legged, praying with a bow in his hands before a stupa. In front of the king are depicted two unadorned images of the Buddha with haloes, seated on the lotus in dhyanmudra and abhaymudra. Chief Curator Fahim Rahimi informed that the famous painting once adorned the drum of a dome at Kakrak and was popularly called the painting of the 'Hunter King'. The main figure of the sovereign, bejewelled and adorned in fabulous robes, wears a crown with three crescents, perhaps symbolizing the triratna of the Buddha, Dhamma and the Sangha. Surprisingly, the Hunter King's arrows have fallen to the ground, symbolizing his renunciation of violence. Stupas placed on pillars separate one image frame from the other.

We retraced our journey to the Bamyan bazaar via a different route through the villages of Hyderabad and Khawal. Hyderabad seemed to be an affluent village with large houses and walled courtyards. There was a modern mosque surrounded by cultivated fields. The village seemed tranquil, like all villages in the Buddha valley. I noticed small children collecting water from streams and women doing household chores by the side of the Kakrak river.

To the Foladi Valley

A third centre of Buddhist art is situated in the Foladi Valley at the western entrance of the Bamyan caves. The caves present an excellent example of stone carvings and mural paintings.

But even as the Foladi Valley beckoned, I had to return to the Bamyan Valley to register at the UNHAS office in order to confirm my return ticket to Kabul by the next day's evening flight. With the electronic ticket in hand, I took off again in the direction of the Silk Road Hotel and drove to Dasht-e-Isa Khan village to reach the Foladi caves. The Bamyan-Foladi road is being tarred by a Japanese-aided project and several bulldozers and heavy machines are stationed along the valley.

In Tarnava village, we parked our vehicle near a school, run by the support of NGOs and the government. Several informal classes were being conducted simultaneously in front of the Foladi caves and the children were distracted by our presence, but the teachers made every effort to hold their attention. We passed the school and continued to walk along the mountain slope till we arrived at a cliff near the village. Here I noticed a high tower built like a stupa. However, the material used appeared to be old bricks and Abbas informed me that it was a watchtower built by the local populace to keep an eye on the invading armies of the Arabs. Or, perhaps it was built to defend the city from the Mongol marauders.

We hiked up the mountainside and finally reached the caves that appeared embedded into the rocks like honeycombs. Many caves had protruding verandah-like structures and we could easily see their beautifully decorated walls and roofs. However, several caves had been occupied illegally by the inhabitants of Tarnava and nearby villages, and were being used as residences, sheds for their cattle and storehouses. Some had been turned into stables for mules and a store for fodder; and many people were actually living with their animals inside the caves. I moved up the mountains and noticed beautiful floral and geometric designs painted on the roofs and walls of many of the caves.

The local story, according to Abbas, is that the mountain was once the home of a Kushan prince who had built a palace inside the hillside, the rock being cut to give way to galleries, large halls and residential quarters with verandahs. The walls and roofs of the rooms were richly decorated with paintings, whose colours were made by grinding local mineral rock stones like malachite, azurite, lapis and cinnabar.

Some supporting structures of the verandahs have crumbled, leaving only the remains of the roof protruding from the cliffs. I climbed up a steep cliff to take a shot of a richly painted roof. The colours were still bright even though centuries have elapsed since they were painted.

Some of these walls were deep inside the mountains and climbing the cliff could risk a long fall. Abbas appeared to be an agile climber and went up the cliff to shoot with my camera. I managed to photograph at least three caves where the paintings had been exposed. On the adjacent mountains, steps seemed to have been cut into the rock walls. The path could take a pilgrim or a resident monk to the caves on the highest cliff where a tower had been built. It cannot be said with certainty whether the structure was a stupa or a watch tower. But the tower, as the only place bricks had been used in construction, one can conclude that it was an important structure built either for worship or security.

After a long photography session, we climbed down the Foladi cliffs to the valley below and reached the road where Sher Hasan was waiting for us. We took a U-turn and drove back towards

Bamyan bazaar. On the way, we stopped at Sabz Poshta (meaning a green embankment) over the Foladi river to check more paintings at a mausoleum belonging to the Ghurid period. A few medieval structures lie along the Foladi Road but we were in a hurry to get back to Bamyan before the Buddha caves closed for the day.

Sandstorm and Rain at the Bamyan Caves

It was 4 p.m. when the car screeched to a halt outside the Bamyan caves. We hurried to the ticket office. But even before I could pull money out, menacingly dark clouds appeared and the sun seemed to melt away. A fierce storm was gathering over the Koh-i-Baba and was fast moving towards us. I could take shelter inside the caves, but Abbas knew that it would be too dark inside even to see the wall paintings once the storm started. Abbas was wary of rain and storm, and was adamant that we head straight to the hotel. Soon, the dust-laden storm brought down fat raindrops. The rains were lashing. Abbas was right. I should return to the hotel. We quickly got back into our vehicle and sped back to Bamyan bazaar. The next day would hopefully be better. I could return to the Bamyan caves again. I'd have five hours to spend at the feet of the giant Buddhas before catching the return flight to Kabul.

I had not eaten a morsel since morning and Sher Hasan and Abbas were also hungry. We made several rounds of the small bazaar looking for a restaurant. We finally stepped into one called 'Safa' and ordered a cheap meal of Kabili pilaf, aloo korma and black tea. The waiter laid a tablecloth onto the carpet—we were to sit eating on the floor! Then we were served large plates of pilaf, korma, naan and a large kettle of black tea. The delicious meal cost me only 340 Afghani (roughly around 350 rupees).

The rain had stopped and after our meal I strolled around the Bamyan bazaar, window shopping. My eyes suddenly fell on an exquisite carpet in a shop. Rows and rows of hand-woven Afghani carpets were stacked inside the shop. Most of these carpets depicted the Bamyan Buddha—the favoured motif for foreign visitors. However, a small section of the shop had been allotted to antiques found in Bamyan. I started turning over some genuine mud-laden Buddhas that perhaps were found in a cave. Through the mud, I could see the golden tinge of the metal. The Buddha wore a brilliant headdress, like that of the Avalokitesvara. Many more Buddhas had been retrieved from the earth and sold to antique dealers. When the shopkeeper, Ghulam Mohammad, found me photographing the idols, he proudly brought out small pieces of a manuscript written on birch paper that was partially burnt. He generously permitted me to photograph the manuscripts. I asked him why he never sold all the Buddhist antiquities to the museum at Bamyan. 'If there was a museum, I'd definitely do so,' he retorted.

Next, we loitered in the Titanic bazaar deep inside one of the market lanes. I was told that the traders here trace their ancestry to India. I was intrigued and decided to find the truth. The India-ancestry story is true. The traders' forefathers, probably from India, had first settled in Kabul and then moved onto Bamyan. They have now set up shops in the makeshift market for toys, hosiery, old clothes and provisions. Obviously, they no longer have any connection with India, but stories abound of how their ancestors picked raw asafoetida (heeng) from the jungles of Afghanistan, and packed dry fruit, camel loads of sarda, the famous white melons of Afghanistan, and woollen shawls made of goat and camel hair and sold it to Indian traders.

It was getting dark when I returned to the hotel for the night. I was informed that due to acute power shortage, the generator would be switched off at 11 p.m. I curled up in bed early. Not too far away from my window, warmth flew in from the Buddha caves and I fell into a deep sleep.

The Buddha Shrines in Bamyan Valley

It was 4.50 a.m. A feeble glow embraced the valley. The faint chirping of birds could be heard from the willow and oak groves nearby. The silvery oak was the first to catch the glow from the sun that was still an hour-and-a-half away somewhere down the horizon. The agricultural fields surrounding the caves were in complete darkness as were the mountains.

A little later, the valley was enveloped in a mist through which the dark Buddha niches were still hidden. The mountains appeared like a huge dark wall against the mist. As if from nowhere, dark clouds gathered over the snowy peaks of the Koh-i-Baba range. The lone road coming from the Foladi Valley, and passing in front of the hotel, was devoid of any traffic. It was very calm except for the barking of stray dogs and the singing of awakening birds.

As the sun approached the horizon, the mountains acquired a light terracotta hue. The oak trees were now completely painted with strokes of silver and the willows swayed in the morning breeze. Many villagers, dressed in their black coats, were now up and about, checking the flow of water in their potato fields facing the giant Buddha caves. The Sitting Buddha cave was the first one to be lit by the rays of the morning sun. The hollow caves of the Standing Buddhas appeared like black ink on a yellow paper. While the entire valley was bathed in light, the sun was yet to appear in the sky.

At 5.30 a.m., the valley was glowing with an ethereal light. The giant caves were beginning to brighten up but the smaller bee-hived ones resembled black dots in the backdrop of the golden-brown mountains. A thick column of smoke rose from a few mud houses beyond the oak forest. Perhaps the hearths had been lit in the nearby Isa Khan village.

At 5.45 a.m., the sun brought its warmth to the scene, setting the valley aflame in a glowing orange light. In the beautiful Bamyan Valley, everyone, everything, was now awake. Farmers trod their fields with their wooden ploughs pulling their oxen behind them and hundreds of children trudged on the Foladi Road to their school near the Bamyan bazaar. Female teachers clad in a chadori (full-length dupatta like a chador that covers the body) walked briskly behind the children.

The main gate to the Buddha caves, too, would soon be unlocked. I prepared to get ready to leave on foot in the direction of the mountains. I was supposed to be at the Bamyan caves at 7 a.m. sharp so that I had enough time for photography and exploration. But Abbas had not arrived and he was not answering my phone calls. Finally, he answered to inform me that I should walk up to the Lantern Crossing and wait there. The distance to the crossing was a short one along the Foladi Road. I got there soon and sat on the bridge over the Foladi stream and waited for Abbas. He arrived after a few minutes and we started walking to the caves, which were about a kilometre away.

On the way to the caves, I came across Tulvara village, where I was told the population was entirely Tajik. The Foladi stream meanders through this village and lends the soil enough nutrients to produce the best potatoes in Afghanistan. Several timber depots could be seen in Tulvara. The depots were laden with felled trees. I wondered how quickly they would fell the entire oak forest of the valley. A children's jail is located on the main road to the caves. I wanted to take a look inside, but the guard at the entrance prohibited me. Entry is by special permission only. I had no permission.

The village road passed by a modern mosque and across potato fields and a row of mud houses to the expansive courtyard of an ancient caravanserai on the main road leading eastwards to the Kakrak Valley. For centuries, this serai catered to the Silk Road travellers coming to Bamyan on their way to Herat or Balkh. It was now in ruins, but it must have been a grand structure during its heyday. We crossed the road running in front of the caves and jumped over a stream to reach the ticket office. A 300-Afghani ticket is valid for the entire day and for all the three sites in Bamyan.

A gateman unlocked the Big Buddha cave. I first noticed the massive left foot of the Giant Buddha. It is still intact while the other feet and the rest of the body are missing. A large storage house near the gate preserves the blown-up parts of the image that are marked and numbered.

Supporting structures of iron railings and wooden roofing have been set up by the Afghan government with the help of UNESCO and Japanese teams to prevent injury to the restorers and excavators from falling rocks. After the 2001 Taliban blast, loose rocks are a potential danger. Surrounding the massive feet of the Buddha are a number of cave shrines cut into the depths of the mountains in a semi-circle. These once held images of Buddhist deities installed on pedestals. The base of the pedestals can still be seen rising a foot-and-a-half from the floor of the cave. Above the pedestals are tall, arched niches that now stand empty, bereft of their gods.

The roofs have been carved with beautiful architectural decorations. The centre of the roof has been carved into a lotus or a protruding lantern; the edges of the roof have a border of geometrical and floral motifs. On the walls and borders of the roof, paintings peep at you from beneath layers of dust and grime. There are several paintings of the Buddha and Buddhist deities separated at regular intervals with floral motifs.

All the caves around the feet of the Buddha appeared to have been cut for the purpose of shrines, almost circular in shape, surrounding the chief deity—the Giant Buddha. The cave walls were once entirely embellished with murals. Only the pedestals below the niches that once held the images of deities remain. Each cave has about five to six such pedestals and tall niches for life-size images.

The caves do not appear to have been the living areas for the monks. They served only as shrines for the Buddhist deities. 'Sufa' or raised structures along the wall of the caves show that either they were sitting places for worshipping monks or resting places for more images. The ceilings of all the caves are embellished with carvings; at the centre hangs a huge clay chandelier wherein burning lamps were placed to light up the caves during evening prayers. During the day, the caves were lit with natural light.

In one cave there is a painting of a spotted animal, probably a lion. A spotted lion in a Buddhist cave could have perhaps portrayed the *Jataka* story of the Buddha's previous life. It could have also portrayed the attack of demon Mara. A similar theme was portrayed in the paintings on the walls of the Varaksha Palace near Bukhara, now displayed at the Tashkent and Samarkand museums. The Varaksha painting depicts a decorated prince or a bodhisattva sitting on the back of an elephant and being attacked by a winged, spotted lion.

We moved on from the Giant Buddha cave to the Sitting Buddha, whose arms rest on the knees and are clearly visible, although the greater part of the Buddha image is missing. Perhaps the Sitting Buddha was in the 'bhumisparsh mudra'—a posture of the Buddha with one hand touching the ground. This cave lies midway between the two Giant Buddhas and is likewise surrounded by hundreds of caves. In the foothills near the Sitting Buddha lie the remains of three stupas. Two were found in a wide open space that once may have been a covered courtyard with a surrounding circumambulatory corridor. The third was locked up in a cave. I tried to peep through the wire meshing of the window. But it was very dark inside and I could only see the faint outlines of a stupa base. Why was the third stupa locked? According to Abbas, the cave is embellished with murals and they might get destroyed by fierce winds and rain that often lash the region. The stupas that lie outside seem to have been of fairly large size with a cruciform base.

As I started walking from the cave of the Sitting Buddha to the cave of the second Giant Buddha, Abbas made a startling disclosure. He told me that I could be walking over the ground that somewhere conceals the Great Reclining Buddha. Believed to be about 1000 feet long, it could be the biggest Buddha ever seen by the world. I was shocked as even the largest Reclining Buddha image at Kushinagar Mahaparinirvana Temple would fall short by several metres. Or, for that matter even the Dushanbe Buddha or the one found at the Krasnaya site, which is now kept at the Hermitage Museum, St Petersburg. I wanted to know more about the concealed image and when it would be open to the public. Abbas informed me that the renowned Afghan archaeologist Professor Zemaryalai Tarzi and his team from DAFA, while exploring the Bamyan site, had perhaps located the probable site of the Reclining Buddha, but had kept it a secret. Because the Buddha is yet concealed under the rocks, it is believed to be intact. For the time being, the Buddha lies in peace.

Some faces of the rocky mountain seemed to have flattened vertically with tools. I learnt that the mountain face was smoothened to accommodate giant images of Buddhist deities. Such smooth vertical faces appear at many places in the valley. It would have been a wondrous sight in those days with several Giant Buddhas placed along the mountains running for several kilometres in a roughly circular shape, as in the Ajanta caves, where a person standing at one end could view the whole valley.

A long walk took me through several storehouses where fragments of the giant Buddhas have been marked and stored. I approached the second Giant Buddha cave, where the silhouette of the image can still be traced clearly. To the left of the image one can notice a steep staircase cut into the mountains, reaching the upper floors of the multi-storeyed caves. I started climbing the steep stairs and somehow staggered to the first floor cave. This cave had a proper verandah with a roof and walls carved and decorated with paintings, the remnants of which can still be seen. Inside it, one can see pedestals along the walls which provide evidence of images that once stood there. Behind the head of the images were painted large circular and oval haloes, faint black traces and impressions of which are still visible.

The chiselled stairway, which becomes steeper and narrower with every step, does not end at the first floor but spirals upwards several steps away to the second-floor cave. To help visitors and restorers climb the precariously steep steps, iron railings have been installed on the walls of the staircase.

Here, on the second floor, the verandah appears fully decorated with paintings that have now faded over the centuries; only some parts of the paintings are visible. The roof of the cave is beautifully designed into a wheel-like structure from which once hung a huge lamp.

The staircase did not stop at the second floor but spiralled yet upwards, even narrower and steeper than before. How the early monks cut the beautiful multi-storeyed caves inside the mountains is a complete wonder. I climbed down carefully and picked up a piece of the rock lying near the feet of the Buddha. It was the most sacred soil of Bamyan, much like the falling leaves of the Bodhi tree at Bodh Gaya.

I did not go back to the hotel as I had hardly any luggage, only a handbag that was already slung on my shoulders. Before heading to the airport, I spent some time at the Bamyan Information Centre where a kind officer provided me a photograph of the lost Kakrak Buddha and of the Bamyan Valley taken several decades before the Taliban regime destroyed them.

At the airport departure terminal, which was temporarily working from a shed, a lone coffee shop was selling woollen fabric made with Afghan goat hair. It was soft, velvet-like. Other woollens were made of camel hair. But there were few buyers as the cold Bamyan air lashed down with full fury at the shed and everyone was waiting impatiently to catch the flight back to Kabul.

Soon the UNHAS aircraft arrived, loaded with UN aid workers. It landed amid a thick whirling cloud of dust. As soon as the overhead rotors halted and passengers alighted, we lined up behind the security officer and marched to the aircraft. Soon, we were above the Buddha caves. The splendorous valley again swung into view. The thin streams of the Foladi and Kakrak came out of their hiding from the silver oak forests. I bade farewell to Bamyan as the aircraft flew towards the horizon.

References

For more details see: Dupree, Nancy H. *A Historical Guide to Afghanistan*

1. Puri, B.N. *Buddhist Tradition Series: Buddhism in Central Asia* (Delhi:

Motilal Banarsidass Publishers Pvt. Ltd., 2000), p. 298
2. Director General, Archaeological Survey of India. *A Challenge to World Heritage* (Delhi: Visual Publication, 2002), p. 3
3. Hwui Li, Shaman and Beal, Samuel (trans.). *The Life of Hieun-Tsiang* (Delhi: D.K. Publishers Distributors Pvt. Ltd., 2001), p. 52-53
4. Hartog, Leo De. *Genghis Khan: Conqueror of the World* (New York: I.B. Tauris Publishers, 1999), p. 113-114
5. Puri, B.N. *Buddhist Tradition Series: Buddhism in Central Asia* (Delhi: Motilal Banarsidass Publishers Pvt. Ltd., 2000), p. 301

The stele of schist from Mes Aynak representing Dipankar Jataka (3rd-5th century AD).
Courtesy: National Museum of Afghanistan, Kabul

Gandhara Buddha in schist from Sarai Khuja representing the 'Miracle of Sravasti' (2nd-3rd century AD).
Courtesy: National Museum of Afghanistan, Kabul

Buddha's Begging Bowl of deep-grey granite found in 1925 at the shrine of Mirwais Baba, Kandahar.
Courtesy: National Museum of Afghanistan, Kabul

Buddha head of clay from Tepe Sardar, Ghazni (5th-7th century AD).

Courtesy: National Museum of Afghanistan, Kabul

Deep corridors with monk cells and niches for images at Top-e-Rustam near Aibak, Samangan (4th-5th century AD).

Niche of the Buddha colossi in the Valley of Bamyan (3rd-4th century AD).

In Search of Naubahar Monastery

The ancient city of Balkh was known by the Greek name Bactra, lending the name 'Bactria' to the region. For a long time, the city is said to have been the seat of the Zoroastrian religion. It was the place where Zoroaster first preached 'Magism'. We learn from Al Beruni that countries up to the frontier of Syria were Buddhist, but Zoroaster went from Azerbaijan and preached his religion in Balkh. Zoroastrianism came into the favour of King Gushtasp and was made the state religion of Persia and Iraq. In consequence, all the Buddhists were banished to the east of Balkh.[1]

The *Si Yu Ki* tells us that even during the time of Hiuen Tsang's travels in AD 630, the city of Balkh was of great antiquity.[2] As early as the 329 BC, Alexander of Macedon crossed the Hindukush and entered the province of Balkh in pursuit of Bessus, the satrap of Bactria, who was in the forefront of the guerrilla warfare that had ravaged and slaughtered the armies of Alexander. Balkh (also called Zariaspa) was made the regional headquarters of the Macedonian army,[3] and it was here that Alexander married the beautiful Roxana, daughter of a Balkh nobleman, Oxyartes.[4]

But the antiquity digs even further in the past. In the 6th century BC, two travellers from Balkh, Trapussa and Bhallika, came to India for trade and met the Buddha after his Enlightenment at Bodh Gaya. They were the first lay disciples of the Buddha, and are said to have built the first stupas at Balkh. This has been mentioned in the memoirs of the Chinese pilgrim, Hiuen Tsang.

Having arrived at Kunduz, the Chinese pilgrim Hiuen Tsang said to have travelled through Tashkurgan westwards to the kingdom of Balkh. In his memoirs, there is an interesting reference to the legend of the two travellers from Central Asia.[5] Apparently, after Buddha's Enlightenment, Trapussa and Bhallika met him at Bodh Gaya. They offered parched grain and honey to the Buddha and received the Five Commandments and Ten Virtues from the Great Master. The Buddha expounded the ways to happiness for men and gods. After they had received the religious teachings, the merchants requested the Buddha for something that they could worship. The Buddha gave them his hair and nail cuttings. Ready to return to their country, the two men beseeched the Buddha for a method to worship. The Buddha took his three garments, folded each four times and placed them on the ground, beginning with the largest and ending with the smallest. Next, he took his begging bowl and placed it upside-down on the garments. Finally, he put his beggar's staff on top and said, 'This is how you should make a stupa.' The merchants went back to Balkh and built a stupa, perhaps the world's first stupa for the relics of the Buddha.[6]

Buddhism is believed to have been popularized in Balkh during the reign of Asoka[7] who spoke of introducing the Dhamma among the people of Gandhara, Kamboja and Yona. The three were neighbouring regions—Kambojas were probably a branch of the Tokhara people while the Yonas were the Bactrian Greeks.[8]

When Hiuen Tsang came to Balkh, he stayed at the New Monastery or the Nav Vihara/Naubahar for a month, and has described it as one of the most splendid monasteries of the Buddhist world. From his description, it can be concluded that the extent of the kingdom of Balkh included a vast territory touching the Oxus on the north and spreading about 800 li (over 200 kilometres) from east to west, including the territory of the modern Hairatan and Samangan. The capital alone was 20 li in circuit.[9] The pilgrim also talks of Balkh as the 'Little Rajgriha', the name probably stemming from the flourishing state of Buddhism there with 100 convents and 3000 monks. Outside the city towards the south-west, Hiuen

Tsang found a convent called Navasangharama, a Buddhist centre where the great Buddhist scholars lived and studied.

At the Navasangharama, Hiuen Tsang saw the great statue of the Buddha which shone by virtue of the precious gems studded onto it. It stood in a hall which was also embellished with rare precious gems. There was also a statue of Vaisravana Deva, who protected the convent. In the Hall of the Buddha, the pilgrim mentioned a dazzling, multicoloured washbasin used by the Buddha. Not far away, the pilgrim informs, lay the yellowish-white shining tooth of the Buddha, about an inch long. The 2 feet and 7 inch sweeping brush of the Buddha, made of the plant 'ka-she' (or kusha grass), with a gem-laden handle was also kept here. To the north of the convent, he saw a stupa, about 200 feet high, reflecting a divine splendour and enclosing a sacred relic. The stupa was covered with a plaster 'as hard as diamonds'.[10] What happened to the these relics no one can tell. But I have heard of a tooth relic of the Buddha being worshipped in a temple at China Town in Singapore.

Interestingly, Xinru Liu in *Silk and Religion*[11] mentions a Chinese pilgrim Wu'kung who is said to have carried away the Buddha's tooth relic (from Balkh?) to China where he was granted official position and honours. In the 7th century AD, the rulers of Kapisa happily parted with the small parietal bone (presumably of the Buddha) in exchange for 4000 bolts of silk, writes Xinru Liu.[12]

It is said that Buddhist pilgrims, walking on the Silk Road, carried bales of silk and velvet pouches spilling with gold and silver to trade them with the relics of the Buddha. The basic motive was to carry the relics to their emperor and gain favours and rewards.

A Journey to Mazar-e-Sharif

Modern-day Balkh is in the northern province of Afghanistan and derives its name from the ancient city which lies 20 kilometres north-west of the capital of Mazar-e-Sharif. Scholars opine that the massive stupa and caves at the Buddhist sites of Top-e-Rustam and

Takht-e-Rustam near Mazar-i-Sharif, 113 kilometres south-east of Balkh, may hold the key to the ancient Naubahar of Hiuen Tsang.

The highway to Mazar-e-Sharif runs north from Kabul and is the most important Ring Road in the country, forming the 2210-kilometre road link between all the important cities of Afghanistan. Starting from Kabul and running through Doshi, Pul-e-Khumri, Mazar-e-Sharif, Faryab, Badghees, Herat and Kandahar, it circles back to Kabul. International highways coming from Pakistan, Iran, Turkmenistan, Uzbekistan, Tajikistan and the Wakhan Corridor from China join this Ring Road at different points on the circuit.

However, I did not take the Ring Road to Mazar; instead, I flew from Kabul. Adhering to the advice of Fauzia, who accompanied me, I packed a burqa. I knew we'd trudge into remote villages of the northern provinces where I must wear the hijab in consonance with the local traditions of Mazar. Hence, both Fauzia and I, clad in long black burqas over our salwar-kameezes and heads covered in a black scarf, boarded the KAM Air flight RQ 243 to Mazar. Ahsanullah, our dear friend, had already reached Mazar a day earlier. He was at the airport to receive us and we headed to Hotel Renaissance near the Indian consulate where Sebastian, the manager, was waiting for us. A kind-hearted man, this Indian has been running the Renaissance for a long time. His hotel is renowned for serving delicious Indian food including mouth-watering dosas and idlis. We noticed a glittering multi-storeyed structure adjacent to a garden which was the super-deluxe part of the same hotel.

Sebastian now showed us to two rooms near the gate, which he said were the only ones available. On entering the rooms, Fauzia threw a fit. The rooms were small and extremely shabby and she was sure they were meant for the guards. After offering her evening namaz, she barged out of the room, proclaiming that she could not spend even a minute at the Renaissance.

Ahsanullah then led us to another part of Mazar to the five star Mazar Palace Hotel, where the manager Shamim offered us their best rooms. With its expansive lobby, art gallery, and dining and breakfast halls, it is one of the best hotels in Mazar. Our rooms were on the second floor and opened onto a massive terrace where several divans had been laid out for a musical evening.

We left our luggage in our rooms and headed straight to the terrace garden and relaxed on the divans till late in the night listening to melodious Hindi and Afghani songs being dramatized on the huge screen erected on the terrace. We snacked on roasted grains, drank sherbet and pea soup and ate melons, bananas and dry fruit till there was no appetite left for dinner. The neighbouring divan was occupied by a young group of boys who smoked chillums and gazed at the Bollywood beauties on the screen.

To Samangan

The following morning, at 6.45 a.m., we left for Samangan to see the Buddhist sites of Takht-e-Rustam and Top-e-Rustam. It is in the ruins of these monastic settlements that scholars have traced the existence of the ancient Naubahar monastery which Hiuen Tsang mentioned in his travelogues.

At this early hour, there were very few cars on the Mazar–Kabul highway. Surprisingly, the pedestrian traffic was high as hundreds of girls, in blue salwar-kameezes and white headscarves, were walking briskly towards their schools. As we left the main shopping area, we saw locals sprinkling water on the pedestrian pathways and sweeping them, cart-loaders washing their carts, and three-wheelers calling out for passengers. We crossed several roundabouts decorated with minarets, statuary art and rose beds—one roundabout even had statues of Buzkashi players.

It was spring in Mazar and summer was slowly unveiling its beauty. With the sun's warmth returning, the plants were covered with blossoms and a sweet flowery fragrance pervaded the air. On the sidewalks, the bony stalks of the pine trees had suddenly burst into new foliage and small, brown pine fruits were raising their heads from green branches. The poplars were already wearing green leaves fluttering with the slightest breeze and the willow trees had expanded their girth.

We crossed the Chaurahe Ali Kuzai and passed through the main taxi stand, where hundreds of taxies and mini buses were calling out for passengers to Hairatan border post near the Friendship Bridge which leads into Termez (Uzbekistan). Another crossing, the Chaurahe Firdausi, was decorated by a minaret surrounded by a beautiful garden.

Travelling eastwards, in the direction of Pul-e-Khumri, we came to the Afghan-Turk Friendship Park. Here, there were multi-storeyed mansions on both sides of the road that were owned by the affluent populace of Mazar. At Chaurahe Kamgar located a market (apparently a labour market) for second-hand cars, perhaps coming from Uzbekistan. Hundreds of jarangs (three-wheelers) were waiting for passengers to nearby Shebergan.

Massive road-building operations were going on along the Mazar–Kabul highway and shining, state-of-art Pakistani buses were plying to and from Kabul through here. A little further down the road was the storage godown for oil coming from Uzbekistan after being refined at the border town of Hairatan. The large campus of the Mazar University, built in collaboration with Pakistan, is an eye-catcher with its huge grounds and modern building. As we drove on, the city now merged into the vast open spaces of the industrial region of Mazar, where several brick-making units dot the area.

We did not turn right at the airport Chaurahe but drove straight down the highway, keeping step with the thick power lines that had been installed all along the highway to Kabul. Most villages appear to be electrified but there is always a power shortage. We were now on the main highway to Pul-e-Khumri. Soon, we crossed the railway line coming from Termez across the Friendship Bridge to Mazar.

After driving for about 30 kilometres, we came to Do Rahe from where a branch road ran north to Hairatan. We carried on straight ahead and arrived in the midst of the richly forested

Marmul mountainous region in the vicinity of Tashkurgan. We were now travelling in the south-east direction, when we came upon a branch road taking a left turn for Khulm. But we drove on towards Pul-e-Khumri. We passed by the ancient walls of the Bagh-e-Jahanuma fort, which is believed to be 300 years old.

In front of us now lay the beautiful mountains of Tangi Tashkurgan whose foothills were covered with thick clusters of almond trees. The mountains here were multi-coloured—green, deep terracotta, ochre and grey—just like the mountains in the Tashkurgan region of the Pamir mountains in Xinjiang. We got off the car now and walked around.

A colourful bazaar had come up along the Tangi Tashkurgan Pass. People here sell not only foodgrains and the famous naan-rotis of Afghanistan, but also handicrafts, fruit and vegetables. The streets are flanked by choykhanas. The hilly slopes provide rich pastures for sheep and milch cattle. The mountains suddenly changed colour from a deep green to a terracotta red while the valley below had a contrasting green colour from the almond forests. Fauzia suddenly pointed to a large chasma (spring) on my right. We turned right and followed a pebbled path to reach the chasma—a clear blue pool of water oozing out of the caves cut into the womb of the mountains. Fauzia and Ahsanullah waded through the chasma and reached the caves. Fauzia offered a short prayer and then returned to the waiting vehicle. I sat on the bank of the river, amazed at the wonders that nature creates in hidden places.

From this point of the chasma, Samangan was still 40 kilometres away.

The highway now turned from the mountains, whose place was taken up by green wheat fields. Once upon a time, these were the red fields of poppy but now red poppies have made way for the brown of wheat.

Further down, the road resembled an unending sheath of yellow. The entire landscape was replete with mustard fields. The best Afghani melons also grow here. But these will be planted only a few weeks later, when the temperature rises. There are vast vineyards too along the road but certainly no fields of poppy.

Soon, we passed through the town of Hazrat-e-Sultan, named after a Sufi saint whose mausoleum lies far away on an isolated cliff. The road takes a deep dip and swings back again. In the grasslands, long-haired goats were grazing placidly. These goats resemble the pashmina goat found in the Tibetan plateau. We come to Ershad Bridge from where the town of Samangan is only 10 kilometres away.

The road from Karti Sohel ran straight to Pul-e-Khumri. But we took a right turn and drove through wheat fields till we came upon a narrow pathway that climbed up a hill top and ended near a huge Buddhist stupa. This is the site of Takht-e-Rustam stupa lying on the main trade route going north towards the Oxus and south through Bamyan and Gandhara towards the Indus and along the Uttarapath and Dakshinapath, it reaches into every province of India.

Our vehicle halted on a landing by the side of the stupa of Takht-e-Rustam. Nowhere in Central Asia had I seen a stupa like this one. Not in Kushinagar, or Kapilavastu or Sarnath. In size it could equal that of Sanchi but the architecture was different. It could be compared to the Mahastupa at Amravati but the latter is in complete ruins. This stupa can only be compared to the Shanti stupa of modern times, established at Dhauli, Vaishali and other places.

The stupa of Takht-e-Rustam is said to have been built in the 2nd century AD. The edges of the stupa are smooth and spherical. The base that is embedded in the rocky soil has long grooves leading into underground water tanks. Abdul informed us that the grooves were meant to divert melting ice water into the tanks to be used for drinking. The stupa seems to have been cut out of a huge cliff but it is difficult to believe how humans could make the top of the stupa so spherical with only hand tools. In those days of measuring strings and hand tools, the rock-cutters must have worked from the top of the cliff to the bottom, like the shrines of Dunhuang, Ajanta and Ellora.

The pradakshina path (circumambulatory corridor) around the stupa is wide enough for two persons to walk side by side, hemmed in between the stupa and the rock wall. Walking around the huge stupa, one could readily believe hundreds of monks were needed to work on the rocks to carve out the stupa and the corridor around it.

The main entrance to the stupa was a wide path along both sides of which lay deep and large caves with windows. The visitors can explore a few caves, but many more interconnected hidden caves also lie within the rocks surrounding the stupa. The natural caves have low roofs but are wide enough for a dozen worshippers to be seated and protected from the harsh weather of the region. Windows were cut into the caves for air circulation. Seating arrangements resemble a huge sufa, a raised bench-like structure along the walls of the caves.

Once inside the caves, there was no fear of inclement weather or attack from wild animals as the site is situated on a high cliff. There was plenty of food from the fertile land that surrounds the site and enough water from the mountain streams and the water tanks below the stupa. The size of the huge stupa, its grandeur, and the multiple caves cut alongside the circumambulatory corridor to accommodate the large multitude of worshipping monks are evidence of the importance accorded to this site.

Another important structure stands over the stupa—a rectangular outcrop with a high empty niche. This probably held a chhatri or a canopy atop the dome of the stupa. Perhaps this was the place which held the Triratna, or the Three Jewels of the Buddha, the Dhamma and the Sangha. Or it could have held an image of the Buddha. The travellers on the northern route from Kabul or Bamyan would have found themselves blessed by the huge image of the Buddha.

Even today, the stupa and the caves have been well-preserved and frequented by the local populace. A garden of pistachio has been planted on the terraced fields below the stupa.

The Caves of Top-e-Rustam

We climbed down the terraced hills, jumping over beds of newly planted pistachio, and approached another hill standing close to the stupa. Even from a distance, we could see a network of closely connected caves inside a massive rocky hill.

Inside it, little known to the outside world, lie massive rectangular and circular halls, courtyards, and galleries whose walls have been decorated with floral motifs. There are deep-arched niches, and on the floor are water tanks cut into the rocks. The interconnected galleries do not seem to be natural; the galleries, halls and walls were certainly carved by humans.

After crossing an open courtyard, we entered an almost circular cave where a kund (cool water body), cut into the floor, welcomes us. Perhaps some stream was led into the tank and the water was stored for drinking purposes. Or, it could portray the scene of the Buddha's nativity, when Queen Mayadevi, after bathing in the pond at the gardens of Lumbini, gave birth to Prince Siddhartha. On the walls are vestiges of floral carvings. There are huge niches inside, where large images of the Buddha once stood.

Over the top of one particularly large arched niche is a huge carving of a tree that resembles the peepal—the Bodhi, the tree of wisdom. Under this tree, the niche perhaps held the image of the Buddha in deep meditation—the first thing any visitor to this cave would notice.

Several lotus flowers are carved on the adjacent walls. They are similar to the lotuses under the feet of the Buddha portrayed at the Chankama at Bodh Gaya, which symbolize the seven steps taken by the Buddha after his Enlightenment.

Galleries connect one part of the hill to another and lead into large congregational halls. One of the several halls into which a gallery opens appears to be several 100-feet long and at least 20-feet wide. There are numerous arches and a broad sufa along the walls. Here, several hundred monks could be seated for a congregation, all facing the stupa on the other hill. Along the galleries deep alcoves are cut for Buddha images that once decorated the entire monastic settlement. From the size of the hill and the number of large halls and connecting galleries, it can be presumed that several hundred monks lived in the monastic settlement.

This could perhaps be the renowned monastery of Naubahar.

After returning to Mazar, I was to take the road to Balkh where the ruins of Masjid-i-Haji Piyada lay, dating to the early 9th century, the famous shrine of Khwaja Parsa and the tomb of the 9th-century poetess Rabia Balkhi. But Abdul brought news that some members of the Taliban had been caught on the main highway to Balkh and the road had been barricaded. It would now be difficult to travel to the remote village where the ruins lay. Haji Piyada was thus dropped from my itinerary.

Instead, Fauzia decided to offer evening prayers at the Blue Mosque, the shrine of Prophet Hazrat Ali, situated in the neighbourhood of the Mazar Palace. The blue-tiled monument is the place where, Muslims believe, lies the tomb of Ali ibn Abi Talib, the cousin and son-in-law of Prophet Mohammad. It is one of the most sacred monuments of Afghanistan.

After praying inside the inner sanctuary of the mausoleum, we took a round of the vast courtyard of the mosque where the sacred flag stands in an enclosure. Here, devotees offer food, clothes and money for charity and pray for the fulfilment of their wishes.

Another charity awaited us on the other side of the mosque—thousands of pearl-white pigeons swooping down in the courtyard to feed on grains offered by the devout. An old maulvi handed me a bowl of grains and mumbled something to the pigeons. A huge flock rushed over my head and swooped down at the plate to feed, nearly scratching my hands. I performed this charity in the hope that my prayers would be answered—that peace and tranquillity may return to this beautiful land of Afghanistan.

References

1. Puri, B.N. *Buddhist Tradition Series: Buddhism in Central Asia* (Delhi: Motilal Banarsidass Publishers Pvt. Ltd., 2000), p. 89
2. Tsiang, Hiuen and Beal, Samuel (trans.). *Si Yu Ki: Buddhist Records of the Western Country*, Book II (Delhi: D.K. Publisher Distributors Pvt. Ltd., 1995), p. 43-45
   Wriggins, Sally. *The Silk Road Journey with Xuanzang* (USA: Westview Press, Perseus Books Group, 2004), p. 41-45
   Bagchi, P.C. *India and Central Asia* (Kolkata: National Council of Education, Bengal, 1955), p. 32
3. Manfredi, V.M. and Halliday, Iian (trans.). *Alexander: The Ends of the Earth,* Volume 3 (London: Pan Macmillan London, 2002), p. 394, 397
4. *Ibid.*, p. 415-419
5. Hwui Li, Shaman and Beal, Samuel (trans.). *The Life of Hieun-Tsiang* (Delhi: D.K. Publishers Distributors Pvt. Ltd., 2001), p. 50
   Wriggins, Sally. *The Silk Road Journey with Xuanzang* (USA: Westview Press, Perseus Books Group, 2004), p. 41-45
   Bagchi, P.C. *India and Central Asia* (Kolkata: National Council of Education, Bengal, 1955), p. 32
6. Tsiang, Hiuen and Beal, Samuel (trans.). *Si Yu Ki: Buddhist Records of the Western Country*, Book I (Delhi: D.K. Publisher Distributors Pvt. Ltd., 1995), p. 43
   Wriggins, Sally. *The Silk Road Journey with Xuanzang* (USA: Westview Press, Perseus Books Group, 2004), p. 41-45
   Bagchi, P.C. *India and Central Asia* (Kolkata: National Council of Education, Bengal, 1955), p. 32
7. Bagchi, P.C. *India and Central Asia* (Kolkata: National Council of Education, Bengal, 1955), p. 32
   Puri, B.N. *Buddhist Tradition Series: Buddhism in Central Asia* (Delhi: Motilal Banarsidass Publishers Pvt. Ltd., 2000), p. 90
8. Puri, B.N. *Buddhist Tradition Series: Buddhism in Central Asia* (Delhi: Motilal Banarsidass Publishers Pvt. Ltd., 2000), p. 90

9. Tsiang, Hiuen and Beal, Samuel (trans.). *Si Yu Ki: Buddhist Records of the Western Country*, Book I (Delhi: D.K. Publisher Distributors Pvt. Ltd., 1995), p. 43
   Wriggins, Sally. *The Silk Road Journey with Xuanzang* (USA: Westview Press, Perseus Books Group, 2004), p. 41-45
10. Tsiang, Hiuen and Beal, Samuel (trans.). *Si Yu Ki: Buddhist Records of the Western Country,* Book I (Delhi: D.K. Publisher Distributors Pvt. Ltd., 1995), p. 43
    Wriggins, Sally. *The Silk Road Journey with Xuanzang* (USA: Westview Press, Perseus Books Group, 2004), p. 41-45
11. Xinru, Liu. *Silk and Religion* (Bombay, Madras, Calcutta: Oxford University Press, 1996), p. 47
12. *Ibid.*, p. 47

Section Two

TAJIKISTAN

Routes into Tajikistan

Several crossing points from Afghanistan led across the Oxus or the Pyanj rivers into the territory of Tajikistan. Among them the well-known crossings lay at Arytam in Uzbekistan and at Aivaz, Dusti and Kharog in Tajikistan. The road from Balkh (Afghanistan) crossed the Oxus river into Arytam village near Termez. Another route led from Kunduz into the region of Aivaz. A third route led eastwards from Kunduz through Taliqan and Faizabad, crossing the Pyanj river at the Afghan-Tajik border near Kharog.

The Pyanj river, a tributary of the Amu Darya (Oxus) runs for over 1100 kilometres to form a considerable part of the Tajik–Afghan border. The river formed by the confluence of the Pamir and the Wakhan near the village of Qil-e-Panj flows westwards, forming the international border. After passing the city of Khorog, capital of the Gorno-Badakshan (autonomous region), it receives water from one of its main tributaries, the Bartang river. It then turns south-west before joining the Vakhsh river to form the greatest river of Central Asia—the Amu Darya.

The Wakhan Corridor route in Afghanistan leads into the Pamir region where it joins the ancient route now covered by the Karakoram Highway to reach Kashgar. The routes from southern Tajikistan dropping into Afghanistan joined the Uttarapath or the Northern High Road (once the Mauryan highway, now approximates to the Grand Trunk Road in India) running from Pataliputra to Taxila and extending up to Kabul. This was the grand route that could take a pilgrim or a trader from Central Asia right up to Chittagong on the Bay of Bengal and further into the regions of South-east Asia or could follow its branches into Tibet, Burma and the Yunnan.

The Chinese pilgrim Hiuen Tsang is believed to have followed the Tajik route into Badakshan and thence to Kunduz while travelling from southern Tajikistan into Afghan territory and taking the road to India from Balkh. It is recorded that Hiuen Tsang, after he passed the land of Termez,[1] did not cross the Oxus at this point to enter the Balkh region of present-day Afghanistan. There was a river crossing at the Arytam village even in ancient times, where we now have the modern Friendship Bridge going into Mazar-e-Sharif, close to ancient Balkh. Instead, the pilgrim travelling eastwards from Termez, crossed into the region of Chaganian, Vakhsh and Khuttal in present-day Tajikistan.

Travellers going into Uzbekistan would take the Balkh–Termez route and those going to Tajikistan would take the Kunduz–Shahrituz route. Those wanting to go to China could take the road through Badakshan and along the Wakhan Corridor into the Pamirs to reach Tashkurgan, the last frontier post near Kashgar.

In *Cities and Routes of the Great Silk Road*, we read about the eastern routes that led through Tajikistan into China and southern routes that led into India. The shortest and the straightest route from Balkh to Kashgar was the Balkh–Termez–Dushanbe–Kashgar route.[2] A second road ran along the right bank of the Amu Darya south-eastwards from Termez to Aivaj in ancient Kobadian. Aivaj served as a ford to Kunduz and the route to India. The northern route through Aivaz leading through the mountains reached Shahrituz. A road from Shahrituz led to Takht-i-Sangin, the monumental edifice of the Oxus Temple near the mouth of the Vaksh where it flows into the Pyanj river. Another road from Shahrituz went along the Kafirnihon river into the Gissar Range and joined the road to China at Dushanbe.

References

1. Tsiang, Hiuen and Beal, Samuel (trans.). *Si Yu Ki: Buddhist Records of the Western Country*, Book I (Delhi: D.K. Publisher Distributors Pvt. Ltd., 1995), p. 39
2. Buryakov, Y.F., Baipakov, K.M., Tashbaeva, K.H., Yakubov, Y. *The Cities and Routes of the Great Silk Road* (Tashkent: Sharg, 1999), p. 73
Also see, map: Tucker, Jonathan. *The Silk Road: Art and History* (New Delhi: Timeless Books, 2003), p. 203, section six

The Great Reclining Buddha at Dushanbe

In the absence of any direct flight into Tajikistan, I had to take the Delhi–Almaty–Dushanbe flight. At Almaty, I was huddled into a tiny aircraft for Dushanbe. As it flew over the ranges of the Tien Shan, the rounded and flattened tops of the mountains covered in several feet of snow came into view. Amid the snowy slopes lay emerald lakes and snaking ice rivers. The sun shone brightly, chasing away woolly white clouds and spreading a blinding glare on the white peaks. So many blue lakes had been trapped in the mountains—terrible earthquakes in this region of Central Asia had caused the mountains to tremor and fall, blocking the path of streams to form the lakes.

The aircraft flew over the territory of the old Silk Route through Bishkek and the cities of Khujand southwards into Dushanbe. Thousands of rivulets flowing down the slopes coalesced to form the giant rivers of Tajikistan which gushed through the mountain valleys and fed hundreds of villages on their way. One of these, the Varzob, was dancing its way south to meet another river, the Kafirnihon. I had entered the Gissar Valley and soon landed in Dushanbe.

At the Avesto Hotel, I hurriedly threw my bag into room 215, and hastened to meet Professor Bobomulloev Saidmurod, director at the National Museum of Antiquities. He was the answer to all my questions and anxieties regarding excavations at the ancient Buddhist sites. Only he could permit me to take photographs of the renowned Reclining Buddha, the largest in Central Asia, from the great monastery of Ajina Tepe and other Buddhist objects from various monastic sites in Tajikistan.

Meeting with Bobomulloev

As I took off my shoes outside the main entry of the museum (as was required), I sensed an unusual quiet about the entire edifice. In the vast pillared verandah, two employees informed me that there was no electricity and hence no exhibits could be seen. Having failed to see the Buddha, I turned my attention to the next important thing on my agenda—to meet the director, Professor Bobomulloev. I enquired about him from the museum staff and they pointed to a figure standing under an apricot tree in the museum garden. As I approached him, he turned towards me, trying to recognize me from our last meeting a year ago at Ashgabat.

I followed him to his room in the adjacent building. We sat down and Bobomulloev looked at my route map, pointing errors in the plan and suggesting a quicker alternate route to the Buddhist sites. From my itinerary, he struck off the Kulob route to Kafirnihon. He suggested a shorter route to Kafirnihon and also a visit to the Buddhist site of Khisht Tepe, nearly 300 kilometres from Dushanbe. However, I dropped the idea later when his assistant told me that nothing remained at the site. It was futile to go there because whatever was found at Khisht Tepe had been brought to the National Museum. That bit of information saved me a lot of hassles. And hours.

Darshan of 'Nirvana Buddha'

There was no electricity in the museum, but I wished to see the Sleeping Buddha even in the dimmest of lights. Bobomulloev agreed. In an enormous upper hall of the museum, the giant Buddha of Ajina Tepe was lying peacefully. The giant image of the 'Buddha in Nirvana', over 12 metres in length, was lying in the traditional posture of the 'Sleeping Lion', clad in red sanghati (robes), lying on his right side.

This famed image of Central Asia was recovered from a corridor or a 'pradikshana path' of the Ajina Tepe monastery, dated somewhere between the 7th-8th century AD. Extraction and conservation of the 'Nirvana Buddha' was a complex and difficult process as all sculptures in Ajina Tepe were made of clay. This particular Buddha had been found in parts and was reconstructed by experts from the Hermitage Museum.

I touched the Buddha's feet in reverence and piety.

The 'Sleeping Buddha of Ajina Tepe' is the chief attraction of the museum. It is the largest and the only intact Reclining Buddha image in Central Asia, much larger than the Nirvana Buddha at the Mahaparinirvana Temple at Kushinagar in India or the one found in Cave 26 of Ajanta. The Reclining Buddha image found in Kyrgyzstan at Krasnaya Rechka village, measuring eight metres, is currently on display at the Hermitage in St Petersburg.

The two large Buddha Halls of the museum display the statuary art and murals recovered during excavations from the monastic centres of Tajikistan. These include several Buddha heads from Ajina Tepe and Kafirnigan, clay seals with Buddhist sutras and votive stupas from Khisht Tepe and the terraced stupa of Ajina Tepe.

Meeting with Rahim Masov

I soon learnt that the permission for photography could only be given by Professor Rahim Masov, director of the Academy of Social Sciences. Later, along with the translator, Mir, I met Masov at the Academy. He was generous enough to grant permission but the museum was about to close for the day and photography would have to wait until the following day. Right now, hunger was gnawing at me. I stepped into The Rohat, the nearest choykhana.

I was looking for some vegetarian food. I could eat salad or naan. But naan never came fresh from the tandoor. It was prepared in bulk and stored. I could also eat the samsa or the samosa with potato fillings, but restaurants usually served it with meat fillings. I could try pilaf or the shorba from which meat had been removed, but as a strict vegetarian I ruled out that option. While Mir ordered mutton shashlik, served with onions and grilled meat balls, I nibbled some bread and tomatoes. It was my only meal of the day. For several days, I would live on naan and salad tossed in red chilli paste.

In the evening I set out with Zarina Khasanova, the proprietor of Pamir and Mountain Travels, on a long walk along the Rudaki Street and arrived at the Somoni Square. Walking past Hotel Tajikistan and the National Library, we entered the city park. Fanned by the cool October breeze and lit by a gigantic moon hanging just over the Rudaki statue, the park was enveloped in a mysterious glow. A glow that lit the hearts of young couples who roamed hand in hand or occupied the dark corners of the park. On Somoni Street, we noticed an old woman selling boiled corn and found a place on the steps of the Square to have a bite. A policeman soon came to oust me from my perch saying I could not sit there for long. Nearby, just across the road was the Asoka restaurant run by two young Indians. Zarina told me that they had captured the heart of the Tajiks with their delicious food and Bollywood music. It was the first and the last time in Tajikistan that I ordered a hearty Indian meal before setting out on a long journey to see the Buddha.

Photography with Bobomulloev

The following day, I was at the museum again. With permission from Rahim Masov, I was ready to shoot. But the museum staff told me bluntly that no written permission for photography had been received from Masov. Since Bobomulloev was in a meeting, and the museum staff could not disturb him, I rushed to Masov again at the Academy for a written permission. On reaching there, I learnt that he had already left for lunch and was not expected to return before 3 p.m. It was a bad day for me. Dejected, I returned to my hotel without stopping anywhere for lunch and tried to rest before venturing to the museum again to meet Bobomulloev, my saviour.

This time I went directly to Bobomulleov's room. His clerk informed me that he was still in a meeting with museum officials and that I should wait. I sat on the plush sofa outside his room and looked out of the window. It was shaded by a lovely quince tree. A branch hung low, heavy with large, bright yellow fruits that resembled oranges. I stretched out a hand and plucked a quince—to taste for the first time—a fruit that did not grow in India. I spent quite a long time struggling to chew the hard, not so juicy or sweet flesh. But it certainly cut the boredom of a long wait.

Finally, Bobomulloev emerged from his room and summoned me to his chamber to discuss my Silk Road journey and the books that I must consult. He very kindly permitted me to photograph the antiquities and himself accompanied me to the various halls. The written permission had arrived by then, I was sure.

Antiquities from Penjikent

Monumental polychromous paintings that once decorated the art galleries of royal abodes of Penjikent now adorn the corridors of the museum. They portray scenes believed to represent the adventures of a hero from Firdousi's *Shahnameh*. Beautiful paintings from Ajina Tepe, Kafir Kala and the Kalai Kafirnigan monastic centres also adorn the walls here.

Images of the Hindu gods Siva and Parvati and of the Four-armed Goddess riding a lion, both from Penjikent, are objects of much interest and curiosity for both local and foreign visitors. The presence of Hindu gods in Tajikistan is evidence of cross-fertilization of the local and Indian cultures during the pre-Islamic period of Central Asia. Renowned Indian scholar S.P. Gupta has noted the worship of five Hindu gods, namely, Brahma,

Indra, Mahadeva (Siva), Narayana and Vaisravana in regions of Central Asia. The Hindu gods, however, had their own local counterparts.[1]

The massive stone altar and Corinthian columns of the Temple of Oxus (Takht-i-Sangin) are the pride of the museum and are displayed in the reception hall. Other antiquities found during excavations at the temple are showcased in a separate hall on the ground floor and include the famous figurine of Marsiyas—the Greek god of the river playing a flute. There is a small head of a Hellenistic ruler believed to be that of Alexander the Great. Several carved objects of ivory recovered from the temple are also on display. These portray scenes of hunting, flying angels and a garden scene with fabulous flowers and birds.

At the museum shop, a special section for 'Badakshan gems' attracts visitors. The most popular gem is the feroza, or turquoise. A blue feroza necklace at $35 a piece was simply irresistible.

By now, I was famished and we headed straight to the Green Bazaar, where I bought some bread and fruits for the long tour scheduled for the following morning. A woman pushed a cartload of boiled eggs which I was tempted to buy. Heaps of boiled corn and loads of meat hung from walls. Bananas were the most expensive item in the bazaar as they do not grow in Tajikistan and have to be imported from India and Iran.

In the evening, I met Zarina again for dinner. We discussed the route, food and lodging in the small towns of Tajikistan. She had arranged a sturdy vehicle—a SUV—for the tough journey and an experienced driver who had been to the Silk Road sites several times before. Suddenly, Zarina asked for my passport and scrutinized it. She pointed out that instead of a tourist visa I had been given a working visa. Before leaving for the Silk Road journey next day, I would first have to visit the Foreigner's Registration office to get my passport stamped. I was despondent. This would delay my tour by a few hours. Thankfully, Avesto Hotel had the authority to stamp my visa. What a great relief!

To the Gissar Fort

At 8 a.m. the following morning, I gorged on a large breakfast and packed some cakes and sweet samsa for the 45-kilometre drive to the Gissar Fort. Crossing Shirin, a sweet factory, we came upon a pumpkin bazaar at Chortepa village. In this region there is a huge demand for pumpkin for making ketchup, vegetable shorpa (curry), and fillings for manty (stuffed dumplings) and samsa. Most villages in the Gissar valley grow only pumpkin and watermelon.

Turtibobo village, besides growing corn was also cultivating grapes. One could see long stretches of vineyards supported on low wooden poles. The Gissar mountains came closer and the valley narrowed as we approached the Chilchanor village. Mominobad presented a picturesque scene as hundreds of women descended onto fields with large sacks on their back picking fluffy balls of cotton. The nearby Sharora is a famous UNESCO village. After the 1986 earthquake, the only survivor was an infant baby girl named Sharora. The new village that came up after the quake has been named after her. The road to the Gissar Fort now passed through a rich agricultural area. Wheat had been harvested and its place taken over by cabbage, tomato and cucumber.

From afar, one can see the massive gateway of the Gissar Fort set within the mountains and the ancient city walls zigzagging for miles. Two massive brick towers framed the wooden gates which opened into the mountains. We parked our vehicle near a choykhana set amid a forest and rambled into the fortress.

A Caravanserai in the Foothills

Mir's job was quickly taken over by a local guide who narrated the history of the fort. Since ancient times, the place on which the fort came up was an important halt on a branch of the southern Silk Road coming from Hindustan and Afghanistan through Termez and Denau and crossing over into the territory of what is today Tajikistan. This route passed through the Gissar Valley and could lead travellers and traders eastwards to China through the ancient city of Kashgar.²

On entering the gateway, one can see massive holes dug into the hill sides which once held the original gates of the fort. A wide pathway between two hillocks leads to the far end of the fort. Gravel and boulders lying on the path are evidence that it was once the bed of the stream flowing near the vicinity of the caravanserai. I do not have to go far into the mountains in search of springs.

The dull, dry road suddenly reached a grassy patch and led down the slopes of a rocky incline to thick bushes and farm land where the mountain spring was being harnessed for irrigation. The spring once brought water to the caravanserai. It still lives on to irrigate the foothills of the fort and has nurtured life for ages. A lovely fragrance of a wild shrub pervades the air. Khul Nazar, the driver, plucked a few purple flowers and presented them to me. They smelled like lavender.

The few mud hutments that lie here once formed part of the palace structure of the Gissar Bek (representative of the Bukharan ruler) who lived here. Remnants of the main palace and its walls can still be seen on the hilltop to the right of the gateway entrance.

The Gissar Fort is said to have been the chief town and the economic, political and cultural centre of the fertile Gissar Valley. The county of Shuman was located here. It is believed to have been settled since the time of legendary hero Afrasiab up to the middle of the 19th century, when it became the residence of the Gissar Bek.³

I tried to explore whatever remained of the chambers on the entrance gateway and climbed several steps to see what lay inside. There was a pentagonal room with a large hole that led to the dark dungeons of the zindan or the prison. There were several hidden spaces inside the chambers and on the outer walls of the fort, from where sharp-shooters rained arrows at the enemy approaching from the valley. The fort walls had loopholes where guards stood with weapons and armours to defend the fort. Even large grenades could be lobbed from the defensive walls.

At the base of the ramp that leads into the fort lies an ancient stump of a mulberry tree. Now it is a shrine to pray for the fulfilment of one's wishes. Several women and children were offering gifts to the spirit that lived on the stump. The practice of tree worship is still prevalent in many parts of Central Asia and travellers can see strips of cloth tied to branches and tree trunks. They are said to carry the prayers to benevolent spirits that are believed to live on trees.

Along the walls of the fort is a mausoleum where a subterranean spring brings sweet water from the mountains. The maulvi, who looked after a tomb in the vicinity, offered me a cup of the holy water. It was cool and fragrant and satiated my thirst. A brother maulvi was imparting Koranic lessons to his disciples under the shade of another mulberry tree. He picked up a handful of sweets from his alms bowl and gave them to me with a blessing. He then looked straight into my eyes and recited some verses which were incomprehensible. I was completely mesmerized by his chanting. I wanted to spend some more time in the company of the maulvi and his disciples. But time was flying and I had yet to see the madrassa and the ruined caravanserai lying just across the road before I returned to Dushanbe.

The ruins of an ancient caravanserai are spread over a vast area in front of the fort gate, by the side of the local museum. It was here that the travellers arrived with their goods and animals. Small living quarters can be traced in the ruins of the serai. The outer courtyard was the place where the travellers rested their cattle, letting them out to graze in the surrounding pastures. Numerous springs brought water from the mountains.

Today, the area seems totally parched. The springs have receded far behind the fort hill, a couple of kilometres away. The madrassa has now been turned into a museum, which records the history of the Gissar Valley in its numerous rooms.

References

1. Gupta, S.P. 'Hindu Gods in Western Central Asia: A Lesser Known Chapter of Indian History'. *Dialogue: A quarterly journal of Astha Bharti* (New Delhi), p. 1-2.
   URL: http://www.asthabharati.org/Dia_April2/Hindu.htm
2. Buryakov, Y.F., Baipakov, K.M., Tashbaeva, K.H., Yakubov, Y. *The Cities and Routes of the Great Silk Road* (Tashkent: Sharg, 1999), p. 71, 75
3. *Ibid.*, p. 77

Buddha along the Kafirnihon and Vakhsh Rivers

It was past 8 a.m.; Mir was waiting in the lobby of the Avesto. Outside, a gigantic Cruiser had its engine revved up for the long journey to southern Tajikistan. This journey would take me to the border of Afghanistan along the Vaksh and the Kafirnihon rivers; and to the points where they merged with the great Oxus, itself a confluence of the Vakhsh and the Pyanj. First on my itinerary was the monastery of Kafirnigan on the banks of the Kafirnihon river.

Kafirnigan was the celebrated city of the Kafirs. It is believed that the Arab forces pushing their way north from Kunduz across the Oxus and along the Kafirnihon river must have encountered many settlements along the river that belonged to a different faith (Buddhist) and hence called them Kafirs (infidels or non-believers). Thus the Buddhist settlement was the kala/village on the river of the Kafirs. Besides the monastery of Kafirnigan on the Kafirnihon river, there is another village/kala on the Vakhsh river, also named after the kafirs living there—the Buddhist site of Kafir Kala.

We drove along the Varzob river on Shirozi street and took Highway A-384 from Saudat. The highway ran smoothly, with little traffic. Soon we were surrounded by mountains of the Karategin range. At Ohonboy village, slopes of mud hills were dotted with herders on horseback who were out to graze their cattle. It seemed nature had heaped layers of clay to form the hills as there were no rocks or boulders. The road ran through Kasimobad like a swing springing up and down through the village that lay on the mountain slope.

After leaving Dushanbe, I had barely seen the Kafirnihon river. Maybe it was flowing far away near the mountains, concealed by the unlevelled ground and cotton fields. But channels drawn from the river passed through every village. These channels get flooded during summers when the river overflows with melted snow water. We passed several villages destroyed by floods on our route to the Kafirnigan site. Chagam village, with only a few mud houses, seemed to have sprung up recently after the devastating floods.

A little ahead of Kasimobad lay a Russian army base; in the dry fields near the mountains were parked dozens of Russian tanks. It's a vast and desolate area with no habitation or village and all the water channels here have dried up, giving the place a parched look. From the army watch towers, soldiers watch every vehicle that passes by.

The road now took a sharp turn to the left towards Khojiboy village, where a division of the Tajik army has been posted. For several kilometres there was no road, only mud tracks, as the road had been completely washed out by floods. At Pistazhor the road became visible again but a huge flock of sheep had kicked up a cloud of dust and blocked the path. They had the right of way. I got down to click photographs of the shepherds and their flock.

We continued to drive ahead to Sharian. From the map, I learnt we were somewhere near the Kafirnigan site. We stopped to make enquiries from villagers, who were raising the new village of Karobochik. One of them, Khudaikum Malin, came forward to show us the way to the Esanboy (Isanbai) village where the ancient monastery is situated.

Buddhist Site of Kafirnigan

The Kafirnigan Buddhist site appears to have been a large settlement spread out over several small hills. Several feet below the settlement flows the Kafirnihon river and beyond are the ranges of the Kurategin mountains, also called the Babatov. The entire settlement is surrounded by an undulating and thick wall that encloses an entire city. Since the settlement is at a height and concealed from the surrounding hills, it is difficult to reach the site from the main highway without guidance. One can easily miss it.

I climbed several hillocks to check out the many rooms, corridors, niches and pedestals that narrate the story of the busy settlement where the monks went about their daily chores, did circumambulations in the corridors around the shrine, sang paeans to the Buddha, studied the Buddhist texts, and ventured on the highway with their begging bowls for their day's meal.

One particularly high hill along a steep incline seemed like a stupa. It appeared like a mountain of small bricks and mud. It was surrounded by monastic structures all around. On reaching the top of this stupa-like hill, I found that extensive digging work had taken place and a heap of broken painted pottery with artistic surfaces lay nearby—some wavy, some with painted lines, some with curved handles of incense holders. Small images of the Buddha and bodhisattvas were recently unearthed from the site, and they presently lie at the museum in Dushanbe.

From the edge of this stupa-like hill one can see the river turning sharply to the left, that is, towards the east, taking an immensely wide sweep and then again turning south to flow towards the Oxus and the borders with Afghanistan. The river, which for some distance had been running at the ground level, ran hundreds of feet below at this point of the monastic settlement. The site for the monastery had been chosen with great care by the early monks. Safety from wild animals was their first concern as the Babatov mountains was known to be full of ferocious predators.

One could also see among the ruins a massive pedestal on which possibly stood a huge Buddha image. But there is no trace of the image at the site. The National Museum at Dushanbe does display several clay heads of immense Buddha statues found at monastic sites in the country. Seeing the high cliff and the menacing river deep down, the possibility of a huge structure falling from the hilltop and being swept away by the river below cannot be ruled out. The extent of terracotta and clay potteries heaped by the side of the excavated site gives an idea that some structure was certainly placed on the great hill or was hidden within it. With time, many clay structures on the hill could also have melted away.

Extensive Digging

On climbing the neighbouring hillocks, I found that extensive digging had taken place at several other ruins. These ruined settlements on small hills were probably monastic cells built around a common open space or a courtyard in which there was a shrine for the Buddha image. Some rooms still have traces of red paint on their walls. Corridors for circumambulation around the main shrine can also be traced. There are big and small niches in the walls of the corridors, which indicate that these were places where lamps were lighted or which were adorned with images of Buddhist deities.

The Kafirnigan site lay on the highway to Shahrituz—the road that leads to the confluence of the Kafirnihon river and the Oxus river (Amu Darya). It could lead travellers onto the highway to Afghanistan and into the Indus Valley. The highway was a particularly busy one with traders coming here from the northern and western regions of India. It provided the wealth needed for the upkeep of the monks and the monastic settlement.

From its great size, the Kafirnigan settlement appears to have catered to a large number of residing monks and also merchants and travellers who halted here. All traffic on the Oxus from Khorezm to Termez—along the road and river routes between India and Central Asia—could be diverted along the Kafirnihon river on which the grand Buddhist site once lay.

Corridor with Polychromous Paintings

According to the museum, the materials from the site of Kalai Kafirnigan, revealed more antiquities connected with Buddhism.[1]

The excavations were done in 1974–1980 under the supervision of renowned archaeologist B.A. Litvinsky. The town with a citadel spread over 3.5 hectares was dated to the 7th and 8th centuries.

A shrine hall surrounded by a corridor was excavated at the centre of the site. The hall had a platform set into a niche in the wall where perhaps stood an image of the Buddha. Records inform that the wooden columns supporting the ceiling were decorated with carvings while the walls, too, were covered with carved wooden panels. A similar building, with a small Buddhist temple, was excavated nearby. But what takes one's breath away are the beautiful polychromous paintings on display at the museum.

The walls and arch were covered with paintings. One famous polychromous painting from the shrine corridor (now in the upper hall of the National Museum) portrays a scene of circumambulating female devotees, bejewelled, clothed in long gowns. A long shawl or a cloak falls over their gown. Beautiful roundels that look like flower petals decorate the cloak. In their hands they hold long tender stems of lotus flowers. They seem to be royal women, their head covered in a cloth or a tight band, perhaps a crown. Their black hair is gathered in a knot at the back of their heads. Long earrings with swaying balls adorn the lobes of their ears and a beautiful necklace clasps their necks. They are accompanied by a monk wearing an orange robe that goes over his left shoulder. His right shoulder is bare and in his right hand he holds a large flower; not a lotus, but a magnolia. There is another worshipper in the frame. He is kneeling on the ground, holding gifts in his hands. The painted corridor, of which this mural was a part, appears to have been a circumambulatory passage around the main shrine, where an image of the Sitting Buddha was found.

Another, two-part painting, from the Kafirnigan site has been preserved. The upper section featured the sitting Buddha with two figures standing on each side of him, and the lower section featured the ceremonial procession.[2]

Excavations continue at the site and many statuettes of the Buddha and bodhisattvas are being recovered. I saw a particularly large bunch of Buddhist statuettes, recently excavated from the site, kept at the National Museum for registration and display.

Road to Shahrituz

From the settlement of Kalai Kafirnigan, we turned south and drove along the banks of the Kafirnihon river. The hills had appeared red in the afternoon sun, as if made of terracotta. The river nowhere seemed wider than near the monastic settlement; the river's sweep to the east and then south was huge and it covered an enormous territory. However, it was very shallow at this point and afforded a crossing point to the travellers coming from Termez into Kalai Kafirnigan after visiting the monasteries of Kara Tepa and Fayaz Tepa and journeying to the rich settlements of Dalverzin Tepa and Khalchayan near Termez.

Many holiday-makers had parked their cars on the bank of the river and descended into the waters for fishing. One of them had caught a fat fish and there was much rejoicing and shouting. We couldn't help but stop our vehicle on the road and venture to the banks to sit awhile and watch the amazing landscape of the deep grey Babatov ranges and the blue-green river flowing along its foothills. Such a moment, such a spot and such a river, I would never see again. How lovely it was to sit there and forget the destination!

I sat with my feet dipped into the river. The water was cold and I sprinkled some onto my face and arms. Silently, I watched the river flow by. I could hear it whispering a sweet song, of the days gone by when travellers and orange-robed inhabitants flocked its banks for their daily chores. After spending some time on the banks, I bade farewell to the river and the fish-catchers and proceeded on my journey to Shahrituz, my next halt.

The road ran close to the river for a few kilometres before going off on a tangent, losing sight of it. Soon, we approached the border post of the Kafirnihon that marked our entry into the restricted zone, the extreme south of Tajikistan. On the other side of the river were vast lands and settlements of the region of southern Uzbekistan. A policeman standing at the post stopped us. After checking our identity, he climbed into the front seat and travelled with us to the next post.

We arrived at Okhmajid village where the population is mostly Uzbek. I learnt that this was a peaceful town and the population belonged to the same family that had grown very large over time and a whole village has been occupied by descendants. At Ishkobad village, a pack of mules loaded with plastic pitchers were fetching water from the Kafirnihon river. Beyond Ishkobad, the road disappeared and our vehicle kicked up a lot of dust while crossing several dry riverbeds. The road continued to evade us up to Jailma village, where more dry river channels full of dust and dirt were waiting to catch us by surprise. The floods had completely devoured the roads. We were jumping from one ditch to another, holding tightly onto our seats. We forgot our travails as the road appeared again, and a wonderful sight welcomed us.

The mountains changed colour—they now appeared black against the green waters of the river. From the Babatov range, we proceeded along the Octov range as we neared Shahrituz. A stream separates from the river and runs wildly into a forested patch. Hidden behind tall grasses, mules and horses were quenching their thirst and enjoying the cool mountain breeze. Numerous nomadic families were camping on the hilly slopes with their herds of cows. They had accumulated loads of fodder and packed grass into large cubes to be transported to other regions of Tajikistan. Close to their yurt (camp) rose hills of animal dung cakes for lighting fire.

As soon as we entered Shahrituz bazaar, we began searching for the UNDP guest house where we were to spend a couple of nights. A large house with several rooms but common toilets, the guesthouse was owned by Akhmadjon and lay behind the bazaar in a quiet residential area. We deposited our luggage in the allocated rooms and assembled in the shady courtyard for a cup of black tea and some sweet buns. It was only 3 p.m. In spite of being very tired after a seven-hour journey from Dushanbe, we did not wish to waste even a single minute. Our next destination was Chiluchor Chasma: a pilgrim spot about 20 kilometres from the Shahrituz bazaar.

The Mysterious Chasma at Shahrituz

The chasma (spring) with 44 streams, located at the base of a hill, is said to be a magical spring with healing properties and blessed with the power of making wishes come true. After all, it was dug by the healing hands of Hazrat Ali himself from under the rocks.

It is said that when Caliph Ali, the son-in-law of Prophet Mohammad, reached this place near Shahrituz, he saw that Ronit, the only river passing through the region, had completely dried up. He cursed the river calling it the 'river without faith' or Kafirnihon (the river of the Kafirs). He raised his hands to pray to Allah for water. He then struck the earth under the rocks and instantly, five springs with clear, cool water burst forth to quench the thirst of his followers. Since then, it has become a place of pilgrimage for the devout from all over Central Asia.

The five main springs are further divided into 39 separate streams. A total of 44 springs thus bring their water into the chasma, which keeps bubbling with clear, cool water and thousands of shiny black fish. These fish are considered holy; so no one eats them.

The magical springs, the source of which remains hidden beneath rocky hills, can be seen flowing from all directions and coalescing to form the lake which is shaded by hundreds of oak and chinar trees bent and twisted with age and with a girth several metres thick. Their roots have penetrated deep into the hills and formed a mesh over the springs like the tentacles of a huge crab. Barely does any sunlight escape through the dense foliage. In order to fetch the holy water, pilgrims walk along the chinar roots and tiny wooden bridges that lead to the centre of the chasma. After running for a few kilometres, no one knows where the springs disappear.

After sprinkling some holy water on myself and making a wish,

I saw that in front of me was another hill where the beautiful mausoleum of Saint Kambar Bobo beckoned. I climbed the steep hillside and reached the top with some discomfort. Here a priestess sat alone at the feet of the saint reading from the Holy Book. She was in charge of the mausoleum and recited prayers for the visitors. She patted the ground and indicated that I should sit down and join the prayers. Although I was in a hurry to return, I followed her instructions and sat quietly with folded hands. My thoughts wandered to the saint's efforts in spreading the new faith in this predominantly Buddhist and Zoroastrian region. He must have been kind and full of love to have been revered by the inhabitants. Outside the mausoleum, at the edge of the hill, are other ancient graves said to be of the companions of the saint.

To Aivaz in Pursuit of Ishrat Bobo

The following morning we were on the road to Aivaz near the border of Afghanistan. Our destination: the monastic settlement of Ushtur Mullo. But first we had to pick up our guide, old Ishrat Bobo, from his residence in Aivaz, and then leave for the mountains of Ushtur Mullo settlement on the right bank of the Oxus.

We passed through the Shahrituz bazaar where I asked Mir to look for a choykhana where I could find some vegetarian breakfast. Zafar mentioned one on Lenin Street where he had already ordered some boiled rice and salted butter. Apart from this, I could munch on freshly baked naan dipped in black tea. On entering the choykhana, I noticed that a bunch of guests from Akhmadjon's guesthouse had already occupied the verandah of the teahouse and were sitting on the huge bed-like divan waiting for their breakfast before leaving for their work in the Tajik villages listed under the UNDP. The courtyard was also full with chattering guests. Large mud tandoors were baking fresh bread that were laid out in big trays and passed around. For the first time, I saw a choykhana serving butter and cream with hot naan.

We walked to the inner hall and were seated at a large dining table on which a teapot with a steaming spout was waiting for us. In no time, we too were served the usual naan. The waiter informed Zafar that the vegetarian meal was not yet ready. Meanwhile, we could eat boiled eggs served in a large wooden bowl. Soon, a big bowl of steaming rice arrived. There was a big chunk of butter melting in the centre. I added some freshly crushed rock salt and devoured the big heap. Rice had never tasted so delicious. On leaving the choykhana, I met the owner and especially thanked him for the rice. He was delighted at the appreciation shown and bade us good luck for our long journey into the mountains.

We crossed the bridge over the Kafirnihon and took the road to Aivaz. Near Lolazor village, we drove over the railway line going westwards into Termez. Lolazor and its surrounding villages are mainly corn- and rice-growing regions interspersed with vegetables farms using drip irrigation by plastic pipes. Amid the fields stand lime-washed mud houses that are large enough to be called bungalows.

In Aivaz, Ishrat Bobo's house was on the main road, surrounded by a forest of poplars. Zafar alighted from the vehicle and shook the front gate and beat at the iron chains as there was no call bell. A lady came out to inform that Bobo was not at home. He was away to his fields a couple of kilometres away across the river channel. Zafar and Mir left for the cotton plantations to look for Ishrat Bobo, who I was sure, had given us the slip.

I sat by the edge of the forest and waited for Zafar to bring back Bobo. What a lovely way to spend time, watching wild hens and birds swooping down from tree branches to peck at the dried leaves and pick worms. At the plantation across the road, women were harvesting cotton.

After a long wait, I got to know that Ishrat Bobo had indeed given us the slip. After promising to guide us to Ushtur Mullo, he had gone away to pluck cotton two kilometres away in a collective farm. When Mir and Zafar caught up with him, he excused himself saying it was impossible to reach the place. It would take hours of trekking over mountains and desert to reach Ushtur Mullo. Besides, he was old and could not take the strain of climbing mountains.

He warned that heavy military 'bandobast' had been made in the border region of Ushtur Mullo following the visit of Russian President Vladimir Putin to Tajikistan for military talks on the subject of Russian bases at key positions near the borders. He suggested that I must present myself at the military post back in Shahrituz and obtain permission to visit this security-sensitive region.

But Bobo had never mentioned all this the previous night. We had travelled 40 kilometres to Aivaz to pick him up. He could have informed us about all this, but he did not. I felt let down and cheated. I had only one more day at my disposal and the permission had to be taken immediately. I had already lost half a day in pursuing the old man and now I must wait at the military station to meet the commander of Shahrituz! I was wringing my hands in desperation at the thought of losing Ushtur Mullo from my itinerary.

Zafar drove back in haste to Shahrituz, and I presented myself at the military station to meet the commander. But it was not easy to get an appointment with him. I waited for a couple of hours outside in the vehicle only to learn that the commander was in an important meeting. However, a military official came out to inspect my documents and permitted me to visit Takht-i-Sangin instead of Ushtur Mullo. I was told to come again the following morning to get a military permit to visit Ushtur Mullo under military escort.

To the Temple of Oxus

It was past 1 p.m. and we immediately sped away on the road to the Takht-i-Sangin military post lying beyond the mountains on the right banks of the Oxus river, directly facing the land of Afghanistan lying across the river. We were asked to drive along the left bank of the Kafirnihon river after crossing the Shahrituz bridge along Lenin street.

We followed the route, asking passersby along the way, and

drove through vast cotton-growing regions and vegetable farms. All the while, a caravan of mules was quietly trudging along the road, laden with huge sacks of cotton for the nearby dumping yard. Many villages had hired trucks to carry their produce to the yard. It was cotton all the way. At the yards, huge piles of cotton lay like tall snow peaks. Here, cotton seeds were separated and taken to oil presses for extracting vegetable oil which fetched a good price in the international market.

Near Khaleli village, the road ended in a T-junction and we turned into a narrow path going right into the mountains. After zigzagging through cotton farms, we reached Teshitosh village (the last border village lying at the tip of southern Tajikistan) from where started climbing.

As we ran into the mountains, the scenery changed from rich agricultural land to a mountain desert completely denuded of even a blade of grass or a trace of water. Dry forest bushes were all that could be seen. The mountains seemed to be made of mud, boulders, pebbles and rocks. The road was unpaved and narrow, just enough for a vehicle to pass. A little ahead there was no road, only the pebbled pathway for military vehicles going to the checkpost bordering the neutral zone right on the river bank.

After meandering through the rocky mountain paths, we reached the top. From this point, one can have a clear view not only of the checkpost far below but also of the vast shining surface of the Oxus river and the land of Afghanistan beyond it. It was a stunning sight. The blue waters of the Amu Darya sparkled in the midday sun like chiselled diamonds. The wide curve of the river sweeps the region of Tajikistan, Uzbekistan and Afghanistan from south-east to west. It was a spectacular sweep seen from the top of the mountains. A rare view seldom seen even by the locals as this was a high security zone where the Tajik and probably Russian militia was monitoring night and day from underground bunkers. Not even a mule could pass unnoticed. I asked Zafar to stop the vehicle for a moment, while I aimed my camera at the landscape far below. Zafar had seen a military vehicle approaching far away from the base, and cautioned me to put away my camera until I had permission to shoot. But by then I had already captured the scenery. The mountain path was so narrow that we sat nervously while Zafar reversed and manoeuvred the car going right up to the edge of the mountains to allow the military vehicle to pass. Mir and I sat with bated breath lest we fall several hundred feet below.

After driving for about two kilometres beyond the mountains in a desert-like area, we reached the military post. A soldier at the gate informed the seniors on his walkie-talkie about our arrival. In no time, military personnel appeared to escort us to the Takht-i-Sangin site, now only five kilometres away on the banks of the Amu Darya. I was relieved. At last, I could actually see the temple in this desert land. And I knew this was a blessing from the river goddess of the Oxus.

It had become quite warm; the midday sun was blazing upon us and we had only one bottle of water between the three of us. We were still driving through desert shrubs and thorns. Thank God, it was an SUV otherwise it was impossible to drive through this rough terrain which gave us hundreds of high-voltage jolts a minute. But I was enjoying every bit of this adventure in the mountains of Aktov and on the banks of the most revered river of Central Asia, the Oxus.

The Sacred Oxus Temple: An Ode to the River

It is said that a dangerous and difficult journey to a temple multiplies its value and beauty. So it was with this temple. I heaved a sigh of relief and was overjoyed on finally reaching the temple. The ruins lay all around me. And the beautiful river stood before my eyes. Beyond it was the sacred land of Afghanistan where the Great Buddha lived in every crevice of its mountains until some time ago. It was a beautiful feeling to have reached this sacred place. After taking several shots of the ruins of the great temple, I sat down in the small shade of a stone pillar to experience the exhilarating moments inside the temple.

In front of me was a deep underground tunnel which seemed to have been dug either to bring the river water to the temple or as a secret exit for those who lived here, perhaps the priests or the worshippers.

Huge stone columns and their round and square bases were evidence of the massive gateway that led to the premises of the temple. It resembled any Indian temple built of stone on the river ghats (banks) with pillared avians (pavilion), vast courtyards, the shrine chamber and corridors around it. Alas! It was now difficult to trace out the plan of the temple from the ruins that lay scattered over a vast area. The evidence that a temple devoted to the Oxus river existed is provided by the stone structures, the river itself and the numerous temple offerings placed in the museum.

Corridors once surrounded the sanctum sanctorum or the garbh griha of the temple. Ruins of several rooms with fading red paint and stone facings could still be seen. Strewn around in the temple premises are bases of stone pillars, high columns and stones carved out into mortars and grinders.

The mountains that lay to my right near the site were evidence that the building materials were collected or mined from these very mountains. The heavy stone pillars and the massive stone altar discovered at the Oxus Temple (now kept at the National Museum) could not have been brought from a long distance. It is possible that the river flowed closer to the mountains then and changed its course over hundreds of years. Mir confirmed that during the spring and the summer season, the river had abundant water that reached the temple precincts.

Was the temple of Oxus an ode to the great river? Or was this a palace of some Greek ruler?

It was in 1976 that archaeologists started excavating the site of the ancient settlement at the confluence of the Vakhsh and Pyanj rivers. At the centre of the vast settlement, they found the ancient temple built of stone, perhaps quarried from the nearby mountains. The belief that the temple was devoted to the divinity of the Oxus river arose from the fact that a small stone altar decorated with a bronze figure of the Greek god Marsyas (a water god) playing a double-barrelled flute was recovered from the site.³ The altar of the water god now adorns the National Museum of Antiquities at Dushanbe.

Temple Treasures

Antiquities found inside the temple are believed to have been gifts brought by the worshippers. They include 5000 ancient objects of Greek–Bactrian times—an ivory sheath with the image of a lion holding a deer, chest facings made of ivory decorated with carvings, weapons of Greek–Macedonian warriors and the biggest collection of arrow tips. The image of Alexander the Great as Hercules was also found here. Many of these are now on display at the museum.

The fact that an eternal fire burned in the temple was gathered from the discovery of an 'ateshgah'—depository of the eternal fire—which is the essential element of a Zoroastrian fire temple. The stone altar too had the following text in ancient Greek: 'according to a vow Atrosok devoted to Oxus'. Atrosok is believed to mean 'possessing a blazing fire' and the name possibly belonged to a fire priest, a Zoroastrian.⁴ According to scholars, this indicated that both the cult of fire and the cult of the river were respected in one and the same temple.

According to museum sources, local inhabitants living along the Oxus river discovered in 1887 a treasure by the river—the 'Treasure of the Oxus'. Believed to be belonging to the temple, this treasure consisted of more than 2000 gold and silver coins and other gold objects, dating back to the 4th-3rd century BC. It is generally thought that the treasure was moved away from the temple in troubled times and buried for safety on the river bank. The treasure was then said to have been sold by the inhabitants to merchants going to India. And finally it fell into the hands of English rulers, then ruling over India. The treasure was brought to England where it finally found its way to the British Museum.

It is ironical that the greatest treasures of the world are outside their native places. The great gold 'Treasure of the Oxus' is at the museum at London; the only Reclining Buddha of the Chuy valley is at the Hermitage Museum, St Petersburg; the gallery of Avalokitesvara from Dunhuang in western China is at the National Museum, Delhi. These are only some of the examples. However, modern historians and archaeologists believe that the precious antiquities cannot belong to any country. They belong to the whole world.

References

1. Masov, R. (ed.), Bobomulloev, S. (ed.), Bubnova, M. (ed.). *National Museum of Antiquities of Tajikistan* (Dushanbe: National Museum of Antiquities of Tajikistan, 2005), p. 167
2. *Ibid.*, p. 169
3. *Ibid.*, p. 93
   Harmatta, J. (ed.). 'The Greek Kingdoms of Central Asia'. *History of Civilizations of Central Asia: The Development of Sedentary and Nomadic Civilizations (700 BC to AD 250)*, Volume II (Delhi: Motilal Banarsidass Pvt. Ltd., 1999), p. 116-118
   Buryakov, Y.F., Baipakov, K.M., Tashbaeva, K.H., Yakubov, Y. *The Cities and Routes of the Great Silk Road* (Tashkent: Sharg, 1999), p. 74
4. Harmatta, J. (ed.). 'The Greek Kingdoms of Central Asia'. *History of Civilizations of Central Asia: The Development of Sedentary and Nomadic Civilizations (700 BC to AD 250)*, Volume II (Delhi: Motilal Banarsidass Pvt. Ltd., 1999), p. 116-118
   Masov, R. (ed.), Bobomulloev, S. (ed.), Bubnova, M. (ed.). *National Museum of Antiquities of Tajikistan* (Dushanbe: National Museum of Antiquities of Tajikistan, 2005), p. 93

Monastery of Ushtur Mullo

I was yet to make the most difficult trip into the no man's land and over the mountains of Aivaz to the monastic settlement of Ushtur Mullo. It seemed that the trip would have to be given up in the absence of a travel permit to the most sensitive area of southern Tajikistan. The army officials at Shahrituz military station seemed reluctant to allow any entry into that zone.

On my return to Shahrituz by afternoon, I made a dash to the military station to find out whether permission had been granted to travel to the Ushtur Mullo site. The army commandant had not yet returned from lunch. The wait was a long one. I left Mir at the military station to deal with the commander as he thought fit and headed to Akhmadjon's guesthouse. I quietly snuggled into my bed for a short nap, losing all hope of ever being able to see Ushtur Mullo. There was no news from Mir till 5 p.m.

I fell into a deep slumber and on waking up, found Mir and Zafar in the lobby watching Putin's visit to Dushanbe on television. They appeared quite relaxed. Surely the army commandant had given us the slip like Ishtar Bobo and the trip to Ushtur Mullo was cancelled. I was despondent.

Suddenly, Mir informed me that we had to pack up early in the morning as the commandant had called us to the military station to give us written permission for visiting Ushtur Mullo. A soldier was to accompany us to the military outpost on the border fencing where the no man's land begins. I was delighted and jumped in disbelief. I think some lobbying by Zarina had worked. Assured of the permission, I again went back to sleep; and dreamt of a stupa on the mountains and cells cut into the sides of the hills. Buddhist chants emanated from the caves. I saw a ship full of orange-robed monks alighting far away on the banks of the Oxus. They walked in a procession; on reaching the foothills, they trudged up the hills and disappeared into holes cut into the mountainside. In a blink, all of them vanished. There was no stupa, only its base. The cells were also empty. Had I seen already what lay on the mountains? Only the following day would tell.

Driving to the Hill Monastery

At the military office, our permit was ready; a soldier sat in the front seat of our vehicle and we drove on the road along the left bank of the Kafirnihon river. I was excited, but the 40-kilometre journey to Ushtur Mullo was risky. We passed through several cotton-growing collective farms belonging to the villages of Oreano and Hoyat. The scene was particularly lively in the Panjosolagi and Jamaoti villages where the morning session of cotton plucking was over and women had opened their bundles of naan and home-made apricot jam for breakfast under the mulberry trees that lined the road.

Gulchin village, as the name denotes, is a 'sugary village' on the way to Sonkh. Mir pointed to a grass factory that prepared a sugary medicine for the liver from the roots of the wild grass that grew along water channels of the Kafirnihon river.

We turned left from Shokh and drove through the streets of a town to an embankment and a dirt track to reach the military outpost—the last outpost that monitors the 'no man's land' along the Oxus river. It was a large outpost and the sentry at the gate took permission from his senior officials on his walkie-talkie before letting our vehicle pass. Another soldier checked our permit and sat with us in the back to accompany us to Ushtur Mullo.

Accompanied by the two soldiers—one in the front seat and

the other squeezed between Mir and I in the back seat—we drove for a few more kilometres in the roadless region of the neutral zone, cutting our way through knee-high desert bushes and boulders. After about four kilometres, the mud tracks too disappeared into the wild growth. Zafar threw up his hands and stopped the vehicle. He would go no further. With great difficulty, we jumped out of the high vehicle onto the shrubs below and waded our way through wild growth to a clearing at the foot of the Ushtur Mullo mountain which was covered with rocks, shrubs and grass.

The army men now informed us that we had to cross four hills before we could reach the Ushtur Mullo site. Even before I could recover from the shock of having to cross four hills, the army men disappeared. The next moment I found them sitting on the top of the hill peering down at me. While they were quick to climb the sharp incline, I held on to shrubs and twigs to pull myself up. There were no steps cut into the hillside and holding onto shrubs and sharp rocks was of no help. Seeing my precarious position, the two army men rushed down to pull me up.

With great difficulty, I reached the hilltop. But three more hills had to be climbed before I could be on the other side of the mountain. Finally, the army men helped me to reach the fourth hill from where the mighty, graceful and bountiful Oxus river came into view. What a beauty! I forgot my travails and sat on a huge rock to catch my breath.

Monk's Shelter

One of the two army men pointed out to a large rocky cave on the hillside. It seemed like a recess, large enough for a small group of people to take shelter from rain and harsh winds that always lash the hillside. Nearby was a collapsed burnt brick structure. Old, flat and square large bricks had been piled, to form the part of a wall. The structure appeared mysterious. It is unthinkable how a burnt brick structure came into existence on the mountains where there were only rocks covered with dry shrubs. Who built this structure on a remote hill? Did the inhabitants bake the bricks? Where did they find the clay for it? Was it a watch tower for the Russians to keep a check on the other shore of the Oxus? Many such questions intrigued me. I had seen such big square bricks only at the ancient Buddhist monasteries in Kapilavastu and Kushinagar (in India) and at Lumbini (in Nepal), where the monk cells were made of large, flat, square, baked bricks. Such big bricks were rarely used in the modern buildings of Tajikistan.

We spent some time at the brick structure, sitting on a rock wall to catch our breath. Looking beyond the shores of the river, the land of northern Afghanistan (the region of Kunduz) came into view. It was somewhere along this point of the river, in the Aivaz region of Tajikistan, that Zaheeruddin Mohammad Babur crossed into Afghanistan on his way to India in the beginning of the 16th century.

Climbing down the steep slope, with the two army men by my side, my attention was drawn to another deep cave in the mountainside where monks could have taken shelter. Shepherds from nearby villages now find it a cosy place to escape from the harsh weather and light fires to warm themselves. We were going from one shelter house in the mountains to another.

Congregational Hall and Stupa

I was yet to come across a large settlement. Soon, I noticed flat, even land that seemed to have served the purpose of a large courtyard or a hall at the foot of the hill. Around this courtyard, the hills had been cut into several shelter houses. This hall or a courtyard must have been a temple surrounded by a monastic settlement on the hills. Very little is known about the antiquities obtained from the monastic site of Ushtur Mullo. But it is reported that a stupa decorated by stone reliefs was discovered here.

Apart from the mountain shelters, caves and brick structures along with a vast levelled courtyard, no ruins of any stupa or monastery can be seen on the ground. According to the authors Davi and Litvinsky, the monastery consisted of 26 buildings which surrounded a square courtyard.[1] In the middle of the north side was a shrine with a circumambulatory corridor. There were small residential cells for individual monks and a large hall for the sangha or the congregational meetings. The shrine was decorated with paintings and alabaster sculptures. Outside the complex was a stupa, the base of which was faced with stone reliefs.

Even the National Museum records attest to this description.[2] It informs that on the right bank of the Amu Darya, in Tajikistan, near the Verblyujya hill, the Buddhist cloister of Ushtur Mullo was investigated by T.I. Zeimal in 1979–1982. The remnants of the stupa were found in the temple and it revealed a 'proto-type stupa consisting of two halves: the lower as a box and the upper as a round dip set into the drum'. The sangharama consisted of a courtyard around which the monastery was built. Of the 26 dwelling places, 14 were used as rooms for the cloister and the rest for a variety of other purposes. In the northern part of the building, there was a big hall measuring about 100 square metres. 'The walls were decorated with inscriptions which were not preserved and of which no transcript exists.'

All these descriptions did not match with what I was looking at. However, what seemed strange is that even the National Museum had no antiquities from this famous monastery of Ushtur Mullo. Professor Bobomulleov also confirmed that much was recovered from the site, including the stupa. In all probability, the antiquarian remains of Ushtur Mullo were transferred to the museums in Russia.

We walked for about two kilometres along a mud track running next to a canal covered with wild flowering bushes. The army man pointed to a shrubby area where the medicinal grass was growing. I pulled out a plant together with its root. It was aromatic, smelling of jaggery and full of juice. This juice which is sweet like sugar is extracted to prepare medicine. Soon, we spotted our vehicle neck-deep in the bushes and somehow we manage to climb inside it.

To the Monastery of Kafir Kala

After dropping the officials at their respective military stations, we took the road to Kholkhozabad. We were now on Highway 384 and driving to the Beshtemur village. On our right were the Aktov mountains. With great excitement, I waited to see the great Vakhsh river. All these days, I was in the proximity of the Kafirnihon and the Oxus. Now, I was to cross the Vakhsh near Kobadiyan. The long bridge over the Vakhsh seemed to swing with the flow of the river. With every passing vehicle, the bridge reverberated. I asked Zafar to drop me at one end of the bridge. While he drove to the other end, I stood in the pedestrian lane over the bridge and started taking photographs. Mir shouted that photography was prohibited on the bridge and nervously looked around for any policemen approaching us. But there was no one there. The river view was simply stunning. Several large streams had contributed to its huge girth, measuring not less than a kilometre in width. The colour of the river, too, varied from stream to stream, some deep green, some clear, while others near the bank were muddy. Like the small islands in the middle of the Brahmaputra, the Vakhsh could also boast river islands near Kobadiyon.

At Yangiobod, a policeman waved and signalled us to stop. He checked my passport and commented that he liked Hindustan and asked me about my views on Tajikistan. I told him that his country was beautiful. He smiled and waved a goodbye.

The landscape henceforth was barren. As we entered Jiliko village, the hills became stark and reflected the heat and glare of the afternoon sun. The rocky mountains changed colour from grey to a shade of terracotta. I noticed a shepherd and his flock of sheep huddled under a large rock to escape the heat. But in the desolate landscape, heaps of watermelons appeared by the roadside as if by magic. They were being brought from the catchment of the Vakhsh lying on the other side of the mountains. Running along with us was the railway line to Kurgan Tube.

At Kafir Kala Monastic Site

We reached Kholkhozabad at 4 p.m., worried that the monastic site of Kafir Kala might be closed. It lay within the city, in the middle of a crowded residential area, and we had to pass through several city streets and narrow lanes before we could reach the site an hour later. Since there was hardly any entrance gate, provision of a security guard or any fencing of the site, it seemed that it was never closed. I thanked my stars.

The monastic ruins, said to be the largest archaeological monuments of the Vakhsh River valley, are believed to have been the early medieval capital of the princedom of Vakhsh, whose rulers practised Buddhism in the 6th–7th century AD.

The ruins of the vast city, together with the citadel, lie like a massive square surrounded on all sides by a wide and deep ditch and protected by walls with towers. The base of the corner projecting towers can still be seen from the pathway over the wide walls. The city walls are in the shape of a broad 5-10-metre rampart which even today appears in good condition. At intervals, the rampart widens, marking the location of the towers.

Excavations here revealed a Buddhist monastery in the southeast corner of the citadel, dating to the 5th–6th century AD. The Buddhist vihara was characterized by a central cella (main sanctuary), encircled by a four-column corridor. During the Arab conquest, the monastery and the stupa were largely destroyed. There remained only fragments of polychrome wall paintings with the depiction of the Buddha, lotuses and ornaments. Some burnt fragments of birch bark were found during the excavations, with characters of Brahmi preserved on them.[3]

A few paintings from Kafir Kala adorn the Buddha Hall of the National Museum in Dushanbe. During excavations, some residential complexes with streets were uncovered. At one site was found a large central hall with an entrance. The walls had deep niches and were decorated with paintings with ornamental motifs. The elevated citadel was uncovered almost entirely. Artefacts found here were dated to the 3rd–4th century AD.

According to the details published by the National Museum of Antiquities,[4] excavations at Kafir Kala palace revealed a large rectangular hall with an entrance. Along the walls ran divan-like benches or 'sufa' made from pakhsa or earth mixture. A large ritual fireplace was found near the hall. A small temple (probably Buddhist) excavated in the citadel consisted of rectangular cells topped with a cupola and surrounded with a corridor on all four sides. The walls were decorated with paintings which are believed to have perished due to moisture in the soil. The town is believed to have come into existence during the Kushan period. The presence of the Buddhist temple at Kafir Kala was confirmed by excavations carried out in the citadel. The religious rituals practised denote that the king and the people of this country were devotees of Buddha.[5]

I reverted to my guide book to see what Dani and Litvinsky have written about the Buddhist temple at Kafir Kala. According to the authors, the southern part of the palace contained the Buddhist vihara and a courtyard. The vihara had a central sanctuary and an ambulatory. The walls of the sanctuary were decorated with polychrome murals depicting the Buddha and other Buddhist deities.[6]

The Kafir Kala Museum is not far from the site. It lay inside the big Central Park. On reaching there I found that the museum was locked as it was past 6 pm. A gardener pointed out to the staff quarters where the in-charge lived. Mir went to fetch him and returned with the curator, Rajab Habibulla. The museum was unlocked and I entered the massive halls where paintings, stone decorations, khums and the site plan of Kafir Kala was showcased. Rajab Habibulla was a kind man and allowed me to photograph the antiquities.

One terracotta-facing brick, perhaps used in decorating the walls of the complex, bore the motif of grapevine. Numerous water pots and large granaries made of baked clay with painted motifs on the surface adorned the halls. A rounded terracotta or gypsum frieze recovered from the site appeared to be a scene from the 'attack of the demon Mara'. It portrayed a lion attacking a male rider on a horse. While the beast, with bared teeth, sprang with all force on the rider, the latter whose face was turned to the right, faced the ferocious creature calmly and fearlessly. The rider, with his hair tied into a top knot and his ears adorned with earrings, appeared like the Buddha.

A polychromous painting that hung on the walls of the Kafir Kala museum, although badly faded, portrayed the Buddha with his disciples. Another painting from Kafir Kala, once polychromous, had now changed colour to dark brown and black. Only a part of the Buddha's head could be seen against the darkened backdrop.

At Ramz in Kurgan Tube

After visiting the Kafir Kala site, we took Highway 384 to Kurgan Tube, which is located in the Vakhsh Valley, 100 kilometres south of Dushanbe. It is believed to have been founded in the 7th century. The city is perched in the centre of a rich oasis.

The territory of modern Kurgan Tube was in the past known as Khuttal and the city itself was known as Levakend or Vakhsh in the Middle Ages. It was famous for its special breed of sheep. Today, Kurgan Tube is one of the largest cities of Tajikistan, the regional centre of Khatlon area, and the seat of several large industrial enterprises, universities, colleges, hotels, fruit and vegetable processing, large dairies, cotton processing units, citrus plants, horticulture, animal husbandry and cotton thread manufacturing units.

While Mir and Zafar arranged to spend the night at a mehmonkhana (guesthouse), they drove me to the nearby Ramz

Hotel for a room. It is a grand five star hotel with all modern amenities. At the counter sat a young woman who was soon to marry her fiancé in Delhi. We immediately became friends.

After the tiring journey from Shahrituz, I found the luxury of Ramz a blessing. My room was on the second floor. It was very large and well furnished. The wall facing the main bazaar was made of glass panels and I spent hours looking at the streets that met at the main road crossing of Kurgan Tube just in front of the hotel. I noticed that even at late hours in the night, the traffic at the crossing was quite busy.

References

Important sources for description of the above monastic settlements are: Litvinsky, B.A. (ed.). 'The Kushano-Sassanian Kingdom'. *History of Civilizations of Central Asia: The crossroads of civilizations (AD 250 to 750)*, Volume III; Masov, R. (ed.), Bobomulloev, S. (ed.), Bubnova, M. (ed.). *National Museum of Antiquities of Tajikistan*

1. Litvinsky, B.A. (ed.). 'The Kushano-Sassanian Kingdom'. *History of Civilizations of Central Asia: The crossroads of civilizations (AD 250 to 750)*, Volume III (Delhi: Motilal Banarsidass Publishers Pvt. Ltd., 1999), p. 113
2. Masov, R. (ed.), Bobomulloev, S. (ed.), Bubnova, M. (ed.). *National Museum of Antiquities of Tajikistan* (Dushanbe: National Museum of Antiquities of Tajikistan, 2005), p. 119, 163
3. Litvinsky, B.A. (ed.). 'Eastern Kushans, Kidarites in Gandhara and Kashmir and Later Hephthalites'. *History of Civilizations of Central Asia: The crossroads of civilizations (AD 250 to 750)*, Volume III (Delhi: Motilal Banarsidass Publishers Pvt. Ltd., 1999), p. 182
Litvinsky, B.A. (ed.). 'Religion and Religious Movements-II'. *History of Civilizations of Central Asia: The Crossroads of Civilizations (AD 250 to 750)*, Volume III (Delhi: Motilal Banarsidass Publishers Pvt. Ltd., 1999), p. 437
4. Masov, R. (ed.), Bobomulloev, S. (ed.), Bubnova, M. (ed.).

National Museum of Antiquities of Tajikistan (Dushanbe: National Museum of Antiquities of Tajikistan, 2005), p. 162-163
5. *Ibid.*, p. 163
6. Litvinsky, B.A. (ed.). 'Eastern Kushans, Kidarites in Gandhara and Kashmir and Later Hephthalites'. *History of Civilizations of Central Asia: The crossroads of civilizations (AD 250 to 750)*, Volume III (Delhi: Motilal Banarsidass Publishers Private Ltd., 1999), p. 182

Burnt clay slab found at Kafir Kala depicting a bodhisattva prince being attacked by a lion (7th century AD).

Courtesy: National Museum of Antiquities of Tajikistan, Dushanbe and Site Museum, Kafir Kala

Clay Buddha head from the monastery of Kalai Kafirnigan (7th-8th century AD).

Courtesy: National Museum of Antiquities of Tajikistan, Dushanbe

A wall painting from a vault of the Ajina Tepa monastery near Kurgan Tube (6th-8th century AD).

Courtesy: National Museum of Antiquities of Tajikistan, Dushanbe

The Reclining Buddha from the monastery of Ajina Tepe, near Kurgan Tube (6th-8th century AD).

Courtesy: National Museum of Antiquities of Tajikistan, Dushanbe

Painting of circumambulating devotees from the monastery of Kalai Kafirnigan (7th-8th century AD).
Courtesy: National Museum of Antiquities of Tajikistan, Dushanbe

Painting of 'gift-givers' from the monastery of Ajina Tepe (7th-8th century AD).
Courtesy: National Museum of Antiquities of Tajikistan, Dushanbe

To the Monastery of Ajina Tepe

We left Kurgan Tube at 7 a.m. and drove east in the Vakhsh Valley for 12 kilometres on the road to Ajina Tepe. Since ancient times, the Vakhsh Valley was the seat of intensive irrigated farming, whose origins, according to B. Litvinsky and T. Zeimal, are traceable to the middle of the 1st millennium BC. The valley is said to have flourished until the Mongol invasion. Its capital was Helaverd where there was a mint for gold and silver coins.

Today, the valley is criss-crossed by a network of modern irrigation canals. The Nurek dam on the Vakhsh is the first of its kind in Central Asia. Near Keirov, a pathway turns right and leads along an iron bridge over a flowing canal to the site of Ajina Tepe. The high mound, which was once a monastery, rises from the ground like a mud hill. The mound lies in the midst of cotton plantations. Legends associate it with evil spirits and, therefore, its name Ajina Tepa or the Devil's hill.

As I climbed up the hill, the agricultural farms and orchards surrounding the site came into view. Canals bring water from the Vakhsh to this agricultural region. The area falls in the lower stream of the Vakhsh in the south of Tajikistan where the valley is surrounded by mountains on three sides.

The ruins of the Buddhist monastery date from the 7th-8th century AD. Only a small part of the ancient site has been excavated by scientists but what was found at the site surpasses anything obtained so far from any Buddhist site, except Krasnaya Rechka in Kyrgyzstan and Kusinara in India.

It was from a corridor or a pradikshana path of Ajina Tepe that a 12-metre Reclining Buddha was found. Mir points to the wall in the back corridor from where the giant image was found. For memory's sake, I stood against the wall to get myself photographed. It was also from here that several images of the Buddha and bodhisattvas were recovered from niches in the wall. Even more amazing was the terraced stupa, found on a high mound in a part of the monastic settlement, which is now preserved in a glass case in the National Museum at Dushanbe.

Monastery and Stupa

Since this was the most famous and complex monastic settlement on the territory of Tajikistan, and to which I could not come a second time, I had requested Bobomulloev to provide me some helpful literature on the site. He very kindly handed me *Ajina-Tepa: Architecture, Painting, Sculpture* by B.A. Litvinsky and T.I. Zeimal and a museum publication, *Antiquities of Tajikistan*. These, he said, were essential for any traveller to Ajina Tepe for learning about the orientation and architecture of the monastery. Especially the numerous corridors that surrounded the courtyards; the high hilly mound that was once the base of the terraced stupa, and the niches in the corridor walls from where interesting antiquarian remains, including the sculptures and paintings were extracted.[1]

The Ajina Tepe ruins consist of two adjoining equal parts—the south-eastern part, close to the entrance, once housed the monastery proper with structures arranged around a square courtyard; and the north-western part, located on the farther end, where once stood a high-rise stupa. Today, the base of the stupa rises like a mound of earth or a small hill. Hundreds of coins found at the site indicated the period during which the monument was in use. According to Litvinski and Zeimal, the period could be from the 7th–8th century, lasting for some 100 years after which it stopped functioning as a Buddhist monastery. This was due to the Arab conquest of the area in the middle of the 8th century. Surrounding the square courtyard of the monastery were corridors with vestibules that led into inner rooms with domed ceilings. The corridors and the walls of the rooms can be easily traced today. In one of the rooms was found a shrine with pedestals and the remains of a miniature stupa. There were decorative paintings and relief panels on the walls. The central figure in the shrine was that of the Buddha. According to the authors, judging by the size of the head, it must have been at least four metres in height.

During excavations, numerous lamps were recovered from the monastic cells. One room alone contained 200 lamps, and countless bottles, coins and ornaments. These were perhaps gifts brought by worshippers of the Buddha. A painting, portraying the 'gift givers of Ajina Tepe', once decorated the monastery walls, and today adorns the National Museum. In some rooms excavators found huge vessels sunk into the floors. These could have been used by the monks for storing or cooking congregational meals.

The Great Nirvana Buddha

During excavations in one of the corridors, a giant image of the 'Buddha in Nirvana' (over 12 metres in length) was found. Lying in the traditional posture of the 'Sleeping Lion', the Buddha, now at the National Museum of Antiquities, Dushanbe, can be seen clad in red sanghati (robes) and lying on his right side, the right arm is bent at the elbow resting on pillows and the left arm is stretched along the body.

Extraction and conservation of the 'Nirvana Buddha' was a difficult process as the image was made of clay. The task was performed by a large number of restorers of the State Hermitage under the supervision of P.I. Kostrov. The Buddha was cut into 92 pieces and then restored. Further restoration was carried out at the A. Donish Institute of History, Archaeology and Ethnography, a faculty of the Academy of Sciences of the Republic of Tajikistan. The final restoration was done at the National Museum of

Antiquities of Tajikistan with the participation of V. Fomin, a specialist from the State Hermitage.[2]

'Descent from Heaven' Stupa

Walking along the corridors of the monastery, the visitor is led into a courtyard in the north-western part of the site. Here, in the centre of the vast courtyard stands the base and drum of a once great rare kind of stupa measuring six metres in height and 28 metres in diameter. The cylindrical drum that topped the base is still intact and stands on the site like a very high mound. Climbing on the drum, one can have a 360-degree view of the surrounding villages.

The remains of the stupa now lie at the Dushanbe Museum, encased in glass. The shape and architecture of the stupa is amazing. It has terraced sides, with flights of stairs like ladders in the middle of every side. We read about a similar type of stupa that had steps in the centre of each side like a flight of stairs in Pema Dorjee's *Stupa and its Technology*. Dorjee calls it the stupa of the 'Descent from Heaven' or the 'stupa offered by the Devas'.[3] This kind of stupa can also be compared to the miniature stupas found at the monastery of Khisht Tepa which has ladders with railings in the centre of each side.

According to Dorjee, the 'Descent from Heaven' was one of the great eight stupas that emerged from the division of the Buddha's relics into eight parts. It was built under the sponsorship of King Suddhodana at the city of Kapilavastu.[4]

Votive stupas offered by worshippers and placed in the corners of the courtyard also adorn the museum. In one of the smaller votive stupas was found a clay tablet inscribed with a Buddhist prayer.

The base of the stupa was made of clay blocks and the brick mass of the drum and lies in ruins at the monastic site. The outer surface of the stupa is said to have been washed with a coating of gypsum and the base was once decorated with relief in alabaster.

The courtyard in which the stupa is located is surrounded by a corridor which once rested on columns. The walls of the corridor were pierced with niches which held Buddhist images. Numerous images of the Seated and the Standing Buddha were recovered during excavations at the site.

Paintings and Sculptures

The richly decorated monastery had its corridors painted from top to bottom. Numerous images of the Buddha adorned the rooms and corridors of the temple. The paintings include compositions like the scene of the Buddha's sermon and gift-givers. The paintings on the arches portrayed the 'Saharsha Buddha' or the 'Thousand Buddhas'. Giant sculptures of Sitting Buddhas stood in deep niches.

Among the beautiful paintings of the Buddha and worshippers decorating the monastic site is the one recovered from the debris of corridor 31. The fragment shows two male figures in white garments kneeling on the ground. In their outstretched arms, they bear gifts in special vessels of gold and silver, offering them to the image of the Buddha placed there, or as Litvinsky points out, to the stupa, in cella 31. The fragment is a multi-tiered painting covering the wall of the passage. The tiers of the painting are separated by a chain of pearls. The worshippers are depicted in special high-necked, full-sleeves, tightly fitting apparel gathered at the waist by a belt.

The main object of worship in the Ajina Tepe monastery appears to have been the giant and awe-inspiring Reclining Buddha. Many other life-sized Buddhist images were placed on pedestals along corridors. The worshippers placed small and large votive stupas as offerings in the courtyard. Generally, the votive stupas carried sutras written on clay tablets that were placed inside them. Clay tablets inscribed with Buddhist mantras can be seen at the National Museum.

From the antiquities displayed in the Buddha Hall of the Museum and the paintings reproduced and described in the works by B.A. Litvinsky and T.I. Zeimal,[5] it can be seen that the decorative paintings used the floral motif of the lotus to separate closely placed figures of the Buddha. The motif of a chain of white pearls separated different tiers of a painting. Contrasting colours were used so that the paintings could be seen in the dim natural light of the monastery. The ceilings of the corridors were covered with the motif of the 'Thousand Buddhas'. The vaults and domes with the Buddha images are believed to have represented a Buddhist heaven filled with innumerable Buddhas and bodhisattvas. The theme of the 'Thousand Buddha' images was a popular Buddhist iconography in both India and Central Asia. The painters created the 'Heaven of the Buddha' on the ceiling of corridors. The dark sky filled with the brightly coloured images of the 'Thousand Buddhas' formed the pradikshana path through which the devout walked.[6]

Back to Dushanbe

We returned to Kurgan Tube to take Highway A-384 back to Dushanbe, about 100 kilometres away. The Vakhsh Valley route goes through the fruit belt of Tajikistan that feeds not only Central Asia but also Russia. From Obekik, the road runs closer to the mountains and sometimes passes through them. They are high and grassy and covered with flowers. At Dakhanakik village, tulips of various hues have overtaken the mountain slopes. The foothills are cultivated for crops and fruits. One can notice large tankers providing drip irrigation through thin cables. The region covered by the villages of Kasimobad and Farakovobad have vast vineyards which supply their produce to breweries.

Monastery of Khisht Tepa

From *Cities and Routes of the Great Silk Road*, we learn of another important Buddhist temple that was excavated at Munk and dated to the 7th and 8th centuries. Munk is believed to have been the largest town in Khutalayan or Khuttal (in present-day Khovaling) in the territory of Tajikistan. Replete with springs and pastures, this was a fertile and wealthy region. Precious metals like gold were quarried here.

The above source informs that the road from Vakhsh went to Khutalayan and passed through Khelaverd to the towns located on lower Pyanj. Caravans went from Khutalayan by the ford, crossed the Pyanj and then entered Badakshan on the way to India.[7]

The monastic settlement lay in the valley of the Obimazar river, near Chepivol village, 12 kilometres from Khovaling. From here, the excavators found a monumental structure with a big votive stupa, miniature stupas, clay inscribed tablets and a circumambulatory corridor around a canopied sanctuary. The Buddhist complex is said to have fallen to decay probably after the Arab conquest of Khuttal in the 7th or 8th century AD.

Khisht Tepa Votive Stupas

After learning that nothing remained at the Khisht Tepa site and that most of the antiquities found during the excavations had been brought to the National Museum at Dushanbe, I dropped my plans of driving 300 kilometres to the site. Instead, I concentrated on objects now on display in the museum. These included several votive stupas and clay tablets.

The votive stupas recovered from the site and the numerous clay tablets on which Buddhist mantras were written have been preserved in perfect condition at the National Museum. I accompanied Bobomulloev to a huge hall of the museum where the antiquities from Khisht Tepa had been preserved. However, the electric bulb emitted a very dim light and the cameras could take only an extremely diffused picture of the stupas. It was quite amazing that the small votive stupas that resembled the huge stupa from Ajina Tepe, were also kept in a section of the same hall. It appeared that the stupa design had been planned by one and the same monastic authority. Or that the same pilgrims offered a similar votive stupa at both monasteries. Or maybe the same craftsmen created similar votive stupas.

According to M. Mullokandov, the excavations of 1985–1988 revealed that the site of Khisht Tepa had concealed a monumental structure, namely an early medieval Buddhist monastery with apparently 20 rooms built of pakhsa (earth mixture) and mud bricks.[8]

The entrance to the monastery was marked by two pylons and led to the central dome chamber which had mud sufas (benches) running along the walls. The sanctuary was encircled from all sides by a corridor. Monastic cells, a room with a big votive stupa, and a large congregational hall for monastic meetings were found by excavators.

The evidence of a canopied sanctuary was provided by four post holes dug in the floor of the sanctuary for holding wooden columns to support a roof over an altar. The niche in this altar once held a Buddhist image.[9]

Nearly 60 intact miniature clay stupas were recovered from Khisht Tepa, the majority from a niche in the platform of the sanctuary. Some of these are showcased at the National Museum. The miniature stupas have been described in detail by M. Mullokandov, historian-archaeologist working on the Khisht Tepa site. In the top part of their hemisphere, the stupas have a small niche for fixing of a harmika (a small platform with a railing on the top of a stupa) and a pin for chattri (umbrella).

In the centre of every side of stupa is a small vertical staircase with a stepped railing; and all of them enclose a clay tablet with a Buddhist prayer (with stamped characters in Brahmi script) reproducing the Buddhist ritual text—the dharma paryayya—that is, the proclamation of Buddhist teachings '*ye dhamma hetu prabhava hetu*'.[10] Such clay tablets with Indian texts of similar inscription '*ye dhamma hetu*' in Tibetan characters was found in the stupa of the Spituk monastery in Leh–Ladakh in India.[11]

According to scholars, there was a practice of inserting various kinds of articles like precious stones, Buddhist prayers written on tablets, and scrolls in the hollow of the stupa. It was widely believed that the greater the number of holy articles inserted in the stupa, the greater would be the power and blessings of the stupa.[12]

I had covered only a few routes of the Silk Road through Tajikistan. Many more remained to be explored. Like the one going to Khorog and the monastic settlement of Vrang in the Pamirs. Zarina dissuaded me as the weather was inclement and the M-41 Pamir Highway, she said, could be blocked. Flights to Khorog had been cancelled. Some other time, she promised. Perhaps, next year.

References

Important source for the description of Ajina Tepa monastery: Litvinsky, B.A. and Zeymal, T.I. *Adzhina-Tepa: Architecture, Painting, Sculpture*

1. Litvinsky, B.A. and Zeymal, T.I. *Adzhina-Tepa: Architecture, Painting, Sculpture* (Tajikistan : A. Donish Institute of History, Archaeology and Ethnography and SSR, 1971), p. 219-244
2. Masov, R. (ed.), Bobomulloev, S. (ed.), Bubnova, M. (ed.). *National Museum of Antiquities of Tajikistan* (Dushanbe: National Museum of Antiquities of Tajikistan, 2005), p. 167
3. Dorjee, Pema. *Stupa and Its Technology* (New Delhi: IGNCA and Motilal Banarsidass Publishers Pvt. Ltd., 2001), p. 52, 56
4. *Ibid.*, p. 133
5. Litvinsky, B.A. and Zeymal, T.I. *Adzhina-Tepa: Architecture, Painting, Sculpture* (Tajikistan : A. Donish Institute of History, Archaeology and Ethnography and SSR, 1971), p. 228, 229
6. *Ibid.*, p. 228, 229
7. Buryakov, Y.F., Baipakov, K.M., Tashbaeva, K.H., Yakubov., Y. *The Cities and Routes of the Great Silk Road* (Tashkent: Sharg, 1999), p. 81-83
8. Mullokandov, M. *Early Medieval Buddhist Monastery Khisht Tepa* (President M. Asimov, The International Association for the Study of the Cultures of Central Asia, Moscow: UNESCO Information

Bulletin-17, 1990), p. 1-5
9. *Ibid.*, p. 1-5
10. Vertogradova, V. *Clay Tablets with Indian Text from Khisht Tepa* (Moscow: President M. Asimov, The International Association for the Study of the Cultures of Central Asia, UNESCO Information Bulletin-17, 1990), p. 25
11. Dorjee, Pema. *Stupa and Its Technology* (New Delhi: IGNCA and Motilal Banarsidass Publishers Pvt. Ltd., 2001), p. 108-109
12. *Ibid.*, p. 41

Penjikent: The City of Divastich

It was easier for me to visit Penjikent from Samarkand, only 70 kilometres away and across the border in Uzbekistan. And so, I visited the village fair of Jartepa, near Samarkand, on my way to Penjikent. The road was jammed with carts, cars, motorcycles and mules. Everywhere, the eye met with loads of vegetables and fruits, especially the famous yellow carrots from the vegetable farms of Penjikent. On the way to the Tajik border were several villages of tobacco growers where the special long-leafed tobacco is cultivated as a major crop. I got down for a while to have a look.

The wait at the border was a long one as it had closed just two minutes before I arrived and was to reopen only after an hour. About two dozen cars were parked in the clearing of fields along a rivulet. Not far away, along the foothills, quince is grown and collected in baskets and sold by vendors sitting by the rivulet with heaps of the rust-coloured fruit. By and by, more villagers carrying baskets of fruit, grains and garments converged here from the fair to cross into the neighbouring Tajik villages.

Finally, the border in-charge arrived and opened the gates of the road into Tajikistan. He checked the passports and allowed people to cross over on foot. Saubek, my Uzbek guide, bade a goodbye as I hurried with the surging crowd to show my passport. He was to wait at the border for the whole day until my return from Penjikent. He parked the car in an overgrown field and hurried off to Jartepa to spend the whole day at the village fair.

On the Tajik side of the border, there was again a long wait for Saidbek Saidov, my guide from Pamir Mountain Travels, who had to accompany me to Penjikent. He arrived quite late. We soon left in a rickety van that made the journey a little more interesting and adventurous.

The road to Penjikent was full of traffic. But the scenery was enchanting. On the skyline, the impressive Fan mountains rose to meet the horizon in columns of purple and deep grey, gradually merging with the sparkling white of its snowy peaks. The sun peeped out from a dense poplar forest that grew on both sides of the road. We whizzed past Sarayosio village, where a wedding meal was being served to villagers and mud tandoors had been laid out by the roadside for baking naan, and numerous vineyards, fruit orchards and wheat fields which lay by the roadside. A strong fragrance of lilies and roses enveloped us in Elipok village, where the flowers were grown commercially and the water of the Zerafshan had been channelized to irrigate the gardens. Near Galubotir village lay a tent colony where hundreds displaced in the 2005 floods were living. Soon we entered the city of Penjikent and stopped for a cup of tea at the Karim Ata restaurant along the Rudaki Street.

The Great Hero Divastich

At the entrance of the town, the great hero of Central Asia and ruler of Penjikent, Divastich, sits astride his horse on his fierce mission against the Arab armies. He ruled over the prosperous kingdom of Penjikent (believed to have been a city of five settlements) and was at the forefront of the anti-Arab rebellion by the Sogdians and who fought against the Islamic armies during the first quarter of the 8th century.

History informs us that the Arabs encountered stubborn resistance from the population of Transoxiana since the very beginning of their raids in Central Asia during AD 680. They were vigorously repulsed by the combined forces of Bukhara, Sogdiana and the Turks and were forced to return to Merv. But trickery and deceit worked in favour of the Arabs. After Qutaiba ibn Muslim (AD 705–715) became the governor of Khurasan, the Arab campaign in Central Asia was intensified.[1]

During AD 720-721, the Sogdians led by Divastich, Karzanj and Ghurak and supported by the Turks, destroyed the Samarkand garrison of the Arabs and expelled them from the town. All attempts to restore Arab power in Samarkand proved unsuccessful. *The Arab Conquest in Central Asia* tells the story of how the brave Divastich ended on a sad note. He was betrayed by his own people and treacherously murdered by the Arabs.

It is said that after realizing that their forces were inadequate, the Sogdian rebels, led by Divastich, and Karzanj, ruler of Pai, escaped to the upper reaches of the Zerafshan, seeking protection from at-Tar, the ruler of Ferghana. But at-Tar secretly informed the Arabs of the rebels' whereabouts at Khujand. In a crushing attack, the Arabs killed thousands of rebels and laid siege to the castle on Mount Mugh, where Divastich had sought refuge. Realizing that further resistance was useless, Divastich is said to have surrendered and was killed in AD 722.[2]

The Penjikent hero would have been forgotten but for the discovery of numerous manuscripts from the ruins of the fort on Mount Mugh, in 1933, where he had taken refuge. The Mug documents describe the social life in Sogdiana prevailing during the 7th century, especially at the time of the Arab conquest. One document (catalogue Donish Institute, No. 593) is a letter from Fatuferna to Divastich. Fatuferna, calling himself a 'poor slave', addresses the latter as 'prince of princes…prince of Sugd…the ruler of Samarkand…' Other documents include a marriage contract written on leather (No. 591) and an application for divorce; a written receipt of helmets and armour; and one interesting document (No. 592) is a loan agreement for 464 bags of wheat flour given for one year.[3] Some of the documents from Mount Mugh are displayed at the State Museum, Samarkand.

At the Excavation Site

Saidov had arranged my meals at an open air restaurant on the banks of the Zerafshan, where I spent a long time watching the river rushing along the foot of the snow-capped Fan mountains. This is the river of gold. It is said to carry golden dust and sometimes even nuggets of precious metal from the mountains. It is, therefore, called the 'gold scattering river' or the Zerafshan that has nurtured its cities, including Penjikent, with gold.

At a little distance from the restaurant, on the banks of the river, lay the ruins of ancient Penjikent, believed to be one of the largest and most prosperous cities on the Silk Road. It is said that the town sprang up in the 5th century or in the beginning of the 6th century AD. But it could have existed much earlier as is proved by the antiquities recovered from here and the neighbouring site of Sarazm. These include objects made of precious metals (silver and gold), a rich collection of beads of turquoises, azurites, agates, different red stones, corals, jade and pearls, brooches, rings, and bracelets. There were amber beads, corals and pearls from the Baltics and from the Southern seas, precious stones from Afghanistan, and sea shells and ivory from India.[4]

Foreign trade with distant countries of the Indus Valley, the Baltics and the Mediterranean, was established long ago as the region was on the trade routes going to Europe, China and India. Rich in mineral ores from its own mountains, abundant water from its rivers, crops from its fertile land, and wood from its dense forests, the region became one of the largest trade depots and metallurgy centres on the Central Asian Silk Road. Because of its riches and wonderful art and crafts, Penjikent was called the 'Pompeii of Central Asia'. (Isakov: *Ancient Penjikent*)

The wealth of the people could be gauged from the fact that even private houses were embellished with marvellous wall paintings and wood panelling with carvings. Deft artistes drew inspiration from the prevailing cultures of near and distant lands and absorbed them in their own local art. The Hindu gods and goddesses, the epic tales and folklore of India as well as incidents from the Buddha's own life, found a place on the artistes' canvas along with the Persian heroes of the *Shahnameh*.[5]

Idol-worshippers of Penjikent

Walking among the ruins of the ancient city, now a vast area covered by hilly mounds of earth, one can still find arched niches of temples where once stood the gods of Penjikent. Some structures are believed to have been workshops and quarters of craftsmen, blocks of single or double storey private and public houses, royal palaces, and temples. Archaeologists have discovered among these ruins, private residences decorated with beautiful wall paintings and embellishments of wood carvings, images of Hindu gods and goddesses made of clay and gypsum. A Christian text and Buddhist inscriptions on pottery have also been unearthed here, throwing light on the multi-religious life of the city.[6]

A museum of antiquities near the ruins displays wall paintings, ancient pottery, stone mortar and pestle and metallic utensils excavated from the site.

Renowned Russian archaeologist Boris Marshak, who spent the greater part of his life excavating and researching ancient Penjikent, has been buried among the ruins. It is said that the city was close to his heart. Even after the independence of Tajikistan from Russia, he continued to supervise the work at Penjikent as director of excavations.

Prominent among the ruins are two temples marked by their huge arches rising from among the hilly mounds. These have been dated to the 5th century AD and are believed to have been used up to the beginning of the 8th century. According to A. Isakov, historian-archaeologist of Tajikistan, the temples represented a complicated set of buildings enclosed within walls and joined by vast yards. Around the main sanctuary of the temple hall ran corridors or open galleries.[7]

From the images and paintings recovered during excavations,

one can assume that the inhabitants of Penjikent were idol-worshippers and that both Buddhism and Hinduism prevailed. The images of gods and goddesses depicted Indian traits. One goddess sat astride a lion, similar to the goddess Durga of the Hindus.[8] The image now adorns the National Museum of Antiquities at Dushanbe.

Historians and archaeologists working at the site found art galleries in palaces, temples and private houses decorated with monumental paintings and statuary art carved out of wood and gypsum. The charred remains of carved wooden images were found in many houses. One is that of the dancer displayed at the Rudaki Museum at Penjikent.

The people of Penjikent were quite obviously art lovers and it was not uncommon to find murals in private houses. The houses of the rich resembled royal palaces. From monumental paintings of the royal abode displayed at the Rudaki Museum, and description by authors and explorers, we can have an idea of the embellishments that lay inside. Entering a rich man's private abode, a visitor was led into a ceremonial hall where his eyes first fell upon a large image of a god or a 'divine patron' peering at him from the opposite wall. Other gods, too, were depicted on other parts of the wall. The visitor could see more compositions of a sacred or religious theme either as a mural painted on the walls or scenes carved out of wood. In addition, the murals depicted scenes of royal feasting, hunting, ceremonial rites or episodes from the *Shahnameh*. Ornamental creepers bordered the lower half of the walls. The ceiling could be wooden with elaborate carvings or paintings with figures of gods, hunting scenes and so on.[9]

The Penjikent paintings, both at the Rudaki Museum and at National Museum of Antiquities at Dushanbe, give us an idea about the religious, cultural and social life of the people of Penjikent.[10] They tell us about the kind of clothes, the motifs that prevailed in those days; the kind of carpets and rugs used by the nobles; the kind of weapons and animal harnesses employed; the kind of entertainments that the people enjoyed.

A carved wooden image of a dancer (Rudaki Museum, Penjikent) that appears to have been damaged in a fire, informs us of the popularity of music and dance. A painting at the site museum near the ruins, portrays a game of chess, still others present the bravery of heroes. These heroes are believed to depict tales from the *Shahnameh*, or perhaps the brave Sogdian rulers Divastich and Karzanj who fought against the Arabs invaders. There are women warriors too, reminding us of the legend of the Amazons whom Alexander the Great encountered in the land of Sogdiana, as early as the 3rd century BC.[11]

Portrayal of Lord Siva

Any visitor to the Rudaki Museum at Penjikent and the National Museum at Dushanbe can immediately identify the Hindu gods and goddesses displayed in the corridors and massive showcases. There are images of the Goddess Riding a Lion (Museum of Antiquities, Dushanbe), Siva and Parvati, Siva with a third eye, and Siva with three heads, to name a few.

At the Rudaki Museum Siva (Maheshvara) is seen sitting in a vast arena appearing like wilderness with his trishul or trident next to him. He seems oblivious of the plight of a woman standing next to him. Perhaps, she is Parvati, whom the demon seems to have abducted. Rustam, the hero portrayed in his act of bravery seems more powerful than Siva who is lost in meditation.

In another painting at the site museum at the Penjikent ruins, we find an Indian sadhu (or a merchant) with matted hair playing a game of chess. Another massive image of Siva and Parvati can be seen in the upper hall of the National Museum at Dushanbe. Among the images of local divinities found in one of the temples, one was identified as that of Uma-Maheshvara (Siva and Parvati) sitting on the Nandi bull.

Excavations in private houses and shops yielded similar sculptural remains and fragments of wall paintings depicting Hindu gods and goddesses, but with local 'overtones'.[12] According to S.P. Gupta, renowned Indian archaeologist and art historian, Hinduism was witnessed in Central Asia in the worship of five gods, namely, Brahma, Indra, Mahadeva (Siva), Narayana, and Vaishravana. The first three were identified with their own local gods—Brahma with Zarvan (described as god with a beard), Indra with Adbad (a god with a third eye), and Siva with Veshparkar (a god with three faces). A four-armed goddess riding a lion was also worshipped in Penjikent. She has been identified with the Iranian goddess Nana. She was sometimes found near the image of Siva and could be identified with Parvati, says Gupta.

Buddhist Iconography at Penjikent Temples

Italian scholar Matteo Compareti has explored the Buddhist iconography in Penjikent. He points to the famous 6th-century painting from Temple II at Penjikent, a copy of which is displayed at the site museum. It is a funerary scene of a figure lying inside a building similar to a stupa, flanked by two columns on top of which are the wheel or the 'chakradhwaja'.[13] Although the funeral has been identified as that of 'Siyavush', one of the heroes of Firdausi's *Shahnameh*, it has similarities with the scene of the 'Great Decease' of the Buddha as portrayed in paintings in the caves of Kuqa and Turfan (fragments now displayed at the National Museum of Delhi) where the mourners slashed their faces, pulled their hair, and disfigured themselves on hearing of the decease of the Buddha.

Compareti also points to a terracotta mould, perhaps used for producing bulk clay images of the Buddha, recovered from inside Temple II of Penjikent, which could indicate that the temple was used by the Buddhists.[14]

One painted representation of the Buddha was recovered in a house with a granary dated between the 7th and 8th centuries. On the left side of the Buddha, a male figure, a bodhisattva, smaller in size and dressed in Indian garments stands with a blooming lotus in his hands. There is a flying figure of a dragon on the right side of the Buddha,[15] possibly representing control over passions or victory over the evil Mara. It could also represent a Naga deity worshipping the Buddha.

That the territory of ancient Penjikent was closely in contact with India for thousands of years is amply borne out by the antiquities dug out from the burial sites in the proto-urban settlement of Sarazm on the road from Samarkand to Penjikent. Located near the Uzbek–Tajik border amid vast fields of tobacco, the settlement of Sarazm, covering about 100 acres, was discovered in 1976 and dated from 3500 BC to 2000 BC.

The World Heritage Site of Sarazm had long-distance trade links with India, Afghanistan, Mesopotamia, and Iran. The shells used for buttons and bracelets were imported from India as they were found in the Indian Ocean. Precious stones were brought from the mountains of Central Asia. This was proved when excavators discovered in a grave the remains of a richly adorned young woman, a princess, wearing two bracelets made of shell, perhaps obtained from India. She was buried in clothes embroidered with lapis lazuli, turquoise, cornelian and steatite beads. Her head and arms were decorated with silver beads. Her hair was entwined in gold and silver beads. Other items found in the grave were four stone mace heads, a bone awl, a bronze mirror and two clay figurines of women.[16]

From the impressive murals and statuary art that now adorn the Rudaki Museum at Penjikent and the National Museum of Antiquities at Dushanbe, it is evident that the people of Tajikistan were not only lovers of Lord Siva and his consort Parvati and worshippers of the Devi on a lion's back but also revered and worshipped the Buddha as in India. In Tajikstan, I saw glimpses of India.

References

1. Litvinsky, B.A. (ed.). *History of Civilizations of Central Asia: The crossroads of civilizations (AD 250 to 750)*, Volume III (Delhi: Motilal

Banarsidass Publishers Pvt. Ltd., 1999), p. 456-460

Gibb, H.A.R. *The Arab Conquests in Central Asia* (Delhi: Cosmo Publications, 2012)

2. Litvinsky, B.A. (ed.). 'The Arab Conquest'. *History of Civilizations of Central Asia: The crossroads of civilizations (AD 250 to 750)*, Volume III (Delhi: Motilal Banarsidass Publishers Pvt. Ltd., 1999), p. 456-460

    Gibb, H.A.R. *The Arab Conquests in Central Asia* (Delhi: Cosmo Publications, 2012)

3. Litvinsky, B.A. (ed.). *History of Civilizations of Central Asia: The crossroads of civilizations (AD 250 to 750)*, Volume III (Delhi: Motilal Banarsidass Publishers Pvt. Ltd., 1999), p. 239, 256, 257-258, 277

    Tucker, Jonathan. *The Silk Road: Art and History* (New Delhi: Timeless Books, 2003), p. 268

    A. Donish Institute. *Drevnosti Tajikistana* (Dushanbe: 1985), p. 246, 247

4. Isakov, A. *Ancient Penjikent* (Dushanbe: A. Donish Institute of Science, History and Ethnography, 1997)

5. Gupta S.P. 'Hindu Gods in Western Central Asia: A Lesser Known Chapter of Indian History'. *Dialogue: A quarterly journal of Astha Bharti* (New Delhi), p. 1-2.

    URL: http://www.asthabharati.org/Dia_April2/Hindu.htm

    Compareti, Matteo. *Sino-Platonic Papers: Traces of Buddhist Art in Sogdiana*, Number 181 (Philadelphia: University of Pennsylvania, August 2008), p. 13-15. URL: www.sino-platonic.org

6. Litvinsky, B.A. (ed.). *History of Civilizations of Central Asia: The crossroads of civilizations (AD 250 to 750)*, Volume III (Delhi: Motilal Banarsidass Publishers Pvt. Ltd., 1999), p. 242, 243, 245

7. Isakov, A. *Ancient Penjikent* (Dushanbe: A. Donish Institute of Science, History and Ethnography, 1977)

8. Litvinsky, B.A. (ed.). *History of Civilizations of Central Asia: The crossroads of civilizations (AD 250 to 750)*, Volume III (Delhi: Motilal Banarsidass Publishers Pvt. Ltd., 1999), p. 250, 253

9. *Ibid.*, p. 245-247, 250-253

10. *Ibid.*, p. 251, 253

11. Manfredi, V.M. and Halliday, Iian (trans.). *Alexander: The Ends of the Earth*, Volume 3 (London: Pan Macmillan Books, 2002), p. 384-385
12. Gupta, S.P. 'Hindu Gods in Western Central Asia: A Lesser Known Chapter of Indian History'. *Dialogue: A quarterly journal of Astha Bharti* (New Delhi), p. 1-2. URL: http://www.asthabharati.org/Dia_April2/Hindu.htm
13. Compareti, Matteo. *Sino-Platonic Papers: Traces of Buddhist Art in Sogdiana*, Number 181 (Philadelphia: University of Pennsylvania, August 2008), p. 13, 15. URL: www.sino-platonic.org
14. *Ibid.*, p. 16
15. *Ibid.*, p. 13-14
16. A. Donnish Institute of History, Archaeology and Ethnography. *Sarazm* (Sarazm: Penjikent Historical and Archaeological Reserve, 2006)

Section Three

TURKMENISTAN

Routes into Turkmenistan

Trade routes ran from several points on the north-western borders of Afghanistan into the lands, now covered by modern Turkmenistan. A traveller could take the route northwards from Herat; alternatively he could take the north-western route from Bala Murghab (fortress on the Murghab) running along the Murghab river to the oasis city of Merv; he could also take the western route along the catchment of the Amu Darya from Balkh into the various settlements inside the Karakum desert. Tracts also ran from the various Afghan oasis cities of Andhkui, Qaramqal and Chapakguzar through the desert. While sardobas provided cool water to the travellers along the way, the desert tracts were discarded when the water bodies dried up. Broken and discarded water bodies can still be seen along tracts in the Karakum.

Today, the main route from Afghanistan into Turkmenistan leads through small oasis settlement of Tagtabazar, on the Murghab river, 214 kilometres south of Mary. The road runs through the town of Kushka (Serhetabad), 90 kilometres from Tagtabazar on the Afghan border. Tagtabazar was known as Panjdeh in the 19th century and formed the setting for a conflict between Britain and Russia during the years of the 'Great Game'.[1] The Mary–Serhetabad Road also extends southwards through Towraghondi into Afghanistan at Herat.

The Cities and Routes of the Great Silk Road informs that in ancient times, on their way from Roman territories to China, caravans passed the fertile valleys of Girkania along the Caspian coast and entered the land of Parthia. The route ran through the large centres of ancient Parthia and medieval Khorasan, namely, the oasis cities of Dehistan, Nisa, Abiverd and Merv located in modern Turkmenistan.[2]

The same source tells us that the caravan route from Dehistan ran eastwards to Nisa and Merv. An independent route from Dehistan went northwards to Khorezm where a chain of caravanserais was discovered. From Nisa, caravans headed eastwards to Bagabat where there was a medieval mosque with dragons on its portals. The road ran further to the oasis cities of Abiverd and Merv and onwards through Amul (Turkmenabat/Chardzhou) to join the caravan route to Bukhara—Samarkand.

Merchants who wanted to deal only with India would turn southwards from Merv and undertake an easy journey through Afghanistan passing through Herat and Seistan and then eastwards to Kandahar. From Kandahar, there were three routes that could be taken: one went south-east to cross the Bolan Pass; a second went north-east to join the Northern Highroad (Uttarapath) coming from India at Kabul; the third route went south from Kandahar to enter India through the sea-route or through low mountains.[3]

The modern Highway M-37, running through the territory of southern Turkmenistan, corresponds to one of the greatest international trade routes that connects the continents of Asia and Europe. Running between the Kopet Dagh mountains and the Karakum desert, the highway nurtured the famous oases cities of Nisa, Bagabat, Abiverd, Merv and Amul.

The strategic importance of these Turkmen cities lay in the fact that they were connected to the Caspian Route that linked India with Russia. This was the most favoured trading route taken by Indians trading in the Black Sea region. The Taxila–Kapisa–Balkh highway took travellers to the Turkmen city of Merv. The Indian traffic on this route is believed to have increased during the Achaemenian period when Punjab was its satrapy and during the Seleucid period when it became the Royal Highway to the west.

The Caspian route into the Black Sea and Mediterranean regions thus opened Turkmenistan and other Central Asian countries to Indian migrants.[4]

References

For the study of trade routes through the territory of Turkmenistan see: Buryakov, Y.F., Baipakov, K.M., Tashbaeva, K.H., Yakubov, Y. *The Cities and Routes of the Great Silk Road*; Warmington, E.H. *The Commerce between the Roman Empire and India*; Tucker, Jonathan. *The Silk Road: Art and History*

1. Brummell, Paul. *Turkmenistan: The Bradt Travel Guide* (Connecticut, USA: Globe Pequot Press Inc., 2005), p. 222
2. Buryakov Y.F., Baipakov, K.M., Tashbaeva, K.H., Yakubov, Y. *The Cities and Routes of the Great Silk Road* (Tashkent: Sharg, 1999), p. 12-31
3. Warmington, E.H. *The Commerce between the Roman Empire and India* (New Delhi: Munshi Ram Manoharlal, 1995), p. 22-24
4. Roy, J.N. (ed.) and Kumar, B.B. (ed.). *India and Central Asia: Classical to Contemporary Periods* (New Delhi: Concept Publishing Company, 2007), p. 9
   Also see: 'Links and Interactions'. *India and Central Asia: Classical to Contemporary Period*

In the Desert City of Ashgabat

There was no question of taking the land route from either Balkh or Herat as the Afghan–Turkmen border region was considered a highly sensitive zone and no travellers were allowed entry. I intended to take a direct flight into Ashgabat—the capital of Turkmenistan. This was the base for my travels on International Highway-37 to the cities of the Buddha in the Turkmen desert of Karakum, namely, Gyaur Kala, Sultan Kala and Erk Kala.

But a one-line message from my travel agent, that my visa had been rejected by the Turkmenistan authorities, sent all my plans of visiting the monastic cities in the deserts of Karakum crashing. I was crestfallen. The chapter on Turkmenistan was now closed. I would have to erase it off my itinerary. I was despondent.

Chinara, my friend in the Turkmenistan Embassy had lent a patient ear to my project on the Silk Road. I concluded my description detailing all I wanted to see in Turkmenistan. Chinara exclaimed, 'Insha Allah! Insha Allah!' She sounded hopeful but I knew it was very difficult to obtain a visa; no travel agency could provide it. I learnt it the hard way after running after one. But I had trust in God and Chinara.

This was in the end of March 2011. Unbelievably, a fortnight later, when I was slumped in the large bed in Room No. 712 of the President's Hotel in Ashgabat, I rubbed my eyes in disbelief. The Buddha of Merv of whom I had only dreamt, had now come alive. I could actually ramble in the fortress of Nisa. And see the rivers and deserts of Karakum. It was in utter disbelief that I was gazing at the landscape outside my glass-walled room. Everything appeared a deep emerald in the surrounding deserts. In fact, there was hardly any desert. It was not as if the glass walls were tinted. Real forests of fir and juniper were growing outside in the vast area stretching up to the horizon.

My room at the President's was particularly large, facing the forests. The menu of its Italian dining too was particularly sumptuous. This fanciest hotel in Ashgabat uses ingredients imported from Italy. Every day for breakfast, I dug into the fat, deliciously stuffed chillies just like our mirch ka salan, gulped mounds of hot butter rice washed down with creamy mushroom soup. The hummus was even better than Damascus where it was rolled in tender grape leaves and served with hot naan.

I had assumed Turkmenistan was a desert nation. But I was dumbfounded at the greenery—rows and rows of water-spewing fountains rising high and dancing as if tapping to music; the sparkling green cypress forests; the cool breeze of a hill station; the moonlight beams that reflected from the marble façade of the tall buildings, as if I was travelling through a milky white path. Tulips of many hues popped their heads out of flowerbeds. Fountains danced at every corner of the road, in front of every monument. They sparkled in sunshine, creating rainbows on the white marble buildings. They seemed to lend life to the city.

Few cities of Central Asia could compare with the 'Marble Valley' of post-independence Ashgabat. In fact, nowhere has such a marble city been built, the dazzle of which is attributed by many to the wealth coming from the subterranean rivers of black gold—the rich oil that lies below the earth. The wealth is apparent in the golden domes of minarets and statues in gold.

Far from being a desert city, Ashgabat had all the trappings of a hill station complete with cypress, fir and pine forests, fruit orchards and flower gardens. Millions of junipers have been planted to add beauty to the landscape and to foil the sandstorms that plague the beautiful city. Water pipes have been laid over the mountains and canals have been dug to irrigate the forests.

Watered by the Karakum canal, the vast Turkmen deserts are being reclaimed for cultivation. It is the largest canal of Central Asia and takes its waters from the Amu Darya at a point where it enters Turkmenistan. Running 1,300 kilometres, it brings water to the chain of oases in south Turkmenistan along Highway-37 and carries water across the entire Karakum desert.

The water of the Amu Darya (River Oxus), apart from greening the desert, also produces the sweetest melons in the catchment of the Karakum canal. In ancient times, cultivators raised pigeons in specially constructed halls and used their droppings as manure for the melons. Just as the fragrant pear grows only in Xinjiang, fragrant melons grow only in Turkmenistan. Along with silk, the Turkmen melons were traded and bartered along the Silk Road. They were brought to India for the kings and nobles.

Turkmenistan: The Land of Buddha

The territory that is now Turkmenistan is believed to have harboured one of Central Asia's largest Buddhist centres in the early medieval times. This was confirmed when two Buddhist monuments were revealed at the site of Gyaur Kala—a large monastery and a Buddhist stupa in the deserts of Margiana where Buddhism is believed to have consolidated its position in the 1st century AD.[1]

It was here that the most amazing discoveries of Buddhist antiquities were made. One was that of a large Buddha head which could have been part of an immense statue, several other images of the Buddha of slate and gilt, a large beautifully painted vase depicting scenes from the life of the Buddha, and birch bark manuscripts in Sanskrit.

While the antiquities from the Buddhist site of Gyaur Kala and Sultan Kala, including several small images of the Buddha and bronze bells engraved with similar (Buddhist) images, were on display at the National Museum of History at Ashgabat and the State Museum at Mary, the immense Buddha head (whose photographs can be seen in old books on Pre-Islamic Central Asia) became an object of mystery.

The discovery of the Gyaur Kala monastery and stupa in the Merv and objects from Sultan Kala oases cities, dated to the 2nd or 3rd century, confirmed that a flourishing Buddhist community had settled in the deserts of Turkmenistan. Further, those Buddhist institutes, where Buddhist texts were not only studied but also translated and commented upon, were set up in Merv. This is clear from the manuscripts that were unearthed from the painted vase, now at Ashgabat Museum. With renewed excavations along the Silk Road going westwards towards the Caspian, the archaeologists may locate other areas where Buddhist communities were set up in the Karakum desert.

M.I. Vorobyova-Desyatovskaya (*Religions and Religious Movements-II-Buddhism*) draws our attention to two stupas—one in Merv and the other in Bairam Ali, from which two Buddhist manuscripts were found. Both were written in Sanskrit in the Brahmi script and inscribed on birch bark. One of them is said to have been restored and preserved at the Institute of Oriental Studies in St Petersburg, and the other is undergoing restoration in Moscow.[2]

The same author mentions some sheets of a manuscript found in Bairam Ali dating from the 3rd or 4th centuries. He also mentions the recovery of a synopsis of a collection of the *Jatakas* and *Avadanas* from Bairam Ali in manuscripts of the 3rd or 4th centuries.[3] Whether they were the same manuscripts, it is difficult to tell, but the fact remains that the manuscripts prove the importance of Turkmenistan as a great Buddhist centre.

I had the opportunity to see a copy of the manuscript recovered from Bairam Ali. It was on display at an exhibition organized by the Bharat Soka Gakkai at the Indira Gandhi National Centre of Arts in Delhi in 2009. The manuscript on birch bark was an excerpt from the canon of Sarvastavadins copied in the 5th century in the Brahmi script. The birch bark seemed to have been painted in a reddish brown colour over which letters had been handwritten in black ink. Other antiquities unearthed in Merv include Buddhist statuary, bronze bells, script on terracotta, masks and parts of a Buddhist sanctuary.

It is believed by scholars that the propagation of Buddhism in the Turkmen oasis cities could have taken place during the time it was part of the Seleucid kingdom by Asoka's missionaries, some of whom, according to Pali sources (*Mahavamsa*), were Greek Buddhist monks.[4]

According to G.A. Koshelenko, at the end of the Parthian and during the Sassanian era, Buddhism had greatly spread along the territory of Merv.[5] Quoting Chinese Buddhist traditions, he informs us that people who practised Buddhism had already been living in Margiana since the 2nd century AD and belonged to different classes of society, among them being a prince (An Shih-kao) of the local dynasty and a merchant (An Huan).[6] By the 1st century AD, he informs, the Parthians had already reached the borders of India and the representatives of the Indo-Parthian dynasty were ruling those regions of India where Buddhism was already widespread.

Buddhist Art in Ashgabat Museum

At the National Museum of Turkmenistan at Ashgabat, there are several depictions of the Buddha from the provinces of Mary and Lebap. There are terracotta and gypsum capitals from ancient Merv. One such capital portrays the Buddha emerging from foliage of acanthus leaves. There is a bejewelled statuette of the bodhisattva Avalokitesvara in a meditational posture from Lebap province occupying the middle reaches of the Amu Darya. The spire of a stupa or a sanctuary in slate and gilt from Merv portrays a series of four Buddhas sitting on a lotus pedestal.

A decoration block cut in blue-black stone depicts the Buddha in 'dhyanmudra'. The head is lost. The base of the two-tiered composition has the central image of Buddha flanked by four worshippers. According to the museum notice, the image is a 'masterpiece of Gandhara Buddhist School'. It has a similarity of theme with the image recovered from the monastery of Fayaz Tepe in Termez depicting the Buddha flanked by disciples. Another statuette in slate and gilt depicts an unadorned 'Smiling Buddha' from Merv. The Buddhist objects are mainly from the monastic city of Gyaur Kala.

A broken part of a pillar base or wall decoration of a temple that depicts the Buddha head protruding from acanthus leaves appears very similar to the 'Ayrtam Frieze' found at a temple in village Ayrtam near Termez in south Uzbekistan and now preserved at the Termez Museum. Here, too, deities appearing as musicians and holding garlands appear from the foliage of acanthus. A frieze portraying 'musicians and garlanders' is also displayed at the State Museum of History, Tashkent. It, too, was recovered from Ayrtam. Portrayal of Buddhist deities on lotus and acanthus leaves on terracotta can be seen among the objects recovered from the ancient monastic establishment of Ambaran near Jammu on the right bank of the Chenab river, in northern India. The acanthus motif was widely used in decorating Buddhist sanctuaries and the foliage was generally carved onto stone pillars or moulded into terracotta or applied to friezes. It was an important motif in Greco-Buddhist art.

A painted ceramic jar portrays events from the life of the Buddha. The unique vase was used for storing Buddhist manuscripts written in the Indian Brahmi script dating back to the 5th century.[7] This text, according to A. Gubaev (*Cultural Integration of Turkmenistan and India in the Early and Medieval Period*), is a part of the Buddhist canon, more precisely of the section containing the rules determining the life of monks in the Buddhist monastery, the 'Vinaya Pitaka'.

However, the head of what could possibly have been the largest image of the Buddha in Central Asia was nowhere to be seen in the prestigious museum of Ashgabat. It measured 75 centimetres high, belonging to a giant statue of Buddha dating back to 2nd–3rd century AD. According to a brochure *Buddhist*

Monuments in Turkmenistan issued by the museum in 1991, the head is supposed to have been one of the first statues of Buddha that became popular with the Buddhist of Central Asia.

Interestingly, the museum brochure mentioned that the head would be restored and exhibited at the Museum of History and Ethnography. But even after more than two decades, the head of the Buddha is missing.

To Ruhi Masjidi: The Grand Mosque

One beautiful morning when it had stopped raining and the sky was clear and radiant, I headed to the Kipchak village, taking the road west of Ashgabat in a direction away from the morning sun. But fierce winds blew, and I was shivering in spite of the sun. The road sped through newly forested areas of fir and pine. Along the road, hundreds of workers could be seen tending the forests. There were rows and rows of mulberry trees which had just shed their leaves. Their branches appeared like a huge brush or a broom held in the centre by their thick trunks. The poplars too appeared bereft of their green cover. Only the apricots and peaches looked resplendent in white and pink inflorescence.

Surrounded by semi-deserts, Yanbas is a surprisingly green village blessed with good agriculture and vast vegetable farms. Special nurseries had arched covers set up to produce cauliflower, tomatoes and bell peppers. Mushrooms cultivated in the village feed the hotels of Ashgabat. The centre of Yanbas appeared like a glistening patch with shiny low-roofed houses amid green fields and dense orchards. The village women were out in their fields with long crowbars to clear weeds and break the earth. Soon I came upon a village bakery where a group of women were baking flat bread in flaming ovens.

Coming to a roundabout near Yanbas, I turned right towards Kipchak to reach the Ruhi, the biggest mosque in Central Asia. It can seat 10,000 people at one time. The golden domes of the grand mosque are enough to blind a person. A golden light emanates from the domes as the sun strikes them. High water fountains draw a shimmering veil of silver over the main entrance. I am overawed by the grandeur of the mosque. Its high portals seemed to touch the sky.

I had not seen anything so splendid; even the Grand Juma Mosque of Kashgar paled in comparison. But Kashgar drew massive crowds that swelled by the hour and there was hardly any place to set foot inside the long galleries of the mosque, whereas the Ruhi Masjidi at Kipchak village lay strangely bereft of worshippers. There was hardly anyone inside the sacred portals, except the grand mufti.

Walking past several fountains, I met the mufti on the marbled steps outside the grand portals. He was wearing a long robe, his head covered with a cap. As I bowed to him, he read a prayer over my head. Inside the large circular prayer hall photography was prohibited. I was surprised to notice that there was no bar on entry of women unlike Urumqi (Xinjiang, China) where I was not allowed to enter even though I pleaded with the Imam. It was so peaceful inside the Ruhi Masjidi that I nearly went into a trance and woke up after a long time.

The grand mufti was waiting to bid goodbye. He appeared to be a noble person who blessed me thrice and walked up to the gates to see me off. By the side of the mosque lies the golden-domed mausoleum of the President Saparmurat Niyazov (1940–2006) and his kinsmen. A statue of an earthquake-devastated female figure trying to snatch her baby from the claws of death, brings back memories of the devastating quake of 1948. Inside the mausoleum lie five tombs; the central one is of the President himself. Others belong to Niyazov's parents and two brothers who died in the earthquake.

Indians in Ashgabat

Many Indians have made Ashgabat their home. I happened to meet some who belonged to my native village, Kushinagar, and had been employed by Pamposh Constructions, an Indian company doing concrete constructions in Ashgabat. Turkmenistan has contracted the best Indian companies and obtained the most beautiful marble from the mines of India to build its monumental institutions. Several hundreds of Indians are working round the clock to lend a hand to the glittering city.

A workers' colony has been set up not far from the city by Pamposh. Here hundreds of workers were living in fabricated rooms that were amazingly clean. Their toilets were sparkling to a fault; their clothes laundered in machines; their food store neatly arranged; and cooks hunched over large pots were rustling up a hearty meal for them. The workers were living like university students with good food, clean clothes and enough entertainment.

Since early times, the Indians are said to have gained access into Turkmenistan which formed the south-east region of the Trans-Caspian. They are recorded to have traded on the Caspian and beyond in the territory of Russia up to modern times.[8] Numerous scholars have studied the extent of Indian trade with Central Asia and the cultural and political exchanges that inevitably followed. Stephen Dale's *Indian Merchants and Eurasian Trade 1600-1750,* Scott Levi's *The Indian Diaspora in Central Asia and Its Trade 1550-1900,* Claude Markovits' *Indian Merchants in Central Asia* and *The Global Work of Indian Merchants 1750-1947: Traders of Sind from Bukhara to Panama*—all inform us of the trade between India and Central Asia which played an important role in the commercial life of both.[9]

It is said that clusters of Multani traders from Punjab and Marwaris from Rajasthan in India were settled in the 17th and 18th century in Astrakhan, the port city of the Caspian.[10] That so many Indians were favouring this Caspian region for trade shows the trading capacity of the region, the profits that could be made, the relative safety of the routes and also most importantly, that a secular atmosphere was prevailing so that the people of all religions could have peaceable trade with their counterparts in the region. It also shows that the region was not such a desertified zone in the sense that it now appears to be; where life was comfortable with means of water, food and shelter to support thousands of caravans that passed that way.

At Ruski Bazaar

It was late evening when I walked into the Ruski bazaar. The market was about to close and the guard was locking the gates. Streams of people were leaving the market though a flurry of activity was still going on inside. I requested the guard to let me have a glimpse of the market; he reluctantly let me in. Ram Ashish, my acquaintance at the Pamposh Constructions, guided me to a shop where a little boy sat behind a pile of raisins. Ashish talked to the boy in Turkmen and pulled out the best raisin at the cheapest price. Nine manat (the local currency) for a kilo was a steal! The boy weighed the raisins, smiled and broke into a Hindi song. His favourite actors were Salman Khan and Mithun Chakraborty.

I was distracted by the ruby-studded gold earrings that most women were wearing. I eye them greedily. I look for the typical Turkmen jewellery next day in Tolkuchka, where they are set in silver but not gold. Instead, I buy a talisman—a black round bead with an eye to ward off evil. At Tolkuchka, Turkmenistan's largest bazaar, it is the carpets and sheepskin hats that take my breath away.

Tolkuchka is certainly bigger than the Kashgar Grand Bazaar, often touted as the biggest in Central Asia. In Kashgar, villagers and herdsmen from the countryside ride their mules and donkey carts, laden with livestock and agricultural produce, directly into the bazaar where the barter system is still prevalent. In comparison, Tolkuchka appeared sophisticated, absolutely clean, with ample space for humans and vehicles.

The light drizzle in the oasis city had sent shivers down my spine. I was thankful I had grudgingly brought along a shawl just in case it became frosty. The strong winds and rain set my teeth chattering, but I was enjoying every bit of the chill in the spring. For two days, the weather gods played truant. When the sun peeped out of the clouds the third day, I set out on a tour of the forests—to the lovely woods, dark and deep.

The beauty of the mountains drew me towards the Kopetdag. I had barely driven a few kilometres into the mountains when I noticed barricades and the cops beckoning me to stop. Instead of halting, the driver sped in another direction, but the cops managed to stop the car. They interrogated the driver and seized his licence as he had crossed the city limits and was close to the international border without a permit. I was dumbfounded. I pleaded with the driver to apologize and settle the matter. After he convinced the cops that it was a mistake, they relented but ordered us to leave the place immediately. We ran for our lives. Literally!

References

1. Puri, B.N. *Buddhist Tradition Series: Buddhism in Central Asia* (Delhi: Motilal Banarsidass Publishers Pvt. Ltd., 2000), p. 101
2. Litvinsky, B.A. (ed.). 'Religion and Religious Movements-II'. *History of Civilizations of Central Asia: The crossroads of civilizations (AD 250 to 750)*, Volume III (Delhi: Motilal Banarsidass Publishers Pvt. Ltd., 1999), p. 437, 445
3. *Ibid.*, p. 441, 444
4. Puri, B.N. *Buddhist Tradition Series: Buddhism in Central Asia* (Delhi: Motilal Banarsidass Publishers Pvt. Ltd., 2000), p. 90, 96
5. Koshelenko, G.A. 'Parthia and India: Political and Cultural Contacts'. Rtveladze, E. (chief coordinator). *India and Central Asia Pre-Islamic* (Tashkent: Academy of Arts and Academy of Sciences of the Republic of Uzbekistan, 2000), p. 32
6. *Ibid.*, p. 32
7. Gubaev, A. 'Cultural Integration of Turkmenistan and India in the Early and Medieval Period'. Rtveladze, E. (chief coordinator). *India and Central Asia Pre-Islamic* (Tashkent: Academy of Arts and Academy of Sciences of the Republic of Uzbekistan, 2000), p. 37
8. Levi, Scott (ed). 'India, Russia, and the Eighteenth Century Transformation of the Central Asian Caravan Trade'. *India and*

Central Asia: Commerce and Culture (1500-1800) (New Delhi: Oxford University Press, 2007), p. 93-114, 107

Levi, Scott (ed.). 'Indian Merchants in Central Asia: The Debate'. *India and Central Asia: Commerce and Culture (1500-1800)* (New Delhi: Oxford University Press, 2007), p. 123-151

9. Levi, Scott (ed.). 'Indian Merchants in Central Asia: The Debate'. *India and Central Asia: Commerce and Culture (1500-1800)* (New Delhi: Oxford University Press, 2007), p. 123
10. *Ibid.*, p. 128

The Dragon Mosque at Bagabat

It is said that trade caravans coming from Persia laden with goods and heading eastwards to Merv and onwards to Bukhara and Samarkand stopped for food and shelter at the ancient city of Bagabat (modern Anau), situated on the edge of the Ashgabat oasis along the northern foothills of the Kopetdag. Small rivers flowing down from the mountains irrigated the town and brought with them rich sediments from the rocks, making it a very fertile region. For this reason, the region is said to have been inhabited since the Neolithic age.[1]

The travellers, besides easily finding food in the rich agricultural belt, could quench their thirst from the clear, cool waters of the huge domed sardoba into which they descended through the narrow steps reaching down the water's edge. They could pray at the beautiful Blue mosque which was known throughout the region as the mosque with the wriggling dragons or the 'Dragonite Mosque'. The striking beauty of this mosque, the colour of its portal tiles and its rare motifs could rival even the great Umayyed mosque at Dimashque, the Tillakari at Samarkand or the Kalon at Bukhara. The peculiar motif in the form of a pair of immense serpents making waves with their bodies caught the attention of the visitors. Far from presenting a frightening spectre, they heralded peace and good omens signified by the flowers dropping from their mouth.

The vegetation depicted on the portals, the brilliant blue of the tiles as if drawn from the precious lapis lazuli mountains of Badakshan, the high dome that shone during the day by the sun and glimmered by the light of the moon, providing direction to the travellers, all combined to impart a grandeur that few mosques in the Islamic world could boast of. The pair of wriggling snakes with dragon-like heads was a powerful motif that set one thinking about the artist and the message he wanted to convey through the fantastic serpents.

Any visitor to the National Museum at Ashgabat, looking at the model of the mosque and the dragon, will agree that the thick stubby claws, looking fierce and ominous, ready to gnaw at some prey, could be the depiction of some evil force. But when the eyes scan the face of the dragons carefully, we see that they hold in their mouth stalks or branches of blooming flowers. They no more appear to be ominous creatures, dreadful or evil. The flowering branches appear to be harbingers of good luck, prosperity, bountiful harvest and good rain in the arid region.

The moving snakes face each other and occupy the space above the main arch, giving evidence of the main theme of portraiture that was perhaps peace and tranquillity attained through a process of turmoil. Such decor is rarely seen in any other Central Asia mosque.

A similar pair of snakes is found wriggling at the feet of bodhisattva 'Padmapani and Vajrapani', at the National Museum, Delhi. The paintings were brought by Aurel Stein from Dunhuang dated between the 9th and 10th centuries. The only difference is that the two snakes in the Dunhuang painting are moving away from each other and instead of carrying branches of flowering stalks in their mouth, they are carrying sparkling gems on their hoods. The paintings depict the bejewelled bodhisattvas Padampani and Vajrapani seated on a lotus flower and holding the lotus and the vajra respectively. The deities draped in Indian-style embroidered blouses and dhotis have two serpents, whose heads are set aglitter by precious 'mani' or gems, almost dancing at their feet. On close scrutiny, the snakes do not look ferocious. They appear, surprisingly noble, just like the dragons of the Bagabat mosque. Was there any connection between the Dunhuang snakes and the Bagabat dragons? The Chinese influence is unmistakable.

Eminent archaeologist and historian Wiktor Sarianidi, who explored the Turkmen Silk Road settlement of Gonur in the region of Margiana, mentions how religious beliefs and cult ceremonies discovered at Gonur centred around human and animal figurines surrounded by snakes and frogs. Sarianidi writes, 'cult vessels, [found at Gonur] intended for drinking haoma, reflect the idea of the abduction of the "semen of the life" as a symbol of continuation of life: wriggling snakes crawl out of the vessel bottom reaching upto the bellies of the animals walking along the upper edge of the vessel.' Also depicted on the seals and amulets found at Gonur was the image of a dragon fighting with a pair of snakes.[2]

Parallels may also be drawn from the Egyptian temple of Debod (rebuilt in Madrid, Spain) belonging to the 2nd century BC and dedicated to the God Amun and Goddess Isis where the author saw two king cobras flanking the winged solar deity on a gateway cornice made of sandstone dated to the 172-170 BC. It was learnt that in the microcosm of all Egyptian temples, the doorway, cornice and lintels were frequently adorned with winged solar deity flanked by two cobras. Whether these cobras were protectors of the treasures of the temple or were some serpent deities who were appeased by worshippers before they entered the sanctum sanctorum, cannot be said with any certainty. But what is certain is that the image of wriggling and coiling serpents on places of worship do have a parallel also in Indian mythology.

In *Indian Mythology: An Encyclopaedia of Myth and Legend,* Jan Knappert informs us that the worship of nature spirits like the *naga* (cobra) has a 'hoary antiquity' in India. In Buddhist stories, too, we come across Naga rajas. In some Buddhist caves, we see the naga deity in anthropomorphic form at the entrance to the courtyard of the main chaitya, the entrance to the shrine courtyard. At Ajanta, the serpents appear on the doorjamb of the vihara and the garbha griha (sanctum sanctorum). In all cases, they are depicted as performing the function of guardian deities, says Knappert.[3] Nagas with a five-hooded canopy are also shown as worshipping the stupa on the facade of Cave 19. The beautiful Nagaraja couple, the lord of the nagas and his consort on his left, are seated in an alcove and a female whisk-bearer standing on his right outside Cave 19. The serpent king is seated on a rocky platform with a seven-headed cobra behind his head. They are lavishly ornamented. At Sanchi, the carved stone panels show the serpent deity worshipping the Buddhist stupa.

John Boardman in 'Central Asia: West and East' (*After Alexander: Central Asia Before Islam*), tells us about iconographic themes found in humanoid and monster figures on monuments. These animals and monsters may not be evil. Among the animals involved, the most spectacular is the snake and the dragon or some animal with a serpentine body.[4] This kind of reptilian figure is also found in Chinese, Central Asian and Indian art.

At the Anau mosque, the reptile has legs that appear to have claws and the body has wave-like, showing movements. Far from hurting anyone, the dragon or the reptile carries flowers in its mouth although it is fearsome in its appearance with a somewhat rounded head, deadly eyes, and curved horns or feelers on its head. However, flowers are the symbol of spring and regeneration. Boardman illustrates one reptilian dragon on a Chinese clay relief tile being fed flowers by another mysterious winged creature.[5]

According to historians and archaeologists, such a decor of the mosque has no parallel in architectural ornamentation of the monuments of Central Asia.[6] The mosque is said to have been built under the rule of Baisunkar Abul-Kasym Babur in 1456.[7]

The huge hoardings at the entrance of the steps leading over the outer wall of the Anau site displays the true structure of the mosque which is difficult to gauge with naked eyes as the mosque now lies in utter ruin due to the earthquake that struck in 1948 and completely destroyed it. We see a beautiful blue structure appearing like a massive hill of precious lapis lazuli.

Old photographs of the mosque, taken before the earthquake,

also portray life in early 19th or 20th century when people mostly travelled by horse or donkey carts. It is still practised in the villages of Xinjiang, where I rode a donkey cart to visit the ancient site of Gaochang in Turfan and the village of Malikawat in Khotan.

Steps lead up a high hill to the ruined mosque whose portal faces a courtyard. The main surviving structures are the base of two columns of the portal decorated with geometrical-shaped blue and turquoise tiles. Just behind the columns lay a huge pile of debris that reminded me of the devastating earthquake.

The focus of the mosque appears to have been a square hall with a high dome. This large domed central building was surrounded and supported by a group of buildings constructed for the purpose of prayer rooms and rest rooms, probably for the imam and those entrusted with the management of the mosque. The side structures, standing like columns, portrayed three-layered niches and was designed to strengthen the main structure.[8]

The column and the massive frontal arch of the mosque appear (from the hoarding at the entrance) to have a blue wavy design and bands portraying undulating lines. The blue waves, the profuse vegetation on the blue portals, the bright light caught by huge openings in the front columns supporting the portals and multi-storeyed side structures all combined to give the mosque a unique splendour. It is said that the artistes and craftsmen who built the structure, were not only picked locally but from many parts of the world, including famous master craftsmen from India who, along with Indian traders, were frequent travellers on the Silk Road to the Eastern Caspian.

As early as the period of Alexander, we find mention of Indian fresco painters and craftsmen working along with 50,000 people from 35 different nations to build the most glorious capital of Darius the Great in Persis.[9] Here the atria of the royal palace—the divine apadana was awe-inspiring. It displayed winged bulls and griffins on its gigantic columns. The precious throne was held by griffins with eyes of rubies. On the walls of the throne room, king Darius himself, in splendorous robes, fought with a winged monster. The monster symbolized 'Ahriman: the genius of evil and of darkness'.[10]

This was a way of Zoroastrian symbolization of the duel between the good and the evil. The same idea seems to be depicted on the portals of the Bagabat mosque where Ahriman represented by the dragons, has been transformed by the noble god Ahura Mazda into harbingers of peace and good luck.

In the courtyard of the mosque, a maulvi sat on a low stool, mumbling prayers as a stream of pilgrims knelt beside the grave of the saint Said Jamal-ad-Din, kissed the cloth spread over it and offered prayers. It is said that in this courtyard once gathered whirling dervishes who sang and played music, went into a trance and attracted a large number of followers. Laymen and women of surrounding villages gathered here to pray and be updated on the current events of the day.

Many women, dressed in long gowns and head covered in scarves were already at the mosque circumambulating a holy structure, concealed under a yellow cloth. What I was able to see was the impression of a pair of hands on two stones lying close to the structure. The women kissed the hands and went around it several times. A stream of women were also seen going through an entrance inside the dilapidated rooms on the right and emerged from another opening after praying inside and tying bands of cloth. I went to the back of the monument. Here, inside the dilapidated rooms, women were tying pieces of ribbons to a wooden beam that once supported the ancient roof. I learnt that these women came here seeking blessings for a child. One miniature cradle was also tied to the wall of the structure. It is said that no one returned empty-handed after praying at the mosque and seeking the blessings of the great saint.

The imagery of the enormous dragons on the front portals of the Bagabat mosque was overwhelming. It refused to fade from my thoughts. The creatures appeared beautiful in a strange way. Instead of displaying viciousness, the commonly dreadful animals looked like benevolent creatures holding the blossoms of peace and goodwill. It appeared as an act of submission in the holy house of the Great Allah.

From the mysterious dragon, I move on to another exquisite object of antiquity, belonging to the Parthian royalty—the carved ivory tusks of elephants, the rhytons. The rhytons were incredibly magnificent, though they served as mundane wine decanters at royal banquets held in the palace halls of Old Nisa—my next destination. The M-37 international highway would take me westwards to the famous Bagir village, the site of excavations at the Parthian fortress where the rhytons were found. I was excited to the last sinew.

References

For the history, design and motifs of the mosque see: Mammedow, Muhammet. *Architectural Complex of Said Jamal ad-Din*
For the Dragon symbol see: Boardman, John. 'Central Asia: West and East'. Hermann, Georgina (ed.) and Cribb, Joe (ed.). *After Alexander: Central Asia before Islam*

1. For detailed description and history of Anau see: Mammedow, Muhammet. *Architectural Complex of Said Jamal ad-Din* (Ashgabat: Turkmen State Publishing Service, 2011)
   For routes in Turkmenistan see: Buryakov, Y.E., Baipakov, K.M., Tashbaeva, K.H., Yakubov, Y. *The Cities and Routes of the Great Silk Road* (Tashkent: Sharg, 1999), p. 12-31
2. Sarianidi, Wiktor. *Margus: Ancient Oriental Kingdom in the Old Delta of the Murgab River* (Germany, Turkmen, Dowlet, Habarlary, Ashgabat: Benatzky Druck & Medien GmbH, 2002), p. 307
3. Knappert, Jan. *An Encyclopaedia of Myth and Legend: Indian Mythology* (London: Diamond Books, 1995), p. 176
4. Cribb, Joe (ed.) and Herman, Georgina (ed.). 'Central Asia: West and East'. *After Alexander: Central Asia before Islam* (New York: Oxford University Press Inc., 2010), p. 14
5. *Ibid.*, p. 17

6. Mammedow, Muhammet. *Architectural Complex of Said Jamal ad-Din* (Ashgabat: Turkmen State Publishing Service, 2011)
7. Buryakov, Y.E., Baipakov, K.M., Tashbaeva, K.H., Yakubov, Y. *The Cities and Routes of the Great Silk Road* (Tashkent: Sharg, 1999), p. 15
8. Mammedow, Muhammet. *Architectural Complex of Said Jamal ad-Din* (Ashgabat: Turkmen State Publishing Service, 2011)
9. Manfredi, V.M. and Halliday, Iian (trans.). *Alexander: The Ends of the Earth*, Volume 3 (London: Pan Macmillan Books, 2002), p. 180-181
10. *Ibid.*, p. 184

Parthian City of Nisa

The very name of Parthia conjures up images of Buddhist savants who worked for the cause of Buddhism in Central Asia and China. This was possible because Parthia itself was in a flourishing state and considered by scholars as a centre of Buddhist activities in the early centuries of the Christian era.[1]

The scholar monks of Parthia were rising stars of the Buddhist world and 'unrivalled' scholars of Sanskrit and Chinese. They preached the wisdom of the Dhamma—wisdom in the form of sutras.

One of them, like Prince Gautama from Kapilavastu, abdicated the Arsacid royal throne and the luxuries of palace life. Donning the orange robes of a monk, he wandered through the deserts of the Karakum. He took the eastern highway passing through Central Asia and arrived in China in AD 148 where he settled as a 'guru' in the renowned White Horse Monastery in Xian and preached the Dhamma to the populace. His name was An Shih-kao or Lokottama. To him alone have been ascribed 179 works of translation of Buddhist scriptures from Sanskrit to Chinese.[2]

Another scholar monk from Parthia, An Hsuan, was famous for his extensive study of the sutras and for his unique style of recitation. His proficiency extended not only to Chinese but also Sanskrit, and he translated the Sanskrit texts orally.[3] Both An Shih-kao and An Hsuan worked towards spreading the Buddhist scriptures.⁴ A number of monks from Parthia took the lead and ventured into other parts of Central Asia and China. They worked in association with the two monks as missionaries in the cause of Buddhism.⁵ Reference is also made to the Parthian An-Fa-chin, engaged in translation of Buddhist texts in the late 3rd century AD.⁶

According to P.C. Bagchi, among the foreign Buddhist missionaries pouring into China from Central Asia, the Parthians contributed immensely to the establishment of Buddhism in China, and also acted as intermediaries in the India–China relations. Their interpretation of Buddhism took China by storm, ushering in Buddhism and Indian culture.

It is believed the land of the Parthians and Sassanians where Buddhism flourished, today includes the territory of southern Turkmenistan. We hear of four monks from Parthia among the translators engaged in rendering the Buddhist scriptures into Chinese.⁷ Quoting the *Mahavamsa*, Bagchi refers to the visit of Mahadeva from Pallavabhoga with 46,000 bhikshus (monks) to Sri Lanka to participate in the celebration at the laying of the 'Great Stupa' in the time of King Dutta-gamini (108–77 BC). The Pallavas have been associated by historians with the Pahlavas, that is, the Parthians and 'Pallavabhoga' as a satrapy of the Parthians.⁸

A Glorious City

The ancient capital of the Parthians was Old Nisa. Inside the glorious city burnt the everlasting fires of the supreme God. Fire temples became popular as Zoroastrianism became the religion of the populace. Interestingly, the Parthian capital was also the city of Siva worshippers. Most of them were Indian settlers from the territory of eastern Iran. One such Indian settlement called 'Hindugan' existed in the neighbourhood of the 'ancient Parthian capital' as indicated by a Parthian ostraca from Nisa.⁹

The wealth of Parthia coming from the Silk Road transit trade was evident in the richly decorated palace complex at Nisa. There were massive halls, embellished with alcoves, where exquisitely carved images of gods and goddesses and royal personages reposed. Lion metopes and paintings decorated the palace walls; libations to the gods and ancestors were offered in exquisitely carved ivory tusks obtained from India's magnificent elephants; craftsmen created magical beings from stone and the most beautiful images of goddesses were sculpted by human hands.

These and more have been discovered at the UNESCO World Heritage Site by the spade of archaeologists of the Turin Centre of Archaeological Research and Excavation for the Middle East and Asia working jointly with the National Department for the Study, Conservation and Restoration of Historical and Artistic Monuments of the Turkmenistan Ministry of Culture. They continue to dig year after year to unfold the treasures of the ancient city of the Parthians. The amazing antiquities from Nisa now lie at the National Museum of Turkmenistan at Ashgabat.

Travels to Nisa

On a bright afternoon, I left Ashgabat for Nisa. My friends Marina, Nilgun, Sarfraz, Rafiq and Radha had already taken their seats in the big van. I climbed in next to Rafiq to learn more about his assignment at Boston where he is currently teaching as a visiting professor from Pakistan. The 30-minute drive to Nisa was spent in mirth amidst a roaring sandstorm that kicked up a lot of dust and sprayed an air mixed with fine sand and mud on the white, high-storeyed marble-façade buildings of modern Ashgabat. Surprisingly, no dust settled on the shiny marble. Our van, engulfed in the rising cloud of mud, lost its colour. The Kopetdag ranges surrounding the city like the edges of a bowl vanished from our sight. The massive forests of fir and pine surrounding Ashgabat swayed violently, the boughs sweeping the ground.

The storm brought a sudden and spectacular change in the landscape. The curling clouds of dust rose high in the horizon as though stalking our speeding van. The storm hissed and squealed like a giant exhaust. With hardly any traffic on the road, we drove on to the ancient city of Nisa, rushing past the residential areas of Ashgabat and spearing through acres of the lush green summer wheat. Unlike India, where in April the summer crops hang heavy with shafts of golden wheat, here, in Ashgabat, the sign of efflorescence was yet to appear. I calculated that the crop would not be harvested before June.

Far in the horizon, many more multi-storeyed buildings were rearing their heads, looming like images draped in marble. Maksat told me that the best white marble comes from India and Afghanistan. Huge lights had been fixed at the base of the buildings to brighten them at night.

As we entered the ancient walls of Nisa, the storm gave way to a drizzle. The Kopetdag reappeared as if on cue just outside the walls. The Bagyr village with shiny roofs and high minarets also swung into view. The rain seemed to have cleansed the dust-laden forests. As usual, Rafiq covered his face and sniffled at the diesel fumes blowing into the back seat where he was sitting. The van had a faulty blower and as luck would have it, every time we moved out of the hotel, Rafiq ended up in the same seat. At first we urged him to bear with it since Nisa was only a short distance from Ashgabat. But soon after, when I looked back, I found him crumpled on the seat, his face in a kerchief. Concerned, we offered him the front seat so that he could escape the fumes and get some fresh air. Soon, Rafiq seemed fit as a fiddle. I almost wondered wickedly to myself—was that a ploy to get the front seat in a crowded van?

Steps ran up the massive walls and across into the portals where we stood gazing at the great city as it lay like a beautiful statue in a large crucible. In its expanse rose a beautiful fortress of mud. The vast area in the front was low-lying, where once royal orchards and farms grew. Several visitors had climbed the walls to have a bird's-eye view of Bagir, its fruit orchards, vineyards and cultivated fields near the great Karakum canal.

I was overwhelmed by the history of the city with its high

bastions and numerous watch towers. It was built by King Mithridates at the foot of the Kopetdag mountains on a hill as the primary capital of the Parthian state. Here, excavators have found palace and temple complexes, wine stores and the treasury of the Parthian kings.

Who Were the Parthians?

According to Eric Hildinger (*Warriors of the Steppes*), the Parthians were Iranian-speaking nomads from the northern steppes who had settled in the Iranian plateau in the eastern regions of the Persian Empire. They dwelt beyond the Persian deserts in the regions south-east of the Caspian Sea.[10] Their name comes from 'the province of Parthava' where they had settled some time before 250 BC.[11] During Alexander's conquest of Persia, the Parthians fought as allies of the Persians at the battle of Arbela.

It is learnt that upon the death of Alexander the Great in 323 BC, the eastern satrapies of Persia, including Parthia, came under General Seleucus. However, in a national uprising led by the brothers Arsaces and Tiridates around 247 BC, Androgoros, the Seleukidan viceroy, was slain and Parthia declared its independence from Greek rule. The famous Arsacid dynasty of Persia was thus founded which endured for nearly five centuries (248 BC–AD 226).[12] Arsaces was crowned the first king of the Parthians. By the 2nd century BC, the Parthian kingdom included practically all the territories of the former Persian Empire.[13]

Rome suffered one of her greatest defeats at the hands of Parthia which fought under General Surena at the Battle of Carrhae in 54 BC.[14] The battle raged till noon, when Parthia suddenly unfurled colourful banners made of Chinese silk, sending out dazzling rays of light under the bright sunshine. The Roman soldiers were blinded and terrified by the dazzling light, and the entire battalion collapsed.[15]

Royal Sanctuary and Temple of Fire

A. Invernizzi (*After Alexander—Central Asia Before Islam*: 164) would have us believe that Nisa was the royal sanctuary of the Parthians and one of its most important centres. One of the special rooms—the Round Hall in the complex of Old Nisa was designed for the purpose of guarding an everlasting fire of the Arsacid dynasty. This prompted scholars to conclude that the inhabitants followed the Zoroastrian religion in which fire altars symbolizing the Supreme God was worshipped.

This most sacred place in the fortification of Old Nisa was surrounded on all sides by corridors that formed a square outside the hall: a circle within a square like the Buddhist mandala. Could it signify an amalgamation of religions, perhaps Zoroastrianism and Buddhism? According to museum records, this hall was considered to be the Fire Temple. The walls were cut into niches that held huge images of the Zoroastrian and Greek gods. The fire burnt in the centre of the hall, and the rising smoke collected in a domed smoke house in the ceiling. The ruins leave everything to imagination.

Apart from being a Fire Temple, the Round Hall is believed to have been a memorial or a temple for King Mithridates himself. This was inferred from the discovery of a fragmentary clay head of a 'portrait of Mithridates I' in the Round Hall.[16] Italian archaeologist, Carlo Lippolis, director of the Turin Mission, present at the site, pointed to the place in the Round Hall from where a part of the statue of King Mithridates was found. According to him, the fragments of sculpture recovered in the room belonged to a monumental statue more than two metres high, made of clay and painted in various colours. This fragment of a partial face and a flowing beard, very likely belonging to a royal person, Mithridates I himself, can be seen today at the National Museum at Ashgabat.

The excavators discovered stamped gypsum balls from various parts of the complex.[17] Perhaps these were offered by worshippers as graffiti or gifts with a prayer marked like a sutra to the numerous divine deities or ancestors of the royal dynasty whose images adorned the tall niches of the Nisa complex. In essence, they are akin to the small votive offerings in Buddhist temples in order to gain merit.

Another large Square Hall lies at the centre of the fortress. It is believed to have served as an audience chamber for the Parthian royalty. Enormous rectangular niches can be seen in the upper tiers of the walls. These were once adorned with large standing statues of divine deities or members of the Arsacid dynasty. The remains of massive, painted clay statues—of men and women found here, including the head of a princely warrior, another with flowing locks of hair and a short beard, heads of warriors with Attic helmets—are now housed in the National Museum.

The hall once had red plastered walls decorated with ornamental paintings. The floor was of alabaster and the wooden ceiling had a hole in the centre for light and air. The architecture of the hall prompted scholars to believe that a gigantic fire burned here.[18]

Ruins of a colossal tower building of brick can also be seen in the southern part of the complex. Archaeologists working at the site recovered several fragments of wall paintings from the debris of the ruined tower. On the top of this tower once stood a citadel that formed the main defence structure of the fortification.[19]

Rare Antiquities

Exotic antiquities in the form of wall paintings of which only fragments were recovered, lion metopea, silver-gilt images of divine creatures, marble statues of goddesses and carved ivory vessels used in ceremonial libation were found by excavators from different parts of the complex.

The statues, mostly belonging to the 2nd century BC, and displayed at the National Museum are believed to be the oldest found in Central Asia. A stone head of Aphrodite draws attention to the softness of its features; the goddess of Nisa, sculpted out of white marble, appears clad in a long heavy dress and a sash wrapped across her chest; Rodoguna, daughter of Mithridates I—in white and grey marble—shows off a bare upper body while the lower garment hangs loosely from the limbs. She appears to be hurriedly emerging from her bath; miniature silver-gilt figures of goddess Athena, a sphinx, a griffin, a winged Nike, glazed pottery with beautiful coloured patterns and other items were all found in the Square Hall. The artefacts prove the superb craftsmanship of the stone-carvers of Nisa.

Elephantine Links with India

In another part of the complex, excavations have uncovered articles of ivory with fabulous decorations and rare treasures lying sealed inside rooms of the massive treasury or the 'Quadrate'. The ivory horns or drinking vessels called rhytons were majestically carved of elephant tusks, depicting Greek gods.[20]

The rhytons used for drinking wine strongly suggest the intimate connection of the Parthian rulers with India, a country known for its elephants with long tusks. The Indian elephant was much prized in the Parthian state and its tusks were put to various ornamental purposes including jewellery, chess pieces and the unique drinking vessels.

We know of Greek, Bactrian and Parthian princes who were always tempted to attack the provinces of north-western regions of India that extended into Afghanistan, Baluchistan and all of Sind, Punjab for its wealth, specially elephants.[21] In 317 BC, Eudemos, commander of Alexander's garrison on the Indus after the latter had left Punjab, obtained 120 elephants by treacherously slaying a native prince.[22]

Seleukos Nikator crossed the Indus in 305 BC in a bid to invade the Ganges Valley, but he was defeated by Chandragupta (321-297 BC) and obliged to conclude a humiliating peace treaty in 303 BC. According to the treaty, Seleukos had to surrender a large part of land to the west of the Indus in exchange for 500 elephants.²³ Antiochus the Great of Syria (223-187 BC) crossed the Hindukush and compelled an Indian king Subhagsena, who ruled in the Kabul Valley, to surrender a considerable number of elephants and a large treasure.²⁴

The ivory rhytons of Nisa, carved from the tusks of elephants that most probably came from India, were found by archaeologists from a chamber of the Square House. Buried for centuries, all the rhytons were miraculously excavated without damage. Unparalleled in the world of art, the carving on the rhytons depict Greek gods. The surface is embellished with gold and silver and set with semi-precious stones, as can be seen at the museum. A written board states that the rhytons were used for cult libations. At the lower end of the rhyton is an opening to let the drink flow out. Some of them had a volume of 1.5 litres.

Trade in Indian Ivory

In *The Commerce between the Roman Empire and India*, E.H. Warmington says that ivory obtained from tusks of Indian elephants formed one of the most important trade articles on the Silk Road. It was used for ornaments and decoration from the earliest times. The best ivory came from the eastern part of India, Orissa. But the western coast of India at Barygaza, Muziris and Nelcynda also exported ivory to the West. It was also traded by the land routes.²⁵

The commerce in Indian ivory was high as it was used in statue decorations, articles of furniture and in temples. A man's riches were counted as 'gold, raiment, slaves and ivory'.²⁶ It was the favoured raw material for carvings as it was durable, hard and yet easy to work.

According to historian Romila Thapar, ivory work remained at a premium requiring as much delicacy and skill as the making of jewellery. Indian merchants were especially active in Central Asia and had established Indian trading stations along the Silk Road. Sources of commercial wealth consisted of produce not only minerals from the mine, but also plant and animal produce.²⁷ And this included ivory tusks from the mammoth elephant.

India was known as the major centre for ivory carving since ancient times. There were famed centres for ivory harvesting and carving, says Thapar. The carvers were familiar not only with the raw material but even with the subject matter since many Indian artistes are reported to have migrated to far-off lands in Persia. We read of many Indian painters being employed in the construction of the royal palace at Persepolis.[28] It is not surprising that Indian carvers were living in Nisa and working in the ivory workshops.

Madustan or Winery

The discovery of a Madustan or Winery by archaeologists in an adjacent building in Nisa shows that the Parthian rulers loved wine and made special arrangement for storing and grading of the product obtained from the state and private vineyards. The Madustan (Madu-wine, stan-place) was situated adjacent to the Treasure House and had the capacity to store half a million litres of wine.[29] Here, invoices on pottery were discovered which provide information about economic and administrative system of the royal town.

According to Gafurov, in the Madustan, wine was preserved in large khums (mud-baked vessels) and graded and entered in the receipt books according to its quality, date, the name of the vineyard, estate, and designation of the wine supplier. Huge wine jars, recovered from the Madustan (wine store), can be seen at the museum in Ashgabat.

To Bekrewe

After taking in the wonders of the Old Nisa, I descended the hill towards the branch canal which feeds the Bagyr village. Many farmers were cutting the embankments of a narrow canal to draw water into their wheat fields. Some were cooling off their hands and feet in the canal waters that ran just below the high hill. I took my cue and dipped my hands and feet into the muddy waters and thought about the ancient channels that filled the Old Nisa's moat. Even today, the water comes from the same river source as in ancient times. Only, its place has now been taken up by the modern Karakum canal.

All along my descent into the fortress and by the embankment into the canal, I had been looking for antiquities that by chance might come my way just as they did in Kaushambi near Allahabad in India, where several terracotta figurines surfaced after rains and inside the Taklamakan near the Rawak stupa. Sadly, a round coin with a square hole which I found in the desert and several pieces of pottery were all taken away by museum officials who were closely following me inside the Khotan desert. It must have been, I thought, an offering to the Great Buddha of Rawak.

Nevertheless, as a matter of habit, I kept looking but alas! Nisa gave up none. On the high hill, adjacent to the one on which we had climbed, were embedded green glass, probably pieces from a used soft drink bottle. The hill was covered with small yellow and purple wild flowers and juicy grass which I sat chewing as I waited for other members of my team to descend from their tour of Old Nisa.

Far away, on the Kopetdag, the hills again appeared hazy. A silvery cover had spread over them and a cool whiff of pleasant breeze was blowing over the ancient town. It must be raining on the mountains, I guessed. Suddenly, my eyes fell on the driver of my coach. I approached him to enquire about the great Karakum canal flowing around Bagir. I ask whether we could take a detour and see the canal and take photos. He replied that the road did not go there and that I could see the canal on my way to the market of Altyn Asyr, 45 kilometres from Ashgabat. However, on several occasions, I was near the canal and managed to take plenty of photos.

On our way back to Ashgabat, we again drove through vineyards and fruit orchards surrounding Bagir. We stopped at

Bekrewe to get some water and chocolates. The water of Bekrewe is as famous as the water of Ganges. It is cool, fresh, sweet and fortified with minerals coming from a mountainous spring. A bottling plant has been set up somewhere near the spring to supply the city and neighbouring areas with sufficient sweet water.

I spotted several women digging at the base of pine trees, clearing the weeds and pulling away dead leaves. Some were sweeping the streets and were covered from head to foot; they had pulled their head scarves over their faces to avoid the harsh sun, wind and dust. Another man was washing the plants. I was amazed at the effort taken by the government and the people to keep the roads clean; and at the trees by the roadside, always green and fresh, even after a heavy storm.

Besides the human hand, vacuum machines were also doing the rounds of roads to collect fine dust from the edges. As we strolled in Bekrewe, I chanced upon a house with a courtyard covered with thick black vine creepers, bereft of leaves and flowers. Soon the efflorescence would set in and small pearly white vine flowers would hang in bunches. Not far was another house with blossoming apricots and peach trees. The branches were full of light pink, white and purple flowers. It was spring in Turkmenistan. Birds flitted from bough to bough, waiting to partake in a grand fruit feast prepared by spring. Every orchard was bursting with life after a deep slumber. We drank the sweet water of Bekrewe and got into our van to drive back to Ashgabat.

The following day, our caravan was to take the M-37 international highway to Mary and Bairam Ali for a visit to the site of ancient Merv in the Karakum desert. The excellent six-lane road M-37 runs up to the border with Uzbekistan at Turkmenabat and Farab before crossing the Oxus to enter Bukhara and onwards to Samarkand and Ferghana in the north-east. The big Karakum canal drawing waters from the Oxus flows along the highway bringing the much-needed water to the desert oases. The road meanders aroud the foot of the Kopetdag mountains and touches Mary on the Murgab river. It is the main highway of Turkmenistan that connects through Uzbekistan and Kyrgyzstan with China at the Irkeshtam pass. The distance between Ashgabat to Mary is only 362 kilometres, and I was enthused at the possibility of seeing more of the desert and villages along the road. But it was not to be. The plan changed. Instead of the road trip, we had to take the 30-minute flight to Mary. Such a disappointment!

References

For details on Old Nisa see: *Exploration Report of Old Nisa* by the Turin Centre of Archaeological Research and Excavation for Middle East and Asia under the direction of A. Invernizzi and C. Lippolis and the National Department for the Study, Conservation and Restoration of Historical and Artistic Monuments of the Turkmenistan Ministry of Culture, headed by V.N. Pilipko; Invernizzi, Antonio. 'The Culture of Parthian Nisa between Steppe and Empire'. Cribb, Joe (ed.) and Herman, Georgina (ed.). *After Alexander: Central Asia Before Islam*

1. Puri, B.N. *Buddhist Tradition Series: Buddhism in Central Asia* (Delhi: Motilal Banarsidass Publishers Pvt. Ltd., 2000), p. 96
2. Bagchi, P.C. *India and China* (Calcutta: Saraswat Press, 2008), p. 113
   Chaudhuri, Saroj Kumar. *Lives of Early Buddhist Monks: The Oldest Extant Biographies of Indian and Central Asian Monks* (New Delhi: Abha Prakashan, 2008), p. 47-53
3. *Ibid.*, p. 56
4. *Ibid.*, p. 56
5. Bagchi, P.C. *India and China* (Calcutta: Saraswat Press, 2008), p. 38-39
6. Puri, B.N. *Buddhist Tradition Series: Buddhism in Central Asia* (Delhi: Motilal Banarsidass Publishers Pvt. Ltd., 2000), p. 101
7. *Ibid.*, p. 102
8. *Ibid.*, p. 96-97 (Puri quotes from W. Geiger. *Mahavamsa*. Op.cit., XXIX, 29)
9. Harmatta, J. (ed.) *History of Civilizations of Central Asia: The*

Development of Sedentary and Nomadic Civilizations (700 BC to AD 250), Volume II (Delhi: Motilal Banarsidass Publishers Pvt. Ltd., 1999), p. 320

10. Smith, Vincent. *History of India,* Volume II (New York: Cosimo Classics, 2006), p. 200
    Hildinger, Eric. *Warriors of the Steppes* (USA: Da Capo Press, 2001), p. 39
11. Hildinger, Eric. *Warriors of the Steppes* (USA: Da Capo Press, 2001), p. 39
12. Smith, Vincent. *History of India,* Volume II (New York: Cosimo Classics, 2006), p. 200
13. Hildinger, Eric. *Warriors of the Steppes* (USA: Da Capo Press, 2001), p. 39
14. *Ibid.*, p. 39
15. Yiping, Zhang and Zhingyi, Jia (trans.). *The Story of the Silk Road* (Beijing: China Intercontinental Press, 2005), p. 30
16. Cribb, Joe (ed.) and Herman, Georgina (ed.). 'The Culture of Parthian Nisa between Steppe and Empire'. *After Alexander: Central Asia before Islam* (New York: Oxford University Press Inc., 2007), p. 164
17. *Ibid.*, p. 164
18. Gafurov, B.G. *Central Asia: Pre-Historic to Pre-Modern Times*, Volume I (Delhi: Shipra Publications, 2005), p. 176
19. *Ibid.,* p. 175
20. *Ibid.,* p. 176
21. Smith, Vincent. *History of India*, Volume II (New York: Cosimo Classics, 2006), p. 107-108, 197-219
22. *Ibid.*, p. 103
23. *Ibid.*, p. 108
24. *Ibid.*, p. 201
25. Warmington, E.H. *The Commerce between the Roman Empire and India* (New Delhi: Munshi Ram Manoharlal, 1995), p. 162-165
26. *Ibid.*, p. 163
27. Thapar, Romila. *The Penguin History of Early India: From the Origins to AD 1300* (New Delhi: Penguin Books, 2003), p. 299, 238

28. Manfredi, V.M. and Halliday, Iian (trans.). *Alexander: The Ends of the Earth*, Volume 3 (London: Pan Macmillan Books, 2002), p.184
29. Gafurov, B.G. *Central Asia: Pre-Historic to Pre-Modern Times*, Volume 1 (Delhi: Shipra Publications, 2005), p. 176

The giant head of the Buddha recovered from the monastery of Gyaur Kala, Ancient Merv (2nd-3rd century AD).
Courtesy: National Museum of Turkmenistan, Ashgabat and State Museum, Mary

A painted vase from the monastery of Gyaur Kala, Ancient Merv (5th century AD).
Courtesy: National Museum of Turkmenistan, Ashgabat

Buddha head emerging from acanthus leaves, found at a monastery in Ancient Merv (1st century BC).
Courtesy: National Museum of Turkmenistan, Ashgabat

An ivory rhyton used for drinking wine from Nisa (2nd century BC).
Courtesy: National Museum of Turkmenistan, Ashgabat

A copy of the Sanskrit manuscript on birch bark recovered from Merv oasis (5th century AD).
Courtesy: Bharat Soka Gakkai, Delhi and Institute of Oriental Studies, St Petersburg

Ruins of the settlement of Kyz Kala in the deserts of Ancient Merv (6th century AD).

Ruins of the Parthian city of Nisa (2nd century BC).

Monastic Site of Ancient Merv

It was in the deserts of the Karakum spreading over thousands of hectares that Merv, one of the largest and most magnificent cities, took root. Ancient Merv, the centre of the sacred province of Margiana, was a brilliant Bronze Age civilization that lay hidden for thousands of years within the layers of the dry Karakum desert. It needed the genius, vision and spade of archaeologists to reveal its glories to the world. The barren desert that we see north of modern Merv is the bed where river channels once ran and a prosperous urban country existed. Far from being a desert in the dry and desolate Karakum, the Trans-Caspian region in which Margiana lay was a green zone as Edvard Rtveladze traces the etymology of 'Margiana' to 'Marg' meaning a meadow or a ground grassed over.[1]

This land also saw the flowering of Dhamma. Buddhist messengers erected stupas, read the holy texts and worshipped the Buddha. The Great Zarathustra is also believed to have lived and preached here. Scientists found traces of the Rig Vedic haoma—the intoxicating nectar—prepared by the inhabitants as a libation for the gods.

One of the greatest cities of the Buddhist and Islamic world, ancient Merv is listed by the UNESCO as a World Heritage Site. Sadly, the Buddhist cities are lost to the fury of nature. Whatever antiquities were recovered from the Buddhist sites of Erk Kala, Gyaur Kala and Sultan Kala can now be seen in the museums at

Ashgabat and Mary. They are perhaps the only link to the country's Buddhist past, when the Buddha's Dhamma had flourished in the deserts of the Karakum. They tell us about the great scholars who rose from the monastic centres of Merv to translate and preach the wisdom of the Buddhist texts to the world.

Spread over an immense area, ancient Merv is believed to date back at least 5,000 years. A series of excavations in the region brought to light monumental fortresses, palaces and temples that led to the conclusion that a magnificent civilization existed along the Murghab river in the Karakum. Viktor Sarianidi (*Margus*) calls it the 'Fifth Centre of the world civilization' competing with the oldest ones of China, India, Mesopotamia and Egypt.[2]

The *Margus* throws light on the close ties of Merv with the Indus Valley. Analogues of ceramics and vessels of the Gonur citadel in Margiana were found in settlements of ancient Indian Harappan civilization, including articles of ivory, probably imported from the Indian subcontinent.[3]

Reading the monumental work of Viktor Sarianidi, one can infer that the earliest settlers of Merv knew about the merits of the sacred 'haoma' which has been mentioned in the Rig Veda. It was here that poppy and hemp were discovered. Huge vessels and drinking bone tubes, special underground furnaces and drainage for waste water and cult figurines imply that the ancient people used to prepare intoxicating divine drinks. Residues of narcotics were found on tub plasters; even mortars and pestles had traces of poppy and ephedra.[4]

On the Banks of the Murghab River

On the last leg of my Silk Road journey in Turkmenistan, I was part of a large delegation touring the desert city of ancient Merv. Here, inside the Karakum desert, lay the remains of various settlements—Kyz Kala, Erk Kala, Gyaur Kala and Sultan Kala. These settlements once lay in the delta of the Murghab river. As the river changed its course, the settlements moved from one place to another and

Merv thus came to be known as a 'city on the move'.

It is believed that the present-day desertified region of Merv was in reality a green zone watered by the Murghab river. The barren desert is the bed where river channels once ran and a prosperous urban country existed. The Trans-Caspian region in which Merv lay was rich and prosperous, drawing its wealth from the trade on the Caspian and the Indus Valley route.

The region was once teeming with inhabitants who were mainly herders who bred, in these Turcoman wastes, superb horses that were sent to India for sale; cultivators who grew crops along the delta of the Murghab river and other water bodies that crisscrossed the land east of Caspian before they shrivelled up and were lost in the sand; artisans who manufactured various goods for traders who frequented the roads leading to the north-western regions of India.

The region was also occupied by pilgrims, scholars and monks who worshipped the Buddha and studied Buddhist texts in the monasteries of Merv. The Buddhist site lay in Gyaur Kala and much has been written about it by historians and archaeologists like A. Gubaev, Z. Usmanova and G. Koshelenko.

To this enchanting desert, I was to take the early morning flight. The airport was located at Mary, the chief town of Merv region which forms the base for excursions into the Karakum deserts lying 30 kilometres east. After a long wait at the Ashgabat airport, I was able to take the 6 a.m. flight along with a huge delegation of historians, archaeologists and scientists who had descended on Ashgabat in connection with an international conference.

In about an hour, we landed at the Mary airport to a rousing reception by men and women dressed in traditional attire while a musical band played folk music. A group of women came with trays loaded with stuffed bread, sweets, dry fruits and cola drinks. I had eaten nothing since morning and I lunged forward for a fat piece of bread stuffed with raisins and black currants. Alas! The stuffing turned out to be pieces of roasted mutton. For a strict vegetarian like me, the dilemma of swallowing the morsel or spitting it out was a grave one. I decided to silently swallow it.

There was much music and feasting as we proceeded in a bus to the city. After crossing the bridge over the Murgab, we turned left and drove for a short distance before arriving at the Mehmankhana in Mary where a sumptuous breakfast was awaiting us. I walked to the Murgab flowing right behind the guesthouse and noticed huge cauldrons set on gas fire in which water was being boiled for preparing hot drinks. Mutton and fish were being roasted and steaming rice pilaf was being laid into large servers. Everything looked superb and mouth-watering; even the mutton shashliks that I could not eat. But at one time, I had tasted platefuls of shashlik served on hot naans in a Khotan bazaar.

I sat on the embankment of Murgab watching the river gently gurgling by. The river flows all the way from its source in the Hindukush and along the southern edge of the Karakum desert and loses itself in the myriad streams of its delta. In the lap of this delta rose the city of Merv located strategically on the north-west route to Astrakhan, north-east route to Bukhara and Samarkand, and south-east route to Afghanistan and India.

On the river front stood an ancient building that resembled a church and a few yards away rose a blue-domed mosque. Not a soul lingered on the banks except a black dog that was leisurely sunning itself. By the time I returned to the Mehmankhana a sumptuous breakfast had been laid out. The spread was lavish even for a vegetarian: vegetable rice pilaf, meatless soup, curd, salad, bread and butter, cheese and jam and, of course, fruits and sherbet.

On a Bus to Bairam Ali

It seemed it had rained all night in Mary. The air was quite chilly and there were puddles of water by the roadside. This was a good sign for the desert travellers as damp sand settles down, making it easier to walk upon.

The bus to Bairam Ali took Highway M-37. Few people were on the street as shopping centres were closed at that early hour.

The Trans-Caspian Railways ran parallel to the road and I spotted a train moving towards Bairam Ali, from where it would turn to Turkmenabat and onwards to Bukhara.

Along the road lay small orchards of apricot and peaches covered in blossoms. Branches of the great Karakum canal crossed the highway at several points to irrigate cultivated fields on both sides of the road. I rarely saw any cotton plantation around the canal. Instead there were large vineyards and wheat fields. Clusters of brick and mud houses, with shiny roofs of tin and asbestos, sped past us. Small choykhanas manned by elderly women, stood at the entrance of villages.

The Karakum canal, like the Oxus, runs almost parallel to the highway. It is the same broad sheet of water that it was near Termez. But it had changed its colour from silvery to green. After nearly an hour of driving, we reached Bairam Ali. A branch road turned left towards the desert. From far away, the walls of a ruined city appeared out of nowhere. The bus tumbled along a narrow road in the desert, brushing against blooming bushes, going around old cemeteries, and finally stopping at the ruins of the ancient Kyzkala.

Sarfaraz, a professor from Peshawar University, came up with an interesting tale about Kyzkala: Once upon a time, beautiful royal maidens lived inside the kala (a settlement or village). Young men of royal blood living in the adjacent kala, in a bid to find partners, threw apples at the maidens. The maiden who caught the apple thrown by a particular youth became his partner. For life or temporarily, Sarfaraz knew not.

We climbed a ramp and went inside the huge kala. Where we stood might have been the second storey of the kala because there was a winding staircase going below. Or, was it a tunnel to the adjacent kala after the apples were accepted as Sarfraz mentioned? Very few of us dared to go down the staircase. I certainly did not. I was in no mood to step into what might have been as dark as a dungeon. The purpose of the ramp was to elevate the level of the ground so that a floor could be built in the basement much like a mezzanine floor built in modern buildings.

The bus moved from Kyzkala to the twin mausoleums of saints where pilgrims come from afar to pray at the tombs of the two companions 'Askhab'; or standard-bearers of the Holy Prophet Mohammad. They were al-Hakim ibn Amr al-Jiffari and Buraida ibn al Huseib al Aslami, who lived in the 7th century. A sardoba lay by the side of the mausoleum where pilgrims not only quenched their thirst but also made a wish and dropped a coin into the deep waters.

Buddhist Monastery at Erk Kala

Our next stop was Erk Kala which stood at the top of a hill that now appeared like a massive earth mound. Ruins of structures could be seen on the hill top. But the climb was difficult as the incline was sharp. What seemed like a high ramp was made up of sand and clay. I kept loitering around the base of Erk Kala, taking photos and trying to look for coins and interesting pottery.

Archaeologist Z.I. Usmanova mentions the recovery of a terracotta head of a human that possibly resembled the face of a Buddhist deity. The image had large eyes and long ears. The photograph given by Usmanova also shows a protuberance on the head—the ushnisa. The image appeared to be made 'in accordance with the traditions of Buddhist plastic art,' says Usmanova.[5]

There is no doubt that a Buddhist monastery existed at Erk Kala and the ruined structure on the hill could possibly have been a monastic settlement. The main evidence of a monastery existing at Erk Kala is the fact that a large Buddhist monastery with a shrine and stupa were found close by in the surrounding settlement of Gyaur Kala. Since a large number of monks and scholars are believed to have lived and studied at this renowned monastic centre of Gyaur Kala, from where copies of Buddhist texts were also found, it is quite possible that the surrounding kalas, too, had been occupied by resident monks.

In the desert around Erk Kala, that formed a part of the Gyaur Kala settlement, lay heaps of broken pottery. A crowd had collected to see the excavated ruins of a mosque, said to be the first mosque in Gyaurkala. And the sardoba too, in whose ruins lay a dried up broken well. There were ruins of ice houses in the desert where water was cooled for the travellers who took the road through the Karakum.

Monastery of Gyaur Kala

The monastery and stupa of Gyaur Kala were supposed to be close by. They should have been visible from quite a distance as they lay atop a high mound. The monastery was particularly a large one and is said to have been one of the largest outside India. Archaeologists excavating at the site in year 1960 recovered a massive Buddha head, part of a large painted statue, several 'Sitting Buddha' images, manuscripts in Brahmi on birch bark, terracotta heads of the Buddha, images of *Jataka* monkeys, inscribed clay tablets from a reliquary and ruins of the monastery itself.

The general layout of the Gyaur Kala monastery, as described by Z. Usmanov, showed that it was typical of the Buddhist monuments of Central Asia.[6] Therefore, the monastery would have included a shrine chamber, the stupa, pradikshana path (circumambulatory corridor), a congregational hall and several monastic cells for residential monks. The basic plan was largely similar to the monastic settlements at Kafirnihon, Ajina Tepa and Khisht Tepa in Tajikistan or the Fayaz Tepa temple at Termez.

From the several illustrations provided by Z. Usmanova (*India and Central Asia: Pre-Islamic Period*), we learn that the monastic centre had well-built rooms with proper windows that allowed for circulation of air and sufficient light. The thick walls of the cells, the niches embedded in them and the windows for light and air were made of adobe, pakhsa (mixture of unbaked mud and straw) and burnt bricks. Some niches were arched. There were corridors, congregational halls for monastic assembly and some rooms had sufa (bench-like raised structures) along the walls.[7]

A. Gubaev informs us of two stupas discovered in Gyaur Kala.

One, dated to the 2nd/3rd century AD built inside the Gyaur Kala settlement and the other built outside the city walls. He writes of the demolition of the 'urban' stupa and the construction of the 'suburban' one, almost 'simultaneously'. He ascribes this to the policy of the local Sassanian authorities aiming at prohibiting the Buddhists of having their sacred places within the city limits but permitting them at the same time to build Buddhist monuments outside the city.[8]

Yet, and surprisingly so, there was no stupa or signs of any monastery in Gyaur Kala where the entire delegation had already reached. I tried to persuade the authorities that accompanied the delegation, to show us the monastery. I was told that the monastic ruins lay further east and the bus could not go there. I noticed that the road through the desert had hit a dead end at the sardoba. There was no road or pathway to the ancient monastery. My heart sank. I asked Maksat, the personnel from the Ministry of Culture, how many kilometres was the distance to the stupa. I actually thought I could cover the distance on foot. The bus could not run on unlevelled and sandy desert in the absence of even a pathway. I was told that it was only two kilometres away along shrub lands that hadn't been cleared.

I wanted to linger around in Gyaur Kala to scan the hilly mounds and low sand dunes in order to locate the monastery. But the bus driver was honking furiously. With a heavy heart, I climbed into the bus and moved on to Sultan Kala where we stopped near the mausoleum of Sultan Sanjar, ruler of the Seljukid Empire. He died in AD 1157 and was interred in the religious complex which was already standing at the site during his rule. The unique squarish monument which has some resemblance to the Samanid mausoleum at Bukhara could be seen by desert travellers from a day's distance.

At the mausoleum, a row of camels dressed in their finery were waiting to carry passengers and tourists in small beautiful yurts set up on their hunches. In ancient times, desert travellers found these yurts, fastened on the back of camels and covered from all sides, very comfortable and it protected them from the sun's heat and glare. I held the reins of a camel and got myself photographed because I was afraid to climb into the yurt after a particularly adventurous experience that I had in the Taklamakan desert in Xinjiang. There a camel had galloped away with me into the mountains. The camel and I could be traced only from the sound of bells ringing around its long neck.

Many yurts had come up in the desert around Sultan Kala. Here, women sat spinning yarn from camel and lamb hair. Some were rolling wool into layers of felt. Inside one yurt, women were sewing and knitting, preparing beautiful caps that men and women usually wear.

Buddha Bells of Sultan Kala

It is believed that in the southern suburbs of the Sultan Kala too lay a Buddhist temple. The evidence for this are the antiquities that were recovered from Sultan Kala in the form of bronze bells and ceramic masks stamped with the image of the Buddha and pressed terracotta with zoomorphic figures displayed at the State Museum at Mary.

The bus was ready to depart to Bairam Ali and all members of the delegation were already seated inside the bus. I, too, trudged back to the bus. My enthusiasm for travelling to Merv was dead. A female guide who sensed my anguish quietly thrust forward a photo of the broken Buddha head found at the monastery and the stairway that led to the stupa of Gyaur Kala. My eyes lit up as I took several shots of the photos. She told me to look for the Buddha head in the museum at Mary. So, there was still a ray of hope left.

At the Mary Museum

From the deserts of ancient Merv, we returned to Mary via Bairam Ali for a visit to the State Museum where I was hopeful of finding the giant Buddha head. Also on display here were other

Buddhist antiquities from the kalas of Merv, namely Sultan Kala and Gyaur Kala. These included numerous bronze bells stamped with images of the Buddha recovered from Sultan Kala. The bells must have once decorated the Buddhist shrine and were perhaps brought as offerings by the devotees. The museum also displayed Buddha figures stamped on terracotta and ceramics. One terracotta fragment was engraved with the image of the sitting Buddha and below the engraving were a few lines inscribed in Brahmi. What exactly was written on the fragment was not mentioned. Since the engravings on the terracotta were barely visible, a clearer image drawn on paper was also displayed. It appeared to be either of a monk or of the Buddha himself. The piece could have been a bulla (clay ball with inscription) for stamping temple offerings like the one found at the temple of Kanka near Tashkent.

Many stamped terracotta figures were reminiscent of the tales from the Buddhist stories of the *Jatakas*. A terracotta fragment from the monastery of Merv, probably a piece from a big jar, depicted a monkey sitting beside a human figure holding a bird. It perhaps symbolized the bird of the *Jatakas*, the famous Sibi Jataka. The story goes that once a bodhisattva was born as King Sibi or Sivi and was reputed for his goodness and virtue. One day a pigeon, chased by a hawk, rushed to his palace and sought protection of King Sibi. The hawk followed the pigeon to the royal court and demanded that pigeon should be given back to him as it was his lawful prey. The king declined to surrender the pigeon and instead struck a bargain to save the little bird's life. He gave the hawk a measure of his own flesh equal to the bird's weight. The bird is seen here in the king's lap.[9]

The image of the monkey, too, could be related to the *Jatakas* (*Mahakapi Jataka*) and to the episodes from the life of the Buddha himself. In the *Mahakapi Jataka*[10] scene engraved on a stone pillar in Sanchi, the bodhisattva is born as chief of a monkey tribe. The tribe lived on the sweet fruits of a mango tree by the side of the Ganga river in the Himalayan region. When the king learnt about the sweet fruits of the tree he surrounded it with his soldiers. The bodhisattva, born as the chief monkey, in order to save his tribe, formed a bridge over the river by tying a bamboo shoot to his waist and stretching his own body to the other end to a tree. He did this so that other monkeys could pass over the bridge and save themselves from the kings's soldiers. All escaped. But Devadutta (Buddha's rival in the sangha, now in the life of a monkey) while passing over the bridge jumped on the chief money, crushing him to death. The king took pity on the dying chief and brought him down. Before his death the monkey delivered a discourse to the king.

Another incident involving the monkeys during Buddha's life time was at Vaishali at the Kutagarshala Vihara built by the Lichhavis for the Buddha. It was at this Vihara that a monkey offered a bowl of honey to the Buddha. It is believed that the monkey took the alm's bowl of the Buddha and climbed up a tree to gather honey for him. The monkey was so overjoyed when Buddha accepted the gift that while leaping from tree to tree he fell down and died. The incident is considered as one of the eight most important events of Buddha's life and is depicted on a panel at Sanchi.

The monkeys at the Vaishali Kutagarshalla Vihara are believed to have dug a water tank for the Buddha whose water was bright and clear. It was called the Markataha-hrada or the monkey tank.

As stories, the *Jatakas* are believed to be full of worldly wisdom and were narrated to the laity to propagate the Dhamma. No wonder, the *Jataka* stories were carved on terracotta and stone walls of the monasteries and facing of the stupas. Thus we find that a synopsis of a collection of *Jatakas* and *Avadanas* was found in Bairam Ali in manuscripts of the 3rd-4th centuries.[11]

Mystery of the Largest Buddha Head

However, the famous head of the giant Buddha recovered from the Gyaur Kala oasis was nowhere to be seen even at the Mary museum. I asked the guide to direct me to this particular exhibit. But she had never seen it during her tenure as a museum guide. She called her senior who explained that the Buddha head can be seen at the Ashgabat Museum. But I had previously taken two rounds of the museum halls at Ashgabat but had not been able to find it. On enquiry at Ashgabat, I was told that it lay at the Mary museum.

Later, I was informed by Maksat, from the Ministry of Culture, that the head that had been recovered from the Buddhist site of Gyaur kala had perhaps been taken away either to Ashgabat or St Petersburg for restoration. I am doubtful if any museum in Turkmenistan displayed the Buddha head.

Photographs shown to me by the guide at Sultan Kala of the steps leading to the Buddhist stupa (or, was it a terraced stupa?) and the Buddha head which she permitted me to photograph were now my only possessions from the monastic site. I later learnt that in recent times no one had seen the stupa and the ruins of the monastery at the site. The recent photographs of Gyaur Kala site uploaded by numerous travel agencies did not show the stupa either. This gave rise to rumours that the stupa had been levelled and there was no trace of the monastery either. In fact, the stupa and the Buddha head can now be seen only in old photographs which were perhaps taken at the time of excavations and which accompany the articles written by historians and archaeologists who had explored the site.

The Buddha head, measuring a little less than a metre, is part of a giant statue and is believed to have been the most amazing discovery in Turkmenistan. One can guess the size of the head from the photograph which shows two excavators struggling to lift the head from the debris with great difficulty. The nose and a part of the huge face appear to be damaged. Compared to the size of the head of the Reclining Buddhas of Kushinagar, Ajina Tepe and the Dazu grottoes, it can be safely said that the head belonged to a giant statue not less than twenty times its size. It would have been the largest image of the Buddha in Central Asia.

However, no one knows whether the Buddha figure was a 'sitting' or a 'standing' one. While a Sitting Buddha could have been enshrined in a roofed building, the Standing figure could only be erected in an open courtyard of the monastic settlement and could have been the first to collapse under the weight of the falling structures of the monastery. There is hope that in the dry climate of Central Asia, the torso of the Buddha is still lying buried somewhere near Gyaur Kala and is waiting for the spades of archaeologists to rescue it.

The sculptured head of the monumental figure of the Buddha is described in detail by Z.I. Usmanov. He tells us that the curls of hair were made of ganch (plaster) and painted blue. Other fragments of the clay sculpture were painted red with traces of golden foil. Only a hand and foot of the sculpture were found.[12]

Delights of a Hot Desert

The delight of my journey into the hot deserts of the Karakum was accentuated by the cooling showers of unexpected rains. The company of lovely friends—Radha, Nilgun, Sarfaraz, Tatiana and Marina, who were all delegates at the conference—enlivened the desert trip. It was a group that stuck together for the days that we spent in Turkmenistan knowing that we may never meet again. We never did.

However, my quest for the stupa in the desert turned out to be a fiasco. I often wonder whether I could have postponed my return to India and requested the authorities for a second visit to the desert. Still, the final choice of allowing a visitor to go near the ruins of the stupa and the monastic settlement was in the hands of the authorities. Had the stupa really melted away as rumoured? Had the giant head been lost during reconstruction? Many theories were floating in my mind when I returned to India. I asked several visitors to Turkmenistan whether they had been able to see the Giant Head of the Buddha or the stupa of Gyaur Kala. No one did. Among the five Central Asian countries, Tajikistan is now the only country to possess and display the Giant Buddha at its Dushanbe Museum. I do not know where the Buddha's head is. Perhaps some day I will see it. I live with that hope.

References

For history of Ancient Merv and Margiana see: Sarianidi, Wiktor. *Margush: Ancient Oriental kingdom in the Old Delta of the Murghab River*; Usmanov, Z.I. 'Historical and Cultural Contacts between Southern Turkmenia and India in Ancient Times'. Rtveladze, E. (chief coordinator). *India and Central Asia Pre-Islamic*; Gubaev, A. 'Cultural Integration of Turkmenistan and India in the Early and Medieval Period'. Rtveladze, E. (chief coordinator). *India and Central Asia Pre-Islamic*

1. Rtveladze, Edvard. *Civilizations, States and Cultures of Central Asia* (Tashkent: University of World Economy and Diplomacy, 2009), p. 17
2. Sarianidi, Wiktor. *Margush: Ancient Oriental Kingdom in the Old Delta of the Murghab River* (Germany, Turkmen, Dowlet, Habarlary, Ashgabat: Benatzky Druck and Medien GmbH, 2002), p. 64, 335
3. *Ibid.*, p. 320-321
4. *Ibid.*, p. 179-197, 308
5. Usmanov, Z.I. 'Historical and Cultural Contacts between Southern Turkmenia and India in Ancient Times'. Rtveladze, E. (chief coordinator). *India and Central Asia Pre-Islamic* (Tashkent: Academy of Arts and Academy of Sciences of the Republic of Uzbekistan, 2000), p. 65-66. Illustrations p. 241-246
6. *Ibid.*, p. 66
7. *Ibid.*, p. 241-246
8. Gubaev, A. 'Cultural Integration of Turkmenistan and India in the Early and Medieval Period'. Rtveladze, E. (chief coordinator). *India and Central Asia Pre-Islamic* (Tashkent: Academy of Arts and Academy of Sciences of the Republic of Uzbekistan, 2000), p. 37
9. Ahir, D.C. *The Influence of the Jatakas on Art and Literature* (Delhi: BRPC-India Ltd., 2000), p. 24
10. *Ibid.*, p. 29
11. Litvinsky, B.A. (ed.). *History of Civilizations of Central Asia: The crossroads of civilizations (AD 250 to 750)*, Volume III (Delhi: Motilal Banarsidass Publishers Pvt. Ltd., 1999), p. 444

12. Usmanov, Z.I. 'Historical and Cultural Contacts between Southern Turkmenia and India in Ancient Times'. Rtveladze, E. (chief coordinator). *India and Central Asia Pre-Islamic* (Tashkent: Academy of Arts and Academy of Sciences of the Republic of Uzbekistan, 2000), p. 65-67

Section Four

UZBEKISTAN

Routes into Uzbekistan

The International Highway M-39—running through the length of Uzbekistan through Tashkent, Samarkand and Termez—crosses southwards into Afghanistan and north-eastwards into Kyrgyzstan and Kazakhstan. It passes into Afghanistan through the Friendship Bridge on the Oxus river. The M-39 connecting three countries of Central Asia is the only route connecting Termez with the city of Hayratam in Afghanistan. The highway approximates to the route taken by Amir Timur over 600 years ago when he marched in 1398 from Samarkand to Delhi.

Another route into Uzbekistan led from the city of Merv in the territory of modern Turkmenistan.[1] This was the main caravan route from Merv going eastwards to the fertile Zerafshan Valley and further into China. The first section of the road led through the desert to ancient Amul (Charjui or modern Turkmenabat) in the mid-flow of the Amu Darya. Amul lay on the crossroads of the land and river routes.[2] The land route led into Bukhara and eastwards through the Ferghana Valley into China; to Russia through Khorezm in the north-west; into Persia through Merv in the south-west, and into India through Balkh in the south. The river route along the Oxus ran right into Khorezm in the north-west.

Goods from India went along this river route to Khorezm and northwards to the land of Khazaria, Russia and Europe.[3]

References

For routes into Uzbekistan see: Buryakov Y.F., Baipakov, K.M., Tashbaeva, K.H., Yakubov, Y. *The Cities and Routes of the Great Silk Road*

1. Buryakov, Y.F., Baipakov, K.M., Tashbaeva, K.H., Yakubov, Y. *The Cities and Routes of the Great Silk Road* (Tashkent: Sharg, 1999), p. 23
2. *Ibid.*, p. 24
3. *Ibid.*, p. 24

A Spring in Tashkent

Tashkent in the sepia pages of history was called Chach. It was destined to be the hub of my travels through Uzbekistan. It forked in four cardinal directions. As if laying at my feet choices I could pick from: if I stepped east, I could be in China; in Europe, if I travelled west; in Russia, if I travelled north; and in India, if I travelled south. I was baffled and mesmerized by the thought.

On a humid afternoon in April 2007, after crossing the beautiful mountains of the Central Asian ranges to the west of the Tien Shan—the celestial mountains of Central Asia—I arrived in the oasis city. The sun was sweltering but the cool winds wafting over the Chirchik river lent a calming effect. I was driving slowly along the streets of Tashkent. Spring had descended and the oasis city was redolent with the whiff of fresh blossoms. The lanes were lined with poplars, fir and pines, grapevine, roses, petunias and marigold. The flowerbeds were a riot of purple, pink, white and crimson. Red poppies were blooming too. Birds were happily chirping and bees were humming oblivious of the woes of the world. The deep blue sky had woolly clouds sailing like small ships on the surface of the sea. The moment seemed like a festival. A festival that is celebrated in the air one breathes, in the colour of flowers, in the freshness of leaves, in the scent of the fruit blossoms, in the gurgling waters of the Chirchik, in the music of one's own being.

The river danced and galloped, swirled and sang, and infused life into the air of Tashkent. Chirchik has blessed the oasis with fertility. Spring is the best time to be in Tashkent. The weather was pleasant. A slight nip in the air still lingered as a vestige of harsh winter but I knew summer was lurking next door.

I had barely stepped into Tashkent but it felt like home. But I could not put my feet up and relax. I was on a quest. And my duty-roster was ready. Before I embarked on my travel, I had to report my arrival to the tourist office at Mirobad kuchasi. I was in Tashkent in search of Buddhist antiquities, which were recovered from the ancient cities during excavations in the region. It was a daunting task, but I had to begin somewhere.

At The Dedeman

In Tashkent, I chose to check into The Dedeman hotel. It is undoubtedly the most sought after and the most stylish of all Tashkent hotels. Huge, sparkling diamond-studded chandeliers hang from ornate ceilings. There's a dainty rose garden in front and manicured lawns all around. It also boasts of the famous Turkuaz restaurant and the kicking Garden Bar where even a dead soul could wake up to a heady potion.

That, however, was not my reason to pick it over other well-appointed hotels. It was its location. The Dedeman is situated in the heart of the city, between Amir Timur and Navoi Streets. From here, everything exciting seemed just at an arm's length; or a few steps away. I could stroll in the tree-covered lanes running along the main street. I could gaze at the tall stately buildings; rest for a while outside the Tashkent University, take a plunge into the tall fountains that spouted waterfall, I could also cool my heels in one of the splendid parks that were cluttered with ancient poplars.

I sank into the soft sofa as a band of musicians played the orchestra in the colossal front hall. That moment, music was not the food of my soul, though. I was planning my next day's itinerary and chewing on my nails. Hunger was gnawing at me and I was jittery about doing some photography inside the Silk Road halls of the premier museums of Tashkent. Will they? Won't they? I was flustered at the thought of the authorities not letting me in with my camera.

Kamol, my guide and interpreter, fathomed my anxiety. But he smiled reassuringly, saying all would be well. He was busy planning my dinner at an Uzbeki restaurant. The famous Turkuaz restaurant and the exciting Garden Bar were barely two steps away but I decided to try some Uzbeki food outside the hotel. I knew nothing about Uzbeki food but I was prepped to dig my fork into something scrumptiously exciting. Kamol talked glowingly of Caravan restaurant, famed for eggs stuffed with red caviar and mushrooms stuffed with olives and cheese apart from assorted meat and pork chops. I whooped at the thought of caviar! Caravan it will be, I told Kamol.

I walked into Caravan and first noticed a central courtyard around which several rooms had been arranged. The menu was extensive, a mix of Russian and Uzbeki fusion cuisine apart from traditional Uzbeki food. Sitting cross-legged on a high cot in the rose garden, I ordered shashlik, shorba, salad accompanied with hot bread. The food was divine.

Full to the gill, I was as happy as a lark. But as soon as I returned to the well-appointed hotel room, the question of photography permits of the Silk Road exhibits in the museums returned to haunt me, and to leave me sleepless.

The following day at the History Museum, the woman behind the counter looked at me stoically and pointed to the signboard. I gulped a breath of relief. I could take photographs. I thanked the Buddha for this mercy. Suddenly, there was added enthusiasm in my gait. My first stop: the Silk Road section on the first floor. Inside, the lights were very dim. They were disastrous for photography but I knew bright light would kill the valuable paintings from Varaksha and other oasis sites in the Surkhandarya region. I forgave the dim light and was happy with whatever I could shoot.

Tashkent on the Buddhist Circuit

Apart from chronicling the Buddhist past of Uzbekistan, the antiquities at the museum threw light on the close cultural connection with India. I tried hard to dig out vestiges of Buddhism in Tashkent. Several travellers and scholars had trudged between India and Central Asia and carried Buddhist beliefs all along the Silk Road to China. Tashkent could not have been an exception. I learnt that Buddhist preachers did come as far as the territories of Chach (Tashkent) where they erected Buddhist buildings.[1]

This prompted me to look for Buddhist monasteries in ancient settlements of Tashkent. About 49 ancient settlements, including 15 settlements around the silver mines in the Angren are shown in an old map of the Chach-Ilak region.[2] Some of these were Kanka, Minguruk, Shashtepa, Aktepa, Khanabad, Kulakli Tepe, Kugai Tepe along the tributaries of the Syr Darya. Extensive excavations in and around Tashkent have brought to light Buddhist antiquities from Minguruk and Kanka.

Ju Buryakov and M. Filanovich mention 'another type' of religious buildings frequently found in the palaces, citadels and the castles of Chach (Tashkent) which showed the influence of the neighbouring regions, Sogd in particular.[3] Many believe this 'another type' of religion to be Buddhism as it was the dominant faith in pre-Islamic Sogd.

In ancient settlements within the limits of modern Tashkent were also found structures where fire was worshipped namely, at Kugai Tepe, Chilanzar Ak Tepe and at Ustrushana next to Chach.[4] Significantly fire altars, generally associated with the Zoroastrians, were also found in Buddhist complexes. At some sites in Uzbekistan, Zoroastrian gods were found in Buddhist temples and ossuaries for the burial of the remains of the dead were found with both Zoroastrian and Buddhist motifs. Scholars point to this intermingling and syncretism of Zoroastrian and Buddhist practices in Central Asia and the contradiction in the practice of Buddhist faith and its depiction as Zoroastrianism.[5]

Some of the ancient temples in the territory of the Tashkent region were also centres of ancestor worship. In one temple mentioned by Buryakov and Filanovich, referring to a Chinese account, inside a palace there was a throne in the centre. Here on the sixth day of the moon a golden urn, with the ashes of the burnt deceased parents of the ruler, were put on the throne. After that the ruler walked around it spreading fragrant flowers and various fruits. The ruler together with nobles brought sacrificial meat. The nobles and others sat down and departed after the end of the meal.[6]

The concept of a shrine with a corridor for circumambulation was a general concept for a Buddhist temple. Inside the shrine were placed idols of Buddhist deities. Such corridors were also constructed around a stupa containing the holy relics and ashes of the Buddha. The temple quoted from the Chinese sources by the authors could be a Buddhist temple where the ruler placed the golden urn containing the holy ashes and circumambulated around it and holding a feast at the end of the prayer service.

We also find mention of an Indian experts arriving in Tashkent to design and build Buddhist shrines. We are informed of a pious artist from Pushkalavati from the region of north-west India (now in Pakistan) who journeyed to this land of 'Asmaka' where he decorated a Buddhist monastery. Many believe this land of stone was Tashkent.[7]

Buddha of Minguruk

Among the Buddhist remains in the museums of Tashkent, brought from various parts of Uzbekistan, such as, Fayaz Tepa, Dalverzin Tepa, Ayrtam and Kuva, I learnt about one or two Buddhist objects found from the ancient settlements of Tashkent. From Minguruk was found a Buddhist statuette pointing to the fact that Buddhism in some form or the other existed in this capital of the Chach region under the reign of the Turks who favoured Buddhism. The statuette was of the Buddha sitting on an inverted lotus in the pose of meditation (dhyanamudra).

At the city of Kanka, the headdress decoration of a Buddhist statue was found during excavations. The Buddhist headdress formed a significant exhibit of the Ikuo Hirayama International Caravan-Sarai of Culture [ICSC] museum at Kanka township in the Tashkent region.[8] ICSC is a Uzbek-Japanese academic and creative centre opened in 2002 to facilitate the revival of the Silk Road traditions and the development of an international dialogue of cultures.

Apart from this, terracotta clay seals called 'bullae' were also found at Kanka. These were found burned by fire. The bullae were said to be used to stamp inscriptions and portraits of priests on temple gifts. Another important discovery from the same region was a terracotta figurine of a woman musician. Kanka appears in the *Mahabharata* with the names of other tribes of Central Asia and was known to the Indians in very early times as it was on the ancient trade routes and kept in touch with India by way of trade.[9]

On my next visit to Tashkent in 2013, in connection with a seminar on Mughal emperor Babur, organized by Professor Zakirjon Mashrobov, I found that the Buddha statuette from Minguruk was not displayed at any museum. What happened to it? I searched the Buddha's galleries of the museums and started enquiring about it from Lola Isamukhamedova, the guide. She called in the scientific researcher of the museum, Dr Tamara Nuriddinova, who too, had no information that such a Buddha statuette was ever present at the museum.

Tamara decided to contact the archaeologist and excavator at Minguruk, Professor Margarita Filonovich, who lived just across the road. We sat in her lovely garden under a grape trellis and waited for her to throw light on the Buddha. But there was no clue from her either. Filonovich informed us that M. Tigran had excavated the Buddhist object in Minguruk and probably he was the right person to give any information. But he resided in Moscow and I could contact him only by phone or mail. Anyway, the photo of the Buddha from Minguruk had already appeared in the museum publication of the year 1991[10] and it was up to the museum to find out where the statuette had gone. Not my job, I thought. So

I did not contact M. Tigran.

Si Yu Ki: Buddhist Records of the Western World, the memoirs of Hiuen Tsang —the intrepid Chinese pilgrim who travelled through Tashkent in AD 629 en route to India—mentions ten towns in the country of Tashkent subjugated by the powerful Turks.[11] This was the time when the Turks were converting to Buddhism, building monasteries, obtaining translations of the Buddhist sutras and setting up Buddhist centres for research. Says Margit Koves in *Buddhism among the Turks of Central Asia* that the faith of the Buddha became known among the Turks when T'opo Khagan (*Khan*) (AD 572–581) came under the influence of Monk Hui-lin. He sent envoys to North Ts'ou to get a Turkish translation of the Buddhist sutras.[12] Another source informs us that Taghpar (AD 572–581)— probably the same T'opo—had converted to Buddhism and was on an ambitious programme of monastery building and sutra translations. The Turk ruler's brother Nivar's (AD 581–587) court became an important centre of Buddhist learning.[13]

But Buddhism was not destined to flourish. Within a century and a half, this great Turkic empire perished along with its monasteries and the monks. The Arabs were beginning to snatch power in Central Asia. All that was left of the flourishing cities of Shashtepa, Minguruk and Kanka was hills of mud and ruins.

Apart from the meagre exhibits from Minguruk, I found no Buddhist antiquities or monuments from the region of Tashkent. Honestly, I was surprised. How did Tashkent fall off the Buddhist map? I wondered. Unfortunately, I had no answers.

An Encounter with Tamerlane

While I diligently searched for the Buddha in the museums, Tamerlane was everywhere. An entire museum had been named after him. My encounter with the great warrior happened at the Amir Timur Mayodani, a walking distance from my hotel. Astride his horse with his cloak billowing in the air, he matched in style with that of the Chinese envoy Zhang Qian, the 'father of the

Silk Road' whose gigantic image can be seen racing his horse in the Gobi near the Jade Gate. Timur's life-size statue lies in the centre of the city park lined with tall trees and dainty flowerbeds. He wears a crown of precious stones, his right arm raised as if addressing his army, while the left holds the rein of his caparisoned horse. His massive boots are held high in the stirrup. The face wears the determination and ferocity of a conqueror on a mission to subdue the world. There are no signs of his physical disability which is believed to have happened some time in AD 1363 when Timur is said to have received an injury which left him lame. This earned him the sobriquet 'Timur the Lame', 'Timurlang' and 'Tamerlane'. After almost 500 years when his tomb was opened in 1941 by Soviet archaeologists, the injuries to both right limbs was confirmed, records Justin Marozzi.[14]

I had enjoyed reading Justin Marozzi's outstanding portraiture of Timur in *Tamerlane: Sword of Islam, Conqueror of the World*, and the hero of the book was now standing before me. Timur's battle-readiness on his horse evoked strange visions of this warrior. Was he reviewing a battle formation on the borders of Siberia in hot pursuit of Tokhtamish, the Khan of the Golden Horde? Was he going to launch one of his fiercest raids across the Indus to 'defeat the infidels and plunder their wealth'? Or, was the hero on his way to 'exterminate the idolaters of China', that was to be his last race towards death? The sensational story by Marozzi, now appeared written before me in stone.

Most evenings in Tashkent were spent sitting on a bench in front of Timur's statue trying to remember whatever little history I had read. Interestingly, this park was occupied by Lenin not many years ago and the resurrection of Timur as Central Asia's hero came in 1993 in the wake of Uzbekistan's independence from Soviet Russia in 1991.

Museum of Timur

Nearby is the Amir Timur Museum constructed in 1996 to mark

the conqueror's 660th anniversary. An impressive building with brilliant blue dome and ornate interiors, the exhibits of Timur and of President Islom Karimov vie for the visitor's attention. Inside, on the ground floor is a massive wall panel where Timur sitting on a decorated marble throne is holding an audience with courtiers. Beneath the dais, several of his minions are prostrating before him. Over the throne, joyous birds and maidens are singing while the fortunate conjunction of sun, moon and stars shine brightly, blessing the reign of the great conqueror. On the left of the panel a tiger roars as a flaming sun rises. The panel is illuminated by a bright gold and crystal chandelier suspended from the great dome. Timur is surrounded by his family, including his most illustrious grandson Ulughbeg Mirzo and great-great-grandson Babur Mirzo, the founder of the Mughal dynasty in India. The dome itself is beautifully designed in gold and turquoise. Kamol informs that over three kilograms of pure gold has gone into the making of this dome.

The first floor of the History Museum also displays a masterpiece: A wall-to-wall panel showing Timur receiving the Spanish envoy Clavijo. The conqueror in all splendour sits on his bejeweled white stallion while the envoy presents his credentials before a huge gathering of courtiers and guards as pigeons flutter over the city gates.

Flavours of Old Tashkent

Leaving behind the sprawling city of modern Tashkent, we drove along the Navoi Street and turned on the Zarqaynar towards the old town. The shimmering glassy skyscrapers, tall water fountains, shady avenues and speeding limousines of modern Tashkent are nowhere to be seen. This was old Tashkent and the city's heart beats in this old town. Squeezing ourselves between old mud-walled and low-roofed houses, we walked through the narrow alleys of an ancient mohalla. Within the old homes, I heard the crackle of innocent laughter. Chubby children were playing football oblivious of the labourers repairing an old mosque and men sitting under the shade of a mulberry tree sharing a lunch. Almost every house has a small courtyard shaded by grapevines or a tree under which lie divans or poster beds. Under the cool shade, women go about their daily chores of cooking, embroidering, and washing clothes and pans.

The alley was immaculately clean, as if someone had scrubbed it diligently. I was amazed. The neighbourhood was densely populated but there is no garbage dump. Kamol explained that there are no municipal sweepers on the payroll of the government. The lady of the house rises with the sun and while others are still sleeping, she sprinkles water and cleans not only her courtyard but also the lane in front of her house. If the lady of the house is unwell, the man or children take it upon themselves to keep the courtyard and lane clean. The law stipulates absolute cleanliness. Deviants are fined heavily.

As we emerged from a lane along an ancient canal, we found ourselves in the midst of the Khast Imom Square—the heart of Muslim Tashkent. It is a huge park where medieval monuments are interspersed with rose-beds. In front of us lay the 16th-century mausoleum of Imam Abu Bakr Kaffal Shoshi, an Islamic scholar of the Shaybanid period. Known as Hazrati Imom, Shoshi was a linguist and a poet. He wrote a number of books on jurisprudence, logic and other fields of science including *Al-Jalal al-Hasan, Javomi al-Kalim, Adab al-Qozly, Ilm al-Jalal* and *Mahosi ash-Shariya*.[15]

The 16th-century madrassa of Bare Khan, a religious school founded by a Shaybanid ruler of Tashkent and a descendant of Timur, is a towering edifice with Koranic inscriptions running across its fine façade amid blue-tiled mosaics. Inside the library lies its greatest treasure: the Holy Koran of Othman also called the *Muskhafi Usmon*. It was written on leather pages in AD 646 with Kufic letters. On some pages are the traces of Caliph Usman's blood. He was killed while reading the book. This copy is considered as one of the rarest manuscripts of the Holy Koran and is supposed to have been brought to Samarkand in AD 1375 by Amir Timur and now kept at the library of the Muslim Board.[16]

This enormous treasure was then taken to Moscow by the Russians in 1868 before being returned to Tashkent by Lenin in 1924.[17]

At Chorsu Bazaar

We left the madrassa by the back door and walked into Chorsu Bazaar, Tashkent's most famous farmers' market. Topped by a giant green dome, the spectacular Chorsu Bazaar is said to have evolved from the ancient caravan city times. Trade roads from all directions came to Tashkent/Chorsu. Around the market hub, sprung neighbourhoods christened after the commodities that were traded there. In the weavers' mohallas lived those trading in fabric; while the Degrez mohalla became home to traders dealing in degs (cooking utensils; called degchis in India). The cattle market was called Tokli Jallob; quite like the ones in Kashgar and Kuqa.

Chorsu Bazaar is a shopaholic's delight. Also a foodie's favourite haunt. One can eat hot samsa and naan straight out of fire, buy truckloads of spices and basketful of fresh fruits like cherries, apricots and peaches coming from the orchards of Samarkand and Bukhara. Luscious pomegranates, melons, persimmons, and tomatoes lend colour and mounds of dry fruits throw in a heady whiff. Resembling the Grape Valley of Turfan, hills of black, green, yellow, brown raisins meet our eyes. In another corner lie walnuts and almonds dipped in sugar. They were deliciously mouthwatering and absolutely sinful.

On a bed of charcoal, hot naans and shashlik were being turned over. Using long tongs, a boy pulled out roasted samsa from an oven dug into the earth. Samsa resembles roasted samosa. We walked around Chorsu Bazaar munching samsa and haggling over black raisins, walnuts and almonds dipped in sugar. In a waif-thin lane, grains tumbled out of sacks and an entire shed was dedicated to dairy products and bread. There were rows and rows of freshly slaughtered livestock. Men were hollering to hawk skull caps, quilted gowns and Kashgaria knives and buyers raised their tones haggling over another penny.

Amid medieval monuments and ancient minarets, I never thought I'd find anything that was so evidently Indian—the India Square in Tashkent. A small square at the junction of the Shastri Road and Mahatma Gandhi Road, it borrows its name from the Indian prime minister, the late Lal Bahadur Shastri (AD 1904–1966). Shastri signed the Tashkent Declaration with President Ayub Khan of Pakistan on 10 January 1966, at Tashkent, then the capital of the Republic of Uzbekistan. The 1965 armed conflict between India and Pakistan was formally brought to an end by the signing this declaration. However, within a few hours of signing the historic Joint Declaration, Shastri died.[18] The Square became a memorial to Shastri. At this Shastri Park, I was among a small group of Indians who had gathered to pay respect to this beloved and great leader of India who gave the slogan: 'Jai Jawan Jai Kisan'.

Along the Chirchik River

I decided to spend a day on the bank of the Charvak reservoir and drive north-east into the suburbs of Tashkent. The vast expanse of verdant fields along the banks of the Chirchik river was once a cotton-growing region. Numerous cotton factories and tractor stations reminiscent of the Soviet days can be seen lying in disuse. This area now boasts of a plentiful wheat crop, green vegetables and fruit orchards. Honey stations, animal farms, fruit growing and kumis-selling are some of the rural sources of livelihood.

Driving along the Chimgan road shaded by dense poplars, we reach the villages of Surum from where the beautiful Chatkal mountains come into view and a mist descends on the horizon. The villages were once state farms aided by a tractor station. Now, they are cooperative farms run by the villagers. In Parkent, at the foothills of the Chatkals, farmers are weeding their wheat and mustard fields. Dala Hovli and Yulduz no longer grow cotton and the nearby cotton factory they were formerly feeding is now defunct. On our right, a small river speeds down a meadow. A little further, we pass through the dense township of Chirchik, boasting of chemical factories and water-heating station for the residents. The Chatkal hills begin from Yangiovy village as the road climbs up and fog descends on the horizon. The grassy meadows present a picture of serene beauty with many families squatting under the shade of fruit trees watching their animals graze. The peaks of the big Chimgan mountains are clearly visible too.

Near the Ugam-Chatkal National Reserve, snow-covered peaks appear out of nowhere. The alpine meadows were bursting into a bright yellow bloom. Dense forests covered the hillside. Wooden cabins had been set up for cowboys and sheds for animals. At an apricot orchard, a group of villagers were picking fruit off the trees. The forest produce can be gathered only for consumption and cannot be sold. One can spot a horse ranch near an apple orchard in Galabasoy village. An old man appeared trotting on a horse and guarding his herd of sheep. He took us to his ranch where his daughter-in-law is selling kumis (fermented mare's milk). I was sipping it for the first time. It tasted like buttermilk. After downing glassfuls of kumis, we squat under the shade of an apricot tree. Over a stove, meat soup was simmering in a large pan as a group of women sat around it. They were all cream and peaches. I wondered where their beauty came from—kumis or the mountain air?

Honey stations have been set up in the meadows on four-wheeled trucks which have been turned into a room with cooking and sleeping facilities. Large honey boxes are kept out for bees that pick nectar off yellow climber roses, cherries, peach and apricot blooms and wild mustard.

At Charvak, hundreds of families have descended for the weekend of fun. Young Uzbek boys are offering their horses for a ride in the mountains and many tourists are saddled up for a journey into the Chatkal. Yurts are also provided for spending a night in the summer pastures. Some tourists are pedalling their mountain bikes and cycling on the dirt tracks around the lake. At the reservoir, the huge green pyramid of the Charvak Oromgohi

Resort welcomes us. It offers a beautiful view of the lake and the mountains. The water takes a deep green hue from the reflection of dense forests on the shores. Fish abound in this lake and are carried to the dozens of eateries on the shores for a delicious meal.

    We returned via the Hojakent–Tashkent Road and stopped at a village chaikhana (also called choykhana) to have a meal of fish caught from the Charvak reservoir. Here, visitors can have their favourite pick from a huge tub lying in the courtyard. The fish is cleaned and barbecued or cooked in gravy on a fire while an oven churns out hot sesame bread. The first floor sitting space is reached through wooden stairs and appears to be suspended from a bunch of ancient trees whose sweeping branches entangle the chaikhana like a snake. The splendid landscape from atop this chaikhana is a painter's delight. Tiny streams running like ribbons across the green meadows and dense forests of the Ugam–Chatkal Nature Preserve are screened by a shimmering blue haze descending from the faraway hills.

Evenings in Tashkent

While evenings are spent in the company of Timur, early mornings are spent in the luscious parks of the Mustaqillik Maydoni (Independence Square). Every day I leave the Dedeman at 6 a.m., strolling along the shaded avenues and listening to the loud chirping of birds as they prepare to leave their nests on the branches of dense poplars. Early risers can be seen sprinkling water in their lanes and gardens. At the square, several women walk their ferocious dogs leashed to gleaming chains. One day I had to cut short my walk to escape being mauled by a dog that had been let loose by its owner to run a marathon in the park! When the sun rises, young boys start arriving at the Square to dive into the pool of the high water fountain. The shiny white edifice in the Square is the Senate building. Ahead sprawls Mustaqillik Maydoni, the largest city square in Central Asia, flanked by public buildings and walls of fountains. In 1992, the Lenin statue was replaced by a globe showing the independent Republic of Uzbekistan.

North of Mustaqillik Maydoni is the Crying Mother sitting in front of the eternal flame. Death cannot defeat her sons. The monument was constructed in 1999 to honour the 4,00,000 Uzbek soldiers who died in World War II. The names of martyrs are etched on the niches along its two corridors. We threw coins in the huge basin of the flame, in the hope that our wishes would come true.

Fountain Park

An evening spent under the cool shade of enormous trees at a Fountain Park restaurant was quite memorable. It was near the Amir Timur Mayodani and faced the huge water fountain. Here, colourful lights turned the fountain into a spectacular sparkler rising up to a height of a 100 feet and falling with such force that the pathways of the open air restaurant were naturally wet and cool. The sky was lit, so were the faces of the visitors in the dark night. Dozens of cars were parked by the roadside and orders were taken from visitors who sat inside their swank cars. If you go there after 7 p.m., you may not find a place to sit.

I was in a different world altogether from the one that I stepped into in the day while roaming about in the mohallas of Eski Shhr, the old city of Tashkent. Here, women were generally clad in long gowns with long sleeves and head scarves, their feet covered in socks and shoes. Near the water fountain young women came in short skirts and high heels with a lot of lipstick and eye make-up. They were rarely alone; they had friends in tow, ordered drinks and sat until late. Kamol told me that these young women were not Uzbek but Russians. The waitresses who moved about with big trays full of drinks and eatables were from China and Korea.

The food came straight from the fire and beer from the glacial ice. The Korean waitress could speak English. She rummaged through the menu card and coaxed us to taste this or that. She said we could eat as much bread and fruits as we liked as it was for free. Only pilaf and shashlik were charged.

The lights were dim and hundreds of cars were parked on the street. Tall trees and thick bushes formed the boundary of the open air restaurant. It was at a walking distance from the Dedeman and I went out every evening to this lovely place to sit until midnight under the starry sky and let the sprays of cool water settle over us in the high breeze. Every night, we listened to the music while the fountain danced and coiled in various colours.

One evening, while I was busy enjoying the cool air from the fountain, an old woman came to me and laid a bunch of roses at my feet. They were beautiful and fragrant. As I brought them close to my chest, the woman pointed to her stomach as if telling me that she was hungry. I realized she was begging for alms. She was poor and famished, but was clad properly. I forgot about the fragrant roses. Her hunger bothered me. I offered her a plate of food. She folded the food in a piece of paper and headed to another table. I watched her as she gingerly picked a morsel. My heart twitched. I prayed to the Buddha to look after her, never to let her go hungry again.

My days in Tashkent were over. It was time to leave for the Sogdian city of Samarkand. As I packed my bags, I moved back and forth in time trying to understand the incongruities in the timeline of Tashkent—the ancient as well as the modern. One of growth and luxury, with the sparkle of gold and crystal; the other content with mud houses, narrow alleys, the thick-waisted mulberry trees in unpaved courtyards and grape trellises hanging on wooden pegs. In Tashkent, I had trudged the ancient and the modern. As I left, in my heart, I carried old Tashkent. Its beauty had stirred my soul. It will remain unforgettable. Forever.

References

For history of Tashkent see: Bearman, P.J. (ed.), Bianquis, T.H. (ed.), Bosworth, C.E. (ed.), Donzel, E.Van (ed.) and Heinrichs, W.P. (ed.). *The Encyclopaedia of Islam*; Buryakov Y.F., Baipakov, K.M., Tashbaeva,

K.H., Yakubov, Y. *The Cities and Routes of the Great Silk Road*; Tucker, Jonathan. *The Silk Road: Art and History*; Buryakov, Ju and Filanovich, M. *Central Asia in the Early Middle Ages: Chach-Ilak History*

1. Litvinsky, B.A. (ed.). 'Sogdiana'. *History of Civilizations of Central Asia: The crossroads of civilizations (AD 250 to 750)*, Volume III (Delhi: Motilal Banarsidass Publishers Pvt. Ltd., 1999), p. 278
2. Buryakov, Ju and Filanovich, M. *Central Asia in the Early Middle Ages: Chach-Ilak History*, p. 78-79, 88, 92. URL: http://www.kroraina.com/ca/h_chach/html
3. *Ibid.*
4. *Ibid.*
5. Haidar, Mansura. *Indo-Central Asian Relations from Early Times to Medieval Period* (New Delhi: Manohar Publishers and Distributor, 2004), p. 39, 40, 46
6. Buryakov, Ju and Filanovich, M. *Central Asia in the Early Middle Ages: Chach-Ilak History*, p. 78-79, 88, 92. URL: http://www.kroraina.com/ca/h_chach/html
7. Harmatta, J. (ed.). 'Cities and Urban Life in the Kushan Kingdom'. *History of Civilizations of Central Asia: The Development of Sedentary and Nomadic Civilizations (700 BC to AD 250)*, Volume II (Delhi: Motilal Banarsidass Publishers Pvt. Ltd., 1999), p. 309
8. Muzaffar, Sakhibjonov. *The Ikuo Hirayama International Caravan-Sarai of Culture at the Crossroads of the Great Silk Road* (Tashkent: Sanat Art). URL: http:www/sanat.orexca.com
9. Roy, J.N. (ed.) and Kumar, B.B. (ed.). 'India and Central Asia: Links and Interactions'. *India and Central Asia: Classical to Contemporary Periods* (New Delhi: Concept Publishing Company, 2007), p. 16
10. *Culture and Art of Ancient Uzbekistan*, Volume II (Moscow: Institute of Archaeology, Academy of Sciences USSR, 1991), p. 75
11. Tsiang, Hiuen and Beal, Samuel (trans.). *Si Yu Ki: Buddhist Records of the Western Country*, Book I (Delhi: D.K. Publisher Distributors Pvt. Ltd., 1995), p. 30
12. Koves, Margit. *Buddhism among the Turks of Central Asia* (New

Delhi: International Academy of Indian Culture and Aditya Prakashan, 2009), p. 33, 35

Litvinsky, B.A. (ed.). 'The Turk Empire'. *History of Civilizations of Central Asia: The crossroads of civilizations (AD 250 to 750)*, Volume III (Delhi: Motilal Banarsidass Publishers Pvt. Ltd., 1999), p. 333-335

13. Litvinsky, B.A., (ed.). 'The Turk Empire'. *History of Civilizations of Central Asia: The Crossroads of Civilizations (AD 250 to 750)*, Volume III (Delhi: Motilal Banarsidass Publishers Pvt. Ltd., 1999), p. 333
14. Marozzi, Justin. *Tamerlane: Sword of Islam, Conqueror of the World* (London, New York, Toronto, Sydney: Harper Collins, 2005), p. 31-32. Also see: p. 166
15. Photo Album. *Uzbekistan: Monuments of Islam* (Tashkent: Press Co. Ltd., 2002), p. 261
16. *Ibid.,* p. 261

    Marozzi, Justin. *Tamerlane: Sword of Islam, Conqueror of the World* (London, New York, Toronto, Sydney: Harper Collins, 2005), p. 175-176
17. Marozzi, Justin. *Tamerlane: Sword of Islam, Conqueror of the World* (London, New York, Toronto, Sydney: Harper Collins, 2005), p. 175-176
18. Refer to: en.wikipedia.org/wiki/lal_bahadur_shastri

Samarkand: Heart of the Silk Road

From the Tashkent checkpoint at Chilanzor, the Highway M-39 runs to Samarkand, 280 kilometres away. The road passes through the fertile Syr Darya vilayat covered in a vast expanse of greenery. The stretch through Kazakhstan has been sealed at Yattisoy and the road runs via Jizzak to the Dehkanobad region of Samarkand.

It was to Samarkand that I was heading. It lay almost at the heart of the Silk Road. Along with Bukhara, it is considered as one of the oldest inhabited cities in the world. Marco Polo described it as 'a very large and splendid city'. The Zaytuni and Kinkob silk, crepes and taffetas invariably pop in any conversation about this Uzbek city that was conquered by Alexander the Great in 399 BC. It was the city of gold brought by Zerafshan river.

Since ancient times, Samarkand has been a trading hub. Caravans laden with goods came from the west through Amul (Chardzou/Turkmenabat), crossing the Oxus into the region of Bukhara and onwards to Samarkand. Other routes into Samarkand came from the south across the mountain passes from India, east from China, and north from Russia. Samarkand's bazaars were famous since the time of Alexander the Great who reached there with his armies in 3rd century BC. He described Samarkand as a fine city overlooking the Zerafshan river.[1] The Chinese traveller, Hiuen Tsang, who visited 'Samokien' some time in 640 AD found it very populous.[2] He writes about the precious merchandise of various countries stored in warehouses, and about Shen, a particular breed of indigenous horse.

Ruy Gonzáles de Clavijo, the Spanish envoy to Timur, provides a lengthy description about the bazaars of Samarkand. He talks of Timur's decree of constructing a street that would cut through the belly of Samarkand. A broad new street was laid by the master builders. Shops were built on both sides, the domed roof had windows for natural light and water fountains were erected at regular intervals down the street.[3]

Beyond the suburbs of Samarkand were well-populated hamlets of immigrants who had been brought by Timur from foreign lands, including India. The 1,50,000-strong population comprised Turks, Arabs, Moors, Greeks, Armenians and Indians. From Damascus came weavers who were deft on silk looms. Gunsmiths came from Turkey; leather and linen from Russia and Tartary; silk and musk from China; ruby and lapis lazuli from Afghanistan; and spices such as nutmeg, cloves, mace, cinnamon and ginger from India. Samarkand produced Zaytuni and Kinkob silk, crepes and taffetas.[4]

Beyond merchandise, lay the bravery of the people. Singing paeans to their bravery, Hiuen Tsang says that they met death as a refuge and no enemy could stand before them.[5] Historians talk of how for almost two years Alexander's forces in Bactria and Sogdiana were harassed by tribal guerrillas. The several-thousand strong garrison of Alexander was slaughtered.[6] Alexander spent the better part of two years scouring the region of Samarkand to eliminate opposition and founding cities to strengthen his base.

For Arabs too the province had to be captured and recaptured due to fierce resistance from the rebellious rulers and inhabitants of Samarkand. The Arab garrisons had to maintain a stubborn fight with the rebellious natives and the powerful Turks who had joined the battle against the Arabs. On several occasions, the Arab garrisons were expelled and exterminated and the provinces reverted to the native ruler.[7]

Two Buddhist Temples

We can get an idea of the extent of Buddhism preached and practised not only in Samarkand but the whole of Sogdiana from the records of Chinese pilgrims, foreign travellers like Ibn Batuta and Marco Polo, Alexander Burnes, Sino Platonic Papers, Saroj Chaudhuri's book *Lives of Early Buddhist Monks*, ancient records found in the Dunhuang and Turfan regions, and from the antiquities discovered in and around Samarkand.

When Hiuen Tsang passed through this region,[8] the king of Samarkand did not believe in the law of the Buddha. He was a fire-worshipper (Zoroastrian). We learn from the pilgrim that in Samarkand, there were two Buddhist temples but, as Hiuen Tsang puts it, 'no priests dwell in them.' If priests from outside sought shelter in those temples, the Zoroastrians chased them with burning fire. Two young 'sramanera' monk disciples of Hiuen Tsang who went to the temple to worship were likewise chased by the 'barbarians' with burning fire. The monks complained to the king who ordered the arrest of the 'fire-carriers' and ordered mutilation of their hands. However, they were saved by Hiuen Tsang because he pleaded against mutilation. Instead, the fire-carriers were beaten up severely and expelled from the city.

The king of Samarkand was so impressed by the discourses on the Buddhist faith delivered by Hiuen Tsang that he requested to be ordained as a disciple. The inhabitants of Samarkand also sought instructions in the Buddhist faith. An assembly was called and the inhabitants were received into priesthood and were established in the convents.[9] The convents perhaps today lie in the debris of the Afrasiab.

Naubahar of Samarkand

W. Barthold in *Turkestan Down to the Mongol Invasion* mentions that in the 10th century, the shahristan of Samarkand (the area of Afrasiab) had four gates. On the east was the Chinese gate which led to the Zarafshan river, and on the west was the Naubahar gate which was also called the Iron gate. On the north was the Bukhara gate and on the south was the Kish gate.[10] Why was the western gate named Naubahar? Did it lead to a monastery—the New Monastery called the Nava Vihara or the Naubahar as the one that already existed at Balkh? All the gates belonged to the pre-Islamic times when Buddhist Viharas were known to exist in Transoxiana.

We also learn that the 'fire-worshippers of Samarkand were exempted from poll tax as they were obliged to repair the lead covered dam located at the Kish gate,[11] which was the best quarters of the town and where they probably lived. Who were these fire-worshippers? It has been pointed out that the fire-worshippers were not only Zoroastrians as is generally thought. The Buddhists too worshipped fire. One can see this in an interesting representation of the Buddha in the Ajanta cave 10 where flames are emanating from his halo. At Amravati, near Nagarjunkonda, there is a representation of Buddha as a pillar of fire. Sculptures of Buddha with flames issuing from the shoulders were found in the Gandhara region and are presently displayed at the National Museum of Afghanistan at Kabul.

'Agni (fire) denotes supreme knowledge and effulgent flames around Buddha would stand for his spiritual light dispelling the darkness of ignorance. The Buddha depicted with flaming aura is not unusual.'[12]

Great Buddhist scholars from Sogdiana (that roughly corresponded to modern Samarkand and Bukhara) known by their pre-fix 'Kang' contributed their might to spread Buddhism. The names of a number of Sogdian translators of Buddhist texts into Chinese have come down to us. The most important among them is K'ang Seng-hui whose Buddhist name was Sanghabhadra.[13] His missionary activities started around AD 247 and continued till his death in AD 280.

House of Idols

At the time of the conquest of Samarkand by the Arabs, there were 'houses of idols (possibly of Buddhist deities) and fire.' The idols were described as being made of wood, gold or silver. When the idols from the main Samarkand 'house of fire' were reduced to ashes, there were found about 50,000 miskals (measurements of weight in old days) of gold. One of the melted Samarkand idols yielded several kilograms of silver.[14]

Uzbek historian-archaeologist Kazim Abdullaev has written about a Buddhist image stamped on an earthenware terracotta plate in Samarkand which was discovered at Sattepa adjoining House No. 118.[15] Abdullaev described it as being similar to the image of bodhisattva Avalokitesvara or a representation of goddess Tara.

From the description of Abdullaev we learn that the figure of the Buddha(Avalokitesvara) sits on a lotus-shaped pedestal. While the left leg is folded, the right is extended and rests on a blooming lotus. The left hand is raised in a blessing. A tall headgear called the 'karanda-mukuta' (Abdullaev) decorates the head. Two layers of a necklace adorn the neck and a winding scarf wraps around the right arm.

The Brahmi and Kharosthi inscriptions on monastic ceramic wares are some of the written sources that point to the territorial spread of Buddhism in Samarkand. The discovery of a clay pot with an inscription in Brahmi at Afrasiab (ancient Samarkand), therefore assumes importance. According to linguists and scholars, ancient forms of Indian writing—Brahmi and Kharosthi—were adopted by the local people (who had no script) to set down their languages. The use of the Indian scripts was confined to a Buddhist context, where they appeared in inscriptions on monastic ceramic wares, on reliquaries and in Buddhist manuscripts.[16]

We also learn of Sogdian pilgrims/merchants, natives of Maimargh near Samarkand and Chach (modern Tashkent), among the numerous visitors on the way to worship Buddhist sacred places in India or by way of trade in the 2nd or 3rd century AD as proved by inscriptions near the Karakoram Highway on the upper reaches of the Indus at Shatial Bridge.[17]

Paintings of Afrasiab

Life in ancient Samarkand centred around the Afrasiab. Today, we see only the ruins of this great city. It lay to the north of the present Registan which formed the catchment of the Zerafshan tributaries. The monumental palaces of the rulers with walls decorated with beautiful paintings, Buddhist Viharas and Zoroastrian temples were all located in the city of Afrasiab. The first mosque was established by Qutaiba in the 7th century after the Arab armies succeeded in breaching the city walls. This was the time when Samarkand was the centre of power in Sogdiana.

According to Xinru Liu (*India and Central Asia*), Buddhist pilgrims and missionaries along with merchant caravans, are said to have travelled frequently between India and China, and along the way through the Tarim basin and Transoxiana they were hosted by Buddhist institutions.[18] Thus, the art of cave excavations, sculpture and mural paintings were adopted.

At Afrasiab, we see the result of this cultural exchange in the monumental paintings on the walls of an excavated palace hall called the 'Hall of Ambassadors' that has now been turned into a museum. The ancient paintings bring to life the stories of the Silk Road; they weave together the threads of the ancient cultures of the land of India, Central Asia and China.

The northern wall of this hall of Afrasiab depicts a boat procession crossing into the land of Samarkand. The river, perhaps the Zerafshan, has bestowed life to the region with abundant crops, minerals and gold. The creatures of the river, the aquatic plants and animals portray a living river. The fish dance and the black snake leaps into the air with joy and gay abandon at the sound of divine music emanating from the 'zither' played by a beautiful woman. A horse swimming through the waters, perhaps symbolizes the divine horse or the ucchraishava. Horses were the subject of many legends. Said to be half dragon, they were born in water and could carry their riders to heaven.[19] They came from the valleys of Sogdiana and Ferghana to the west of the Pamirs. The joy of regeneration is depicted in the bird dropping the 'nectar of life' into the young one's beak while the princess aboard the ship feeds the fish and aquatic beings from her dainty hands.

A Chinese woman, who appears to be a princess from her richly woven robe and hair elaborately styled in a chignon, sits in a boat. She is crossing the river to reach the palace of Varkhuman, the ruler of Samarkand or perhaps the Khan of the Western Turks, whom she must wed. It relates the story of intermarriages between Chinese princesses and the Turk khagans (rulers).

In Susan Whitfield's *Life Along the Silk Road* we read about the Chinese imperial princess Taihe[20] from the Chinese capital of Changan, who was the sister of the emperor who rode on a howdah on a Bactrian camel with her female attendants riding beside her on treasured Ferghana horses. The princess had been chosen as a tribute and was on her way to wed a Uighur khagan to cement their countries' friendship. She was travelling through the Central Asian steppe in the autumn of 821.[21] Taihe was the fourth Chinese princess promised to a Uighur khagan.

It is an exact parallel of the southern wall where another royal personage is arriving at Samarkand palace on a caparisoned elephant along with a retinue of officials and followed by a caravan of elephants, horses and camels and footmen. It perhaps depicts the story of the princess in the howdah going to marry the king of the western regions; the connection it might have with India, the land of elephants. Possibly the royal personage sitting in the howdah too is from India, followed by the best steeds in brown, black and grey from the region of Dawan.

On the western wall facing the entrance, the ambassadors from various countries are in a queue to meet the ruler of Samarkand and have brought gifts for him. Perhaps the occasion is the ruler's marriage to the brides approaching in processions on the northern and the southern wall. Or his coronation as the king of Samarkand, as pointed out by scholars.[22]

Many more palaces, as Batuta said, perhaps lie buried in the ruins of the Afrasiab. They are said to rival even the imperial Chinese palaces in opulence. The tale of a resplendent era of the rulers who had subdued the Arabs is history. But the rulers and their opulent palaces still live in the paintings, the gods still live in some ancient inscriptions; the shrines, the palaces, the ariks (canals to bring water), the warriors, the queens and princesses all come to life on the walls of the excavated halls of Afrasiab. The Hall of Ambassadors brings to life the opulence and grandeur of the forgotten rulers of Samarkand, whether they were Tarkhun, Ghurak or Varkhuman. It enlivens the links with India, the land of the elephant on which rode the princess to the palace at Samarkand. It connects with the Buddhist institutions of India where the geese and the swan lived, where the great Vessantara elephant lived. Where the Central Asians heard the preaching of the Buddha and related Buddhist stories in paintings on the walls of the monastic caves, depicting royal processions moving on elephants.

Samarkand: The City of Timur

Today, Samarkand is the city of Timur. While the ancient city lies in the ruins at Afrasiab and the innumerable stories of her brave and brilliant rulers and warriors lie buried in history books, the glory of Samarkand, studded with the stunning jewels of Timurid structures revolve around Timur, the World Conqueror.

In the heart of Samarkand, Timur sits on a massive throne. Having conquered the nations around him, he is no more a mere 'Amir'. He is lord and emperor of Asia and monarch of much of the land along the Mediterranean. A galaxy of subdued nations lies at his feet. This enormous legend in marble and stone is surrounded by his stunning creations—a world-class city, the likes of which dreams are made of, but never seen.

Wrapped in adornments of gold and lapis lazuli, this city of the Timurids is truly a wonder of the world. The famous gardens of Samarkand described by Clavijo still live by the side of every road, the fountains at every crossing, the bazaars at every square and monuments with blue domes and decorated columned front arch defining the skyline.

In the 14th century, when Ibn Batuta journeyed to Samarkand, he wrote about the old city, mainly that which remained on the territory of Afrasiab. He described it as one of the largest and most perfectly beautiful cities in the world. It was built on the bank of a river where the inhabitants promenaded after the afternoon prayer.[23] But alas! It is in complete ruins. The Arabs, according to historians, had captured the city from the Persians in AD 704, while Genghis Khan snatched it from the Sultan of Khwarezm in AD 1220, pillaged and destroyed it.[24]

In 1370, Timur was to make Samarkand his capital city and restore it to its ancient splendour. In the suburbs, he settled the captive craftsmen from India, West Asia and Europe who were put into the task of monument building.[25] Today, the eyes look in amazement at the creation of these craftsmen as one moves from the Registan to the Bibi Khanum Mosque, the Shah-i-Zinda and the Gur-e-Amir.

Today, any visitor to Samarkand is awestruck by the splendour of the Registan Square with the three madrassas and the central fountain, the surrounding bazaars overflowing with silk, jewellery and fruits, the spotlessly clean alleys, lush gardens and beautiful orchards, and above all, the lovely people, so warm and friendly. The lively restaurants are the places where music flows with wine. Beautiful women with cream and peaches complexions, dressed in long skirts, still do a semblance of a whirl dance with men at their elbows. The hot, scrumptious kebabs and mutton pilaf downed with local beer, shashlik heaped on soft naans, shorpa and red juice of watermelons become the stuff of an evening meal.

The Bibi Khanum Mosque was built in memory of the mother of Timur's wife, the Great Khanum. Timur personally oversaw the construction.[26] The Registan Square is believed to be once the catchment of the Zerafshan tributaries. The river changed its course, leaving behind the sandy bed on which the Registan Square later came up. In the 14th century, during Timur's reign, there was a Central Market on this square. During Ulughbek's (Timur's grandson) rule, the setting up of the first university of the East began with the construction of the Ulughbek madrassa in 1417. Such world-famous poets as Abdurabman Jami and Alisher Navoi came here to study. Ulughbek also brought more than 100 scientists to work with him at the famous Samarkand (Ulughbek's) observatory.[27]

Timur's Roots at Shakhrisabz

From the ancient to the medieval and closer to India, a visit to Samarkand is incomplete without visiting Shakhrisabz—the green city of Timur where lay his grandest dream, the most beautiful Ak Sarai. Walking along the Victory Park flushed with a colourful array of flowerbeds and green shrubs, my eyes fall on the towering sculpture of Timur. He stands in front of his most lavish palace and his seat of power, the Ak Sarai. Two mighty, ornamental towers, covered in splendid majolica tile work, rise from the ground to form a welcome arch for the emperor. But the once intimidating entrance to the Ak Sarai is now lost to the vagaries of nature. Only the lower half of the columns remains. The grand palace too has been reduced to stumps.

While many young couples were getting themselves photographed at Timur's feet, scores of tourists had climbed the high entrance towers to have a 360-degree view around Shakhrisabz—the dome of mosques, madrassas, bustling bazaars, the suburbs with a few scattered villages and the winding road that joined the main highway M-39.

We entered the palace area through the huge entrance flanked by gorgeous pillars. Inside were the ruins of the palace and vast open spaces.

It is difficult to imagine what kind of structures were present here during the time of Timur but we can still have an idea from the descriptions of Clavijo about the Ak Sarai and his meetings with Timur and his queens.

One can still see the arches with blue tiles in geometric designs and beautiful calligraphy. Ak Sarai was probably Timur's most ambitious project and took thousands of craftsmen including the best from India taken along with Timur when he raided India in 1398 and settled them in the suburbs around Samarkand.[28]

We walked down the main street from the palace towards the busy market place and were led first into the area of the blue-domed Kok Gumbaz. A narrow path lead to a building complex called Dorussiadat (Seat of Power and Might). Here lay the tomb of Jehangir, Timur's eldest son who died at 22. It was also the resting place for another son, Umar Sheikh. Adjacent to the mausoleum, steps lead to an underground room where lay the crypt of Timur—a stone casket believed to have been intended for Timur himself. But his remains lie in Gur-e-Amir mausoleum at Samarkand. On the wall near the crypt is carved a huge tear drop—symbolizing a father's grief over the death of his most favourite son.

I left Samarkand heartbroken. I had seen glimpses of Buddha in peeled paintings and desecrated statues. However, on my journey to Termez, it was a tear drop that was haunting me. The big tear drop on the wall of the Dorussiadat. The tear drop of Timur at the death of his beloved son. We all know of the victories of Timur, of his grand dreams and conquests, but not many know of his tears, of his pain, of the tragedy of being a great conqueror and a bereaved father. Timur had a heart. And a tear drop too!

References

For more on Timur see: Gonzalez de Clavijo, Ruy and Guy Le, Strange (trans.). *Embassy to Tamerlane (1403-1406), The Broadway Travellers;* Marozzi, Justin. *Tamerlane: Sword of Islam, Conqueror of the World*

1. Manfredi, V.M. and Halliday, Iian (trans.). *Alexander: The Ends of the Earth*, Volume 3 (London: Pan Macmillan Books, 2002), p. 358
2. Tsiang, Hiuen and Beal, Samuel (trans.). *Si Yu Ki: Buddhist Records of the Western Country*, Book II (Delhi: D.K. Publisher Distributors Pvt. Ltd., 1995), p. 32
3. Gonzalez de Clavijo, Ruy and Guy Le, Strange (trans.). *Embassy to Tamerlane (1403-1406), The Broadway Travellers* (London, New York: Harper and Brothers, 1928), p. 278-300
4. *Ibid.,* p. 278-300
5. Tsiang, Hiuen and Beal, Samuel (trans.). *Si Yu Ki: Buddhist Records of the Western Country*, Book II (Delhi: D.K. Publisher Distributors Pvt. Ltd., 1995), p. 32
6. Manfredi, V.M. and Halliday, Iian (trans.). *Alexander: The Ends of the Earth*, Volume 3 (London: Pan Macmillan Books, 2002), p. 382
7. Barthold, W. *Turkestan Down to the Mongol Invasion* (Great Britain: E.J.W. Gibbs Memorial Trust and Oxbow Books, 2012), p. 186-187
8. Hwui Li, Shaman and Beal, Samuel (trans.). *The Life of Hieun-Tsiang* (Delhi: D.K. Publishers Distributors Pvt. Ltd., 2001), p. 45-46
9. *Ibid.*, p. 46
10. Barthold, W. *Turkestan Down to the Mongol Invasion* (Great Britain: E.J.W. Gibbs Memorial Trust and Oxbow Books, 2012), p. 85
11. *Ibid.,* p. 85
12. Ghosh, A. (ed.). *Ajanta Murals* (Delhi: Archaeological Survey of India, 1996), p. 39
13. Bagchi, P.C. *India and China* (Calcutta: Saraswat Press, 2008), p. 40

Chaudhuri, Saroj Kumar. *Lives of Early Buddhist Monks: The Oldest Extant Biographies of Indian and Central Asian Monks* (New Delhi: Abha Prakashan, 2008), p. 59-64
14. Gafurov, B.G. *Central Asia: Pre-Historic to Pre-Modern Times*, Volume 1 (Delhi: Shipra Publications, 2005), p. 421-422
15. Abdullaev, Kazim. *Buddhist Image Discovered in Samarkand*, Volume 55, No. 1 (Creative Commons: Asian Art, 2000), p. 173-175
16. Litvinsky, B.A. (ed.). *History of Civilizations of Central Asia: The crossroads of civilizations (AD 250 to 750)*, Volume III (Delhi: Motilal Banarsidass Pvt. Ltd., 1999), p. 432-433, 434
17. Rtveladze, E. *Civilization, States and Cultures of Central Asia* (Tashkent: Forum of Culture and Arts of Uzbekistan foundation and University of World Economy and Diplomacy, 2009), p. 149
18. Liu, Xinru. *India and Central Asia* (Ranikhet, India: Permanent Black, 2012), p. 19-20
19. Whitfield, Susan. *Life along the Silk Road* (London: John Murray Hodder, Hadline, 2004), p. 97
20. *Ibid.*, p. 95, 102
21. *Ibid.*, p. 102
22. For an interesting interpretation of the paintings on the walls of Afrasiab see: Compareti, Matteo, and Waught, D.C. (ed.). *The Silk Road*, Volume 4, No. 2 (Washington: Silk Road Foundation, 2007), p. 32-39
23. Gibb, H.A.R. *Ibn Batuta: Travels in Asia and Africa* (New Delhi: Manohar Publishers and Distributers, 2006), p. 174
24. Weatherford, Jack. *Genghis Khan and the Making of the Modern World* (New York: Three Rivers Press, 2004), p. 9
    Hartog, Leo De. *Genghis Khan: Conqueror of the World* (New York: I.B. Tauris Publishers, 1999), p. 101
25. Gonzalez de Clavijo, Ruy and Guy Le, Strange (trans.). *Embassy to Tamerlane (1403-1406), The Broadway Travellers* (London, New York: Harper and Brothers, 1928), p. 278-300
26. *Ibid.*, p. 280
27. *Samarkand: Registon Ansambli* (Samarkand: Graphic Press, 2007)

28. Gonzalez de Clavijo, Ruy and Guy Le, Strange (trans.). *Embassy to Tamerlane (1403-1406), The Broadway Travellers* (London, New York: Harper and Brothers, 1928), p. 278-300
Manfredi, V.M. and Halliday, Iian (trans.). *Alexander: The Ends of the Earth*, Volume 3 (London: Pan Macmillan Books, 2002), p. 208

Maghoki Attari Mosque that has its roots in an ancient Buddhist temple found at Archaeological Park, Bukhara (10th century AD).

Bodhisattva on Elephant. Painting from Varaksha near Bukhara (8th century AD).

Courtesy: State Historical Museum of Uzbekistan, Tashkent

Buddhist temple at Kuva, near Ferghana (7th-8th century AD).

Buddha with a 'third eye' from Kuva, near Ferghana (7th-8th century AD).

Courtesy: State Museum of Fine Arts, Tashkent

Buddhist deities (Manjushri) worshipped at Kuva, near Ferghana.

Courtesy: State Historical Museum of Uzbekistan, Tashkent

The Kalta Minar inside Ichon Kala fortress, Khiva (19th century AD).

Frieze depicting musicians and garlanders from Ayrtam (2nd century AD).

Courtesy: State Historical Museum of Uzbekistan, Tashkent

Bodhisattva from Dalverzin Tepa (2nd-3rd century AD).

Courtesy: State Fine Arts Museum, Tashkent

Stupa of Fayaz Tepe monastery, Old Termez (1st century AD).

Caves and stupa courtyard at Kara Tepa, Old Termez (2nd century AD).

To the Oasis of Bukhara

That early morning, as Nur's car sputtered to life, I left Samarkand. After rambling through the deserted city streets, we were on the Royal Road, now Highway A-38 to Bukhara which lay 300 kilometres away. The Shah Rah or the Shahi Marg (Royal Road) was one of the most famous and busiest routes for caravans travelling between China and Central Asia. In ancient times, the caravans took about a week to cover the Bukhara–Samarkand distance. The royal entourage of kings and princes trudged on this route. Of course, there were the traders and travellers and all the facilities that lay on this route—warehouses, rest houses, sardobas (water and ice houses) and houses for worship. Even educational centres sprang up along the road! Pottery-manufacturing centres churned out beautiful glazed pottery for sale and barter.

Gold dust brought in by the Zerafshan river was annealed into exquisite jewellery. Precious and semi-precious stones were inlaid in ornaments and monuments. The gold hub lay in the mining belt of the Zerafshan and Uchhkud. Traders exchanged goods, replenished their stocks, took care of their animals, and exchanged ideas and news.

One of the most imposing serais—the Rabbat-I-Malik—known as the Prince's caravanserai lay on this route. It was built in 1078 by the Shams al-Mulk, the Karakhanid ruler.[1] Located between Karminia and Dabusia and placed in the steppe zone, it was the favourite halting place for merchants. It was so spacious that an entire caravan could settle in the courtyard where there was always enough water and fodder for animals.

Shakarkent provided fine clay for the pottery-making village of Gidjuvan, which has been a ceramic centre for nearly 2000 years. I met Abdulla Narzullayev, a potter, who, over a cup of hot tea and salted apricot seeds, talked of the distinct style of Gidjuvan pottery—lustrous lead glaze, a unique turquoise-blue colour and the use of floral motifs combined with geometric patterns.

Xargosh village drew its fame from the great traveller Ibn Batuta who is believed to have spent a night here in 1340 and described it as 'a small beautiful town with many gardens and rivers.'

Idol-worshippers of Bukhara

I was caught in the ancient past of Bukhara. A past which belonged, if the accounts of historians are to be believed, to the idol worshippers and Buddhist Viharas; of a time when craftsmen sculpted figurines of deities and painted picture stories on the walls of the ancient palaces. Decorated in the garb of bodhisattvas, they narrated stories of royals riding on the backs of magnificent elephants in all grandeur, slaying evil, yet looking peaceful. I thought of temples with Buddhist images; others in which the goddess of wealth and fertility was worshipped, much like the goddesses of India. In the museums and monuments of Bukhara, the ancient past is still alive.

It is believed that pre-Islamic Bukhara was home to Buddhists, Zoroastrians and Christians. There were temples where images of the Buddha were installed, palace paintings which portrayed the prince (bodhisattva) and common peoples' house gates engraved with idols announced their religious preferences. There were temples where fire was worshipped and villages which were marked as Christian villages. The name of the city itself is believed to have come from the Sanskrit 'Vihara' meaning Buddhist temple and monastery. The famous historian of Bukhara, Narshakhi (Trans. Frye, Richard N. *al-Narshakhi's The History of Bukhara*) wrote about the predominance of idol-worshippers in Bukhara before being supplanted by Islam in the 8th century AD.[2]

W. Barthold in *Turkestan: Down to the Mongol Invasion*, mentions the large village of Tawawis. Named so by the Arabs in AD 710, when they saw peacocks in the village, it had a temple of idols and a temple of fire.[3] However, no one can say with surety whether the idols belonged to Buddha or gods from the Hindu pantheon. In olden times, a 10-day bazaar was held here annually in late autumn. Merchants from the various districts of Transoxiana, even from Ferghana and Chach gathered. Strangely, very close to Tawawis was a village called Kukshibaghan, which in Hindi translates into garden of birds. The Indian merchants lived in Kukshibaghan and offered prayers in the temple. The name appears similar to the Kukshi Vihara situated at the foot of the Gridhakuta Hills at the Rajgir Buddhist site in India. I thought of the possibility of the inhabitants of Tawawis migrating from Rajgir.

Maghoki Attari: A Buddhist Temple

Among the seven gates of the shahristan (ancient city) at Bukhara, one particular gate is mentioned by Barthold as the bazaar gate which was subsequently called 'attaran' (gate of the spice sellers). In the pre-Muslim era, there was a Buddhist temple and great importance was attached to the locality near the 'Gate of the mosque of Makh' where the Makh-ruz bazaar was held twice a year.[4]

Barthold believes that Buddhist figurines were sold here, a custom prevalent even under the Samanids. History tells us that the Prince of Makh started this tradition. Who was he? Was he Shir-i-Kishvar or his successor, who having married a Buddhist princess from China, subsequently became Buddhist and promoted the sale of idols of the Buddha, sitting in a throne in the sacred grove under the shade of a tree? Later, that spot became the temple of fire-worshippers.

The present site of Maghoki Attari mosque is believed by many to have been originally a Buddhist temple. Later, in the 5th century, a Zoroastrian temple was built on the site. The temple was destroyed by the Arabs and in its place a mosque was built in the 12th century. The mosque was named Maghoki Attari (the pit of the herbalists) after the nearby spice market.[5]

If you speak to the Bukharan Jews, living in the deep lanes running along the Nadir Diwan Begi Khanaka, just near the Maghoki Attari mosque, the in-charge of the Jewish temple will narrate their long history and show you ancient books kept in cloth-covered almirahs. The forefathers of this Jewish community used the site of Attari mosque as a synagogue until the 16th century when the mosque was reconstructed. An earthquake destroyed the mosque in 1860. It was excavated and restored in 1930 during which the earlier structures were found.

There was another locality in the shahristan, where lived fire-worshippers (or were they idol worshippers/Buddhists?). They are said to be 'rich merchants of foreign descent who were called 'Kash-kushans'.[6] They gave up their houses to the Arabs and built 700 castles for themselves. The locality was called 'Castle of the Magians'. On their gates, the so-called fire-worshippers carved images of the deities they worshipped (as mentioned by Barthold).

In his *Travels into Bokhara,* Alexander Burnes mentions that the 'natives of Bokhara were also firm believers in magic; but they referred to India as the seat of that science. According to the Bokharans, the art of magic was daily practised by the women of Surat. In Bengal, it was practised by men'.[7] This was perhaps a reference to the practice of Tantricism and Vajrayana of the Buddhist school prevailing in Bengal. The Bukharans knew about the tantras practised in India as a consequence of trade and exchange with Indians since very early times.

The Indian traders were a visible community in Bukhara and lived in serais of their own. Till recently, the Hindu Serai was a popular tourist area of the Bukhara Bazaar. Hindu traders from India came with loads of sugar, salt, various kinds of spices and the best white cotton fabric. A diminutive room that once must have been a part of a large arched corridor leads into a spacious paved courtyard of the Hindu Serai. Over a 100 years ago, the Indian Hindu traders rented rooms to live and store their goods. Their animals were tied to posts in the large open courtyard and firewood for the hearth was kept in a corner. During Burnes' visit, there were about 300 Hindus (mainly natives of Shikarpur in Sind) living in the Hindu Serai in Bukhara.

Buddhist Pagoda at Ramitan

Ramitan was situated in the neighbourhood of Bukhara and was the ancient winter residence of the rulers of Bukhara. The Turkic successor to Shir-i-Kishvar (Tardu, son of Khagan of the Western Turks), ruler of Bukhara, is said to have married a Chinese princess. When the Buddhist princess of China brought to Bukhara a Buddhist pagoda in her trousseau, it was placed in the village of Ramitan. Ramitan and several other villages of Bukhara had been set up during the rule of Shir-i Kishvar to accommodate the growing population accumulating in the fertile lands of Bukhara.[8]

Inside the citadel of Bukhara there was an idol temple (possibly a Buddhist temple).[9] In AD 712-713, Qutaiba built a grand mosque inside the citadel on the place where previously a temple stood. Qutaiba had ordered the people of Bukhara to assemble at the mosque every Friday. He offered two dirhams to anyone who attended Friday prayers. The newly converted Bukharans were unable to understand the Koran in Arabic and said their prayers in Persian. When it was time for bowing or prostration during prayers, a man from behind shouted instructions![10]

History tells us the Muslim armies raided Bukhara in summer and departed in winter after converting the inhabitants to Islam. But each time the Muslims withdrew, they apostatized. Qutaiba converted the inhabitants to Islam three times, yet they apostatized and became infidels. The fourth time he captured Bukhara and established Islam making it difficult for practitioners of other religions.[11]

To Paikend and Varaksha

Before leaving for Khiva, I wished to visit Paikend and Varaksha, two ancient sites outside Bukhara. But Nur, the driver, dissuaded me. That day in June was burning hot. I could not have done a short trip because the two sites lay in opposite directions–Paikend, about 50 kilometres south-west and Varaksha about 60 kilometres north-west from Bukhara. Visiting both in one day would add up to 200 kilometres. On my agenda was photographing the sites and a visit to Paikend museum. Nur was flustered. Adamant. I could hear him murmuring something to Shaknoza in Uzbek. Everything was getting lost in translation but his frustration was writ large. He did not want to go. I argued with him that my itinerary listed both the sites and that I wanted to speak to his superiors in the travel agency. Silence fell. Nur opened the car door. Peace seemed to have fallen between us.

Even before I had gone a few miles—the heat was killing me—the car had faulty air-conditioning, though I had paid through my nose for a comfortable drive through the Silk Road. I failed to count the number of canals, orchards and fields I had crossed but I did see many rooftops covered completely in gold from the peaches and apricots drying in the sun. It was the fruit season—even the animals were happily nibbling away at the plums. In several villages, women were driving mule carts loaded with fodder, sacks full of fruits and huge Bukhara melons for sale in the market.

Paikend, the city of rulers, lay in ruins. The ruins lay over a wide area. I climbed up the hill to walk inside the ruins. A young boy was scouring the ruins. He was rummaging through the debris. Suddenly, he showed me pieces of burnt pottery on which were etched wavy designs. Inspired, I too, started looking for some more pottery. I was lucky. I found a few pottery shards scattered along the walls. They had fascinating geometrical designs. I packed some for a memory of a forgotten glory.

During excavations at the site, archaeologists found a fragment of a painting (now kept at the Paikand museum) that appears to be that of some beautiful god. It must have formed a part of the temple or palace decoration. It is said that when Qutaiba conquered Paikand, a city of merchants trading with the countries of India, China and the Caspian, he found an idol of silver (presumably of the Buddha) in a temple with a weight of 4000 dirhams. He also found silver goblets and two pearls of the size of a pigeon's egg. All the treasures that Qutaiba found were sent to the governor of Khorasan (Hajjaj).[12] The above painting at the museum must have decorated this temple where the massive idol of silver was found and in the worship of whom the people offered pearls and other gems and where silver goblets were used in the rituals.

Bodhisattva of Varaksha

Touted as more ancient than Bukhara, Varaksha was the private property of the Bukhhar Khudat. This village was confiscated by the Samanids who wanted to build a cathedral mosque but were unable to do so, perhaps due to the opposition of the local populace. That Indians travelled to Varaksha was evident from the writings of travellers like Burnes, who mentions inscription on stone in letters resembling Hindi (possibly Brahmi). Burnes also talks of numerous antiques representing figures of men and animals cut out of cornelian and other stones found there. Some of these bore a writing—that 'resembled Hindee'. He saw innumerable small turtles/tortoises sculpted from stones brought from the higher ranges of the Himalayas.[13]

Some of the ganch (clay plaster) images found in the excavations at Varaksha and kept in the museum at Samarkand resembled that of the bodhisattva Avalokitesvara with a halo around the head and the right hand raised holding a scarf or a banner. Several fragments of the ganch decorations were found at Varaksha and Paikand during excavations and which now adorn the museums of Tashkent and Paikand.

The famous wall paintings of Varaksha namely, the panel of 'Prince on Elephant' found at the royal palace, now adorn the museums of Tashkent and Samarkand. They seem to have parallels with murals found in the Buddhist Viharas of India, especially at Ajanta. Considered as the fountain head of Buddhist art throughout the world, Ajanta has stories of the supernatural elephants of the *Vessantara Jataka* and the *Chhaddanta Jataka* painted on its walls.

The Varaksha painting shows a fancy beast in the form of a spotted, golden, winged lion, attacking a bejewelled prince sitting on a caparisoned elephant. The elephant symbol has been associated with both Buddha and bodhisattva Samantabhadra. As the tradition goes, the bodhisattva Gautama entered Queen Mayadevi's womb in the form of a white elephant with six tusks. In many Dunhuang paintings we see bodhisattva Samantabhadra seated on a six-tusked white elephant. He is believed to be the protector of the Dhamma.

The similarity of Varaksha paintings with that of Ajanta is not surprising. Both lay on an ancient arterial trade route connecting the Indus and the Oxus Valleys. Ajanta was a meeting place for traders and pilgrims coming from the distant lands of China, Central Asia and the Mediterranean world. Likewise, Varaksha too, was a meeting place for traders and pilgrims from India, China, and those coming from areas around the Caspian Sea.

At the National Archaeological Park

I stepped out of the Bukhara Palace hotel for a journey into the National Archaeological Park, also a World Heritage Site. I flinched at the heat and quickly bought an umbrella and a bottle of chilled water for myself. Passing through the handicrafts bazaar, we reached the Samanid monuments of the 9th–10th centuries. One of the oldest monuments in the park is the Ismail Samani mausoleum. Built in the Samanid era (between 892 and 905), the tomb is believed to contain the remains of Ismail Samani, the founder of the Samanid dynasty, the last Persian dynasty to rule in Central Asia.[14]

Professor Kamoliddin of the Uzbekistan Academy of Sciences,

Tashkent, points to the Buddhist symbols in the architecture and design of the square Samanid mausoleum which is another link of Bukhara with Buddhism. Here the design on the stone façade of squares within squares and a circle in the middle is said to have been drawn from the Buddhist mandala.

According to him, precisely the same symbol is represented in the paintings on the walls of Dunhuang caves. He says that Samanids were sympathetic to Buddhism and included it in the representation of the Buddhist gods and symbols in their coins and in the archaeology of their monuments.[15] Kamoliddin, after deducing several opinions and data, says that the origin of the name Saman, was probably connected with Buddhism and Samankhuda was a Buddhist as Buddhism enjoyed the dominant position in Balkh where the Saman-khuda founded a settlement named Saman.

Dark Dungeons of the Emir's Palace

The main road runs in front of the Bolo Hauz along the Registan. We crossed the road and walked towards the Execution Square which forever buzzes with the story of crime and punishment, of an Emir and two British men. It was the site of an ancient citadel—the Bukhara Ark (royal fortress) which had been home of the Bukhara rulers since ancient times. All that remains now is a large mound and ruins of a great citadel and parts of a palace structure. And, of course, the story of two British officers who were beheaded and buried in Registan on the orders of Nasrullah Khan, Emir of Bukhara.[16] I stood there, as if beamed back to that fateful day in 1842. I could hear the crowd baying for blood. I could see the Emir's haughty smile as the heads gathered dust. I could smell fresh blood. I shuddered. I stood numb.

The sight of the dark dungeons was quite unnerving. The paved entrance to the Ark is flanked by shops selling everything under the sun—from sepia-toned booklets about legends of Bukhara, to jewellery, old photographs, miniature paintings... Before I climbed into the shop, Shakhnoza asked me to look below the steps. There was a small aperture in the basement, ragged, dust-laden, full of cobwebs, humid and foul-smelling. It was difficult to see what lay inside the dark basement room. These were the dungeons where the enthusiastic British officers, players of the Great Game had been imprisoned by the Khan. There was no entrance to the dark dungeons—a rope was used for throwing in and taking out the prisoners!

As I stepped from the dungeon towards the Emir's palace, I felt I was walking from hell to heaven. The paved entrance street that ran along the Juma Mosque had been swept clean. I wondered whether this was the mosque mentioned by Narshakhi in *The History of Bukhara* that had idols engraved on its gates—their faces scratched, their bodies untouched.[17] Quite like the caves of Bezeklik in Kizil where the Buddha's faces have been scratched out. But Shakhnoza dispelled all similarities. She said that this one was built much later, in the 17th century.

The street lead to the reception area of the palace. A massive courtyard used to be the treasury. The Emir sat on a gem-studded throne and white lions guarded the treasury. A few steps away lay the domed 'chatkhor' which opened on four sides. Those who entered the throne room walked halfway without seeing the Emir as the throne lay behind a screen. The courtiers sitting in the aiwan (a columned verandah) kept a hawk's eye on all visitors. A large part of the citadel was used as a warehouse and army quarters. Another courtyard served as a stable for the Emir's horses. Not too far was his harem. The real lions are no more, they have been replaced by lions sculpted in stone. The courtiers are gone too. Now, all you see is traders hawking their wares. The harem is empty. All that remains are stories.

Jews of Bukhara

In days of yore, the pathway of the bazaar was so slender that only small carts were allowed in. Today, the street is broad and paved and vehicular traffic is no longer prohibited. Vendors can be seen selling fresh ice cream made by churning real fruit pulp with cream and ice. Cola vendors are everywhere. There were mounds of ice—coloured, scraped and piled into heaps. I am not surprised. Even in old times, there was an abundance of ice in Bukhara. Said to be 'one of the greatest luxuries of Bukhara', even a beggar was wont to throw a few ice cubes in his glass of water.

We took a turn towards the towering Kalon minaret said to be Bukhara's 'finest landmark'. Dating back to AD 1127 and built by the Karakhan ruler Arslan Khan, it was used by the Bukharan rulers not only as a watch tower and the muezzin's prayer tower but also to push infidel prisoners to their death.[18]

Shakhnoza lead me into a narrow lane behind the Nadir Diwan Begi Madrassa. It was a long, narrow lane culminating into the headquarters of the Jewish population of Bukhara. The Jewish head politely walked with me around the temple where an ancient scripture was kept locked in a painted wooden almirah. I was curious about the Jews of Bukhara. The head patiently took me back into time, into the beginning of the Bukharan Jews. The first Jewish settlements in Central Asia, I learnt, developed from the Babylonian-Persian community.[19] The presence of Jews in pre-Islamic Central Asia was numerous; their wealth largely sustained by the trade on the Silk Route.

Soon, we were at another door. Shakhnoza jangled the brass rings nailed into the door. A woman opened the cracked wooden doors and lead us inside. Inside lay grandeur and opulence. The floor was marble, the rooms richly carpeted. A spiralling staircase would lead us to the upper floor while a very narrow one lead to the underground floor which was pitch dark. The owner fetched a candle and showed us the basement which was the dwelling of the master's servants. The slaves were not allowed to eat in the master's kitchen—they prepared their own food, slept on the floor in the airless dungeon, only to get up the following morning to drudge for their masters

We heard that Bukhara slaves were mainly of Persian descent, brought as captives from Turkistan and traded in the Sunday slave market. The slaves were kept in stalls and examined like cattle. Alexander Burnes, an Englishman, had undertaken the long journey from India through Kabul to Bukhara. In 1831–1833, when he visited the bazaar, he found six slave girls who were being examined physically for leprosy or any other disease during interrogation about their religion and parentage.[20]

An Evening at Lyabi Hauz

It was my last evening in Bukhara. The following day I would take the desert road to Khiva, Urgench. I decide to spend the last evening at the Lyabi Hauz. The setting sun had cast a spell of burnished orange on the waters of the Lyabi Hauz. Countless Bukharans and tourists from all over the world had descended at the central plaza for a pleasant evening by the side of the medieval Hauz. They were following an age-old tradition—for eons, the population of the old Bukhara bazaar and Kalon complex gathered by the pool at the day's end. People came dressed in their traditional 'choga'—the quilted gown or the chapan. That was the time when there was no recorded music, no electricity. The oil lamps were lit by the pool, musicians played the dutar while a melodious voice regaled the Bukharans with a lively song. The merchants feasted, gossiped and revelled in the entertainment for a little celebration, after they had found a good bargain for their wares or after they had made their purchases.

From the location of the plaza, one could hazard a guess about the vast population it catered to—the Nadir Divan Begi madrassa and khanaka (a halting station for traders and roaming dervishes) adjacent to it; the Kukeldash madrassa, the biggest Islamic school in Central Asia just across the street. To the west and north of Lyabi Hauz were the medieval multi-domed shopping arcades where money-changers, cap makers and jewellers resided. A lane from the plaza radiated to the Maghoki Attari mosque where Muslims as well as the Jews gathered. This was the holiest spot.

After scouring the Bukhara bazaar and Kalon Complex—where splendid mosques and madrassas stood—and trying all sorts of adornments at the Toki Farrushan and Toki Zargaron, I took the lane to Lyabi Hauz and found the plaza bursting with people. It had been swept clean and sprayed with scented water. Beautiful canopies had been set under the mulberry trees. Old silk trees had spread their arms into the pool as if to draw its water. Hundreds of birds were chirping, eagerly looking for their nests. And Mulla Nasruddin—the wise fool, rode on his mule through a poplar forest by the side of the pool.

The plaza was so crowded that I had to wait long to find a seat under a mulberry tree. The setting sun brought more cheers at the Hauz as more crowds joined. The water of the pool was set aflame and a cool breeze blew from the surrounding groves. As the evening progressed, the sound of lilting music grew louder.

Another show was going on at the Nadir Diwan Begi Khanaka. Young Bukharan girls in short skirts and high heels were rubbing shoulders with women in long flowing gowns. Dozens of foreigners were occupying the front sofas inside the khanaka along with their guides who were enthusiastically narrating the history of the Begi and how he managed to construct the Lyabi Hauz.

By the time I reached the khanaka of Diwan Begi, the music got cacophonous. The guests were tapping their feet to an old Indian song, 'Dam dam Diga diga, mausam bhiga bhiga', as women dressed in yellow skirts and feathered caps got into a slow rhythmic dance. Indian songs were popular there and the audience seemed spellbound by the music and the beautiful women. The courtyards must have once been a caravanserai where travellers stored their goods and rented rooms for the night. But now they are decorated with grape trellises and shaded by poplars.

It was in serais like this that merchants from all corners of the Silk Road converged to sell and exchange their wares. The Indians did not lag behind with their sugar and spices. Their serai was just next door. With its big walled courtyard and double-storey rooms, the Hindu Serai suddenly came alive with the flames of a burning fire—a thick smoke billowing from the courtyard. The hired mules tied to the post and the lofty camels crouching outside enjoying their respite after the drudgery of the day. As the music dies and the evening melts into the night, I take a step. Away from the ancient past of Bukhara. To a new city. To Samarkand.

References

For more details on Bukhara see: Barthold, W. *Turkestan Down to the Mongol Invasion*; Frye, R.N. *al-Narshakhi's The History of Bukhara*

1. Barthold, W. *Turkestan Down to the Mongol Invasion* (Great Britain: E.J.W. Gibbs Memorial Trust and Oxbow books, 2012), p. 315
   Buryakov, Y.F., Baipakov, K.M., Tashbaeva, K.H., Yakubov, Y. *The Cities and Routes of the Great Silk Road* (Tashkent: Sharg, 1999), p. 42-43
2. Narshakhi and Frye, R.N. (trans.). *al-Narshakhi's The History of Bukhara* (Princeton: Markus Wiener Publishers, 2007), p. 25-26
   Barthold, W. *Turkestan Down to the Mongol Invasion* (UK: E.J.W. Gibbs Memorial Trust and Oxbow books, 2012), p. 108-109
3. Barthold, W. *Turkestan Down to the Mongol Invasion* (UK: E.J.W. Gibbs Memorial Trust and Oxbow books, 2012), p. 98
   Narshakhi and Frye, R.N. (trans.). *al-Narshakhi's The History of Bukhara* (Princeton: Markus Wiener Publishers, 2007), p. 14
4. Barthold, W. *Turkestan Down to the Mongol Invasion* (UK: E.J.W. Gibbs Memorial Trust and Oxbow books, 2012), p. 101, 107
   Narshakhi and Frye, R.N. (trans.). *al-Narshakhi's The History of Bukhara* (Princeton: Markus Wiener Publishers, 2007), p. 25-26
5. Barthold, W. *Turkestan Down to the Mongol Invasion* (UK: E.J.W. Gibbs Memorial Trust and Oxbow books, 2012), p. 101, 107
6. *Ibid.*, p. 108
7. Burnes, Alexander. *Travels Into Bokhara: A Journey from India to Cabool, Tartary and Persia (1831–1833)*, Volume I (New Delhi, Chennai: Asian Educational Services, 2009), p. 321
8. Narshakhi and Frye, R.N. (trans.). *al-Narshakhi's The History of*

Bukhara (Princeton: Markus Wiener Publishers, 2007), p. 7
Barthold, W. *Turkestan Down to the Mongol Invasion* (UK: E.J.W. Gibbs Memorial Trust and Oxbow books, 2012), p. 116
9. Narshakhi and Frye, R. N. (trans.). *al-Narshakhi's The History of Bukhara* (Princeton: Markus Wiener Publishers, 2007), p. 67
10. *Ibid.*, p. 67
11. *Ibid.*, p. 65
12. *Ibid.*, p. 62
13. Burnes, Alexander. *Travels Into Bokhara: A Journey from India to Cabool, Tartary and Persia (1831-1833)*, Volume I (New Delhi, Chennai: Asian Educational Services, 2009), p. 320
14. A Photo Album. *Uzbekistan: The Monuments of Islam* (Tashkent: Press Co. Ltd., 2002), p. 210.
15. Shamsiddin, Kamoliddin. *On the Religion of the Samanid Ancestors* (Tashkent: Uzbekistan Academy of Sciences)
16. Hopkirk, Peter. *The Great Game: The Struggle for Empire in Central Asia* (New York, Tokyo, London: Kodansha International, 1994), p. 2, 233, 236, 278
17. Narshakhi and Frye, R. N. (trans.). *al-Narshakhi's The History of Bukhara* (Princeton: Markus Wiener Publishers, 2007), p. 67-71
18. A Photo Album. *Uzbekistan: The Monuments of Islam* (Tashkent: Press Co. Ltd., 2002), p. 214-215
19. Ochildeiv, David. *A History of Bukharan Jews* (New York: Mir Collection, 2005), p. 24
    Burnes, Alexander. *Travels Into Bokhara: A Journey from India to Cabool, Tartary and Persia (1831-1833)*, Volume I (New Delhi, Chennai: Asian Educational Services, 2009), p. 274-275
20. *Ibid.*, p. 282

To the City of Khiva

Highway A-380 runs through the Kyzlkum desert to Urgench, capital of Khorezm province. The route from Bukhara passes through the villages of Ramintan and Gazli. The mighty Amu and the Syr Darya rivers dwindle as they traverse the desert and are nearly sucked into the hot sands of the Kyzlkum before reaching the Aral Sea. Few villages lie on this shiny six-lane desert road. In the barren landscape there are green villages like Shoroxon, Tortkol and Rashidov where channels from the Oxus have been diverted to irrigate cotton fields. The road crosses the Oxus and enters the Khorezmian, capital city of Urgench, from where Khiva is only 35 kilometres.

I am no Ibn Batuta—the 14th-century intrepid traveller. But that day, however, I was feeling like him. I was going where he had been before. I was on the old Silk Route from Bukhara to Khorezm. The route meandered through Caspian Sea to reach Astrakhan on the Volga river and wound its way to the shores of the Black Sea and thence to the Mediterranean region. It was on this much-travelled route that Ibn Batuta (AD 1304-1369) travelled from Constantinople to Khorezm on way to India. He had trudged 40 days through the harsh desert to reach Khorezm which, according to him, 'is the largest, greatest, most beautiful and most important city of the Turks. It shakes under the weight of its population.'[1] My primary purpose was to visit the towns of Urgench, Khiva and the ancient settlements or Kalas inside the Kyzlkum desert across the Oxus river in the Karakalpakstan region.

Not too far in the past, the province of Khorezm was one of the most prosperous regions on the Silk Road because of its location on the Oxus and the Caspian route, enabling a thriving trade with Khazaria in the north and west of the Caspian. Khorezmians imported the best animal furs, wood, sheep and slaves in return for luscious water melons, fish, grapes, raisins, satin silk and carpets. The region was famed for its excellent fish that was exported all along the Silk Road.[2] It was one of the biggest cotton growing belts in Central Asia and continues to be so. The Khorezmians were also trading with Indians who lived on the shores of the Caspian. These Indians were engaged in trade with the Caspian region and beyond in the territory of Russia up to modern times. A colony of Indian settlers is recorded to have existed in Astrakhan.[3] The documents recovered from the Kalas of Khorezm reveal names of inhabitants that sound similar to Indian names. Perhaps Indians were employed as agriculturists in the delta region of the Oxus in the Kyzlkum desert.

The immense wealth and strategic location of Khorezm attracted the attention of the invaders: Arab general Qutaiba in the 7th century, Genghis Khan in the 13th century, and Timur in the 14th century. All of them ravaged the region ruthlessly.[4] It is learnt that by the 17th century, Khiva emerged as the principal town of Khorezm and capital of the newly named Khivan Khanate of the Uzbeks.

Inside Ichon Kala Fortress at Khiva

At Urgench, Sayeeda, my friend, was waiting for me. We drove around Urgench city for a couple of hours. There was nothing ancient about this new city. Its modernism was very unattractive. So, I decided to head off immediately to Khiva, barely 35 kilometres south-west through the Black Sand desert.

Within an hour, we crossed the Dishan Kala gates and headed towards the Asia Khiva hotel across the southern gate of the monumental Ichon Kala fortress, a World Heritage Site. As our car entered the driveway, a group of children ran after us shouting in welcome. I waved out to them, but Sayeeda dissuaded me. She whispered that it would encourage the children to follow me everywhere. I stopped waving. The children gradually vanished and my mind got cluttered with vignettes of ancient bazaars, residential quarters, tea houses and hotels.

Soon, Sayeeda and I were at the massive western gate, the Ata Darwaza, built into the high walls of the fortress. Inside the fortress, the minarets stood tallest against the skyline. In Central Asia, Khiva has the largest number of preserved minarets. The oldest of them is the 10th-century Juma Mosque's minaret; the tallest, grandest, and youngest is Islam Hoja minaret; and the largest of them and the nearest to Ata Darwaza is the green Kalta Minar, which was left unfinished by the death of the Khan of Khiva. From the minarets, the muezzins invoked the gods and the infidels were pushed to death.

Ichon Kala's Indian Connection

As we entered the Juma Mosque, Sayeeda talked of the mosque's carved wooden pillars that were brought from India. One of them had a swastika carved on it and another one had an elephant-head motif. The Juma Mosque was structurally unique: it had no portals, domes, galleries and courtyard. Inside, there was a large hall with the ceiling resting on 213 wooden columns.

It is said that there were more than a 100 mosques in the Khiva Khanate where prayers were offered five times a day. Inside the mosque, I was reminded of Batuta's praise of the Khorezmians' unusual prayer custom: each muezzin would go around the houses adjoining his mosque warning residents to attend the service. Anyone absenting himself from the communal prayers was flogged by the qadi (whip) in public and fined five dinars. Today, there are no whips. There are no muezzins coaxing the believers to attend the prayers.

At the nearby Sher Ghazi madrassa, the in-charge tells me that late Indian Prime Minister Rajiv Gandhi's great-grandfather studied here. The fact took me by surprise. The in-charge wasn't too sure whether it was Gandhi's maternal or paternal great-grandfather. I guessed it must have been Gandhi's paternal great-grandfather. After all, his father Feroze Gandhi is believed to have been of Persian descent and during those days several Persians enrolled at the renowned academic colleges of Khiva.

Khiva had the largest number of madrassas in the Middle Asia, I was told. These residential institutions of higher learning were both secular and religious and were founded by the rich and the prosperous. Situated at the centre of Ichan Kala in front of the entrance to Pahlavan Mahmud mausoleum, this madrassa was erected by slaves captured in 1718 by Sherghazi Khan during his raid on Khorasan and Meshhed.

I found more of India in the Pahlavan Mahmud mausoleum which had the largest dome in Khiva. Covered with blue glazed tiles and a gilded top, it was the mausoleum of Pahalvan Pir (AD 1247–1320) who was born in Khiva. From an epitaph, I learnt that he was a fur-maker and an invincible wrestler. He was also a poet and a philosopher and one of the founders of Sufi trend of Islam. He is said to have fought with Indian wrestlers on the Indian soil and won bouts. By winning the wrestling match in India 'he saved the Khorezmian people from becoming the slaves of India.' Or, so a notice on the walls of the mausoleum proclaimed. India honoured him as a patron of wrestlers.

Nearby is the Museum of Avesto which has lines from the holy book written on bull skin. A museum note tells us that in the 3rd century BC, during the invasion of Central Asia and Iran by Alexander the Great, the Avesta written in gold letters on 12,000 bull skins was found.

Harem of Kunya Ark

Inside Ichon Kala, the Khans and their families lived in palaces, which were also used as a government office. There's more than one palace in Khiva that has remained intact architecturally. The most beautiful of all the palaces is the 17th-century Khan's Palace—the Kunya Ark. Apart from a fortress, it housed the Khan's residence, his harem, judiciary, arsenal, mint, winter and summer mosques, kitchens, stables and guardrooms.

The harem was located in the northern part of Kunya Ark. The rooms for the Khan's four wives and female relatived surrounded a vast rectangular courtyard. I walked inside the long corridors of the harem to check the beautifully tiled rooms but felt claustrophobic. I wondered how the countless queens and concubines lived in such cloistered dwellings. I imagined their predicament—they lived in the fear of being discarded by the Khan. Every day, new women arrived; every moment, the women manipulated and schemed for the affection of the flamboyant Khan and for their survival in the palace. There are stories about how the harem women would walk around dripping with gold jewellery, often weighing several kilograms. They knew they could be dismissed any time and at dismissal, they were only permitted to take whatever jewellery they were wearing. Hence, they walked around weighed down by gold. And fear.

A winding staircase leads to the terrace of the Kunya Ark. Many tourists had climbed to the top to have a bird's-eye view of the entire Ichon Kala with its lovely minarets, majolica-tiled palace aiwans, blue and gilded domes of madrassas. Surrounding the palace were several handicraft centres running inside the Tims (bazaars), caravanserais and at the medieval madrassas.

Life inside the Fortress

In the evening, Sayeeda left for her home in Urgench, 35 kilometres away. I was on my own, free to loiter around the Ichon Kala fortress. Sayeeda had warned me not to do so. But the Tash Darwaza of the fortress was at a stone's throw from my room. There was no ticket collector at one of the exit gates and I was free to venture in and out as many times as I could—both in the late evenings and early mornings before the official visiting time began. I was virtually living inside the fortress. My days were spent roaming around and sipping tea in the choykhanas. Soon, I learnt by heart all the lanes and bylanes and was no longer scared of the dogs following me in and out of the Kala.

Until 1873, there used to be a slave market near this Darwaza. In the niches inside the gates, fugitive and rebellious slaves awaited their fate. The Khan's farmans (decrees) were also read at this gate. Those convicted of serious offence were thrown down the high minarets or whipped by the qadi.

After Sayeeda was gone, the young boys were my guide. An entire battalion followed me from house to house and monument to monument. Sayeeda had warned me about it, but these kids were my friends now. I shunned Sayeeda's warnings. Mind it, they were not seeking money as I learned later when I tried to hand over some change to them. They refused. A boy, about 11, told me I was his friend and he could not accept money from me. He said he liked me. And all young boys sang a chorus in Uzbeki language. I did not know what. But I was humbled. And embarrassed.

The quarters of the fortress were spilling with residents. A family I had befriended invited me for lunch into their two-room house that had a courtyard covered with vine and grape bunches hanging from the trellis. The kitchenette was very small and pilaf was simmering in a gigantic aluminium pot. A big bundle of naan was hanging on a nail in the wall. In a basket some brinjal, tomatoes and onions were kept for the dinner. I, along with members of the family, sat around a low table for a meal of hot pilaf, naan and jam. A young girl took out a set of hand-embroidered napkins from a drawer and displayed them for sale. I apologized because I was not carrying any money. I promised to visit again and write to them from India. I never kept that promise.

True Descendants of Ichon Kala

The descendants of the original settlers of the Ichon Kala were still residing inside the fortress. Their quarters lay near the left alley of the Tash Darwaza. The legacy of the Ichon Kala has been kept alive by these descendants. After the end of the Khiva Khanate, and with it the rule of the Khans, they are the only residents of the Ichon Kala who have remained inside the old quarters. They are the ones who have kept the fires burning, running choykhanas.

Some residents sell embroidery work and jewellery. The most popular piece of jewellery is the gold earring inlaid with large rubies. Near the Oq Masjid, a dozen women sell carpets displayed from the parapet of the Masjid. Still others displayed various kinds of fur caps on the street corner near the Jami Mosque. The Khans themselves were fond of wearing fur caps as their portraits inside the museums reveal. It was not merely a macho-style statement; the caps were a necessity in the cruel Khiva winters.

Near the carpet corner was the music museum where antique musical instruments were on display. They remind us of the early days of the Kala when sound from the various instruments were used on different occasions—small bells to make way for the palanquins; the sound of trumpets announcing the sultan's arrival; large drums for official proclamations, and stringed lutes for weddings.

The Famous Kheivak

There was a time when there was plenty of water inside the Kala. The Kheivak Well was famous for its sweet water and all the caravans coming from Caspian Sea rested near the well on the spot where the Ichon Kala came up. The underground water source was the Amu Darya river delta that emptied into the Aral Sea. There was enough fodder and water for the camels. But the sea had nearly dried up due to excessive use of the Amu and the underground water reserves were dwindling. Today, there is an acute shortage of water inside the Ichon Kala.

Life at Ichon Kala has changed over the centuries. No caravan stops here. The residents, too, have not drawn water from the Kheivak. The Khan's palace is deserted. His harems are empty. But the fires are still burning—churning out scrumptious meals for travellers living in the luxurious guesthouses. The connoisseurs of art loosen their purse strings for exquisite carpets and woodwork. They are the modern Khans of Khiva. It is around them that life of Ichon Kala revolves.

Travels into the desert of Khorezm

Early in the morning, Sayeeda and I planned a trip into the deserts of Khorezm to see the kalas or ancient settlements and fortresses, belonging to the 3rd–4th centuries. These desert villages and the ancient kalas were located along the various delta streams of the Amu Darya. The kalas were wealthy settlements of rich farmers who cultivated crops and planted vineyards with the help of slave labour from neighbouring regions and possibly by migrants from the far away but closely connected regions of India. Trade as well as human traffic from India must have taken the Oxus route into Khorezm. This can be gauged from the Indian names of families once living in one of the settlements in the Kyzlkum desert along the river.[5]

We took the Khiva–Urgench road passing through the Dishon Kala gate. Crossing the Avesto Square, we soon came upon the banks of the Amu Darya. Here, all traffic crossing the river was moving over a pontoon bridge. At the far end in the haze over the river, I could see silhouettes of workers building a new bridge. We drove past the villages of Khamam and Beruni. The latter village was the birthplace of Abu Rayhan Alberuni (AD 973–1048), the famous author of *Alberuni's India* who was closely connected with India.

At Ayaz Kala

Ten kilometres from Beruni begins the Kyzlkum desert. We soon arrived at the T-junction from where we turned left for Ayaz Kala. At the ancient site of Ayaz Kala, a road was being laid. A bulldozer and dozens of workers were levelling the ground. Before we climbed the hill top city of Ayaz Kala, we noticed a dozen yurts set up in the desert to provide a night stay for tourists and excavators.

The dry steppes and deserts of Central Asia looked dull during the day but turned into fairylands in the starry night and under the gaze of the silver moon. In the vicinity of the Sultanuvais mountains and the Ayaz Lake, a night stay at Ayaz Kala is like a fulfilled dream. All around there are ancient settlements dating before the Christian era. Although there is not a single tree to provide shelter or a metalled road to ensure a smooth drive, you can take a camel ride into the foothills and go fishing at the lake. In the evening, as you dig your fork into a sumptuous meal cooked over wood fire, desert dwellers descend on the camp to entertain with folk music.

After parking our vehicle at some distance from this camp, we walked to the settlement of Ayaz Kala perched on a hill. There was a wide path that formed the corridor encircling the settlement. Parts of this corridor had arched roofs indicating that it was once a covered pathway surrounding the settlement. The high walls of the settlement were also visible in some parts. They had long slits, perhaps for defence purposes. In one entrance, ancient clay bricks are still visible. They have not withered with age and still support the high and thick walls of the kala.

The entrance to the inner precincts lead into a vast central yard which is believed to have been used as a reception room or a royal living room surrounded by small rooms. These could have been the guard rooms. Sayeeda informed that from the ruins of Ayaz Kala were unearthed vine presses and golden images that were carried away to St Petersburg. From the uppermost structures of the settlement, we had a bird's-eye view of the surrounding desert, the radiant peaks of the Sultanuvais mountains shining in the midday sun and the glistening surface of the Ayaz Lake. Below, on different levels were ancient settlements called Ayaz 1 and Ayaz 2. Here lived the soldiers and the common people who guarded the rulers' palace from nomadic invasions and tilled the rulers' land.

To Toprak Kala

We descend from the Ayaz Kala hill and drove back to the T-point from where we turned right to take the road to Toprak Kala. A canal carrying water from the Amu Darya ran alongside the road. The canal was almost besieged by desert bushes laden with wild pink flowers. adding beauty to an otherwise drab landscape.

Toprak Kala was discovered by S.P. Tolstov in 1938 and excavated in 1945.

Today, a visitor to the beautiful Toprak Kala site can see only dug-out walls of the citadel, the ruined palace and remnants of paints on its walls. At the site, there are no murals, no stucco works, and no engravings. The sculptures of kings and goddesses too, have been taken away by the excavators. Neither is there any site museum to showcase the remaining antiquities of the desert settlements.

At Toprak Kala, the ramp lead into a pathway between two high mounds which must have been the gateway. This lead to the inner precincts—a vast courtyard that could have served as the royal reception area. Corridors at the various floors of the palace are set at different levels of the hill like a terraced mountain slope. One of the floors had a large rectangular room, now lying roofless. The walls were thick and at regular intervals high-arched niches had been cut into the walls. There were also traces of red paint. These were perhaps the halls that we read about in the history books with life-size statues of kings and warriors. Another large hall had traces of paint in its oval niches which had frescoes of birds and animals. The images and frescoes were also cut and taken away by excavators, said Sayeeda.

From the reception yard of the palace complex, I noticed a corridor leading to a small door. When the door opened, I dropped my jaw at an amazing structure. It was a large vaulted room with an opening in the roof. The rear wall of the vaulted room had a large niche cut into its wall. A wide arch divided the room into two parts—the rear part and the frontal space. It lead into a chamber that had niches cut into its walls. According to Sayeeda, this was the Zoroastrian temple of the fire where the rulers living in the Toprak Kala palace worshipped. I thought it was the place where the images of the Goddess Anahita and the goddess of water and fertility were installed. They were excavated from this palace of Toprak Kala and now find a place in the Museum of Avesto at Ichon Kala in Khiva.

After walking over the walls of several rooms and narrow corridors, we reached the topmost floor of the palace. Here, dozens of rooms were placed in rows. All around there was a vast expanse of steppes. It was amazing how this huge multi-storey structure was built of clay and clay bricks. How was clay brought here? Maybe the slaves had dug the canal and lugged it up. Or, the Amu Darya had brought the clay as debris. It was therefore no surprise that at Toprak Kala the ruler had installed the goddess of river/water in the sanctum of the temple of his palace.

What intrigued me the most was the Indian-sounding names in households at Toprak Kala. In his book *Economy and Social System in Central Asia*, A.R. Mukhamedjanov provides a peek into ancient Khorezmian society and their use of slave labour. Documents in Toprak Kala palace archive have names of the head of the 'family household' and of 'house owners', their son, son-in-law and slaves. The names appear similar to Indian names. Perhaps Indians were being used as slave labour in the fields of Khoresmian castles/kalas. There is one household of Gausimava/Gausimha (lion among the cows) from document number 8. Gausimha had a family of 21 males including 17 slaves showing that he was a rich landlord several slaves to work in his farm. Another big family was the 'House of Vavansira'/Babanshira/Babbarsher (the Lion), a common Indian name.[6]

On the top of the Kala, it was very windy. My cap flew away. Sayeeda ran after it, but it landed below the settlement down the hill. We walked down the ramp and reached the foot where my cap lay peacefully on the sands on a dry bush of camel thorn. I was happy to have my cap back.

I was certain from the description of historians and archaeologists who excavated the desert settlements of Kyzlkum that the region was hardly a desert. Being the delta of the Oxus, there was great wealth from agriculture and slaves were required to cultivate the land. Multi-storey palaces were built as royal residences. Artistes were employed to decorate the structures with murals, carvings and stucco images. Imagine the beauty of the white lilies on a sky blue background with pink borders that once decorated the 'Hall of Kings', the floral motifs engraved on alabaster, the sculptures of royal personages feasting in the company of the goddess of victory, and the ferocious black painted warriors with armour of chainmail on their bodies.[7]

Missing Buddhist Links

It is widely believed that Khorezm was in contact with the Kushan empire and was influenced by Kushan art and culture.[8] The extent of Kushan influence gives rise to presumptions regarding the existence of Buddhism in the region.

B.N. Puri (*Buddhism in Central Asia*) does not talk of Buddhism in the Khorezmian settlements but points to the Kushana connection. He suggests that the sculptural finds from Toprak Kala like the head of alabaster, a stone readily available in Afghanistan, has 'stylistic affinity to the Indo-Hellenic art of the Kusanas'. Stucco and painted decorations too suggest influence by Hellenistic works.[9]

I was intrigued. How come no reliable evidence has been

found about the prevalence of Buddhism in the area? It will be presumptuous to say that Buddhism did not exist in Khorezm. How can one forget the startling discovery of a Buddhist figurine at the site of Kazakliyatkan in the Beruni district of Karakalpakstan in 1999?

It was a terracotta statuette of a headless Buddha or a bodhisattva that perhaps dated back to 1st century AD, as cited by V.N. Yagodin in *New Findings Relating to the Historical and Cultural Relations between India and Khorezm*. The statuette was of a deity sitting cross-legged. The upper bare body has the marks of a necklace, a belt and a sash adorn the body. From the waist down, the figurine is draped in a cloth that falls in pleats like a 'dhoti'. The left hand rests on the hip. The position of the fragment of the right arm suggests it was raised.[10] It can be said to belong to the Buddha sitting cross-legged with the right hand raised in 'abhaymudra' or in the posture of blessing. Was it really Buddha's? I wondered.

However, according to E.E. Nerazik and P.G. Bulgakov there is no indisputable evidence that Buddhism was commonly practised in Khorezm.[11]

I brooded over the mysterious missing Buddhist links of Khorezm. Termez was my next destination. It involved a long road journey from Samarkand along the M-39 highway.

References

1. Gibb, H.A.R. *Ibn Batuta: Travels in Asia and Africa* (New Delhi: Manohar Publishers and Distributers, 2006), p. 167-172
2. Tucker, Jonathan. *The Silk Road: Art and History* (New Delhi: Timeless Books, 2003), p. 240
3. Levi, Scott (ed.). 'Indian Merchants in Central Asia: The Debate'. *India and Central Asia: Commerce and Culture (1500-1800)* (New Delhi: Oxford University Press, 2007), p. 123-146,128
   Roy, J.N. (ed.) and Kumar, B.B. (ed.). 'India and Central Asia: Links and Interactions'. *India and Central Asia: Classical to Contemporary Periods* (New Delhi: Concept Publishing Company, 2007), p. 20

4. Tucker, Jonathan. *The Silk Road: Art and History* (New Delhi: Timeless Books, 2003), p. 237-245
5. Rtveladze, E. *Civilization, States and Cultures of Central Asia* (Tashkent: Forum of Culture and Arts of Uzbekistan foundation and University of World Economy and Diplomacy, 2009), p. 161
   Harmatta, J. (ed.). 'Economy and Social System in Central Asia in the Kushan Age.' *History of Civilizations of Central Asia: The Development of Sedentary and Nomadic Civilizations (700 BC to AD 250)*, Volume II (Delhi: Motilal Banarsidass Publishers Pvt. Ltd., 1999), p. 289
   Litvinsky, B.A. (ed.). 'Khwarizm: History and Culture of Khwarizm'. *History of Civilizations of Central Asia: The crossroads of civilizations (AD 250 to 750)*, Volume III (Delhi: Motilal Banarsidass Publishers Pvt. Ltd., 1999), p. 207-218
6. Harmatta, J. (ed.). 'Economy and Social System in Central Asia in the Kushan Age'. *History of Civilizations of Central Asia: The Development of Sedentary and Nomadic Civilizations (700 BC to AD 250)*, Volume II (Delhi: Motilal Banarsidass Publishers Pvt. Ltd., 1999), p. 289
7. Puri, B.N. *Buddhist Tradition Series: Buddhism in Central Asia* (Delhi: Motilal Banarsidass Publishers Pvt. Ltd., 2000), p. 295-296
8. *Ibid.*, p. 295
9. *Ibid.*, p. 295
   Rtveladze, E. *Civilization, States and Cultures of Central Asia* (Tashkent: Forum of Culture and Arts of Uzbekistan foundation and University of World Economy and Diplomacy, 2009), p. 161
10. Yagodin, B. 'New Findings Relating to the Historical and Cultural Relations between India and Khorezm'. Rtveladze, E. (chief coordinator). *India and Central Asia Pre-Islamic* (Tashkent: Academy of Arts and Academy of Sciences of the Republic of Uzbekistan, 2000), p. 59-62
11. Litvinsky, B.A. (ed.). 'Khwarizm: History and Culture of Khwarizm'. *History of Civilizations of Central Asia: The crossroads of civilizations (AD 250 to 750)*, Volume III (Delhi: Motilal Banarsidass Publishers Pvt. Ltd., 1999), p. 221

The Stupas of Termez

Never before has a highway so fascinated me. Never before have I walked on a highway so steeped in history. Perhaps, never before was a highway wrapped in stories and history instead of tar and bitumen. They call it Highway M-39. That is its contemporary name. There was a time when it was nameless. It surely could not have had such a staccato monosyllabic name. M-39. The name is too dreary for a highway that formed the north–south corridor between India and Central Asia. It existed even before Timur and Babur. Most traffic to India passed through this corridor via Afghanistan. Compare M-39 with Highway A-312 of China. A-312 approximates the route taken by travellers on their journey from the Chinese capital to the western regions. At the border of Xinjiang near Jarkent, the A-312 joins the M-39 loop coming from Almaty. Is it any surprise that M-39 is considered the lifeline of Central Asia connecting India, Pakistan and Afghanistan with the Xinjiang province of China through the territories of Central Asia?

One fateful day, I was on M-39. Professor Turgunov Bahadur Azizovich, the head of the Uzbek–Japanese expedition was expecting me at Dalverzin Tepe near Termez. He had excavated not only at Dalverzin Tepe but also at Khalchayan and unearthed exquisite antiquities from the earth's womb. After a quick early breakfast, Shakhnoza and I left Samarkand. One last time, I looked at the majestic statue of Timur. I bade a silent farewell to the valiant invader. We crossed the southern gate of Samarkand leading towards Termez. If I took the straight route, I'd find myself in India. I knew that because that gate was also called 'the gateway to India'.

Soon, we were on highway M-39—the international highway which linked Almaty through Bishkek, Tashkent and Samarkand and ran towards Termez through the Kashkadarya and the Surkhandarya provinces. The M-39, connecting three countries of Central Asia, was the only route to Termez. In 1398, this was the route taken by Timur when he marched from Samarkand to Delhi.

The Mountain Road

That summer day was dry. Parched. The journey was long—seven hours from Samarkand to Termez. The road started climbing almost immediately after leaving Samarkand, meandering through the ranges of the Zerafshan. The drive through the mountains brought in the fragrance of wilderness and the beauty of raw nature. Mountain streams interspersed with picturesque green hills. The beefy mountains are said to be the habitat of the Asian bear and the quick-footed deer—mountains that harbour in their belly semi-precious stones, metals and building materials. It is said that this was the shortest path from Bactria to Sogdiana and was used by the marauding armies of Alexander the Great, the Arabs and Genghis Khan to cross into the trans-Oxus region.[1]

Dozens of small villages lie in the lap of groves, pasturelands or on the slopes of green hills and are visible from the road. On high altitudes, there are plenty of orchards of wild walnut, apricots and pine trees. Young shepherd boys sitting on mules or horseback guard their flocks of white sheep. Nur (name changed), the driver, had other plans. He was unhappy with the cragged roads of M-39. He was imploring that we spend a full day at Shakrisabz. I was oblivious of the potholes because the mountains had taken over my mindspace.

Orchards at Gulistan

The heat was searing, and so we stopped at Gulistan village to borrow a breath of fresh air from the apple orchards and vineyards. Shakhnoza noticed the dark recesses which were caves leading into the depth of the mountains. As the road passed through high mountains, Nur pointed to the ruins of a medieval caravanserai. Here, archaeologists discovered a massive cattleshed, resting cells for travellers, and workshops for blacksmiths who forged horseshoes for donkeys.

The road climbed dangerously uphill till it reached the Takhtakaracha Pass near Tumaniga and crossed into Kashkadaria. In medieval times, Kesh (Shakhrisabz) was situated in the area of Kashkadaria (what is now Kitob). We learnt of one bodhisattva impression recovered from the Takhtakaracha Pass in the neighbourhood of Samarkand as illustrated by E. Rtveladze.[2]

Several villages and orchards later, we bade farewell to Kashkadaria and entered the Surkandaria province near Novabad. The M-39 got potholed from Akrabad. But the landscape was stunning. Mountains appeared blue and misty over the colourful earth covered in green grass and wild yellow, blue and pink flowers. The colour of the high mountains soon changed from greyish blue to a deep red. This was the Gissar range.

Peep into history and you learn that this was a historic route traversed through ages by caravans crossing into India. After a two-day ride from Shakhrisabz, informs Justin Marozzi (the modern historian, biographer who followed the campaign of Timur on his march to India), Timur and his army taking this very road, that is now highway M-39, rode through the famous Iron Gates of Derbend in the Baysun Tau mountains.[3] In AD 629 the Chinese pilgrim Hiuen Tsang too took this route and in the early 15th century, Clavjio, the Spanish ambassador (AD 1403-1406) travelled this way to Timur's court.

Suddenly, the car screeched to a halt. It had been flagged down by a cop. Nur stepped out clutching a bunch of papers. Shakhnoza and I waited for him. When he returned, he was red with anger.

He had been fined 1200 dollars because he was carrying a gas cylinder. He was in a foul mood and hit the steering wheel with a vengeance. We stopped at a choykhana (tea house) near Angkor in Mozrabad district. Here, a group of Afghanis were enjoying a game of chess over tea. They welcomed us warmly and as if on cue, everyone broke into a jig to an Indian song. Termez was only 50 kilometres away from here on the Oxus.

At Termez

After a gruelling drive, we reached Termez in the afternoon. I checked into the Meridian Hotel situated in the heart of the city. There, I was in for a big surprise. The hotel had generously upgraded me from a standard room to a suite. I could not believe my good fortune. I peeped out of the large glass window and saw an old mohalla. I narrowed my gaze on to the beautiful house with walls of mud bricks, clay-plastered and lime-washed. I was tired but I had to see the house.

A nap and few hours later, I opened the wooden gate of the enchanting mud house. A young boy was sweeping the yard; another child, perhaps his brother, was sprinkling water to settle the dust that blew like a storm from the unpaved courtyard. Minutes later, an elderly man pulled a cot, careened and played a beautiful tune on his harmonica. He was deft. I recognized the melody—it was from an old Hindi film. The women were huddled around a teapot and a tray of naan, raisins and apricots. I joined them. The boy lopped off fresh apricots from the garden and I quaffed countless cups of black tea.

In Termez, everyday, an old woman (guide) took me around the ancient sites and the surrounding areas. One evening she invited me for dinner. The temptation: rich rice pilaf cooked by her Afghani tenant. Dressed for dinner, I headed to the lobby where the guide was waiting. As soon as our eyes met, I noticed a tear drop trickling down her cragged skin. I was bewildered. Her tenant had not returned from the market, and thus the pilaf could not be cooked. She was profusely apologetic and offered to take me to the nearby Termez Club. It was a lovely idea. We sat in the lush green lawns of the club and ordered some shorpa and shashlik with naan.

I had forgotten about the pilaf. The music was loud and I joined the merrymakers in the banquet hall. The delightful evening turned into a dizzy night when suddenly a loud noise drowned the music. Everyone stood stunned. The transformer had tripped. The lights went off and I could hear a terrible storm gathering. We waited for the storm to subside and then walked from the restaurant to the Meridian covering our faces with paper napkins. After the storm came fat raindrops. That night it rained so heavily that I feared my trip to Dalverzin Tepe would be cancelled.

The rain gods relented. The next morning, we left for Dalverzin Tepe to see the ancient site and watch the ongoing excavations first-hand. It was here that I was to meet Azizovich. I had never seen him, only heard stories about him from Shakhnoza.

To Ayrtam

An 18-kilometre drive took us first to the village of Ayrtam. On reaching the border post, we realized that we needed an official permit to go beyond that point. It started raining heavily and we sat outside the border post waiting for a permit. The wait was futile. The permit was denied. I was crestfallen. I looked beyond the fence at what was once Ayrtam. The ancient site, we learnt, had been levelled by the Russians to build the Friendship Bridge.

The famous idol of Pharro-Ardoxso, the 'Siva-Parvati' of Ayrtam, was found here during excavations in 1979. The stone idol with inscriptions at its base, now adorns the History Museum at Tashkent.

It (the Bactrian inscription from Ayrtam) attests the rule of the Kushan king Huvishka in the year AD 30.[4] It was an important Buddhist centre in Bactria where the Buddhist missionaries were active.

Professor Turgunov Bahadur Azizovich, whom I met later

at Dalverzin Tepe village, talked at length about Professor D.N. Mukherji from India who tried to read the inscriptions etched at the base of the Siva-Parvati statue. It was a tedious task—nearly 90 of the 380 letters of the inscription had been damaged.

A museum notice at Tashkent displayed the readings of inscriptions and informed that in AD 164-174 Kushan king Huvishka sent his officer Sodila as treasurer to the sanctuary at Ayrtam and had a Pharro-Ardoxso (Siva-Parvati) image prepared and installed. Later, when the river changed its course and the sanctuary became waterless, he had the divinities transferred to another place. Then, by his officer Sodila, he had a well and a water conduit dug and having ensured the water supply, he re-settled the cult of Pharro and Ardoxso into the sanctuary of Ayrtam.[5]

It is said that with the penetration of Buddhism into north Bactria at the turn of the millennium, a mass construction of Buddhist shrines began in Ayrtam. A large Buddhist centre consisting of a temple and a monastery came up in Ayrtam along the Amu Darya river.[6]

After taking a photo of the Ayrtam site where tractors were running and a fence went along the Afghanistan border, we returned to the Oxenbober flyover and took the Dushanbe road to Dalverzin Tepe. There were fields of cotton and wheat and not far away pine forests popped up on the horizon. Because of the lush greenery and fresh air from the pine forests, a sanatorium had been set up at Jagroxona. TB patients were treated with special minerals found in the mountains and pine air to cure them. We were in the midst of dense forests of poplars and pines at Oqtepa village. Soon we arrived at Chegra, the border zone with Afghanistan and crossed the bridge over the Surkhandaria near Ismail Tepe. The railway line to Dushanbe, built by the Russians in 1925, ran along to our left.

Seventy-two kilometres from Termez, Highway-41 runs over a dam on a mountain river at Makedon village. Parallel to the road are the ancient ruins of the Bandehon bridge which is connected with Surkhandaria between the borders of Jarkurgan and Qomkurgan.

Soon, we were in Dalverzin Tepe village and turned right from the highway.

Dalverzin Tepe was an important town on the Great Silk Road situated along the Termez–Dushanbe Road not very far from Denau. The thick ancient wall could be seen running along a moat. A part of the site had been turned into a graveyard. Walking through the slush and sticky mud, we reached the dugout area which was spilling with rain water. There was nothing to protect the site from the vagaries of nature.

The town is said to have been founded during the Greek–Bactrian time and reached its glory in the Kushan period. During excavations, large residential houses with lobbies, baths, rooms and reception halls were discovered. There was also a rich collection of utensils and adornments.[7]

Two 2nd–3rd century Buddhist temples were found inside and outside the territory of the town. The local guide pointed to the spot where the huge Buddha statue and massive gold hoard had been discovered. The antiquities dug out at Dalverzin Tepe indicated the volume of trade between India and Central Asia. The gold treasure found in Dalverzin Tepe had Indian inscriptions in Kharosthi which indicated the weight measures of the bars. Among the adornments, were delicate necklaces and inlaid badges. The travellers are said to have carried huge amounts of gold as currency for trading with their counterparts in Central Asia.[8] It is also possible that the hoard was an offering to the Buddhist deities in the temples of the Dalverzin Tepe town.

From the site, we drove to the hostel where Professor Azizovich and other archaeologists were camping. It was a double-storey house where a working laboratory, store and a small museum were set up. For Azizovich, it was as good as home. He had been working in Dalverzin Tepe for 46 years! We sat in the reception hall waiting for Azizovich. This doubled as a residence for the Japanese archaeologists and as a locker room for valuables taken out from the Dalverzin Tepe site. It was here that the huge statue of Buddha stood for some time before being shifted to the Termez museum. A huge poster of the statue stared from the wall behind me. The precious gold excavated from the site along with the huge jar was also kept in this room.

We sat in Azizovich's laboratory and discussed the expedition. He showed me a copy of the 1st century BC Indian ivory chess figurines excavated from the site. I wanted to see the gold hoard, but I stood no chance. It had been stacked away in the country's presidential palace (or so it is said) to which very few have access.

Azizovich recounted that on 25 September 1972 the excavators, including Azizovich himself, found the 21 slices of pure gold replete with ancient Indian letters. The jar was 34 cm in length with a diameter of 8.5 cm. Since 1989-94, Uzbekistan has been jointly working with Japan and such famed archaeologists as Professor Kutzo Kato, Professor V.A. Livshits and Professor E.V. Rtveladze to read the inscriptions. He took us around the museum where a recently dug ossuary was lying against a wall. It was intact and covered with a lid. A skeleton lay inside.

After taking a round of the village, we planned to return to Termez, cutting off our trip to Khalchayan due to heavy rains.

To Buddhist sites of Old Termez

Our next destination in Old Termez was the Buddhist sites of Kara Tepe and Fayaz Tepe belonging to the early centuries of our era. The old city of Termez was the largest city of the upper Amu Darya. The Amu Darya river was the lifeline of the thriving city situated on the main Silk Route coming from Balkh. The markets and streets were paved. The ruins of old Termez occupied an area of more than 400 hectares and were situated in several kilometres to the west of the modern capital of Surkhandaria province. During the Kushan epoch, Termez became a crossroad between Sogd and Bactria. The town grew steadily and sprawled over 100 hectares.[9]

Fayaz Tepe: From the main street of Termez, we turned north on Highway M-39 towards Samarkand. A few kilometres later we stopped outside a huge stupa that was clearly visible from the highway. It was the site of 3rd-century Buddhist monastery of Fayaz Tepe. Discovered in 1968, it was restored and partially rebuilt with support from the UNESCO. The huge dome that we saw outside was actually a protective covering within which the ancient brick stupa lay for over 1700 years.

Along with the stupa, the Fayaz Tepe site, along the banks of the Amu Darya seems to consist of three parts. While the stupa appears as a separate, independent entity now, at one time it must have been in the same enclosure as the monastic complex. The plan resembles the Buddhist complex at Kushinagar Mahaparinirvana site where the order of the structures appears to be the same. The main stupa lies near the Reclining Buddha temple along with smaller brick stupas of monks while the monastic complex is aligned in a perpendicular line. The modern entry point to the Kushinagar site takes a visitor first to the monastic complex, then to the temple of the Reclining Buddha and last of all, to the stupa. However, the entrance in ancient times could have been from the northern side when the visitors could see all three parts aligned in a line exactly like the Fayaz Tepe site.

The Fayaz Tepe complex was adorned with beautiful paintings of the Buddha and bodhisattvas and portrayed processions of the laity and the monks. The paintings are now displayed at the History Museum of Tashkent. According to the museum notices, some Fayaz Tepe paintings portray scenes of conversion of the local populace to Buddhism. A sculpture of Buddha flanked by two worshippers chiselled out of white limestone was found here and is now displayed in the Tashkent Museum of History.

Standing within the monastic complex, one can see a massive square yard in which once existed a Buddhist shrine. Numerous rooms with separate entrances surround the courtyard. Along the walls of the yard runs a 'sufa' (raised platform). There are remains of the base of columns on which once stood pillars which supported the roof over the corridor and the raised platforms. Shakhnoza points to the south-western part of the yard where the shrine stood. Near the entrance to this shrine was found paintings of the Buddha, monks and laymen. A great number of pottery pieces with inscriptions in Kharosthi, Brahmi and Bactrian were also found. In the debris were found coins of the Kushan rulers, Vima Kadphises, Kanishka, Huvishka and Vasudeva.[10] Many of the coins now lie at the Termez museum.

At several places, the outer as well as the inner walls of the complex have been dug out for paintings but only a few can be seen at the museums in Tashkent and Termez. A wall facing the entrance has three large niches. These were said to hold the figures of the Buddha in three different postures. Other niches held the images of bodhisattvas. Small niches were meant for oil lamps. A well was found in one of the rooms surrounding the courtyard while in another room was a wall-to-wall platform that could have been a bed for several monks.

To the north-east from the temple stands the large stupa and a smaller round stupa bricked-up inside, believed to date back from the 1st century BC to the 4th century AD.

Many American tourists had gathered here and were peeping through the glass window. We all discovered that the small space actually opened into a kind of circumambulatory path around the ancient stupa inside. It was probably used for cleaning and restoration work. I found it difficult to hold myself back and climbed into the circumambulatory path, taking a round of the main stupa amid chants of 'Buddham Sharanam gacchami'. I was overawed by the antiquity of this small stupa. I was certain that Buddha's relics were brought here by some revered monk to be buried inside the stupa around which sprang the monastery. All tourists sat on the stairs leading up to the giant dome to get themselves photographed. Shakhnoza was close at hand to shoot my pictures.

Caves of Kara Tepe: From Fayaz Tepe, we turned south-west. The metalled road gave way to a broad gravel tract along a fenced border that resembled a semi-desert area. The afternoon was extremely hot; the vegetation was sparse. I noticed a large number of dilapidated army-type quarters and rusting machinery. It must have been a cantonment now fallen into disuse. Photography was prohibited in the military zone, so I adhered to the rule. Touring this area needed a special permit and Shakhnoza had worked hard on it so that I could visit the cave monasteries of Termez.

After crossing the arid stretch, we stopped at an armed post. After the verification of my papers, an army official sat in our vehicle and we drove towards the main army office built on a high ground. From there, I could see the great Amu Darya flowing beyond the fence. The water was clean as crystal and a million suns were reflected on the river's surface. It formed the boundary between Afghanistan and Uzbekistan.

Our papers were ready and the army official accompanied us to the 2nd-century Kara Tepe caves. Here, we found separate groups of caves that constituted the monastic complexes of the Kara Tepe hills. Shakhnoza pointed to seven such complexes inside the mountains. We entered one cave that led from a massive courtyard outside the hill into a large arched entrance built of mud bricks and plastered with clay. I was able to trace several high-roofed galleries coming out of one hill and entering another. Even a very tall person could walk upright into the labyrinth of the dark caves. The galleries were neither very narrow and two to three persons could move inside together. After short intervals, there were small openings in the between hills in the roof for daylight. Small niches in the walls were the places where once burned lamps for lighting up the dark caves in the evening. Along the galleries lay small arched rooms that were the shrines of the Buddha.

The walls of the caves exhibited remnants of red, white and black pigments giving evidence of paintings that once adorned the caves. A visitor could gaze for hours at the walls and the splashed pigments to keep guessing what the images could have been. I noticed one wall with large patches of red and black paint that seemed like life-sized human figures, all looking towards their right to a point where sat another diffused image resembling the Buddha. Numerous inscriptions can still be seen on the temple walls perhaps written by foreign pilgrims and monks.

I peeped through a hole inside a walled-up cave and noticed piles of human bones. These are believed to have come when the caves were used as a burial site in later times after the monks had left.

Other monastic complexes had been built over the land at a little distance from the Kara Tepe hills. Several large and small rooms with courtyards and bases of columns could be seen here. One massive stupa similar to the brick stupa at Fayaz Tepe lay on a high rectangular base made of mud and bricks.

To Zurmala: In our race against time and rough weather conditions of Termez and our eagerness to see the two important sites of Old Termez—the Fayaz Tepe and Kara Tepe, we completely forget about the beautiful Zurmala tower situated in the west of the town and headed towards our hotel. I checked my diary and realized that one more site had to be seen. I promptly asked Nur to turn around for Zurmala. But he paid no heed. He mumbled something that sounded like an Uzbeki curse. I knew he was angry because he had no time to rest and had been driving since early morning in the heavy downpour.

I tried hard to convince the local guide and Shakhnoza how important it was for me to pray at the ancient Buddhist stupa. Nur's heart melted and he turned the car around towards the tower. A few miles later, he shut the engine. The tower was about five kilometers away across several cotton fields. I spotted a broad mud track that led along the fields and implored Nur to take me to the nearest spot. He declined.

The elderly guide could not walk and Shakhnoza was stumped for choice between walking such a long distance and staying back in the car. However, my mind was made up. I could not go away without seeing Zurmala. I started walking along the green cotton fields. Soon, I realized that this was the most beautiful stretch of the day. Acres and acres of green fields of cotton planted with such precision in straight furrows that only a machine could manage.

The cotton plants were full of buds and some had bloomed into pearly white flowers. So silky that one could think that silk grew on plants. Far away, a tractor was running through a cotton field pulling out weeds. In my heart, I thanked Nur for stopping the car on the road and compelling me to undertake the long walk. I had, for the first time, touched the leaves of a cotton plant and rubbed the silken flowers between my fingers.

Soon, fear overtook me. A burly black dog had been following me for a long distance. If it were to attack me, no one was at hand to save me. I got scared. I changed track and started walking into a field. Thankfully, the dog went away. Although I had walked more than a couple of kilometres, the tower was still a long distance away. I took out my camera and zoomed in. It was another Buddhist edifice—a monumental tower built of raw bricks and terracotta slabs. The walls of the tower were once decorated with the scenes from Buddhist stories.[11]

From far, Zurmala appeared to be similar in shape to the Dhamek stupa at Sarnath, near Varanasi (Uttar Pradesh, India). I believe that it was the site where probably some Buddhist relics might have been buried centuries ago. It was a calm and peaceful place surrounded by intense greenery unlike the sites of Fayaz Tepe and Kara Tepe where hot dusty winds blew into our face. In the last rays of the setting sun, my eyes were fixed on the Zurmala. It appeared beautiful in the red glow of the flaming ball of fire. I said a short prayer to Buddha and thanked him for my journey to the beautiful land of Uzbekistan.

The mausoleum of Al-Hakim al-Termezi, the 9th-century Sufi philosopher and the city's patron saint was close by. The place was being renovated. After paying respects to the great saint who is known to fulfil every wish of the visitor, I looked for a place to rest under the shade a huge tree. Looking around, I noticed that the great saint had chosen his abode in a picturesque setting, among lush greenery on the banks of the great Oxus river. During his lifetime, he composed over 400 literary works including *Secrets of Holy Trips and Rare Stories about Prophet Rasul*. He was educated in Balkh and became a Haji at 27. The great saint died in AD 869 and his mausoleum came up where he lived.[12]

My days in Termez came to an end, and I headed to the airport, completely oblivious of what was brewing in Nur's head. I had forgotten about the 1200-dollar fine that was imposed on him for carrying a gas cylinder in the car. I was thinking of Ferghana, my next destination. Then, Shakhnoza whispered that I had to pay 1200 dollars to Nur. The fine was due on me. I was taken aback. Why me? I had not implored Nur to carry the gas cylinder. It was his doing, his mistake. Why should I pay for it? I argued. But all my pleas fell on deaf ears. I relented. Basically, I changed the tactic and offered to pay but only after speaking to the manager of the Advantour, my travel agent.

Shahknoza conveyed the offer to Nur. He turned red with anger. He was furious. Agitated. He said I could not speak with the manager. I insisted. I knew the ploy would work. I pulled out my phone and started dialling the manager's number. Suddenly, Nur changed gear. He started pleading with me not to speak with the manager. I did not. As I headed to the departure terminal, I knew I was wiser by 1200 dollars. In Termez, the Buddha had lent me a handful of wisdom. I carried it to Ferghana.

References

1. Buryakov, Y.F., Baipakov, K.M., Tashbaeva, K.H., Yakubov, Y. *The Cities and Routes of the Great Silk Road* (Tashkent: Sharg, 1999), p. 53
2. Rtveladze, E. *Civilization, States and Cultures of Central Asia* (Tashkent: Forum of Culture and Arts of Uzbekistan foundation and University of World Economy and Diplomacy, 2009), p. 173-174. Illustration, p. 174
3. Marozzi, Justin. *Tamerlane: Sword of Islam, Conqueror of the World* (London, New York, Toronto, Sydney: Harper Collins, 2005), p. 245
4. Harmatta, J. (ed.). *History of Civilizations of Central Asia: The*

Development of Sedentary and Nomadic Civilizations (700 BC to AD 250), Volume II (Delhi: Motilal Banarsidass Publishers Pvt. Ltd., 1999), p. 432-433

5. Harmatta, J. (ed.). *History of Civilizations of Central Asia: The Development of Sedentary and Nomadic Civilizations (700 BC to AD 250)*, Volume II (Delhi: Motilal Banarsidass Publishers Pvt. Ltd., 1999), p. 326
   Also see: Tashkent State Museum of History
6. Abdullaev, K.A., Rtveladze, E.V., Shishkina, G.V. *Culture and Art of Ancient Uzbekistan*, Volume I (Fayaz Tepe, Moscow: 1991), p. 145 [Exhibition Catalogue]
   The Ministry of Culture of Uzbek SSR and The Khamza Fine Arts Research Centre, Soka University. *Antiquities of Southern Uzbekistan* (Japan: Soka University Press, 1991), p. 44, 49
7. Buryakov, Y.F., Baipakov, K.M., Tashbaeva, K.H., Yakubov, Y. *The Cities and Routes of the Great Silk Road* (Tashkent: Sharg, 1999), p. 57
8. *Ibid.*, p. 57-58
   Also see: The Ministry of Culture of Uzbek SSR and The Khamza Fine Arts Research Centre, Soka University. *Antiquities of Southern Uzbekistan* (Japan: Soka University Press, 1991), p. 44, 49
9. Buryakov, Y.F., Baipakov, K.M., Tashbaeva, K.H., Yakubov, Y. *The Cities and Routes of the Great Silk Road* (Tashkent: Sharg, 1999), p. 55-56
10. *Ibid.*, p. 56
    Also see: Abdullaev, K.A., Rtveladze, E., Shishkina, G.V. *Culture and Art of Ancient Uzbekistan*, Volume I (Fayaz Tepe, Moscow: 1991), p. 107-112 [Exhibition Catalogue]
11. Buryakov, Y.F., Baipakov, K.M., Tashbaeva, K.H., Yakubov, Y. *The Cities and Routes of the Great Silk Road* (Tashkent: Sharg, 1999), p. 56
12. Marozzi, Justin. *Tamerlane: Sword of Islam, Conqueror of the World* (London, New York, Toronto, Sydney: Harper Collins, 2005), p. 248
    Buryakov, Y.F., Baipakov, K.M., Tashbaeva, K.H., Yakubov, Y. *The*

Cities and Routes of the Great Silk Road (Tashkent: Sharg, 1999), p. 56

A Photo Album. *Uzbekistan: The Monuments of Islam* (Tashkent: Press Co. Ltd., 2002), p. 210

In the Valley of Ferghana

The 400-kilometre-long mountain road A-373 passing through the Chatkal ranges runs along the coal city of Angren and, crawling over the high Kamchik Pass, drops into the Ferghana Valley. Crossing the Syr Darya near Kokand, the road reaches the city of Ferghana across the Great Ferghana Canal.

As I packed my bags for the Ferghana Valley, all around me picture postcards lay scattered. Pictures of the famous Bagh-e-Babur in Andijan; the soft mulberry silk of Margilan; of glazed pottery of Rishtan; the 'blood-sweating' horses and the splendid wines of Dawan; sweet almonds and melons from the orchards of Khojand, and precious gems from the mountains of Tien Shan. So many pictures; so many vignettes lay scattered around me. But I ignored them all. I was told that the best way to see the 'Pearl of Central Asia' was from an altitude. No picture postcard could ever capture the beauty of the picturesque valley.

After the arid deserts of Termez, the rich and fertile valley of Ferghana was a sight for sore eyes. I could see the grand valley surrounded by mountains, the meandering Syr Darya river, green farms of alfa-alfa and the golden of the ripening wheat, and the lush orchards and meadows with hundreds of cows and horses grazing on the nourishing pastures. Fine weather awaited me in this huge oasis.

Hasanbey, my translator/guide, was waiting for me at the Asia

Ferghana hotel. My room opened onto a park encircled by a high stone wall that was covered with fragrant climber roses. The park abounded in fruit trees and in the centre a fountain danced with the breeze as melodious music flowed from the flower beds. Soon, I was to explore the beauty of the valley that lay outside the stone wall of the hotel. The beauty of the famous Sridevi—the goddess of Ferghana—and the giant bejewelled and compassionate Avalokitesvara who guarded the valley as well as the Buddha who had a mysterious third eye like Lord Siva.

The enormous valley ran east to west for about 300 kilometres and formed a wide corridor through which flowed the Syr Darya. Historically, this corridor was an important trade route for goods and people travelling from India in the south through the passes that descended into Kashgar, the hub of trade routes coming over the Himalayas and along the Tarim Basin routes from China. The routes led to the Trans-Caspian regions, Middle-East and Europe.

The valley was the foremost trade hub of Central Asia, renowned for its high-quality Kuva glass, Margilani silk, Ferghana steeds, grains, fruits, wine, fur and leather goods. Owing to its rich, fertile soil, pleasant climate and abundant water from its two rivers, Naryn and Karadarya, that joined to form the mighty Syr Darya, the richest crops grew here and Ferghana was often referred to as the 'Food Bowl of Central Asia' and the 'Valley of Gold'.[1]

This was also the route for itinerant Buddhist monks and pilgrims who travelled to the famous Buddhist shrine at Kuva that lay 35 kilometres from the main town of Ferghana. Here, from atop a hill, the giant Buddha guarded the valley and blessed the travellers and pilgrims coming from all over Central Asia, India and China. This happened centuries before the days of Zaheeruddin Mohammad Babur, the first Mughal emperor of India, who came from the mighty Valley of Ferghana.

To the Buddhist Temple at Kuva

The following day, I started my journey into the valley. My first destination was Kuva, 35 kilometres north-east of Ferghana. Kuva is believed to have flourished from the late 1st millennium BC to 13th century AD. The town was famous as one of the trade centres of the valley on the road to China.[2] Situated on the banks of the Kuva river that flowed into the Syr Darya, the town had a good supply of water and was cluttered with gardens and fruit orchards. Even in present times, informs Hasanbey, the climate is just perfect for fruits, specially strawberries and pomegranate. The berries start arriving by May and are soon followed by yellow, juicy pineapples.

The road goes through dense forests, vineyards and orchards of apple, apricot and quinces, interspersed with vast fields of cotton and wheat. Flowers abound. On both sides of the road were beds of hollyhocks and roses and the air was redolent with their fragrance. At village Sreder, the fields are aflame with orange lilies and red roses that are grown commercially.

Soon, we arrived at village Begat. We parked our vehicle in a lane by the side of the Al-Fergoni Park, named after the great geographer and astrologer Ahmad Al-Fergoni (AD 797–861) whose marble statue stands in the centre of the park. He hailed from Kuva and achieved great fame as a scientist. Known in the West as Alfraganus, he set up two observatories in Damascus and Baghdad.

At Kuva, I set off to meet Rekhbar Karim Jon, director of the Kuva Museum to seek his permission to photograph the famous goddess of Kuva. I crossed several rose gardens to reach Karim Jon's office. He was elated to have a visitor from India. He accompanied me for a round of the museum halls. I was impatient. I wanted to see the famous exhibit—the Buddhist goddess, Sridevi.

As I stood before the goddess, I was mesmerized by her face. There was a mysterious spell about her. Her eyes seemed heavily intoxicated. They were large and slanting and bulging out of their sockets. The heavy eyelids seemed to fall over the eyes as if in a trance. The mouth had full lips and the colour of her face was a pale yellow. She wore a crown through which fell a fringe of curls on her forehead. Her hair was combed with a middle parting. She was found during excavations at the Buddhist temple in Kuva.

Just as in India and Tibet, it is learnt that the inhabitants of Ferghana worshipped Goddess Sridevi. She could have been either a Hindu or a Buddhist deity. Karim Jon allowed me to take a few photos of the goddess.

David Kinsley in *Hindu Goddesses—Vision of the Divine Feminine in the Hindu Religious Tradition*, describes the goddess 'Sri' as the 'divine feminine in Hinduism'.[3] In the Hindu tradition, the goddess Sri or Sridevi is also known by the name Lakshmi since pre-Buddhist times[4] and is one of the most popular goddesses of the Hindu pantheon. Sri suggests 'capability, power and advantageous skills', says Kinsley. As an external quality, Sri suggests 'beauty, lustre, glory and high rank.'

In Taranath's *History of Buddhism*, we read about kings who obtained wealth and glory by propitiating the 'Goddess Sri' and King Virasena, who obtained inexhaustible treasure by propitiating the 'Goddess Sri, the consort of Kuvera'. The king used his wealth to entertain monks all around and worshipped all the chaityas in the world with a hundred items of offerings for each. Another scholar Vagisvarakirti frequently received the vision of Goddess Tara in particular and acquired the proficiency of defeating many rivals. He became the western gate-keeper of Vikramsila Vihar.[5]

Since devotion to feminine divinities was one of the features of Vajrayana—a form of Buddhism based on the Tantras and incantation of magical formulae, it is believed that Kuva perhaps was a centre for Vajrayana where the goddess Sridevi was worshipped along with the Buddha–Avalokitesvara. According to *Buddhanusmriti*, Vajrayana is considered as an offshoot of the Mahayana.[6] The sect is named after its symbol Vajra, which means a thunderbolt or a diamond, the object used for worship.

As I moved further, I found a series of photographs of the extensive archaeological diggings that took place in Kuva. Antiquarian remains of a Buddhist settlement belonging to the 4th–3rd century BC was found here. In 1979, archaeologists excavated a religious complex, including a Buddha temple. Images of the

Buddha were found buried here. The unique sculpture of Buddha modelled in clay on a wooden frame and a sculpture of Sridevi, along with other pre-Islamic Turkic gods, were recovered from the centre of the temple. A large number of utensils and clay pots were also recovered.

Parts of the sculptures are on display at the museum, including a huge hand of the Buddha, parts of the head with ringlets, a number of ancient clay and metallic pottery that were used in temple rituals. The body parts on display give an idea of how colossal the sculpture must have been. A newspaper cutting of the excavations is also on display. One photograph of the statue of the Buddha recovered from the depths of the temple informs us that it was a gigantic Buddha, like the ones that adorn the Great Silk Road passing through China.

The archaeologists led by V.A. Bulatova discovered stone stairs leading to the Buddhist temple that was built on a natural hill and the colossal Buddha towered over the whole settlement. According to Karim Jon, the complex consisted of a monastery and a shrine which was built of adobe bricks and pakhsa (rammed loam and straw mixture) and was covered with a wooden roof. Inside the shrine was a high altar where the Buddhist deities were worshipped, offerings of flowers and fruits were made and incense was burned.

In the Buddhist complex, the excavators found the strange wrathful, divine deities with terribly fierce faces. They wore a garland or a head decoration of skulls. These were perhaps the Vajrayana deities that scholars believed were worshipped by the inhabitants of the valley, and which clearly had their antecedents in the divine but wrathful deities worshipped in India, Nepal and Tibet namely, the Mahakaal, Kalbhairava and Yamanataka who were endowed with supreme powers—powers that were invoked by the chanting of incantations.

One image from Kuva, has been denoted as that of Manjushri, the great bodhisattva. He has large terrifying eyes hanging from the sockets and a fearful face. Generally, bodhisattva Manjushri (or Manjunath, Manjughosh) meaning sweet or pleasant, is also

Vagisvara or the 'Lord of Speech'. He is a god supposed to be of Central Asia origin.[7] He is shown sitting on his 'vahan'/ carrier—the bejewelled lion, like the one in the cave paintings of the Dunhuang and Yulin grottoes in China and Alchi in Ladakh, India. Since only the head was retrieved, it is possible that his 'vahan' was lost. He is portrayed as the 'god of wisdom'. His hair appears ruffled. His eyes wide open, he looks at his worshippers and opens his mouth to bless them.

Broken and intact ceramic bowls used for keeping fruits, incense and other offerings were also kept at the museum. The temple is supposed to have been at its glorious best in the 7th/8th century when Kuva was at the peak of trade and commerce. This was the time when traders came looking for goods like mulberry silk, the famous 'blood-sweating heavenly horses' and high-quality leather, fruits and grains. They sought the blessings of the Buddha and paid obeisance to the goddess.

Another image on a stele found at the Kuva temple shows a semi-nude god. The figure is described as Kuber, sitting with a jug, perhaps of the sweet nectar and a large wineskin full of some intoxicating drink that was made in abundance in the Valley of Ferghana. The figure perhaps could be the god who blessed the valley that produced the best wines of Ferghana.

The images of the Turkic gods and goddesses from Ferghana are also displayed at the Tashkent Museum of History. They show similarities with the Hindu gods and goddesses in India where goddess worship is still prevalent. The image of Buddha with the 'third eye' of Lord Siva, recovered from Kuva, is also on display at the Sanat Museum of Fine Arts.

Buddhism in the Ferghana Valley

Close trade relations of the Ferghanians with the Indians promoted Buddhism in the Ferghana valley. There were many important trading posts along the Silk Road passing through the valley. Indian traders were travelling to the valley for its glass, metal ores and glazed pottery among other things.

Uzbek archaeologist A.R. Mukhamedjanov mentions that iron, gold, silver and nephrite were mined in the mountains of Ferghana and Sogdiana.[8] There were craftsmen producing metal ware and adornments for women, bronze vessels, mirrors, bracelets, earrings, and rings. The economy of Central Asia was considerably rich during the 1st to the 3rd centuries AD and handicrafts were a major occupation. The large Central Asian cities such as Bukhara, Samarkand and Ershi, among others, became centres for handicraft production and trade and were frequently visited by merchants coming with their caravans from India, western Asia and China.[9]

The archaeologists discovered the ruins of a medieval town with a citadel in the eastern suburbs of Kuva. There were bazaars, palaces and prisons, a mosque and a mint. Traces of industry such as metallurgy, pottery, glass-making was discovered. From archaeological excavations, it is clear that Kuva was a centre of trade and handicraft. The craftsmen lived in the village settlements of Kuva and engaged in crafts of varied nature, including glass-making. Kuva is believed to have possessed the best silica sand suitable for glass-making and had the best glass-blowers. Kuva glass had a market throughout Asia.[10]

The proximity of India with Central Asia through ancient routes encouraged exchange of goods, ideas and faith. Historian Romila Thapar informs that during the construction of the Karakoram Highway, it was found that the ancient route, branches of the ancient Silk Road, linked the Upper Indus through the Hunza Valley to the route going towards Samarkand, Tashkurgan and Yarkand. Inscriptions in Kharosthi, Brahmi and Bactrian and engravings of Buddhist images and themes along the way date the ancient route to the start of the Christian era. According to Thapar, the occasional depiction of horses suggests an early trade of Ferghanian 'blood-sweating horses' with India.[11]

Even before the Chinese ambassador Zang Chien had travelled west and learnt about the celestial horse of Ferghana, Indians knew about the divine Ferghanian horse and weaved its divinity into their mythology. It is related to the great Uchchaishrava or the divine horse, arising out of the ocean during samudramanthan or the 'great churning' of the ocean by the gods and the demons. The 'snow white, seven-headed, flying horse' obtained from the ocean was the king of horses, the vahana of Indra, the god-king of heaven and also of the demons. The horse rose from the ocean of milk along with other treasures like amrita (elixir of life).[12]

Even the Buddha was associated with the divine horse. In a painting of Vairochana Buddha from Balawaste in the ancient Buddhist site of the Domoko oasis (from Central Asia, displayed at the National Museum, Delhi), there is a fragment of a wall painting depicting the Buddha with various symbols, including the galloping horse, perhaps the divine horse, Uchchaishrava.

It is believed that the Western Turkic Khagnate in Ferghana was mainly responsible for the growing influence of Buddhism in the region of the Syr Darya.[13] Since the long corridor of the Ferghana Valley was a vantage part of the Silk Routes, having the best soil and climate and the best fodder for the 'blood-sweating' horses and stock-breeding, the Turks focused their energies on the Ferghana Valley and wanted to retain it at all costs even through an alliance with the Chinese or the Tibetan suited the occasion. However, both alliances worked in favour of the spread of Buddhism in Ferghana.

Many Turks had married Chinese princesses and converted to Buddhism, while some had been converted by the great Buddhist scholars passing through their territories.[14] During the period of alliance with China there were several Chinese and Turkish intermarriages due to which Buddhist influence was growing as the Chinese princesses coming to the Turkish land installed Buddhist idols in their temples. An alliance of the western Turks with Tibetans is also said to have promoted Buddhism, especially the Vajrayana school.[15]

Silk City of Margilan

Margilan was and still is famous for its silk which was exported to India, China, West Asia and Europe through the ancient trade routes. Weavers from all over Central Asia came to Margilani institutes and silk weaving centres to learn how the best silk was made, woven and dyed. Nevertheless, 'Benarasi' silk with gold and silver weavings from India left an imprint on the Margilani centres and 'Benaras' silk fabric became popular at Margilan.

At the Silk Museum of Yodgorlik, I noticed the gigantic ovens on which sat heavy iron pots in which thousands of small silk cocoons were bobbing. A woman sat behind the pot extracting silk threads from the cocoons and running them over a spindle which was hand drawn by another woman. In another room, the spindles were turned into reels of silk thread to be woven into silk fabric by deft weavers. In another section, Ikat/abr silk fabric was being designed.

Many researchers believe that the Ferghana Valley is the birthplace of abr fabric, known for its special dyeing technique called abrband. Dyes are made from extracts of roots, fruit and leaves of native plants including madder, pomegranate, walnut, acacia, onion and saffron. Black tea, indigo, cochineal and henna were also used. Another section at Yodgorlik produces fine carpets and semi-silks such as bekasab, benaras and adras.

Between Qashqar and Qumqagal villages, I could trace the outline of huge mountains in the backdrop of which flowed the Syr Darya. A left turn from Batah brought me to the banks of the river. Far from being a sandy bank, there was soft mud all around. I walked through a stretch of muddy banks to reach the river. I dipped my hands into the waters which appeared muddy like the Ganges. But not cold, unlike the latter, which is a glacial river. Also known as the Jaxartes or the Sayhoun, Syr Darya once marked the northernmost limits of the conquests of Alexander the Great. According to historians, the conqueror founded the city of Alexandria Eschate (literally Alexandria, the Farthest) on the Syr as his permanent garrison (present-day Khojand).

Khudoyar Khan's Palace

A few kilometres later, I reached Kokand, called the 'City of Winds' and the 'City of Khans'. This windy city, I was told, was home to a succession of 29 Khans in the 170-year history of the Khanate until its annexation to Russia in 1876. Since ancient times it was on the travellers' route from India to China. From here, a route branched to Tashkent in the north-west and another to Khojand in the west. In medieval times it was one of the most important religious centres of Central Asia, with more than 300 mosques.

A visit to the magnificent Palace of the last Khan of the Kokand Khanate, Khudoyar Khan (1845-1876) can inspire awe. Thousands of best craftsmen from Bukhara, Khorezm and all over the Ferghana Valley are said to have been brought to Kokand to build the beautiful palace with a brilliant blue façade of glazed ceramic work. A high ramp running across a three-metre high foundation leads into the palace.

A walk through the verandahs and courtyards of the palace brings alive the history of the Khanate men and women occupying the quarters, be it the royal personages or the workers as humble as the carriage pullers. Some hand-pulled carriages can still be seen lying in the verandahs of the palace. There are several courtyards full of trees. Walking through them, one can imagine a gaggle of women going about their daily chores in those courtyards. Of these, only a few were wives; others were concubines. The last Khan is said to have four wives and 40 concubines.

Mansoora, in-charge of the palace museum, guided me to the rooms inside the palace. In one, displayed prominently, was a top-to-toe veil—a black burqa made of horse hair. The hair was so fine that the woman wearing it would not feel suffocated, air could pass through it and she would not feel hot. An outsider could not judge the form nor see the face of the wearer but the burqa wearer could see everything very clearly. For a few seconds, I put on the veil. It was too heavy. I removed it hurriedly.

Mansoora informed me that before the Soviet occupation, it

was mandatory for all grown-up women to wear the head-to-foot veil. According to prevailing custom, they were not permitted to appear in public unless heavily veiled. In 1927, the Soviet government launched an offensive agitation against this oppressive custom. Many women were in the forefront of the agitation against the veil. Even though many of them were beaten by their husbands, killed and maimed, they continued to defy the oppressive system. In the end, they won and the women of Uzbekistan threw away their veil.

From the artefacts preserved at the Palace Museum, one can imagine the rich costumes that the Khans wore and the exotic jewellery that their consorts wore, some wearing up to five kilos of jewellery on their bodies from top to toe. The Khan himself wore a quilted chapan (resembling a sherwani) richly woven in stripes, gold-embroidered and embellished with glittering gems.

The small town of Rishtan, situated 50 kilometres from Ferghana, is the oldest centre of ceramic art in Central Asia. Master craftsmen have set up schools for pottery production using local clay and mineral colours in traditional designs. This glazed earthenware pottery was the hallmark of the Ferghana Valley and was exported worldwide. The most characteristic colouring of this earthenware (ceramics) is turquoise, dark blue and brown on a milky background. A special glaze made from plant ash gives the earthenware its radiance.

To Andijan, the Land of Babur

Leaving Kuva, we headed east to Andijan, nearly 55 kilometres away. Andijan borrows its fame from a boy born here in 1483—Mughal emperor Zahiruddin Mohammad Babur, founder of the Mughal dynasty that sprawled over much of today's India, Pakistan and Afghanistan. He is perhaps the most captivating personality in the history of conquerors—the conqueror who came to settle down in the heat and dust of India and become a part of the great land for howsoever short a period—only about four years—in which he gave birth to a dynasty, the Mughal, and an empire of wealth and splendour, of great learning and sciences and patronage of art.[16]

Babur, the son of Umar Sheikh and the great-great-great-grandson of Timur, symbolized the link between Central Asia and India. He was the emperor and conqueror who wrote his own memoirs, 'in his own hand, in his own tongue', in the medieval age of the 15th century when few emperors took up the pen to write their own history—one of the most captivating of all memoirs written so far. His contribution to world history is his contribution to world literature. His memoir—the *Tazooki Baburi* or the *Baburnama* entailed the personal story of his rise from the small kingdom of Ferghana to the mighty throne of Hindustan.

Babur's home—the city of Andijan was an important stop on the Silk Road, lying roughly between Kashgar and Khojand. Known as the eastern gate of the Ferghana Valley, it became the capital of Ferghana for three centuries.

The drive to Andijan was absolutely picturesque. Every little cottage along the road was hidden behind a veil of vine, tall hollyhocks and surrounded by a garden full of blooming roses and fruit-laden trees. Lost in the scenic beauty along the road, I reached Bagh-e-Babur in no time. The Bagh was actually a huge nature reserve on the Andijan hills, 15 kilometres away from the city.

Here, amid the beautiful landscape of rose gardens, fruit orchards, splendid fountains and enormous shady trees and above all, the most befitting literary museum (named after Babur), signifying his love for books, lay the mausoleum of Emperor Babur built from the earth brought from Agra (where he passed away) and Kabul (where he was buried). It is said that Babur loved to read prose and poetry and would carry books, even on his campaigns. Sometimes he was so greatly fascinated by nature, its bounties and its profound beauty that he even composed and inscribed poetry on rocks. His intense love for the Syr Darya and the Ferghana Valley prompted him to look for his paradise and kingdom beside the Kabul river in Afghanistan and beside the Yamuna in India.

Hundreds visit the mausoleum every day and sit quietly in remembrance of the great son of Ferghana whose memoirs, women into poetry, outshine and outlive his dynasty.

At the Babur Literary Museum, Ahmedova Roza Khan guided me through the artefacts. I met Professor Zakirjaan Mashrabov, director of the expedition *In the Footsteps of Babur*. He travelled to India several times from Andijan by road in search of books and manuscripts related to Babur. He brought more than 300 books on history from India from various universities which were displayed in glass cases inside the museum.

Zakirjaan asked me about the dynasty of Babur, especially about the great-granddaughters of Bahadur Shah Zafar II. Honestly, I knew nothing about them. Zakirjaan does. He told me that Tahira Sultan Begum now lives in England and her sister Pakiza Sultan Begum lives in Delhi.

I returned to Andijan city where Hasanbey guided me to Babur's madrassa. Outside the huge gates of the ancient madrassa, women clad in long skirts and head scarves could be seen selling suzma (white dry balls of hung curd) and dolma (a dish prepared from cow's milk). I walked inside the huge ancient gates and headed straight to the statue of Babur sitting in the midst of a garden. The walls of the madrassa had been repaired with terracotta bricks. Inside the rooms arranged around a courtyard were fabulous paintings depicting scenes from the *Baburnama*. I went from room to room admiring the artefacts that were once used by the madrassa some 500 years ago. The statue has now been moved to the Babur Literary Museum.

During his lifetime, Babur never forgot Ferghana from where he ventured south covering thousands of miles over mountains, rivers and plains to the golden land of the Sindhu, the Ganga and the Yamuna—the land that gave him the throne and a dynasty. Yet, he never grew tired of praising the excellence of Ferghana and the beauty of its numerous towns. Any traveller to Ferghana would agree with Babur. No traveller will ever tire of praising Ferghana. Such is its splendour.

References

1. Buryakov, Y.F., Baipakov, K.M., Tashbaeva, K.H., Yakubov, Y. *The Cities and Routes of the Great Silk Road* (Tashkent: Sharg, 1999), p. 62-63
   Tucker, Jonathan. *The Silk Road: Art and History* (New Delhi: Timeless Books, 2003), p. 271-274
2. Buryakov, Y.F., Baipakov, K.M., Tashbaeva, K.H., Yakubov, Y. *The Cities and Routes of the Great Silk Road* (Tashkent: Sharg, 1999), p. 63
   Tucker, Jonathan. *The Silk Road: Art and History* (New Delhi: Timeless Books, 2003), p. 273
3. Kinsley, David. *Hindu Goddesses: Vision of the Divine Feminine in the Hindu Religious Tradition* (New Delhi: Motilal Banarsidass Publishers Pvt. Ltd., 2005), p. 2
4. *Ibid.*, p. 19
5. Chattopadhyay, Debiprasad (ed.), Tibetan Lama Chimpa (trans.), Chattopadhyay, Alaka (trans.). *Taranath's History of Buddhism*. (Delhi: Motilal Banarsidass Publishers Pvt. Ltd., 2004), p. 79, 299, 295 n
6. Acharya, Alka. *Buddhanusmriti: A Glossary of Buddhist terms* (Mumbai, New Delhi: Somaiya Publications, 2002), p. 217, 218
7. Eliot, Charles. *Hinduism and Buddhism: A Historical Sketch*, Volume II (Delhi: Sri Satguru Publications, Indian Books Centre, 1988), p. 18-21
   Puri, B.N. *Buddhist Tradition Series: Buddhism in Central Asia* (Delhi: Motilal Banarsidass Publishers Pvt. Ltd., 2000), p. 337
8. Harmatta, J. (ed.). 'Economy and Social System in Central Asia in the Kushan Age'. *History of Civilizations of Central Asia: The Development of Sedentary and Nomadic Civilizations (700 BC to AD 250)*, Volume II, (Delhi: Motilal Banarsidass Publishers Pvt. Ltd., 1999), p. 278-279
9. *Ibid.*, p. 279
10. Buryakov, Y.F., Baipakov, K.M., Tashbaeva, K.H., Yakubov, Y. *The Cities and Routes of the Great Silk Road* (Tashkent: Sharg, 1999), p. 63

Tucker, Jonathan. *The Silk Road: Art and History* (New Delhi: Timeless Books, 2003), p. 27
11. Thapar, Romila. *The Penguin History of Early India: From the Origins to AD 1300* (New Delhi: Penguin Books, 2003), p. 222
12. Banerji, P. *New Light on Central Asian Art and Iconography* (Delhi: Abha Prakashan, 1992), p. 16-23
13. Koves, Margit. *Buddhism among the Turks of Central Asia* (New Delhi: International Academy of Indian Culture and Aditya Prakashan, 2009), p. 33
14. *Ibid.*, p. 32
15. *Ibid.*, p. 32, 34, 95
16. Lamb, Harold. *Babur the Tiger: First of the Great Mughals* (Dehra Dun: Natraj Publishers, 2003)
    Thackston, W.M. *The Baburnama: Memoirs of Babur, Prince and Emperor* (New York: Modern Library, 2002)
    Lane-Poole, Stanley and Hunter, W.W. (ed.). *Rulers of India* (New Delhi: Low Price Publications, 2005)

Section Five
KYRGYZSTAN

Routes into Kyrgyzstan

It is said that travellers from China and India generally took the Pamir Route to enter the land of Kyrgyzstan. To enter this icy region of the Pamir, the travellers could take the northern foot of the Kunlun mountains to reach Kashgar, the last point on the Silk Road through China. From Kashgar they crossed the snow-covered Pamirs into the Kyrgyz territory via the passes on the Kyrgyz–China border at Torugart or Irkeshtam and reached the Ferghana Valley through the city of Osh.[1]

From ancient times, the territory of Kyrgyzstan was in contact with Russia, China and India through trade routes leading westwards and north-westwards to the Caspian and the Aral regions, through passes on the Silk Road entering the Xinjiang province of China at the points of Aksu (through the Bedel Pass) in the north and Kashgar (through the Torugart and Irkeshtam Passes) in the south. From Kashgar and Yarkand, trade routes dropped southwards into the Kashmir and Ladakh regions of India.

Today, there are a number of modern highways that approximate to the ancient Silk Routes running through the territory of Kyrgyzstan. These brought trade caravans not only from India and China over the Pamirs and along the foothills of the Tien Shan mountains but also from the Mediterranean, Black Sea and Caspian Sea regions along the east–west corridor of the Chuy Valley.

One of the most prominent and picturesque highways of

Central Asia, and also one of the longest, running north to south is the Pamir Highway M-41. It covers the tracks of the ancient Silk Route cruising through the territories of Kyrgyzstan, Uzbekistan and Tajikistan. The highway coming from Termez (Uzbekistan) through Dushanbe (Tajikistan) touches Osh (Kyrgyzstan), the main hub of this route. Then it runs for 650 kilometres from Osh through Jalalabad, Tashkomur and Toktogul to reach Kara-Balta and joins the M-39 Highway to Bishkek.

Another important highway passing through Kyrgyzstan is M-39. It is Bishkek's key link with Almaty in the north and Taraz in the west (both in southern Kazakhstan). The northerly M-39 International Highway, corresponding to the ancient trade route coming from Termez, Samarkand and Tashkent, continues north-eastwards to enter Kyrgyzstan, past Kara-Balta to Bishkek. This route continues further north-east into Almaty or to the Issyk Kul lake eastwards through the Chuy Valley.

Irkeshtam–Osh Route: From Kashgar via the Irkeshtam Pass, the westward route from the Tarim Basin (Xinjiang province of China) crossed the Alay Valley to the Kara Darya river and thence into Uzgen and Osh.

Torugart–Naryn Route: The 700-kilometre Bishkek–Balykchy–Naryn–Torugart route running into Kashgar—the A-365, winds up in the Boom gorge towards Kochkor, a stopover on way to Naryn. From Naryn via At Bashy and Tash Rabat, it runs to the Torugart pass into Kashgar.

Kokart–Osh Route: Eighty kilometres south-west of the Torugart Pass is the Kokart Pass. The road A-370 presently joins Kokart to the Highway M-41 into Osh.

Bedel Pass Route: The Bedel Pass Route was an important path connecting China to the Chuy Valley of Kyrgyzstan and was known as the Hiuen Tsang Route, named after the Chinese pilgrim Hiuen Tsang who took this route in 629 AD to reach the shores of southern Issyk Kul from Aksu in the Xinjiang region of China.[2] The Highway A-364 passing near the Bedel Pass runs up to Barskon on south Issyk Kul and joins the A-363 to Balykchy.

References

For ancient travel routes and modern highways of Kyrgyzstan see: Buryakov, Y.F., Baipakov, K.M., Tashbaeva, K.H., Yakubov, Y. *The Cities and Routes of the Great Silk Road;* Lawrence, Mitchell. *Kyrgyzstan: The Bradt Travel Guide;* Author's own travels in Kyrgyzstan

1. Buryakov, Y.F., Baipakov, K.M., Tashbaeva, K.H., Yakubov, Y. *The Cities and Routes of the Great Silk Road* (Tashkent: Sharg, 1999), p. 84-97
   Author's own travels along the road: M-41 Highway, Bishkek to Osh, Highway M-39 (A2) to Almaty via Kordai, Andijan-Osh Road, Chuy Valley, Northern Issyk Kul and Kegeti Valley routes
   Lawrence, Mitchell. *Kyrgyzstan: The Bradt Travel Guide* (Connecticut, England: The Globe Pequot Press Inc., 2008), p. 128-129. Also see, map: p. 1; Introduction: p. 190, 116
   Lonely Planet: Central Asia (Australia: Lonely Planet Publication Pvt. Ltd., 2000), p. 392. Also see, map: p. 393
2. Tsiang, Hiuen and Beal, Samuel (trans.). *Si Yu Ki: Buddhist Records of the Western Country,* Book II (Delhi: D.K. Publisher Distributors Pvt. Ltd., 1995), p. 24-28
   Watters, Thomas. *On Yuan Chwang's Travels in India: 629-645 AD* (New Delhi: Munshiram Manoharlal Publisher Pvt. Ltd., 2012), p. 66-67

Gods of the Osh Caves

The drive into Kyrgyzstan was a short one. From Andijan (in the Uzbek part of the Ferghana Valley), Natasha and I drove in a van eastwards to Osh (in the Kyrgyz part of the valley). The two-hour journey through the valley was a picturesque one along streams, through cotton cultivations, wheat fields and orchards of walnuts, cherry and plum.

The road from Ferghana ran via Andijan to the border at Dostylik, only 115 kilometres away. This check point, barely 40 kilometres from Andijan, opens into the city of Osh lying at the foot of the holy mountains of Sulaiman-Too. Prophet Solomon is believed to have taken shelter here while the great emperor Babur, found solace in the depth of the myriad mountain caves.

On reaching Osh, our stomachs were growling with hunger. We forgot all about history. All we needed was an eatery. After driving through a maze of lanes and markets, we found one in the midst of an apple orchard—a choykhana called 'Kashgar'. A small carved wooden screen, a little beyond the entrance to the restaurant, concealed the vast courtyard from the noise of vehicles sputtering on the main road. Rabbits and cats roamed freely and boughs of green apples swung right over our heads. I stretched out an arm to pluck an apple, biting into the juicy flesh while we waited for the meal of shorpa with shashlik and a huge platter of salad and laghman (flat homemade noodles served with chopped vegetables) that Natasha had ordered. Soon, a huge bowl of broth arrived with pieces of meat and flat, boiled noodles. Steamed dumplings and fried sheep liver, round balls of sour cheese, the ubiquitous naan and fresh salad completed the scrumptious meal.

Osh or Osh-e-lini

Osh was an important crossroad on the ancient Silk Routes and a major trading point of the Ferghana Valley. It still holds the reputation of being one of the oldest and biggest markets in Central Asia. Sprawled along the valley of the Akbura river, the city forms the hub of the modern Pamir Highway M-41. Northwards, the highway crosses into Kazakhstan through Kara-Balta; southwards it crosses into Tajikistan through the Kyzlart Pass; south-eastwards through a branch road it enters into China via the Irkeshtam Pass and Kashgar. From Kashgar, the routes lead southwards into India.

The name, however, reminded me of the sacred Buddhist convent of Osh-e-lini in Xinjiang, which apparently has some connection with Osh. Maybe an itinerant monk from Osh had set up the Osh-e-lini convent: the 'extraordinary and sacred' Osh-e-lini, where the great monk Hiuen Tsang had set foot in the province of Kuqa, in East Turkestan on his way to the western regions. But the similarity ends there: Osh in Kyrgyzstan was different from the Osh-e-lini of Kuqa. It never had a Buddhist convent or even if it did, it was never found by any historian or dug up by the spade of any archaeologist. However, in the recesses of the sacred Sulaiman-Too mountain are mysterious caves similar to the caves found near the Black Jade river (Karakash) in the suburbs of Khotan, which were inhabited by mendicants in ancient times.

After a tiring journey through the long and difficult routes of the Pamirs, the ancient travellers would find rest, food and plenty of water in Osh. They could seek shelter in the caravanserais of Osh Bazaar. However, most chose the enormous natural shelter houses in the mountains along the Akbura. Here lay several deep caves, large enough for caravans and families to live safely and comfortably, with abundant water from the Akbura river flowing along the foothills. The large cave shelters with rock paintings today provide evidence of human habitation in the Sulaiman-Too, that rises like a phoenix in the middle of the city of Osh.

Sacred Cult Mountain

The UNESCO heritage site of Sulaiman-Too has been the most sacred Central Asian mountain for several millennia. Many believe the carvings and paintings were related to the idea of fertility, magic treatment, sun worship and shamanism. They belong to a time when the settlers worshipped the sun, wind and the rain gods. Most importantly, the temple faced the north where the light never faded, from sunrise to sunset. There is also mention of an Arab legend that Prophet Sulaiman (Solomon) stayed in the sacred mountains at Osh.[1]

According to an assessment report of important Kyrgyz sites, prepared by Yelena Khorosh for UNESCO, the sacred mountain has a continuous tradition of pilgrimage 'blending both Islamic and pre-Islamic beliefs and practices'. The mountains are believed to possess a large concentration of various cult objects and constitute the historic core of Osh.[2]

From the base of the mountain, steps lead into the caves that portray the history of the Kyrgyz people. Two Buddhist images from the Ferghana Valley of which Osh was a part are displayed at the entrance cave highlighting the Buddhist past of the region. The gilded images belonging to the 7th and 8th centuries are those of Avalokitesvara and Sridevi, as the notice board mentions.

The life-sized bejewelled image of Avalokitesvara sits cross-legged in 'Bhumisparsh mudra' with the left hand touching the earth. His body is wrapped in a tight pleated robe. A three-tiered, gem-laden crown with an image of the Amitabha Buddha in the centre rests on the head while two rows of a necklace with a huge pendant falls on the chest. The earrings are so large they almost touch the shoulders and armlets clasp the upper arms. A third eye in the forehead destroys every evil and bestows blessing on all human beings.

The glorious golden image of Goddess Sridevi, one of the most popular goddesses of the Hindu pantheon, symbolizes wealth and beauty. Propitiating the goddess and devotion to the feminine deity was one of the important features of Buddhism in the Ferghanna Valley.

Images of the Avalokitesvara and Goddess Sridevi found in other parts of the Ferghana Valley and Chuy Valley have been displayed in the museums of Kyrgyzstan and Uzbekistan corroborating the popularity of these Buddhist deities in Central Asia. According to scholars, several factors were responsible for the spread of Buddhism in the Ferghana Valley of which the Osh region was a part. The foremost was the interaction of Ferghanians with Indians. Ferghana was an important staging post on the Silk Road for the sale and exchange of goods and Indian traders were travelling to the valley for its horses, wine, glass, metal ores and glazed pottery, among other things. This encouraged exchange of ideas and faith.

A Decorated Cave Shrine

One cave was deep within the belly of the mountain. Through steps leading from the base to the peak, it opened into a wide terrace shaped like a multi-layered arch facing the north. From this opening, built like an aivan or verandah of a huge monument, one could see a panoramic view of the city below. Even in ancient times the mountain is said to have been a reference point for travellers and passing caravans and also a military watchpost for defending the trade routes. Like the caves in the oasis cities along the Tarim Basin, it must have provided not only solitude for itinerant mendicants but also safety from wild animals. It looked like a natural, multi-tiered cave. Today, hundreds of visitors jostle with each other to reach the top of the spacious arched portal.

The naturally lit cave is the site of numerous rock paintings and appears to have been a shrine at one time. The cave-shrine where no central image can be seen today is very similar to the Buddhist cave-shrines of the Gansu Corridor in China. If we compare the Sulaiman-Too cave with the Majishan cave paintings, we notice the similarity in the motifs. In the latter, apsaras can be seen showering flowers from heaven. Rare birds and animals are depicted on the walls. One cave ceiling depicts the heavenly horse galloping away. In the Osh cave (which has been turned into a museum), on close examination, the motifs appear like clouds sailing in the sky and flowers being showered from heaven. Some motifs have the form of animals, and there are hundreds of such motifs on the rock walls.

Rock paintings in red and black pigments, point to the fact that the caves were occupied by people who used it as a special place, perhaps for ritual worship. Although there are no sculptures or images of gods, it can be said that the inhabitants did worship some god that occupied the centre of the massive cave.

All over the ceiling and walls of the caves there are impressions of primitive drawings, which on closer scrutiny, appear like some kind of a narrative with the help of animal figures and geometrical drawings and form a backdrop for the central object of the cave. Why else was the huge cave decorated with motifs that appear like flowers being showered from heaven? Or resemble a landscape where men and animals moved about? Did the inhabitants have a story to tell? Did they embellish the caves for a central deity? No one knows. Because no images were found here.

Rock engravings are found all over the mountains and inside the caves. They resemble solar signs. Many are web-like impressions of a hand, perhaps of a deity or a stream of flower petals.

Some of the mountain parts are believed to have healing properties. One can see women sliding along the polished surface of rocks as a cure for infertility. Some of the rocksides have extremely shiny and polished surfaces, a smoothening that has taken place over centuries of pilgrims sliding along them to cure infertility, headaches and backaches. The most dramatic is a huge sloping rock, shaped liked an inclined bed on which barren women slide. While many believe that benevolent spirits living on the rocks bless the pilgrims, others says that sliding on the mountain slope acts like acupressure, activating body hormones and restoring fertility. Standing on the pathway running along the sloping rock, one can see the sprawling Osh mosque that appears to be newly built. Three other mosques are built on the mountains—the Takht-i-Sulaiman mosque, Abdullah Khan mosque and Asaf-ibn-Burkhiya mausoleum.

At the base of the caves are fruit orchards. Here a three-tiered yurt has been set up for visitors. The spacious yurt has its inner walls and floors completely covered with patterned carpets and complete with a heating arrangement in the centre to ensure warmth during winter months.

A Trek to Babur's House

The highpoint of a visit to Osh is a half-day trek to Babur's house atop the Takht-i-Sulaiman. The trek along the hillside to the silver-roofed cave, where Babur is believed to have sometimes sought refuge, is a long one. It was here in the rock shelter of the Bara Koh mountains that Babur often sat alone to ponder over his life and strategy to win back his kingdom.

Not many tourists had reached the top so early in the morning; I was among the few who had. As I climbed, I could see a red flag fluttering atop the mountains in the fierce winds. The incline was steep, and the climb exhausting, but it was fun going to the top. I have always admired Babur and wanted to see every place mentioned in his *Baburnama*. I had already seen Andijan, his birthplace. Now, I was in his refuge. I was elated.

Babur called this place Bara Koh. He mentions that on the summit of the Bara Koh, Sultan Mahmud Khan built a pavilion but further down on the spur of the same mountains Babur himself had built a pavilion in 1496–97. From here, Babur had a bird's-eye view of the entire town and its fringes. When he mentioned the river that 'passes through the area around Osh and goes on to Andijan', he meant the Akbura.

On the lower slopes of the Bara Koh, Babur mentions the Gemini mosque whose outer courtyard was a 'delightful, shady field of clover where every traveller and wayfarer stopped to rest.' He also mentions a 'large main irrigation canal' flowing from the direction of the mountains which channelized the waters of the Akbura for irrigation. During the days of Babur, the Akbura river had gardens on both its banks.[3] We learn about a beautiful red stone with white variegated lines found in the Bara Koh which was used to make knife handles and belt-buckles, among other things. Babur was pleased with the good climate, abundance of water and beautiful spring of Osh: 'In all of Fergana Province no town has air as good as that in Osh'.[4] He also mentions the Osh fortress, of which only a wall and some gates now exist.

Finally, after a long trek, I reached the Takht-i-Sulaiman mosque and sat on its rocky floor. The oval-shaped mosque had a low arched ceiling. Its floor was depressed in the centre and I found myself sliding towards the cave entrance as I sat tightly holding myself against the walls of the small mosque. The maulvi uttered a prayer for me and spoke a smattering of English. He elaborated on the importance Babur accorded this place. There was something so peaceful about the domed sanctuary.

The area along the Akbura river is said to have been the site of the ancient town, dating back to the 3rd century BC. Here, several feet below the modern road, the river snakes through a narrow valley. People were swimming and bathing. Many were playing cards on the banks or just leisurely sunbathing for the perfect tan. Close by was the Jeyma market, one of the largest markets of Central Asia and one that has been running at the same place for centuries. I had to literally push my way through the crowded bylanes to buy fruit and other eatables for the next day's journey.

After spending a day in Osh, I was to leave for the Kyrgyz capital of Bishkek which would be my camping station for a week and from where would begin my foray into Chuy Valley. This was the 'Valley of the Buddha' and the gateway to the region of 'Thousand Springs' traversed by no less a pilgrim than Hiuen Tsang himself on his way to India.

References

1. Khorosh, Yelena. Report on the Assessment Mission to Kyrgyzstan, Tajikistan and Uzbekistan carried out for UNESCO in June–July–August 2006. Site 11: Sulaiman-Too Mountain. Obtained courtesy B. Amanbaeva/Abuseitova. Report submitted in 2010 by the National Commission of the Republic of Kyrgyz to UNESCO. Ref. 5518, p. 6
Also see: UNESCO World Heritage Centre. *Sulaiman-Too: Sacred Mountain.* URL: whc.unesco.org//en/list/1230
2. *Ibid.*
3. Thackston, W.M. *The Baburnama: Memoirs of Babur, Prince and Emperor* (New York: Modern Library, 2002), p. 3-5
4. *Ibid.*, p. 3-5

The Mountain Road to Bishkek

Natasha had warned me of the beautiful but risky mountain journey from Osh to Bishkek; of the falling rocks and landslides; of the high icy cold passes which were filled with snow for six months a year and became dangerous when the snow started melting, deep gorges and the immense yawning valleys. Recently, there had been avalanches, especially on the Toktogul–Bishkek stretch.

I had already travelled through the high altitude of the Himalayas and the Trans-Himalayas while covering the Buddhist sites in Himachal Pradesh, Arunachal Pradesh and Leh–Ladakh. The terrifying rockfalls and mountain slides of the Spiti Valley on the Hindustan–Tibet Road began to haunt me. Fear overtook me. I was in no mood to risk my life and be buried under a large, falling rock. I could choose to fly into Bishkek.

But the adventures of travelling on the roof of the world would be lost. I remembered the Chinese pilgrim's escapades on the icy route to Issyk Kul through the Aksu and Bedel Passes and took strength. Soon I found myself clutching the windows of a rickety van and cruising on the road to Karabalta and Bishkek through high passes and dark, fearsome tunnels. But the scenery was awesome and I thanked myself for ignoring the fervent pleas of Natasha who sat behind, cursing me under her breath.

Any traveller on this route would find M-41 the most beautiful highway in Central Asia despite being detained at mountain passes due to engine failure, burning and bursting tyres and leaking coolants. Such mishaps take one closer to the mountains, to the banks of singing rivers, in the lap of the valleys and provide them the warmth of the local inhabitants.

The road heading towards Tashkomur and Karakol ran along the Uzbek border, hugging the Ferghana ranges and passing through the rich agricultural region of Jalalabad, Bazarkorgan, Massy and Kochkor Ata. The region is popularly known as the food belt of Kyrgyzstan due to its enormous fertility.

The road runs along the lower reaches of the Naryn, hugging the massive Toktogul Reservoir. Here a series of dams have been built to harness hydro power. The road skirts round the massive Toktogul Reservoir. One of the largest manmade lakes on the Naryn has been built for the generation of electricity. The bank of the reservoir is lined with resthouses where meals are served to travellers. The land along the reservoir is fertile and well irrigated. Farmers grow vegetables, crops and cotton.

There is a long line of choykhanas and car-washing and service stations lining the highway. The van stopped here for a while and we get down for some beautiful photos of the mountain scape and a breath of refreshing air. Tea, hot naan and salad had already been laid out on the table for bus passengers. From my perch at the choykhana, I could see the river and vegetable farms. A series of dams had been constructed for the generation of hydro-power.

The road runs northwards as it approaches the beautiful Zoological Reserve fed by the Chychkan river. Here the green meadows weave a life of beauty and wealth. The herders can be seen living inside rail wagons parked on the meadows, their cattle, grazing on the rich pastures. Cream, milk, cheese and dried yoghurt balls are sold in large quantities along the highway.

The road swings up and down as it reaches the mountain passes at Otmok and the Too Ashuu. From the top of the pass, one can see the vast expanse of the valley and the road threading between the mountains. One can find many vehicles piled up by the roadside after suffering from tyre bursts.

The smell of burning rubber and smoke suddenly started

spreading inside the van and passengers panicked. The driver stopped the van just outside the tunnel and noticed that the tyres were heated and smoke was emanating from them. The journey had to be halted for the tyres to cool down. To prevent the tyres from burning, the van had to be stopped at several points of the mountainous route.

At several points on the highway, protective road coverings have been built along mountainsides to prevent falling rocks from hitting the vehicles. Deep tunnels have been cut into the mountains to reduce the distance between Bishkek and Osh. The 3-kilometre long mountain tunnel of Atin Dagi, boring through the Kyrgyz Alatoo at a height of over 2500 metres, is a manmade wonder. It is said to be one of the longest mountain tunnels of Central Asia.

The scenery is picturesque as the highway runs between high mountains and along the bubbling rivers. Many vehicles lose their coolants even before entering the mountains. Here, as I had feared, the coolant came pouring out even before the mountain journey had begun. It seemed to be a major catastrophe as we had yet to cover nearly 600 kilometres of the journey. The driver rushed to the Karabalta river with a can, and fetched some river water which was poured into the cooling tank. To my surprise, the bus ran more smoothly than before.

The road further runs into the large city of Karabalta. It lies on the Karabalta river by the same name on the northern slopes of the Kyrgyz Alatoo in the western part of the Chu province on the Bishkek–Taraz Road. Karabalta is a prosperous town due to its uranium processing industry. Uranium was brought here for processing from the mountains of Kazakhstan and Kyrgyzstan during Soviet times.

At Karabalta, the M-41 splits from the M-39, 60 kilometres west from Bishkek. The M-39 highway continues towards the Kazakh city of Taraz and goes on to the Uzbek capital of Tashkent. Another branch turns south towards M-41 highway, running for almost 700 kilometres through mountains, across rivers and along beautiful meadows to reach Jalalabad and Osh.

The 60-kilometre drive from Karabalta to Bishkek goes through the small but famous town of Sokuluk. The town lies 30 kilometres west of Bishkek and stands at the mouth of the Sokuluk river passing through a valley that leads up to the Sokuluk Pass at over 3000 metres.

It was from a mound in Sokuluk that the image of Avalokitesvara was found. The deity wore a gem-laden crown with a protuberance in the centre, which was possibly a small image of a deity. The sitting posture of the bodhisattva is unique. While one hand bestows flowers, the other rests on his thighs. The deity's lotus throne is missing.

As is true for all travellers passing through Kyrgyzstan, the capital city of Bishkek forms the most important halting station for a peep into the various museums of antiquities, where objects excavated from the Silk Road have been showcased. In Bishkek, I set about cruising through the streets, soaking in the flavours of *shora* (a national non-alcoholic drink made of roasted grains) and the beauty of the splendid Oak Park, Alatoo Square, Philharmonic and the Victory Square.

In the evening, I returned to my hotel to rest and prepare for a really long and exciting journey to the Silk Road sites along the Chu river and the famous Issyk Kul Lake.

Known as the Switzerland of the East, this beautiful country in the heart of Central Asia rests in the lap of the heavenly mountains of the Tien Shan and the Pamirs. Here, I seemed to forget the travails of my journey through the desert and steppe lands. I was here to look for the enchanting Buddhas that had lived in the meadowlands along the Chu river a long, long time ago.

References

For Route M-41 Highway see, Lawrence, Mitchell. *Kyrgyzstan: The Bradt Travel Guide* (Connecticut, England: The Globe Pequot Press Inc., 2008), p. 240

Chuy: The Valley of the Buddha

In Bishkek, I lost no time in reaching the State Historical Museum, the biggest in Kyrgyzstan. And here I hoped to see the gallery of the Buddha and bodhisattva Avalokitesvara and numerous other deities recovered in the ancient cities of the Chuy Valley by Kyrgyz and Russian scientists and explorers.

Chuy was the valley of the Buddha where lay some of the historic cities of the Buddhist world—Krasnayarechka, Novopokrovka, Suyab (Ak-Beshim), Balasagun, Sokuluk, to name a few.

Krasnayarechka was made famous by the discovery of the Great Reclining Buddha image from the corridor of a shrine and also a gigantic 'Sitting Buddha'; Suyab's name was etched in the diary of no less a traveller than the Chinese pilgrim Hiuen Tsang who halted there on his way to India; Balasagun earned the epithet 'Gobalik' or the 'good city' by no other than Genghis Khan. Excavations at Novopokrovka brought to light Buddhist figurines and structures from what could have possibly been a monastery. And few would have imagined the beauty of the bejewelled Avalokitesvara of Sokuluk wearing large flaming ornaments and a lotus-shaped headgear. The cities flourished as great Buddhist centres of art and learning in the heart of Asia.

The sacred valley of the Chuy river was the place where the Ekdasa-mukha (eleven-headed) Avalokitesvara was worshipped. Here Buddhist preachers were revered and their images carved in stones. Numerous images of the Buddha and bodhisattvas were recovered from the above sites during excavations by Kyrgyz and Russian scientists.

A Legacy of Turks

The Buddhist legacy of the Chuy Valley belonged to the Turks who were greatly influenced by the teachings of the Buddha. During the middle of the 6th century, the western Turks are said to have been in control of the rich Chuy Valley and where they set up their capital at Suyab. Apart from the beauty of its land and a fine weather, the valley had abundant water from the Chuy and its tributaries and river wealth in the form of fish, black fertile soil that gave abundant crops of red millet and grapes, and enormous pastures for the rearing of domestic animals.

Most importantly, the Silk Road passed through the Chuy Valley and the Turks controlled the traffic of goods passing through their capital cities. All caravans coming from China in the east passed through the Chuy Valley in order to move to the Caspian or the Aral Sea regions and to enter the Caucasus, the Black Sea and the Mediterranean regions. Caravans from India had a choice of routes into the Chuy Valley. They could join the Kashgar route through the Pamirs or take the Yarkand route into Kashgar. They could alternatively join the Balkh route through Termez, Samarkand and Tashkent and through Shymkent eastwards into the Talas and the Chuy Valleys.

Margit Koves in *Buddhism among the Turks of Central Asia* gives us detailed information about the spread of Buddhism among the Turks. It is said that the Khan of the Turks, Topo Khagan (AD 572–581), son of Bumyn, came under the influence of Buddhist monk Hui-lin of North Ts'ou. We also learn that the Gandharan monk Jinagupta stayed for some time with Topo Khagan and, along with some lamas, translated the sutras for him. There followed a spate of monastery building in the land of the Turks and the translation of Buddhist sutras into Turkish.[1]

There was an inflow of Buddhism into the land of the Turks

during the period of the Chinese–Turkish alliance, when much intermingling and intermarriages took place between the Turks and the Chinese. The Turks were also in alliance with the Tibetans during the first quarter of the 8th century, when the Tibetans wrested control of the Chinese trade routes of the Tarim Basin.[2]

It is said that in the monasteries and settlements of Central Asia (including those in the Chuy Valley), Sanskrit texts were translated into Chinese, Khotanese, Tocharian, Sogdian and Tibetan.[3] The *Nirvana-sutra* and *Suvarnaprabhasa-sutra* were some of the famous sutras that were translated by scholar monks in these monasteries. Says Koves, not only were the monks and nuns supposed to know Sanskrit and recite their confessions in Sanskrit, but the laymen were also expected to know enough Sanskrit so that the titles of holy works and certain Buddhist terms did not become corrupted.[4]

A Big Shock

But here I was in for a great shock that brought tears rolling down my face and caused much pain in my heart. I was totally at a loss for words as I shook hands with the museum staff. The most prestigious State Historical Museum of Kyrgyzstan did not display either the Reclining Buddha of Krasnaya, which I learnt had been taken away in pieces by the Hermitage, or the recently unearthed 'Sitting Buddha' from Krasnaya. Barring the head of the Ak-beshim Buddha and some temple decorations, no Buddhist antiquities from the Chuy Valley could be seen in the galleries of the museum.

I was informed that most Buddhist antiquities had been stored in the locker room of the museum and it was not open to the public. There was thus no question of photographing them. The kind museum director, however, paid heed to my pleas and permitted me to take photos of the Buddha from a booklet. It carried a photo of the Ak-Beshim (Suyab) 'Crowned Buddha' portrayed in a 'tribhanga' posture of a dancer and a few other Buddhist antiquities. But the myriad Buddhas of the Chuy Valley had no place even in the museum brochure and this too, was not for sale at the sales counter. Totally dejected, I turned my attention to another museum—that of the Kyrgyz Russian Slavic University. Here the museum was locked. I was told by the guide to visit the site museums at Suyab (Ak Beshim), Krasnaya Rechka, Novopokrovka and Balasaghun where some Buddhist antiquities might be displayed. Strictly following the guide's advice, I made a dash to the ancient villages in the Chuy Valley.

The Road to Novopokrovka

It was barely 6 a.m. when I took the road eastwards from Bishkek. There was hardly any traffic at this hour. Passing along the village of Novopokrovka and turning left onto the village road, I drove for a few kilometres inside the village expecting to find some vestiges of the ancient city where excavations had been carried out by archaeologists and Buddhist antiquities unearthed. Having failed in my effort to find the excavation site, I returned to the highway.

I was informed that, formerly, on the ancient Buddhist site of Novopokrovka, on the road to Tokmok, stood an arts centre. Attention was drawn to the existence of ancient ruins when the floor of the arts centre started to sink suddenly. The art centre building was demolished and excavations started at the site in 2004 under the supervision of Phillip Rott, professor at the Russian–Kyrgyz Slavic University and supported by the Swiss Society for the Exploration of Eurasia.

According to a report by the Society for the Exploration of Eurasia (president Dr Christopher Baumer), archaeologists previously digging at this site in 1965 and 1966 discovered several small Buddhist objects, including a stone relief 'in the Gandharan style', the head of the Buddha made of clay, as well as bronze Buddhist figurines.[5] Based on the findings of the site, one can assume that Novopokrovka had a Buddhist building, possibly a monastery. A small statuette of the Sitting Buddha from Novopokrovka, was found in 1965.

According to a report of the National Academy of Sciences at Bishkek and photos provided to me by an Indian Embassy staffer Bhargav Mitra, rare bronze images of bodhisattvas were found at the site. The adorned Boshisattvas sit on stylized lotus thrones. They wear peculiar pointed crowns and hold in one hand a pot of sweet nectar—the nectar of life with which they healed and nourished mankind. In the other hand is an object which appears to be a Vajra or a thunderbolt. The deity's elongated throne is a kind of pin which could have been held in the niche of an altar.

To Krasnaya Rechka

I followed the road running along the Chuy river. It is the longest river in Kyrgyzstan and is formed by the confluence of the Joon, Aryk and Kochkor in the district of Naryn and on its way draws abundant waters from hundreds of tributaries that mingle joyously with it. As the river flows through the valley, it forms the border between Kyrgyzstan and Kazakhstan for more than a 100 kilometres. Within this flat valley are situated the Kyrgyz capital of Bishkek and the Kazak city of Shu.

As I proceeded further into the valley, on my left was the Chuy river, the natural boundary with Kazakhstan. On the way, hidden behind a beautiful garden with tall trees and a stream flowing by, was Cafe B—famous for its hummus and baked trout. Then followed a long stretch of waterway surrounded by wild grass and interspersed with a profusion of pink flowers. Natasha informed me about the bounties of the Chuy river and its tributaries in the form of its splendid varieties of fish. This is true for all mountain rivers of Kyrgyzstan; famous among the various species of fish found here are the rainbow trout, the Osman and the Amu Darya trout. Trout is the predominant species in the Kyrgyz rivers and popular fishing tours are organized along the Chuy and its tributaries.

Thirty kilometres from Novopokrovka, on the road to Balykchy, lay the village of Krasnaya Rechka (Red river). The village rose to fame when a Buddhist complex was unearthed and images of a gigantic, 8-metre-long Reclining Buddha in Nirvana and a Sitting Buddha were discovered by the excavating team of the Academy of Sciences of Kyrgyzstan.

In ancient times, this Silk Road settlement was called Navekat—a flourishing trade centre from the 6th to the 12th centuries and one of the largest settlements of the Chuy Valley. Lying on the banks of the Red river or the Krasnaya Rechka, the village was placed strategically on the trade route passing through the Chuy Valley. This was a region which formed a belt where not only abundant crops grew due to extensive irrigation but it was also a place for production of high quality wool.

Two ancient highways met in the valley—one coming along the northern banks of the lake which gathered tributary pathways from the south and eastern regions of Kazakhstan and another running along the southern banks of the lake which gathered the tributary roads from across the Tarim Basin and Kashmir.

Krasnaya, was thus directly linked to the Tarim region of Aksu, Kuqa, Kashgar and Yarkand of the present-day Xinjiang province of China and to the Kashmir and Ladakh region of northern India via routes through the Karakoram ranges. The village was a trading hub where Buddhist preachers found fertile soil for the spread of the message of the Buddha. The wealthy town set up rich temples endowed with gigantic images of the Buddha, employing artistes to decorate the temples.

It is said that site was accidently discovered by a farmer who while ploughing his field struck into a gold burial mask. Late archaeological explorations in the area revealed a Buddhist temple with the remains of monumental Reclining Buddha of clay, said to be originally painted red. Some images of bodhisattvas were discovered in another corridor. These all are now in the Hermitage Museum in St Petersburg.

At the Village

A narrow tarred road ran inside the village for a few kilometres along corn fields, took a right turn, and ended in front of a couple of yellow brick houses. It seemed to be a thinly populated village with only a few houses, the habitation surrounded by vast fields fringed by a thick forest line of oak and poplars.

The village had woken up. The cattle were driven out for grazing. They were followed by huge dogs and men on horseback. They ran up the grassy hills in search of pasture. A small tractor was roaring away in a field and in a cloud of dust, a flock of yellow-necked cranes dived into the freshly dug earth.

However, almost all sides of the village appeared to be surrounded by low hills or earth mounds which were possibly ruins of ancient settlements. The village must have been a prosperous one considering the number of settlements indicated by the low hills. Up the mounds ran undulating pathways to the flat top where ancient walls and mud structures of a massive citadel had been unearthed during excavations.

The unpaved road bent around a mound and ended at a signpost which pointed to the excavated citadel atop a mud hill. It was dated to 7th–12th century AD. A large part of the citadel was, however, still under earth. The excavated structures appeared to be large halls and corridors, some opening into rooms on a lower level, indicating that the citadels might be a double-story structure. Clay and unburnt bricks peeped out of the walls revealing a sturdy structure inside. One particularly large opening that led from the foot of the hill appeared to have been used as the gateway to the citadel.

Another hill arose at the far end of the village. On top of this hill were mud structures propped up by iron pillars under a shed. Walking down from the citadel hill, I crossed stubby fields and thin streams to reach the second hill over which the shed had been erected. This was the second Buddhist temple belonging to 7th–8th century AD. It had been fenced by the Archaeology Department of the Academy of Sciences. Beyond the fence lay a huge stupa–like structure and a high altar. By the side of the locked gate was a small passage that had been left open for single entry, and soon I was inside the temple.

This was the sanctuary from where the massive 8-metre-long sculpture of the Reclining Buddha was discovered from a 10-metre-long pedestal.[6] The image lies at the Hermitage in a broken condition. From a photograph sent by the Hermitage to me for use in this book, one can clearly see the folds of the robe that covered the lower half of the body. The wooden armature used for creating the clay image is visible. As in all clay images, this too, was built over a wooden frame.

In *New Findings of the Indo-Buddhist Culture in Kyrgyzstan*, V.D. Goryacheva dwelt in detail upon the findings of Buddhist sculptures in Krasnaya Rechka. He mentions that in the western corridor of the sanctuary were found fragments of paintings with drawings of flowers, volutes and pearls. In another corner in the south-western part of the sanctuary was found a niche where a small ganch mould for making the ringlets of the Buddha head, some coins dating back to the second half of the 8th century and a cowrie were found.[7]

In one of the galleries, clay fragments of the left foot and hand belonging to a large statue of the Buddha were found. The dimensions of the fragments of the limbs allowed the archaeologists to estimate that the height of the statue of the 'Sitting Buddha' was up to 6 metres. Images of bodhisattvas were found in the southern corridor and at the sanctuary entrance.[8]

Other discoveries at the site included a birchbark manuscript written in the Brahmi script in Sanskrit language.[9] These were treasured relics and objects of worship in the Buddhist sanctuaries of Central Asia. Krasnaya was no exception. Passing monks and pilgrims who halted at the Buddhist centres offered scrolls of Buddhist sutra written in Sanskrit as an invocation to the Buddhist deities. Rolls of Buddhist sutras or tablets were also sealed inside hollow images and votive stupas.

Under the metallic shed, the thick clay walls rise to meet the roof. The mud structure resembles a clay stupa whose sides had caved in. But it was actually a large hall whose clay walls once enclosed a Buddhist shrine. A wide circamambulatory path went around the shrine inside which an image of the Reclining Buddha had once been installed. An altar had been built into one of the walls where worshippers offered prayers and gifts for the Buddha.

One wall of the Buddhist temple was thicker than the others and it seemed as if it held the main image of the gigantic Buddha. The alignment of the temple appeared to be in line with the citadel and it must have once been a part of the citadel.

Monk with a Bodhi Sapling

Among the various images found at the site of Krasnaya was a rare cast bronze sculpture with traces of gilding. This discovery stokes the fire of one's imagination. The image published by V. Goryacheva in *New Findings of the Indo-Buddhist Culture in Kyrgyzstan (India and Central Asia Pre-Islamic)* is depicted as a preacher or a 'Buddhist monk'.[10] He seems to have arrived in the village (or the country of the Turks) with the branch of the Bodhi tree. The preacher/monk wears a headgear decorated with the image of a deity, perhaps that of the Buddha, indicating that the wearer was a Buddhist 'dhammmaduta or mahamatta' (Buddhist preacher) carrying the message of the Buddha.

The 'sanghati' or monk's robe covers his body and falls up to the knees. He holds an akshamala (rosary) in one hand. A heavy necklace with a pendant falls on his chest. He holds what appears to be a sapling with a small leaves. Considering that the image is that of a Buddhist teacher or a monk, it brings to mind the possibility that the leafy branch could be that of the sacred Bodhi tree at Bodh Gaya, where the Great Buddha attained Enlightenment. It could also allude to a branch of the Bodhi tree carried by Mauryan Emperor Asoka's son, Mahindra, to Sri Lanka for the propagation of the faith. It also alludes to the despatch of the mahamattas and dhammadutas (religious messengers of Asoka) to countries far and wide, including Central Asia. It also goes to prove that the craftsmen and monks living at the monastic settlements of the Chuy Valley were aware of the Buddha's Enlightenment under the Bodhi tree.

The Bodhi tree at Bodh Gaya (India) was regarded as sacred not only in the Chuy Valley but also in the monasteries of Russian Siberia (belonging to the 16th/17th centuries), where among the Buddhist relics are remnants of the sacred Bodhi tree believed to have been cultivated from the seeds of the holy Bodhi tree at Bodh Gaya.

Archaeologists from the Kyrgyz Academy of Sciences and the Russian Hermitage Museum in St Petersburg have unearthed another massive clay sculpture of the Buddha at Krasnaya Rechka village. The Buddha, measuring between 1.5 to 2 metres high, was found in the sitting lotus position and has been dated between the 8th and 10th centuries AD.[11]

Today, most images of the Buddha can be seen only on paper. The great wealth of Kyrgyzstan lies at the Hermitage Museum, St Petersburg. The image of the 8-metre-long Reclining Buddha from Krasnaya Rechka village is away from the land where it belonged. The 12-metre-long Reclining Buddha recovered by archaeologists from the Vakhsh river valley from the site of Ajina Tepe is now the only Nirvana Buddha of Central Asia. It adorns the National Museum of Dushanbe. These Buddhas are tangible. You can see and touch them only in the museum. But Buddha as a thought lives eternally in the Chuy Valley. Time can never obliterate Buddha from history, or from the minds of believers.

References

1. Koves, Margit. *Buddhism among the Turks of Central Asia* (New Delhi: International Academy of Indian Culture and Aditya Prakashan, 2009), p. 33
2. *Ibid.*, p. 31-33
3. *Ibid.*, p. 9
4. *Ibid.*, p. 9
5. Baumer, Christopher. Report on Excavations at Novopokrovka by Society for the Exploration of Eurasia
6. Jansen, Michael. *Kyrgyzstan-Krasnaya Rechka: Heritage at Risk*

(Germany, Kyrgyzstan: ICOMOS, 2005)

Goryacheva, V.D. 'New Findings of the Indo-Buddhist Culture in Kyrgyzstan'. Rtveladze, E., (chief coordinator). *India and Central Asia Pre-Islamic* (Tashkent: Academy of Arts and Academy of Sciences of the Republic of Uzbekistan, 2000), p. 99-106. Illustrations by Goryachev, V.D., p. 99

7. Goryacheva, V.D. 'New Findings of the Indo-Buddhist Culture in Kyrgyzstan'. Rtveladze, E. (chief coordinator). *India and Central Asia Pre-Islamic* (Tashkent: Academy of Arts and Academy of Sciences of the Republic of Uzbekistan, 2000), p. 99-106. Illustrations by Goryachev, V.D., p. 99

8. *Ibid.*, p. 283-288

9. Jansen, Michael. *Kyrgyzstan-Krasnaya Rechka: Heritage at Risk* (Germany, Kyrgyzstan: ICOMOS, 2005) p. 165

    Raina, Radha. *Beyond Legend Cultural Convergences India and Kyrgyzstan* (New Delhi: RHI Printographics Pvt. Ltd., 2007), p. 63

    Goryacheva, V.D. 'New Findings of the Indo-Buddhist Culture in Kyrgyzstan'. Rtveladze, E. (chief coordinator). *India and Central Asia Pre-Islamic* (Tashkent: Academy of Arts and Academy of Sciences of the Republic of Uzbekistan, 2000), p. 99-106. Illustrations by Goryachev, V.D., p. 283-288

10. Goryacheva, V.D. 'New Findings of the Indo-Buddhist Culture in Kyrgyzstan'. Rtveladze, E. (chief coordinator). *India and Central Asia Pre-Islamic* (Tashkent: Academy of Arts and Academy of Sciences of the Republic of Uzbekistan, 2000), p. 99-106. Illustrations by Goryachev, V.D., p. 283-288, 101

11. Dr Kolchenko Valery. Speaking at the International Scientific Conference: '40 Years of South Kazakhstan Comprehensive Archaeological Expedition: Results and Prospects for Research, Restoration of Objects of the Excavation, the Issues Museumfication Monuments, tourism development'. Organized at Otrar by the A.K. Margulan Institute of Archaeology, Academy of Sciences, Republic of Kazakhstan. 18-19 October 2011

    State Hermitage Museum. 'Unique Findings of the Tian Shan

Expedition of the State Hermitage' (Petersberg: Krasnaya Site, News archive, 2011)
Press TV, 'Buddha Statue Found Near Kyrgyz Capital'. 19 July 2011, TE/MMAs

[I was provided important photographs of the Buddha and bodhisattvas from the Chuy Valley by Professor Bakyt Amanbaeva and Dr Elena Popova of the Academy of Sciences, Republic of Kyrgyzstan, and Bhargav Mitra of the Indian embassy at Bishkek.]

To Ak-Beshim and Balasaghun

The 60-kilometre drive to Ak-Beshim goes through green meadows, cultivated fields, and over numerous streams that bring snow water to the vast expanse of pasturelands. On the way lies Tokmok, which is a town peopled with Kyrgyz and Russians who have lived here for generations. From Tokmok, the road turns right, and an ancient mosque with a silver dome comes into view. The road swings to the right and left, up and down till we come upon an area full of high mounds, some covered with grass, others left exposed after digging. On approaching the Ak-Beshim site, we notice an ancient cemetery on our left and the beautiful snow peaks of the Tien Shan right before us.

At the village of Ak-Beshim, the wheat is about to be harvested. At several places, tall grass has completely covered the high mounds of earth that once must have been residential quarters of the inhabitants, Christian churches or perhaps Buddhist Viharas that are still awaiting the spade of archaeologists. The numerous mounds give ample evidence of a large flourishing city in the Chuy Valley. The modern inhabitants of Ak-Beshim—among whom many are Russians—live in an old colony, a few kilometres from the excavation site. My friend Vladimir Alexandrovich is one of them.

Before going to Vladimir's house, in the Russian colony nearby, we walked to one of the high mounds where a board announced the settlement of Suyab. This Silk Road trading town arose as one of the largest settlements of the Sogdian merchants along the river

Ab, a tributary of the Chuy (or Chuy/Suy) hence became known as the Chuy yab or Suyab.

Hiuen Tsang's encounter with Khan

In the *Si Yu Ki*, Hiuen Tsang mentions Suyab—probably the first city visited by the pilgrim after turning northwards from Aksu in the Tarim Basin and crossing the Tien Shan mountains to reach the Issyk Kul Lake region. Following the southern borders of the lake in a north-west direction, Hiuen Tsang came to Suyab, where he encountered the Khan of the Western Turks called Yeh-hu who was then on a hunting expedition. The Khan's chief officer Ta-mo-chi, we are told, conducted him to a large tent and arranged for his comfort. After three days, the Khan returned from hunting and took the pilgrim inside his tent, which was a large pavilion adorned with glittering golden flower ornaments.[1]

When Hiuen Tsang reached Suyab in 629, he did not see any citadel or Buddhist temple. However, we learn of the wealth of Suyab from his descriptions of the fine horses and the silk, satin, fur and hair garments of the Khan and his courtiers. Glittering flower ornaments made of gold adorned the pavilion of the Khan. The pilgrim was presented numerous pieces of silk and vestments. A rich meal of honey, cream and sugar was brought for the pilgrim, and a large quantity of wine and music accompanied the wine-drinking session of the Turks. The pilgrim mentions in detail everything that happened during his meeting with the Turkic Khagan. But he did not mention the temple. The Buddhist temple (dated to the end of the 7th or 8th century) was possibly built after the Khan converted to the Buddhist faith after hearing the discourses of the Chinese pilgrim.

Prior to this, we learn that the Turks, whom Hiuen Tsang met, were 'fire-worshippers' and did not use wooden seats because wood was inflammable. Instead, they spread padded mats on the ground for seating. When everyone was seated, the Khan ordered that wine be offered to the sound of music. While the Khan and his ministers drank wine, Tsang was offered grape juice. Soon, boiled quarters of mutton and veal were brought for the gathering but Hiuen Tsang was served 'rice cakes, cream, sugar-candy, honey-sticks, raisins'.[2]

The Khan was apparently receptive to the teachings of the Buddha. Expounding the doctrines of the Buddhist faith, Hiuen Tsang spoke on the 'Ten Precepts', preservation of life, the 'Paramitas' (perfections) and steps to final deliverance. Raising his hands, the Khan is said to have humbly prostrated himself on the ground and joyously accepted the teachings of the Master.[3]

Crowned Buddha

A rare image of a beautiful Crowned Buddha made of bronze and inlaid with copper and silver, depicted somewhat in the posture of a dancing Siva, was recovered from the Suyab site and now adorns the State Historical Museum. The Buddha has been dated to the 6th–7th century AD. The Buddha in the Tribhangasana[4] or the triple-bent position of the body, resembling a dancer, was found to be decorated with silver and copper. It is the traditional pose in which Indian deities are portrayed namely, Lord Krishna, who plays the flute while standing in Tribhangasana. The eyes and urna (circular mark on the forehead or the third eye) are inlaid with silver while the lips are inlaid with copper. Massive earrings or kundalas hang from the ears and the neck is clasped by a necklace made of large pearls. There are bracelets on the slender arms and kangans (bangles) on the hands. The sanghati (robe) seems to be translucent and wraps around the body, leaving the right shoulder uncovered.

The Buddha is seldom depicted in such heavy jewellery, although the bodhisattva Avalokitesvara, as we see him in the galleries of the National Museum, Delhi, appears beautifully bejewelled. The image found at Ak-Beshim resembles the bejewelled image of Avalokitesvara from Dunhuang. The posture of Tribhangasana is rarely used for depicting the Buddha but may be used to depict the Avalokitesvara as in some paintings from Dunhuang which are displayed at the National Museum, Delhi.

Excavations at the site were carried out by L.R. Kyzlasov, historian-archaeologist (Moscow State University), and the shrine was dated to the end of 7th and early 8th century AD when the control of the region had been taken over by the Chinese Tang dynasty.[5] Located some 250 metres east of the first shrine, another Buddhist shrine was discovered by L.P. Zyablin, archaeologist and explorer of the Ak-Beshim site.[6] Along with the two Buddhist shrines was found a Zoroastrian cemetery and a necropolis and two Nestorian churches that provide evidence of flourishing Christianity in the Semirechye region.[7]

The finds at Suyab also include medallions of the seated Buddha. A stone image of a bodhisattva carved in relief is displayed in the upper hall of the State Historical Museum. Another image of a preaching Buddha carved in stone is flanked by his disciples and appears similar to the one found at Fayaz Tepe near Termez. The Buddha sits on a lotus throne. Below the blooming lotus are seen two lions worshipping the stupa.

Most of the ruined rooms at Suyab were found decorated with remnants of wall paintings, fragments of which showed traces of gold,[8] perhaps pasted by pilgrims. Even today pilgrims to Buddhist temples paste gold foil on the images.

At the House of Vladimir

Vladimir, a native of Ak-Beshim, had invited us to a sumptuous breakfast of rose and peach jam that his wife had prepared. I still feel hungry at the thought. On way to Vladimir's cottage, I noticed vestiges of a modern past—a statue of Lenin waving to the fields and old houses and a defunct Chinese paper factory.

Vladimir's cottage looked straight out of a fairytale. Flowering bougainvilleas arched over the wooden gate, as did branches of cherries and wild pink roses. As I admired the beauty of the old gate, a huge dog leapt out and started barking at us. Vladimir told me that he had been out of the town for a week and the dog was very happy at his master's return. On hearing the loud barking, a beautiful woman came out to take a look. She was Vladimir's wife. She welcomed us graciously. There was a shaded porch at the back entrance of the house covered by vine creepers from which large bunches of grapes were hanging. There was also a pet corner where huge black cats were growling at us. We entered the house and took a seat in the dining room. The room had lead pipes to carry heated water during the winter months when the temperature dips below freezing point. Soon, Mrs Vladimir brought out a tray full of cakes and bread with different kinds of jams and jelly prepared at home. I felt so relaxed in the cosy cottage that I plonked on a sofa and fell into a short nap.

To the Ruined City of Balasagun

After our tasty and filling breakfast (and my short nap) we drove through mustard fields, cotton-growing areas and villages with low-roofed wooden and mud houses, to reach Balasagun, barely a few kilometres from Suyab. We parked our vehicle under the shade of a tree and walked down a gravelled path leading to the Burana Tower, a large minaret in the Chuy Valley and the ancient ruins of the 6th-century city of Balasagun.

Like Suyab, Balasagun was among the 10 major Sogdian colonies (under the protection of the Turks) discovered in the Chuy Valley by Russian archaeologist A.N. Bernshtam.[9] Since the early centuries of the Christian era, Sogdians were successful merchants who organized trade between Sogdiana and China. They set up colonies along the Silk Road. As such, there were many Sogdian colonies in the river valleys through which their caravans passed along the Silk Routes. According to Mariko Namba Walters (editor, *Sino Platonic Papers*), these Sogdians were not only 'carriers of goods but were also cultural transmitters of many religions such as Buddhism, Zoroastrianism, Manichaeism, and Nestorian Christianity'.[10]

The ancient city of Balasagun lay at the foot of the tributary river valleys of the Chuy—the Shamsy and the Kegeti on the road going eastwards to China. It was one of the big cities of the Silk Road and one of the largest towns of Semirechye or the Seven Rivers region. A fertile and rich region irrigated by numerous streams, it lay at the end of a day's march from Suyab.

Here lived a population that was believed to have been predominantly Buddhist and Christian until the ruling Khan converted to Islam and made it a state religion. Thus in the 10th and 11th centuries, Balasagun saw the construction of its first mosque and the minaret on the ruins of earlier temples and churches. History would have us believe that at the beginning of the 10th century, Islam was adopted by the Karakhanid ruler Satuk Bogra Khan who proclaimed it as the state religion in AD 960. Gradually, the new religion spread among the populace.[11]

Several earthquakes through the centuries caused much damage to the mosque and the 46-metre-high minaret, reducing its size to half. The structure of the mosque appears to have been totally ruined but the minaret still exists as the Burana Tower.

A few yards from the minaret lie the high mounds of the ruins of the ancient city of Balasagun. The fragments of gold foil, still visible on some walls of the ruins, which were pasted by pilgrims to the site, show that the excavated structure is regarded as an ancient temple. The practice of offering gold to deities still continues at many temples in India and China, especially at the Buddhist shrines where pilgrims paste gold and silver foil on the central image of the Buddha; they are offered in the belief that Buddhist relics might be lying buried under the ruins or that the ruins belong to an ancient Buddhist shrine.

Only a part of the ancient city has been excavated. The small hill with the ruins was found to conceal a palace and a temple complex which existed before the Karakhanids built the new town.

It is said that the Sacred Mountain of Balasagun along the Chuy river had been under the control of the western Turks who followed the cult of the sacred mountains which they believed to be their ruler's seat of power. And for the Turks in Semirechye, the mountains of Balasagun were as sacred as the Sulaiman-Too in the city of Osh. Such sacred mountains possessed various cult objects and were the highpoints of the cultural landscape.[12] The cult of the sacred mountains has existed not only in Kyrgyzstan but also in India where the Himalayas were revered as the abode of Siva; in China, the Mount Emei (Si Chuyan province) where bodhisattva Samantabhadra is believed to have resided; and in Tibet, where the holy Mount Kailash is considered as the abode of Siva.

Balbals or Stone Images

Just outside the Balasagun temple or palace complex are a group of stone images with human faces, called balbals, said to be gravestones dating from the 6th century when the western Turks lived in the region. According to the literature provided by the site museum, the stone carvings located at Burana Tower are tombstones serving as monumental memorials to honour deceased warriors.[13] The balbals are believed to have appeared on the territory of Kyrgyzstan from the middle of the 6th century, following the establishment of the first Turkic Khanate. This Khanate incorporated Tian Shan, Semirechye and part of East Turkestan. Since then, ancient Turkic people began to settle in the region, bringing with them their burial customs, especially the tradition of constructing stone sculptures in memory of their ancestors.[14]

Today, rock carvings from Chuy, Issyk Kul and Naryn oblasts can be seen at the open air museum in Burana. Among the carvings, one can clearly distinguish sculptures of men carrying vessels in their hands. What do these vessels hold? Do they symbolize offerings of food and drinks for the deceased? Are the balbals divine spirits guarding the graves, not very different from the strange animal figures which we notice at the burial chambers in Turfan?

Ekdasa-mukha Avalokitesvara

Like Dunhuang, the Chuy Valley was the place where the eleven-headed Avalokitesvara was worshipped. A beautiful image of an eleven-headed Avalokitesvara, cast in bronze with gilding, dating between the 12th and 14th centuries, has been recovered from the valley. The image appears to have a close analogy with the paintings of the eleven-headed Avalokitesvara displayed in the National Museum Delhi at the gallery of Avalokitesvara paintings brought from Dunhuang by Aurel Stein.

In several paintings, Avalokitesvara has been depicted with more than one head (the count ranged from eight to 11 heads). Ekdasa-mukha Avalokitesvara or the eleven-headed Avalokitesvara has 11 heads arranged in a pyramidal sequence. The topmost head is that of Amitabha. The 11 heads and 11 pairs of eyes symbolize that the deity 'sees every object, destroys every evil and bestows benediction on all living things'.[15] The Avalokitesvara holds a jug of sweet nectar, perhaps the heavenly 'somrasa' which only the immortals drink. He holds aloft the thunderbolt or vajra of Indra and the lotus of the 'True Law'. In some paintings, the deity holds the sun and the moon. In others, he has the attributes of God Siva holding tridents in both hands.

According to Lokesh Chandra, the legend behind the 11 heads is that the bodhisattva once descended into hell, converted the wicked, liberated them, and conducted them to the Sukhavati of his spiritual father, Amitabha. But for every wicked person thus converted another sprang up to take his place. In grief at the extent of wickedness in the world, Avalokitesvara's head split into 10 pieces. Amitabha turned each piece into a head and placed them on the body of Avalokitesvara in three tiers of three each with the tenth head on top and his own image above them all.[16] Chandra further elaborates that the 10 heads symbolize the 'synthesis of space' and explains that 'the spatial perfections go back as early as the Saddharma-pundarika (Lotus sutra) where Avalokitesvara has been termed samanta-mukha which means facing all directions'.

At another instance, he explains that the 10 heads represent the Ten Paramitas (perfections) and the eleventh head is the attainment of Enlightenment.

The Chuy Valley was the valley of the Buddha. The Buddha lived and breathed in the numerous shrines and monasteries along the river. In one of the monasteries, he breathed his last, and attained Nirvana. The 8-metre-long image of the Reclining Buddha was built in memory of that moment at Kushinagar—a moment when his teachings became a lamp unto the inhabitants of the sacred valley. The Turks, newly enamoured of the faith, built temples and monasteries whose ruins we now see and from where great many images have been recovered. The powerful empire of the Turks saw both peace and power in the Buddha.

It was a valley through which the Buddha's messengers—the monk scholars—travelled with trade caravans and preached the Wisdom and Perfection of the Buddha. Under their influence, the Turks built monasteries where they sang Buddhist sutras. The travelling monks, like Monk Jinagupta of Gandhara, had the privilege of staying at the Turkish courts to preach and translate the Buddhist sutras.

Even formidable mountains, rivers and treacherous piles of ice on high passes could not hold back links between the Chuy Valley and India. The threads of the Silk Road routes wound closely with the land of the Buddha.

References

1. Hwui Li, Shaman and Beal, Samuel (trans.). *The Life of Hieun-Tsiang* (Delhi: D.K. Publishers Distributors Pvt. Ltd., 2001), p. 42
2. *Ibid.*, p. 43-44
3. *Ibid.*, p. 43
4. The museum brochure of State Historical Museum, Bishkek, contains large-size photographs of the Avalokitesvara
   Goryacheva, V.D. 'New Findings of the Indo-Buddhist Culture

in Kyrgyzstan'. Rtveladze, E. (chief coordinator). *India and Central Asia Pre-Islamic* (Tashkent: Academy of Arts and Academy of Sciences of the Republic of Uzbekistan, 2000), p. 99-106. Illustrations by Goryachev, V.D., p. 283-288. Crowned Buddha photo, p. 287

5. Semenov, G. 'Suye and Journey to the West'. Chandra, Lokesh (ed.) and Banerjee, Radha (ed.). *Xuanzang and the Silk Road* (Delhi: Munshiram Manoharlal Publishers Pvt. Ltd., 2008), p.259

   Raina, Radha. *Beyond Legend Cultural Convergences India and Kyrgyzstan* (New Delhi: RHI Printographics Pvt. Ltd., 2007), p. 63
6. *Ibid.*
7. Semenov, G. 'Suye and Journey to the West'. Chandra, Lokesh (ed.) and Banerjee, Radha (ed.). *Xuanzang and the Silk Road* (Delhi: Munshiram Manoharlal Publishers Pvt. Ltd., 2008), p. 261
8. UNESCO World Heritage Convention. *Silk Road Sites in Kyrgyzstan*. Report submitted in 2010 by the National Commission of the Republic of Kyrgyz to UNESCO. Ref. 5518, p. 6
9. Walter, Mariko Namba. *Sino-Platonic Papers: Sogdians and Buddhism*, Number 174 (November 2006), p. 18. URL: www.sino-platonic.org
10. *Ibid.*, p. 3
11. Ross, E. D. (trans.). *A History of Moghuls of Central Asia (The Tarikhh-i-Rashidi of Mirza Muhammad Haidar Dughlat)*, Volume II (New Delhi: ABI Prints & Publishing Co., 2006), p. 286-287 n
12. Khorosh, Yelena. Report on the Assessment Mission to Kyrgyzstan, Tajikistan and Uzbekistan carried out for UNESCO in June–July–August 2006. Site 11: Sulaiman-Too Mountain. Obtained courtesy B. Amanbaeva/Abuseitova. Report submitted in 2010 by the National Commission of the Republic of Kyrgyz to UNESCO. Ref. 5518, p. 6
13. Tabaldiev, K.S., Shamenova, A.A., and Reeves, Madeleine (trans.). *The Stone Carvings at Burana Tower* (Bishkek: Kyrgyz-Turkish Manas University and Archaeological and Architectural Museum at Burana Tower)

14. Baipakov, K.M., Kapekova, G.A., Voyakin, D.A., Maryashev, A.N. *Treasures of Ancient and Medieval Taraz and Zhambyl Regions*. Archaeological Expertise Baipakov, K.M. (Taraz: 2011), p. 209
15. Gupta, S.P. (ed.). 'Masterpieces from National Museum Collection'. *Central Asian Antiquities* (New Delhi: National Museum, Catalogue-Chhaya Hesner)
16. For descriptions of Avalokitesvara see: Chandra, Lokesh. *Transcendental Art of Tibet: Indo-Asian Literatures,* Volume 385 (New Delhi: Aditya Prakashan, 1996)

Sacred cult mountain of Sulaiman-Too in Osh.

Ekdasa-mukha Avalokitesvara from Chuy Valley (8th-9th century AD).

Courtesy: State Historical Museum of Kyrgyzstan, Bishkek

A 'Sitting Buddha' from Chuy Valley (8th-9th century AD).

Courtesy: State Historical Museum of Kyrgyzstan, Bishkek

Temple of Krasnaya Rechka from where the eight-metre long Reclining Buddha image was found (7th-9th century AD).

Crowned Buddha of Ak-Beshim, Suyab (8th century AD).

Courtesy: State Historical Museum of Kyrgyzstan, Bishkek

Reclining Buddha Image found at Krasnaya Rechka (7th-9th century AD).

Courtesy: The State Hermitage Museum, St Petersburg

On the Banks of Lake Issyk Kul

Roads, they say, are just a path. But some roads have history written on them. Like the Hiuen Tsang Road that ran along the southern shores of the Issyk Kul Lake and was named after the intrepid Chinese traveller who walked through it in 629 AD. The pilgrim's route that passed through the Bedel Pass, Seok Pass, Arabel Valley, Sari Moinok, Barskon Pass, through the Barskoon river valley to the southern shores of the Lake Issyk Kul, was active till the recent times.[1]

It is said that during medieval times, the road through the Bedel Pass and southern Issyk Kul was in regular use as caravans feared taking the Ferghana Road due to civil disturbances in the valley. Besides, the headquarters of the western Turks was located in the Suyab region and the Turks were the biggest consumers of the Silk Road goods.[2]

Today, Highway A-365 goes via Tokmak and through the Boom gorge runs towards Balykchy and Cholpon Ata to reach Lake Issyk Kul. The main route to China is to the south of this lake through Barskon. From here, the route ascends through the Barskon gorge in the Tian Shan mountains and over the 4000-metre Bedel Pass, it crosses into the Xinjiang region of China. The Bedel Pass is an ancient crossing point on the Kyrgyz–China border and is only 200 kilometres north-west of the important Chinese Silk Road town of Aksu. It was this route that Hiuen Tsang, the Chinese traveller, took on his way to India.[3]

I took the Jibek Jolie road from Bishkek going eastwards along the Chu river. This road was originally built by the Russians more than a century ago. Through Tokmak I entered the Chonkemin region where the Chu Valley appeared at its glorious best. In the rolling meadows, the landscape is dotted with thousands of sheep grazing on fine pastures. There is grass even on high mountains and far away lie the snow-laden peaks of the Kungey Alatau. As I drive along, the valley disappears and the forests of poplars give way to pine. Hundreds of black felt yurts belonging to herders can be seen all along the road.

The herders not only look after their cattle but also collect wool, weave astrakhans from the skins of young lamb, and make cheese and yoghurt balls from sour milk. Some of them also collect honey and wax from the wild bees.

Soon I was in the Boom canyon which is like a conduit between the Chu Valley and the Issyk Kul region. Along the 24-kilometre-long canyon, the Chu river, approaching on the right from Naryn does not drop into the lake but turns left towards Bishkek. I drove straight towards the lake. The railway line to Balykchy, built by the Russians in 1948, runs parallel to the road. As I entered the Issyk Kul region, new railway tracks came into view. The line, I am told, will soon run from Balykchy to the Chinese border at Torugart, connecting Kyrgyzstan with China.

Balykchy: The Gateway to Issyk Kul

By the time I reached Balykchy, it was 8 a.m. Sitting on the western bank of the lake, Balykchy is the gateway to Issyk Kul. It was the site of the earliest settlement on the lake, Salamat Bulak, where 1,000 stone tools were found by archaeologists. Balykchy was, till recently, famous as a shipyard and a rich and busy port. Even today one can notice dozens of white luxury yachts bobbing on the lake's surface. The town is still the main transport hub for the gigantic fishing industry operating on the lake. The daily fish catch is loaded at Balykchy and sent to all parts of Central Asia.

Wool processing is also a major industry here. Since ancient times, shearing of wool has taken place on the banks of the Issyk Kul lying on the main east–west caravan route to China. It was here that the traders picked up the best wool from sheep that grew up on the lush pastures surrounding the lake.

Balykchy is crowded with numerous vendors selling the famous smoked Issyk Kul fish. There are vendors hawking jars of honey from their trolleys lining the road. Surprisingly, the trolleys are made of abandoned railway wagons that are lined with upholstery and collapsible beds and racks from the old bogies to store honey.

The A-365 splits at Balykchy into the northern and southern lake routes, much like the routes splitting around the Tarim Basin in the Xinjiang province of China. While the branch road, A-363, skirts around the lake, the main A-365 starts on a long and arduous journey across the alpine ranges of Naryn province in central Kyrgyzstan to the Chinese border at the Torugart.

History tells us that an important branch of the main Silk Road passed through the Chu Valley and the Issyk Kul depression. Branches of this route covered the entire territory of the Semirechye and Tian Shan regions. The largest settlements, about 80 in number, were situated in the Chuy Valley. The caravans travelling along this route could stop at any town or settlement.[4]

Ten kilometres from the eastern tip of the lake is the fertile region of Karakol, lying close to the border of China, only 150 kilometres away over the central Tian Shan mountains. Here lies the famous Holy Trinity Cathedral, a wooden mosque and the grave of the Russian explorer, Nicolai M. Przhevalsky (1839-1888) after whom the town is also known.

Ancient caravans going to China or India took this route (now A-363) from Karakol to Barskoon—a major caravan city on the ancient Silk Road. It is known as the native land of the famous 11th-century Uighur scholar, Mahmud-al-Kashgari who wrote the first comprehensive dictionary of the Turkic languages: *Diwanu-I-Lugat-al-Turk*. I happened to see his tomb while travelling in the Pamir region along the Karakoram Highway to Tashkurgan. It lies a few kilometres off the main road near the city of Kashgar. A branch road—the modern A-364—passes through the Barskoon Valley and approximates to the ancient Silk Road passing over the Bedel Pass into the town of Aksu in China.[5]

Herders on the Lake

Leaving behind Balykchy, I was soon on the northern shores of the lake. Dark clouds gathered overhead and I dreaded that the rains would hamper my photography. It had already started drizzling. Unmindful of the wet weather, herders drove thousands of sheep into the rich pastures along the lake. These appeared like small dots on a green canvas around the bluish-grey lake.

Since ancient times, the lake was the camping ground for nomads and herders who carried out most of their shearing and wool gathering here. This was a lake that never froze even in the coldest winters due to its sheltered position between the Tian Shan and the Altai mountains. In *Life Along the Silk Road*, Susan Whitfield describes the shearing of the sheep's best wool on the banks of the Issyk Kul. There would be plenty of wool for sale. The best wool of the dumba sheep was sheared here as these fat-tailed creatures were not found further east. Astrakhans or karakuls, hats made of the skin of 14-day-old slaughtered lambs, were also sold here.

It is said that Sogdian traders dealing in wool took the road east from Chach (Tashkent region) and followed the path through low mountains to reach the lake. It was on the shores of this lake that the Kaghan (Khan) of the western Turks moved his court, his army and his herds for the winter. At this time the pastures on either side of the road would be filled with tens of thousands of horses, sheep, cattle and camel.[6] Susan Whitfield transports us back to the days of the migration in her picturesque descriptions in *A Merchant's Tale*. Hundreds of tents made of white felt would have been pitched in the meadows. Khan's courtiers and other officials would have been adorned with dazzling silks and brocades with their hair braided in long plaits. And his guards and soldiers would have been wearing coarse fabric.

Cholpon Ata: A Tourist Haven

I crossed Tamchy and reached Cholpon Ata, a resort town for holidayers and nature lovers and the administrative centre of the Issyk Kul district. The town is crowded with hotels, guesthouses and sanatoria to accommodate the rush of summer tourists from all parts of Central Asia. Close by lies a petroglyph site, dating back to 1st millennium BC. But I decided to spend the entire day at the lake and see the petroglyphs on my return.

Seeing the Fisherman's Hut at Cholpon, I sat down on the wooden benches of the garden restaurant. After drinking some hot tea, I hungrily opened my snack box packed by the hotel for the day. I hated the cold eggs and dry bread and tried to snack on some fruits. Besides, the breakfast was meagre and barely enough for one person. I offered it to Natasha and Vladimir, who had been driving with me since morning. I waited for the sky to become clear and then gathered my equipment and headed towards the nearest resort for a shortcut to the beach where a vast stretch of the shimmering bluish-grey lake lay before me. The imposing Tian Shan range adorned with a glittering crown of snow rose like a giant on the other side of the lake.

Here I sat for a long time on the silken sand watching the high curling walls of dark waves running menacingly towards the shores. A dense undergrowth of sea buckthorns appeared to have engulfed quite a part of the beach. Now and then it became drenched as towering waves lashed the shores and threatened to swallow whatever came its way. Black clouds seemed again to have descended onto the lake, lending it a mysterious darkness and igniting it now and then with burning shafts of lightning.

We have a first-hand account from the Chinese pilgrim of the fierce weather that threatened the lives of travellers on the route from Aksu to the southern shores of the Issyk Kul lake. After visiting tens of sangharams (monasteries) in Baluka or Aksu (in the foothills of the Tien Shan mountains), Hiuen Tsang travelled north-west to cross a stony desert and arrive at the Ling Shan, the ice mountains of the Tien Shan ranges. He describes the fierce dragons that lived on the lake and molested travellers and impeded their movement. Travelling for a distance in these mountains, the pilgrim arrives at the great Tsing lake—the Issyk Kul.[7]

Hiuen Tsang too must have seen terrifying tides when he wrote:

'The waves of this lake roll along tumultuously as they expand themselves. Dragons and fishes inhabit it together. At certain occasions scaly monsters rise to the surface, on which travellers passing by put up their prayers for good fortune. Although the water animals are numerous, no one dares to catch them by fishing.'—

But there are no monsters, only the countless varieties of fish that sometimes come rolling with the waves.

A dirt track led from the beach to an isolated patch on the lake shores. The path seemed to have been paved by hand. It went through a dense undergrowth of sea buckthorns and other wild thorny plants. Hidden under the thorns and silvery leaves, dozens of ducks and other birds had made it their homes. I noticed that the rough path led to a group of hutments made of mud and tin. This was one of the many settlements of fishermen who stayed back on the beach after a hard day of fishing while sending their catch to Balykchy and restaurants in Cholpon Ata.

The Issyk Kul Lake region was the biggest trading zone of ancient and medieval Kyrgyzstan. Caravans laden with goods passed along the lake on the east–west corridor between China and Europe. A necklace of cowries (seashells) displayed at the museum points to the trade with India. The cowries are believed to be used as currency and in jewellery art.

Mani stones with inscriptions 'Om Mani Padme Hum' in Tibetan found from the lake region at Alabash and Tamga give evidence of small Buddhist settlements around the lake.[8] Tamga, a small village on the southern shores of the lake near Barskoon derives its name from a Buddhist inscribed rock 'Tamga Tash' found at some distance from the village. It is a large stone carved with the 'Buddhist mantra' (Hail the jewel in the lotus) in Tibetan. More Buddhist stones are reported from Tamga river gorge.[9] The stones, dated between the 7th and 8th centuries, are believed to correspond to the period of Tibetan expansion in northern Kyrgyzstan.

Archaeological excavations in and around the lake have also revealed underwater ruins, one of them near Cholpon Ata. Even Timur is said to have built a castle or a jail on an island on the lake for prisoners. Another ruler is said to have built a fortress on the lake at Koy Soo. Some of the ruined structures now lie under water. The 'Kamenskiy Treasure', found from the bottom of the lake in 1954, included bronze sacrificial tables, cauldrons, and censers decorated with figures of animals.[10] The treasures are displayed at the Issyk Kul Historical State Museum.

Close to Cholpon Ata another site was waiting to be explored. This was the splendid art gallery created on rocks by the early inhabitants settled around the lake. These consist of thousands of petroglyphs, said to have been created in the 'Saka-Scythian' animal style by the Saka tribes living in the region between the 8th and 3rd centuries BC. There are images of rock goats with rolled and branching horns, large deer and wolves or wild dogs

It is believed that the site lying on the western end of Cholpon Ata served as a gigantic temple where the ancient inhabitants worshipped nature and performed mysterious rituals much like the inhabitants of the Tamgaly petroglyph region near Karabastau village in Kazakhstan.

By evening, the road to Balykchy was crowded. The day's catch from the lake had already arrived and fisherwomen were hollering at passersby to taste their freshly roasted fish or to buy raw fish. The fishermen were literally shoving fish into the faces of passersby while women were huddled over large fish, scaling them with hot ash. Mounds of fish had already been roasted and hung on a string at the bus stand. A large group of fishermen had stacked their stuff on trolleys and had set off to the railway station from where the fish would be transported to other regions of Central Asia.

Hiuen Tsang's Route to Suyab

History would have us believe that Hiuen Tsang on his journey through the Chuy Valley could have taken the route running between the southern shores of the Lake Issyk Kul and the city of Suyab. Traditionally, it is considered that the route from the southern shores of the Issyk Kul ran along its south-western coast and crossed the Boom Gorge to pass into the Chuy Valley.

From the pilgrim's travel records, we learn that he trudged roughly 500 li or around 250 kilometres (Chinese measure of distance one li is nearly half a kilometre) to the north-west of the Tsing lake (Issyk Kul) and arrived at the town of Suyeh (Suyab/ Ak- Beshim).[11] This was a big town where 'merchants from surrounding countries congregate and dwell'. The pilgrim further informs us that the soil of the town was fertile and red millet and grapes grew here. The forests were not thick, and the weather so 'windy and cold' that people wore twilled wool.[12]

The pilgrim's path ran through the modern Chu district of Kyrgyzstan. The district itself is situated in the eastern part of the Chu Valley. Its southern part spreads into the Kyrgyz Ala-Too mountains. The Chu river and its tributaries—the Shamshy and the Kegeti—are the main water carriers of the Chu district. Their enormous water content is fed by a number of glaciers of the Kyrgyz Ala-Too range, such as the Shamshy and the Kulter glaciers.

In order to reach Suyab, the pilgrim could have trudged through the valleys of either the Shamsy or the Kegeti rivers before he came to the region of Suyab. But at the jailoo (meadows of the valley), he halted as he met Tung Yabgu, the Khan of the western Turks, who after receiving him went off on a hunting expedition.

What beauty lay before the pilgrim depended on the season of his travels through the Chu district. Since the pilgrim wrote about the good soil and crops such as red millet and grapes, he must have travelled during the summer months when the valley wore a mantle of green and was covered with wild flowers, and when fruits such as luscious grapes hung from the trellises of every courtyard. Such a lovely sight I had witnessed at Tokmok. On my journey along the small streams and rivers that joined the Chu, the weather was exactly what the pilgrim had mentioned—'windy and cold'. Even during the month of June, the valley of the Kegeti river was extremely cold due to rain and trekkers were huddled around a fire in an abandoned railway wagon to keep themselves warm.

Route through Kegeti Valley

About 10 kilometres from Balasagun is the mouth of the Kegeti Valley. There are also plenty of side valleys for hiking. The one that I took headed to the waterfall and onwards to a camping area inside the pine forests. A pebbled path goes along the river for several kilometres before crossing to the other side of the mountains. Trekkers generally leave their car at the wooden gates located just before the waterfall and take the gravelled path passing through high grassy mountains and glacial streams.

The valley, which at first appears narrow, gradually opens into a broad stretch running through the mountains of the Kyrgyz Ala-Too. The snowy waters of the Kegeti snake through the valley. Along the river runs a narrow gravelled path for trekkers. The river rushes down, dancing and hissing to meet the Chu, quite like the other tributaries that run almost parallel to it—the Shamshy and the Issyk Ata. All three rivers have their own valleys cutting through the massive ranges of the Alay mountains, their own share of meadows, their own water bodies. They are home to wild animals and birds. In their rich pasturelands, herders descend with their animals during spring and summer when the snow has melted.

In the month of June, the mountains appeared not only a deep green but now and then painted with strokes of yellow, white and blue of the wild flowers that grew profusely along the slopes. As I went further inside the mountains, the air turned crisp and it became quite cold. Gradually, the soft hissing of the river turned into a crescendo and hidden between the fold of a mountain I could see a huge waterfall.

Just before the waterfall was a wooden barricade which was the checkpost and where visitors to the valley had to present their papers. I walked to a rock to sit by the side of the fall. It seemed like a sheet of liquid snow raining down the gorge. The weather was beautiful; the grass soft beneath my feet, and a sweet fragrance from the flowery slopes of the mountain pervaded the air.

Vladimir gave a signal to return as the trek inside the valley was long and I had to be back in Bishkek by evening. Reluctantly, I proceed to the yurt camp set up further into the mountains. The valley opened into vast meadows and the snow-laden peaks of the Ala-Too receded far away behind the forest line. Hundreds of sheep, goats, cows and horses could be seen grazing on the lush pastures. Surprisingly, I did not see any shepherds. A little ahead, an abandoned railway wagon turned into a hutment stood proudly by the river welcoming tourists to the valley of the Kegeti. Inside a clearing, half a dozen yurts had been set up. As I left the mountain road and walked towards the camping site, a couple of dogs started barking furiously as if angered by a visitors' arrival. It seemed to me that most monuments and tourist sites in Central Asia are guarded by ferocious dogs.

The road runs deeper into the mountains and passes over it to join the main road going to Kochkor and onwards to Naryn—the main highway A-365 that runs to the Torugart Pass into China.

I spent about an hour inside the yurt resting and warming myself by the fire as the weather had turned for the worse due to rain. The yurt owner brought in hot soup with noodles and boiled eggs. Vladimir explained the weather cycle in the valley and the adaptation by the shepherds and their flocks. When it starts getting cold in September, the herders prepare to leave the meadows. By October, when the first snow falls on these mountains, the meadows are already deserted and become bereft of life. Up to April, there is deep snow in the mountain passes. As the valley warms up in May-June, a carpet of grass starts covering the mountain slopes and the meadows. On this emerald carpet nature weaves lovely multi-hued flowers. The high passes become clear as the snow melts and human and animal life reappear to claim the meadows and the milky streams. Herders and their flocks of sheep and cows are the first to descend on the jailoos or pastures. Here, along the forest line, they build temporary shelters to pass the four cosy months from June to September; moving with their herds from one jailoo to another until the next snowfall.

During these four months, the herders have a hectic schedule on hand. They have to replenish their stock of wool for the season's sale. The soft locks on the back of sheep are sheared and packed away. The animals are fattened on the green pastures in preparation for the lean months ahead. Flesh from hunted wild animals and jungle fowls are cured, dried and packed. The herders then fold away their temporary shelters, pile them on the back of their cattle, and leave for the depressions along the warm Lake Issyk Kul. There, they spend the winter months on surrounding pastures far away from the freezing mountains.

The journey to Lake Issyk Kul and the valley of the Kegeti was in essence a journey with the great pilgrim Hiuen Tsang. Although his memoirs do not say much about the 500 li distance that he covered between the south shores of the lake and the city of Suyab, there was nothing that he did not inform us about. In a few words, the pilgrim had described everything that we came across. The densely forested valley lying before us still harboured plenty of game. It was here that the Great Khan went hunting and returned with game to meet the pilgrim. The pastureland that rolled out like a vast sheet of emerald fed and fattened thousands of animals. The undulating path running through the meadows were ancient strands of the trade routes that brought luxuries for the Khan and his nobles. And the monastic ruins that still lay here were evidence of the Turks' receptivity to the Buddhist faith.[13]

No one knows the exact route of Hiuen Tsang from the south-western shores of the Lake Issyk Kul into Suyab, where he met the Khan of the western Turks. But it is possible that he would have chosen one of the tributaries of the Chuy river for an easy trek into Tokmok region. And this could have been the beautiful Kegeti Valley that leads to Balasagun only 8 kilometres from Suyab.

References

For roads and highways in Kyrgyzstan see: Mitchell, Lawrence. *Kyrgyzstan: The Bradt Travel Guide*; *Lonely Planet: Central Asia*. Lonely Planet Publication Pvt. Ltd. For Hiuen Tsang's Route see: *Silk Road Sites in Kyrgyzstan: UNESCO World Heritage Centre*

1. *Silk Road Sites in Kyrgyzstan: UNESCO World Heritage Centre*. World Heritage Convention, UNESCO, submitted in 2010 by National Commission of the Kyrgyz Republic for UNESCO. Ref. 5518, p. 1-12
2. Khorosh, Yelena. Report on the Assessment Mission to Kyrgyzstan, Tajikistan and Uzbekistan carried out for UNESCO in June–July–August 2006. Site 11: Sulaiman-Too Mountain. Obtained courtesy B. Amanbaeva/Abuseitova. Report submitted in 2010 by the National Commission of the Republic of Kyrgyz to UNESCO. Ref. 5518
3. For routes check: Buryakov, Y.F., Baipakov, K.M., Tashbaeva, K.H., Yakubov, Y. *The Cities and Routes of the Great Silk Road* (Tashkent: Sharg, 1999), p. 84-97
   Lawrence, Mitchell. *Kyrgyzstan: The Bradt Travel Guide* (Connecticut, England: The Globe Pequot Press Inc., 2008)
4. *Ibid.*
5. Lawrence, Mitchell. *Kyrgyzstan: The Bradt Travel Guide* (Connecticut, England: The Globe Pequot Press Inc., 2008). Also see, maps: p.158, 182, 201
6. Whitfield, Susan. *Life along the Silk Road* (London: John Murray Hodder, Hadline, 2004), p. 40
7. Tsiang, Hiuen and Beal, Samuel (trans.). *Si Yu Ki: Buddhist Records of the Western Country,* Book II (Delhi: D.K. Publisher Distributors

Pvt. Ltd., 1995), p. 26

Hwui Li, Shaman and Beal, Samuel (trans.). *The Life of Hieun-Tsiang* (Delhi: D.K. Publishers Distributors Pvt. Ltd., 2001), p. 42-44

8. Raina, Radha. *Beyond Legend: Cultural Convergences India and Kyrgyzstan* (New Delhi: RHI Printographics Pvt. Ltd., 2007), p. 78

   Ysmanova, K., Rymbekova, N., Nurmametov, R. *Issyk-Kul: The Guard of Ancient* (Issyk Kul: Issyk Kul Museum)

   Lawrence, Mitchell. *Kyrgyzstan: The Bradt Travel Guide* (Connecticut, England: The Globe Pequot Press Inc., 2008), p. 183, 185

9. Lawrence, Mitchell. *Kyrgyzstan: The Bradt Travel Guide* (Connecticut, England: The Globe Pequot Press Inc., 2008), p. 183, 185

10. Ysmanova, K., Rymbekova, N., Nurmametov, R. *Issyk-Kul: The Guard of Ancient* (Issyk Kul: Issyk Kul Museum)

11. Tsiang, Hiuen and Beal, Samuel (trans.). *Si Yu Ki: Buddhist Records of the Western Country,* Book II (Delhi: D.K. Publisher Distributors Pvt. Ltd., 1995), p. 26

12. *Ibid.*, p. 26

13. *Ibid.*, p. 26

    Hwui Li, Shaman and Beal, Samuel (trans.). *The Life of Hieun-Tsiang* (Delhi: D.K. Publishers Distributors Pvt. Ltd., 2001), p. 42-44

Section Six

KAZAKHSTAN

Routes into Kazakhstan

It is said that the traders, monks and scholars travelling from India through Central Asia towards China took the route through the Kashmir region to Yarkand and onwards to Kashgar where the routes coming from south Kazakhstan and the Semirechye region met through several mountain passes on the Xinjiang border. Several routes from south Kazakhstan looped round the Issyk Kul Lake and ran towards Aksu, north-east of Kashgar. Another route running along the Ili and passing through the region occupied by the present Altyn Emel Park met the Urumqi route at Khorgos. Other routes ran north-east of the Semirechye region and joined the Alakol route to the Dzungarian Gate connecting with north-west China.

Routes from north-western parts of India ran through the Khyber Pass and onwards to Balkh, meeting the southern route coming from the Seven Rivers region or Semirechye through Tashkent, Samarkand and Termez.

The most popular route from Europe and Russia to China was through the Seven Rivers area and southern Kazakhstan. Records tell us that from Tashkent the road went through Turbat and Ispijab into the Talas Vallley. Ispijab, lying 15 kilometres east of Shymkent, has been identified with Sairam, one of the largest trade centres on the Silk Road, drawing merchants from all over Asia.

From the Talas Valley caravans reached the ancient town of Taraz and eastwards to Kulan. The road ran to Navaket, or Novgorod or 'new town', one of the largest towns of the Semirechey and the residence of the Turkic Kaghan. From Navaket the road went to the largest town of the Seven Rivers area: Suyab (modern Ak-Beshim), the capital of the western Turks. From Suyab it went through the northern and southern banks of the Issyk Kul Lake. These led to the Bedel Pass into Aksu (Xinjiang) and onwards to China. The southern branch turned south from Barskoon and led through Naryn and Tashrabat to the Irkeshtam Pass into Kashgar.

Another route ran from the Issyk Kul hollow through Santash Pass and the Karkara Valley to the Ili valley and then through Zarkent and Khorgos to Huocheng and onwards to Hami and Turfan in the Xinjiang region of China. There is a border crossing into Kazakhstan at Khorgos, where the road continues to Zharkent in Panfilov district.

Separate branches of the Silk Road also ran north from Navaket and Balasagun to meet at the Kastek Pass and through Kaskelen to reach Alma Ata and along the Ili valley it took the Almalik route. Another branch led through the Talgar river up to the ford on the Ili river near the Kapchagai gorge and through the Altyn-Emel Pass to the Koksu Valley to reach Ikioguz (Equius town, as mentioned by traveller Rubruk (1253) on a journey to Kayalik.

In *On Yuan Chwang's Travels in India,* Thomas Watters informs us about a route through the Muzart Pass that connected the Ili Valley with the Tarim Basin, a direct and short route linking Kashgar, Yarkand and Khotan with Kulja (Ili). This was also the southern route from Kazakhstan into India.

References

For details of routes see:
Buryakov, Y.F., Baipakov, K.M., Tashbaeva, K.H., Yakubov, Y. *The Cities and Routes of the Great Silk Road* (Tashkent: Sharg, 1999), p. 100-118; Watters, Thomas. *On Yuan Chwang's Travels in India: 629-645 AD* (New Delhi: Munshiram Manoharlal Publisher Pvt. Ltd., 2012), p. 67; Author's own travels through Kazakhstan; Hakluyt, Richard,

Beazley, Charles, Giovanni, Raymond, Van Ruysbroeck, Willem. *The Texts and Versions of John de Plano Carpini and William De Rubruquis: As Printed for the First Time by Hakluyt in 1598, Together with Some Short Pieces* (London: Cambridge University Press, 1903), p. 227-229

Buddhist Rock Art on Almaty Highway

It was a bright sunny morning (in June 2007) when I started on Highway M-33, a branch of the M-39 from Bishkek to Almaty. My Russian friends, Natasha and Vladimir, drove me to the Kyrgyz border near Kordai village, where we got stuck at the immigration checkpoint for several hours. After a thorough checking of my luggage and currency, we were allowed to cross the border. On the Kazakh side, we drove 25 kilometres to Targan village where in a choykhana we waited for Anastasia, my guide and interpreter, on the Kazakh Silk Road. Behind the teahouse, in a small bamboo forest, stood a bear spouting water. Not a real bear. A sculpted one! Had I been here years ago, I would have probably seen the real bears—not too far in the hoary past, burly wild bears roamed around here. Or, so they say. From behind the bear, peeps a silhouette. It is Anastasia.

I hopped into the wagon and found Alisher, from the State Archaeology Institute at Almaty, hunched over a huge map of Kazakhastan. Alisher knew all about ancient sites spread over the Kazakh steppes. On the map, he marked a tiny dot on a pencil-thin road—Tamgaly, a UNESCO Heritage Site belonging to the Bronze Age.

We drove for about 25 kilometres on Highway A-2. On both sides were steppe lands with no trees, only grass and some dry shrubs. Soon we took a left turn and drove along a decrepit narrow road full of potholes and dust. Faraway, a group of wild asses could be sighted burying their heads in the wild grass. Horses and cows became a common sight as we reached Kopa. Here and there lay ruins of cattle-farms built of thatched mud. The steppe herders are said to come here with their cattle during the winter months when the mountains are covered in snow.

The bumpy ride nearly exhausted me but the steppe lands were beautiful. After every mile, the grass acquires a new hue, from green to brown and golden. The land rose and fell like a swing. Animals grazing on high grassy mounds formed a part of the beautiful landscape. A railway line passed through Kopa village and ran towards Almaty.

At Karabastau we stopped at a grassy hill where a path led to the Tamgaly UNESCO Heritage Site. There stood an isolated yurt where the in-charge of the Tamgaly petroglyphs lived. A bullterrier sat at the entrance of the yurt. Anastasia went out to seek permission for entry to the petroglyph area. The dog seemed to know Anastasia, licked her feet but suddenly getting the scent of unknown persons, started barking and whirling like a merry-go-round and then darted in my direction. He was there to catch thieves and unauthorized persons stealing inside the petroglyph area. Even at Khotan (in Xinjiang province of China) a ferocious dog guarded the museum of antiquities. Anastasia returned with the permit and the guard followed the bullterrier with a leash, pulled him away and unlocked the gate of the site.

After walking for a kilometre through low hills and a dry bed of streams, we arrived at the petroglyphs perched high up on the mountains.

Alisher led us through tight spaces between the rocks up to the high cliffs where several thousand years ago man expressed himself through paintings on the rocky canvas. He sketched his life, his gods, his animals and his entire environment as engravings on the mountains that were his home and his shrine. The ancestors of the Kazakh people played with the rocks, worshipped nature—the earth, the trees, the animals that gave them food, clothing and daily comforts.[1]

We climbed up a steep hill where a cliff had been decorated with a picture gallery portraying an elaborate scene of sun worship. A sun-headed deity stood at the centre of a religious ceremony that included festivity and dancing by humans. There were scenes from everyday life showing hunting and ploughing of the field. We spent a long time on the mountains photographing the rock paintings.

Finally, we were back to our wagon and taking a U-turn from Karabastau, we drove towards a high mound, which could be one of the many burial sites that ran along the low mountains of Kazakhstan. As we stopped to savour the landscape before us, Anastasia brought down a big box containing our lunch from the back of the wagon and laid out a lovely meal of homemade apricot jam, naan, boiled eggs and yoghurt on the grass in the backdrop of the petroglyphs.

We were again on the road eastwards to Kopa. Westwards, the same road joined the highway to Lake Balkash, 300 kilometres away. At Targan we joined the highway to Almaty.

Almaty was crowded and choked with vehicular traffic moving slower than a snail. We literally crawled to the Astana International Hotel on the busy Baitursynov street. The rooms were too small, too cluttered. I wanted to check into another hotel, but the shift would have to wait until the three-day tour to Zharkent on the Kazakh–Chinese border.

I forgot about the tiny room when Taimur, the proprietor of the travel agency that had arranged our visit in Central Asia, came to take us out for dinner. We walked two squares to reach Swagat, a famous Punjabi restaurant. The table was laid for 10 persons. The waitresses were wearing Indian outfits and bhangra music piped through the room. A portrait of Mughul Emperor Babur stared from a wall and Noor Jahan peeped from another corner. Taimur was waiting for a special guest. Soon, Panditji—a dear Indian friend of Taimur—arrived, sporting a dhoti and kurta. Panditji was a vegetarian and teetotaller and often came to Almaty to perform puja for his Kazakh friends. He went into a spiel about how Indian women followed the tradition of not touching alcohol. However, when vodka was ordered for all guests, Panditji was a little embarrassed. He looked with amazement as women all around him downed glassfuls of the drink and hurried through platefuls of butter chicken. Almaty seemed so Indian. Or, so I thought.

Buddha on the Ili Valley Route

My journey over the next week involved exploring the ancient Buddhist sites near Lake Capshagai and traversing the Silk Road through the Altyn Emel region to the borders of China at Zharkent/Korgas. Driving along Highway A-350, we reached Lake Capshagai where the Ili river has been dammed. We left the main highway and turned left into a narrow road going along the river and after a short drive, stopped amid tall grasses on the banks. Walking towards the nearby mountains we came to a high cliff where, on vertically flat rock face, were perched the Buddhist petroglyphs, dating back to the 8th century.

It is said that since early times, Tamgaly Tas was a crossing on the Ili river. At its narrowest part, it could be forded by the travellers going north-east along the trade routes leading into China. The river and its tributaries running across deserts and steppes nourished the local tribes of the land.

At the river ford, Buddha and other Buddhist deities sat on the face of high, treeless cliffs guarding the Ili river route to and from China and blessing pilgrims and travellers who sought the Buddha's protection. The travellers were imperilled by wild animals, demons and robbers who killed and plundered caravans. The flooded river added to their woes. Below the carved images of Buddhist deities are inscriptions in Tibetan reading 'Om mani padme hum' meaning 'Hail the Jewel within the lotus'—a mantra that encapsulates all teachings of the Buddha. Chanting or viewing the written mantra is believed to invoke the benevolence of Avalokitesvara.

The drawings on rock depicting the Buddha and the inscriptions in Tibetan, Pali and Mongolian is said to relate to Lamaism that had become popular in the Semirechye region and southern Kazakhstan.[2] These were magic mantras chanted by pilgrims in praise of the Buddha. Three images hewn on stone portrayed the 'All Compassionate and Merciful' Avalokitesvara, flanked on either side by the carvings of the unadorned Enlightened Buddha sitting under the Bodhi tree after discovering the Truth of Life and the Healing Buddha or the 'Buddha of Medicine'.[3] The 'Healer' wears the robe of a monk and holds a pot of nectar—the medicine that wipes out the sufferings of mankind.

The Avalokitesvara is believed to have been highly popular in Central Asia because of his compassionate nature and concern for suffering humanity. The deity is depicted sitting on a blooming lotus and wearing a gem-laden crown. He holds aloft the Lotus of the 'True Law' like Siva raises the trident and with his 'third eye' destroys all evil.

Similar inscriptions have been found at other places in Kazakhstan, such as at Taygak village, written on rock faces as I was to soon discover while exploring a river gorge in the Altyn Emel National Reserve.

The vast blue stretch of the Ili appears irresistible in the heat of the day. It is the biggest river of southern Kazakhstan flowing from China, coursing over 1,000 kilometres. Before reaching the Buddha's cliff, it forms a huge reservoir at Capchagai, covering an area of 1800 square kilometres. It runs northwards, finally emptying into Lake Balkash, one of the largest in Asia, sprawling over 16,000 square kilometres and harbouring the richest uranium town of Balkash.

Wild flowering grass and weeds were in full bloom after the severe winter, enveloping the foreground of the Buddhist petroglyph and undulating around the river. I waded through the tall feather grass and the pink flowering bushes to reach the shores. For a long time, I sat on the grassy banks, dipping my hands into the shallow edge of the river and enjoying the cool breeze that blew through the valley. Instead of lunching at the Taygak village as planned in my itinerary, I decided to picnic on the Ili for the sake of memory. Anastasia laid out a simple meal of naan and fruit jam on the banks of the river covered with wild flowers right under the shadow of the Buddha.

Buddhist Sutras in a River Gorge

The sun was right overhead and we returned to the highway encircling Lake Capshagai. We drove east for several kilometres before we entered the nature reserve of the Altyn Emel. For the next few hours we drove into the steppes on dusty untarred roads till we reached a log hut beyond which there was fencing and we could go no further. The driver looked for the sign of a narrow gorge inside the mountains and turned the vehicle towards it. We drove for several kilometres on a pebbled path running along a bubbly stream going deep into the mountains. Finally, we came to a clearing surrounded by a forest of wild apples. In the midst of this clearing stood a wooden hut—the guesthouse. Nearby were small fabricated structures that made up the village of Taygak located right in the middle of high mountains and dense foliage. A tiny stream flowed by the side of our hut.

In the high mountain caves, I was told, lived animals like the bear, sheep, wolves, wild ass, goats, horses and the nilgai. Suddenly I spotted three huge brown and hairy wild hunting dogs and a dozen cows sitting in the shade of the gorge. They all leaped to their feet and started running towards us. Anastasia said they always do this when new guests arrive. But they were harmless creatures who guarded the guesthouse.

Shepherd Feroze who lived in the Taygak village informed me of a nearby gorge where archaeologists had found Buddhist inscriptions written in ancient Indian script. While everyone settled in the lovely environs of the hut, Alisher and I set out with Feroze into the narrow gorge. The grassy pathways went along a thin stream. A couple of cows followed us as well. We waded through tall grass and wild plantain bushes. Feroze pointed to an inscription written on a high cliff—'Om mani padme hum' in Tibetan by some passing travellers or monks, on their way eastwards to China. Deeper into the gorge, more inscriptions were found written on high walls.

Afraid of wild animals, the travellers perhaps had climbed the high mountains during the evening to take shelter and had written the magic mantra to ward off evil. Or, they might have spent a few days in the gorge, meditating and worshipping the Buddha. Close by is the watershed of the stream, where the main route to the Chinese border begins. We took several photos of the passage through the mountains and the inscriptions, and felt honoured to stand beside Feroze, who led us into the gorge.

It was getting dark and we decided to return to our hut where a woman was preparing dough for flat noodles. Before the noodles were ready, Anastasia brought out some salad, cola and buns which we shared with Feroze. He appeared too shy to accept the goodies. We coaxed him to snack with us, after which he retired to his shepherd's room in the foothills.

As night fell, the lady of the guesthouse beckoned us to the sitting room for dinner. There was no electricity, earthen lamps had been lit and everything appeared lovely in the dim lighting. After a hearty meal, we retired for the night. From the low windows, the dense foliage of apple orchards appeared dark and eerie. A half moon peeped through chinks in the foliage, playing hide and seek in the gentle breeze that blew in the gorge. The hunting dogs growled and nilgai came knocking at the fence surrounding the hut. The cows had climbed onto a wooden platform set under the orchard for collecting apples and apricots. They lay there at leisure, munching green apples through the night.

As the valley filled up with the morning glow, wild fowls were the first to make an appearance by flying past the window and pecking for worms in the garden. There was music in the cacophony created by the birds chirping wildly around their nests and the meowing of the shepherd's cats and barking of the wild dogs while the pitter-patter of the blue bulls faded away.

A blue mist hung over the mountains as the sun lurked

somewhere behind the high peaks. It was 8 a.m. The jungle was alive and kicking. High on the mountains, I could faintly see a cave outside from which a fox-like creature and her three babies emerged for a sunbath. Herds of mountain goats strolled into the valley and filed past into the gorge to drink from the stream. Feroze opened the sheep pen and led his two dozen sheep into the gorge. The cows followed them. Feroze went last of all with his dogs and a long stick. He was wearing an old coat and a cap and his feet were covered in long boots. This was his daily routine in the reserve park where he and his family had been living with their cattle for the past several months moving from place to place in search of pastures.

Next morning, we had to scour the national reserve park for the Saka burial mounds—the Beshtyr. I hoped to see some wild animals on the way. For hours my camera stayed in full focus to spot any animals on the high mountain slopes and near streams where they might come to drink water. Unfortunately, I saw none. We drove on dirt tracks through the steppes with the mountains on our left. After a few hours of driving through semi-desert land, where nothing except dwarfed, pale plants were growing, we turned left and drove towards the mountains. Coming close at the foot of some low hills in an open ground we saw numerous mounds of chip stones covering huge protuberances. Nearby, huge pieces of rocks had been piled in a mysterious arrangement. Three huge rocks stood vertical while two lay down in a parallel arrangement.

There were barrows like a stupa made of earth and rocky soil. According to Alisher, these barrows, which are believed to be the burial places of some Scythian (Saks) royalty, belong to the 7th century BC. The burials were surrounded by groups of pillars believed to serve a ritual purpose. The largest barrows were nearly 17 metres high and belonged to an unknown Saka king.

Choykhana in the Steppes

I almost lost track of our direction as we journeyed through the steppes on dirt tracks alongside mountains of various hues and heights. A couple of hours brought us to a vast watering body, perhaps a part of the Capshagai, where a flock of large-necked cranes were scouring for fish and aquatic animals.

We drove for long distance through the steppes till we reached a grove of old, thick-waisted, and twisted mulberry trees, where under the shade lay a small pond with a mud embankment and beside it a choykhana. A wooden house had been built with a kitchen to provide lodging and meals for visitors. Wooden chairs and divans had been set up in private enclosures near the pond. A samovar was burning to provide boiling water for tea.

In no time the lady caretaker, a young woman, spread out a light refreshment of melons, grapes, dry fruits, naan and black tea. I lay down on the wooden divan and looked around the choykhana noticed live fish, snails, crabs and ducks swimming in the pond. The lady told me that the pond was a part of the choykhana. I could choose any fish and she would cook it for lunch. Near the pond was a big reed basket which covered dozens of chirpy chicks and hens loitered nearby. I could order anything but I did not have the heart to kill the steppe animals for a morsel of food.

She brought more food—steaming hot soup in bowls, a salad of onions and greens topped with lemon slices, a pot of honey, steaming rice, and chicken broth. I had never seen the working of a samovar. I was curious and requested the lady to show me how a samovar functions. She brought out another smaller one, opened it and stuffed it with some wood scrapings and put a piece of burning coal into it. The water could be boiled and kept hot on the slow fire for the whole day. After taking a short nap, lying down under the shade of the grove at the open air choykhana, we resumed our journey through the steppes again.

Our next destination in the wild steppe lands was the singing sand dunes or the barchans. Just like the ones near Dunhuang in China, there was a several-kilometre long stretch of golden sand emerging from the steppe lands and surrounded by the rocky mountains. Where did the sand hills come from? Some say the sand grains had been deposited by the Ili river. It is said that the heated sand is therapeutic for all kinds of ailments. If one dug a hole into the sand and sat inside covering oneself with sand, the heat and the micronutrients in the soil would heal the bones and cure blood ailments. That moment, I was not interested in facts. All I wanted to do was to enjoy the music of the dunes. So, Anastasia and I climbed up the dunes. The sand was burning hot. We came down together laughing and enjoying the sound of an aeroplane emerging from the heated sand as we slipped down to its base.

All around in the sandy environs of the barchans, wild herbs and bushes grew and all kinds of insects, lizards and reptiles sped past us. It could also have been a butterfly park as thousands of butterflies nested in the wild bushes. Alisher stopped near a bush to take photographs of insects and reptiles.

It is said that below the mounds of sand hills, a clear spring of sweet water flows and the medicinal properties of the sand is believed to come from the sacred spring.

A Night at Baschi Village

We were to spend the night in the village of Baschi. With plenty of time on hand, we decided to meet Kurmanaliyev Sauytbek Kurmanaliyevich, director general of the Altyn Emel National Park. We were to take a round of the museum to see the flora and fauna of the park, the largest of its kind in Central Asia. In the evening I set out to stroll through Baschi. I thought I would find nothing except some mud huts and sheep. To my amazement I found a caravan of camels journeying through the village, perhaps like us, on their way to the Chinese border near Zharkent. The village also boasts of lovely, although old, one-storey brick houses with lime plaster and wooden gates. The lone church looked old, and is not used much now, but tells of the Christian (mostly Russian) population in the village. But the church lay locked and some of its doors and windows were sealed.

After a round of the village, I stopped at an old rickety wooden gate half closed with piled-up bricks. Inside the compound was a cluster of houses lying back to back, all belonging to one big joint family still living together but cooking their meals separately. An old woman, perhaps the head of the family, was sitting by a wood fire, burning a sheep's head and ridding it of its skin and hair. After it turned black from scalding, she picked up a scraper and started scraping the head. It needed some strength to pull out the burnt skin. She boiled some hot water and poured it over the burnt head, cleaning it thoroughly and scraping it again and again. She then washed the head in soap water and scrubbed it clean.

The log fire hearth had been set up in the verandah of the house. The old woman set up a large quantity of water in an iron basin and dipped the sheep's head in it for making some delicious soup. She threw in some carrots, potatoes and spinach. The mother-in-law, being the head of the family, had the privilege to prepare it and serve it to all the members of the big joint family. The daughter-in-law was frying cheese cakes. As I sat watching all the preparation, the lady brought some cheese cakes and black tea for me. The family was in a joyous mood. The occasion was special—it was the birth anniversary of one of the daughters-in-law. I was invited to the anniversary picnic on the steppe lands by the side of a stream. What a lovely day it would have been! But I had to leave for Zharkent to be at the Chinese border.

Before departing, I visited the old lady again the following morning to offer a small present to the birthday girl. I had nothing to call a proper gift and all I could think of as a present was a pair of new Chinese pearl hair pins that adorned my hair. I pulled them off from my hair and gave them to the lady. She was really happy and got herself photographed with me. She locked her curly hair in the pins. After a photo session, we left for Zharkent. I have never forgotten that happy evening in Baschi and the lovely cheese cakes.

On way to Zharkent, on the Kazakh–Chinese border, we drove through the steppe for about an hour before catching the main road, A-253. This time we were lucky to find wild asses in droves.

In the middle of the dirt track, running through the wild steppes, our way was blocked by hundreds of wild asses crossing the road. They were quick to escape into the wilderness. We tried to chase them but were left far behind.

Monastery of Sumbe

The Zharkent bazar was loaded with summer fruits as women sat with baskets of apricots and plums by the roadside, beckoning buyers. We stopped our vehicle at the nearby Russian Orthodox Church and sauntered through the market for a small meal before venturing into the Dungan mosque. Instead of a mosque, it looked more like a Chinese pagoda. Even the entrance gate was topped by a double-storey pagoda similar to the ones of a Buddhist shrine. The green-roofed mosque, built mainly of wood was surrounded by a corridor supported on red pillars. The low ceiling of the corridor had intricate wood carvings with painted floral borders. Large upturned eaves on the corners dispelled any idea of a mosque.

Inside, the wooden structure said to have been built without nails, was brightly painted in red. The central hall was very spacious but there was hardly any visitor. The huge Chinese lantern, hanging from the ceiling provided lighting and beauty to the structure. The minbar at the far end of the congregational hall resembled the pulpit of a lama facing the east as seen in the Himalayan monasteries of India. The mosque has no parallels even in the neighbouring and contiguous Xinjiang region (formerly eastern Turkestan) of China.

A branch road cut from the Almaty–Zharkent highway eastwards to Khorgos, a town that straddles both sides of the Kazakh–China border. On the Kazakh side of the border, hundreds of people had queued up at the immigration counter to cross over to the recently constructed trade zone in the Xinjiang province of China. They usually made purchases at the wholesale market and the giant shopping mall here and brought back manufactured goods, mainly clothing and electronics to sell back home. The border town is the highlight of Kazakh–China relations as the proposed gas pipeline from the Caspian to the Xinjiang province of China is slated to pass through it.

We turned back towards Highway A-352 and headed into the steppes again to have a glimpse of the 154-kilometre-long Charyn canyon, one of the most exotic places in the Ili river valley. The Charyn river, a tributary of the Ili, while passing through rocks, leaves strange forms and depressions forming sculptures in the mountains that are called 'Valley of castles'. As I stood atop a rock castle, Alisher pointed far beyond the canyon in the direction of the Buddhist site of Sumbe. The site lay north of Kegen in the Almaty region. Its ruins were found on the right bank of the Sumbe river, a tributary of the Tekes, in the foothills of Shartaas.

I requested Alisher to take a detour through Sumbe while returning to Almaty from Charyn so that we could see the monastery. But it turned out that the monastery had suffered a major fire and all that remained were now at the Institute of Archaeology in Almaty. These included bells that once decorated the entrance of the monastery and stones with Buddhist inscriptions.

Details of the monastery of Sumbe were recorded by the famous Russian explorer C.C. Valikhonov in 1854, 10 years before the destruction of the monastery along with other Buddhist temples during the Dungan uprising.

Alisher was himself present at the excavations at Sumbe which revealed roof tiles decorated with peonies, chrysanthemums, lotuses, butterflies and heads of fantastic monsters and dragons.[4]

Interesting facts emerge about the monastery from an article written by Kazakh archaeologist A.K. Akishev. The article informs that the Sumbe monastery functioned actively in the late 1850s to the early 1860s.[5] In May 1859, it was seen by A. Golubev, who stayed in the monastery for several days and found that about 30 monks were living there. The structure consisted of a joss house. The shrine had many bells hanging from its entrance which rang with the sound of the wind. Inside the shrine were big idols perhaps of the Buddha and other Buddhist deities and their consorts.

By evening, we were back in Almaty after spending three days in the steppes of Kazakhstan and visiting the borders of China from where Highway A-312 goes to Urumqi and running through the Gansu Corridor reaches Xian. Instead of going back to the hotel, I decided to spend a couple of days on the Almaty hills just 60 kilometres from the city, at the Tay House Resort. Situated in the prime location of the State National Park, it is a tourist's delight. Dozens of multi-cuisine restaurants run round the clock, providing culinary delights from every corner of the globe.

A visit to the A.K. Margulan Institute of Archaeology, brought me face-to-face with splendid images on display from the burnt temple of Kuiryktobe in Keder. Excavations in this temple town, situated near Otrar, led by Professor Karl Baipakov,[6] brought to light amazing figures of gods. The gods sat on 'zoomorphic' thrones carved on wooden boards that decorated the temple walls. The god holding the sun and the moon in raised hands gave rise to exciting conjectures about the figure resembling the Avalokitesvara. I got curious about this temple town and tried to find out more about it and the gods who resided therein.

The burnt, yet beautiful gods on the wooden frieze, I learnt, now adorn the Museum at Otrar situated in Shauldar village. It was one among the many amazing antiquities discovered during excavations at Otrar. The figure's resemblance to a Buddhist deity evoked curiosity. The comparison was not impossible. If the Chuy Valley could be a home to the Buddha, then why couldn't the Syr and its tributary, the Arys, be a region of southern Kazakhstan ruled by the Turks in the 7th and the 8th centuries AD. Buddhism was prevalent among these Turks.

But the journey to this unique temple town on the way to Sauran, would have to be kept on hold until I had completed travels on Route 2 to the site of Talgar, in the proximity of Almaty, and on Route 3 to the sites of Kayalik and the Tekeli, both reached through the city of Taldykorgan.

References

1. Zheleznyakov, Boris. 'In Search of Ancient Sanctuaries, Nomad Kazakhstan'. No. 3, (Almaty: 2005)
2. Baipakov, K.M. 'New Data on Buddhism in Semirechye and Southern Kazakhstan'. Rtveladze, E. (chief coordinator). *India and Central Asia Pre-Islamic* (Tashkent: Academy of Arts and Academy of Sciences of the Republic of Uzbekistan, 2000), p. 96-97
3. *Ibid.*, p. 96-97
4. Akishev, A.K. and Grigorev, F.P. 'Sumbe: Buddhist Datsan in the Mountains of Shartaas'. (Made available courtesy Alisher Akisher)
5. *Ibid.*
6. Baipakov, K.M. *The Site of Kuiryktobe Town Keder* (Almaty: A.K. Margulan Institute of Archaeology, 2005)

Ivory Buddha of Talgar

I was slumped in the Air Astana seat for the second time on the Delhi–Almaty flight in 2011. This time my extensive journey along the Silk Routes had the support of the Archaeological Expertise Scientific Research Organization—the leading non-state body in the field of archaeological researches in Kazakhstan. The organization, headed by Dr Dmitry Voyakin, had provided me the essentials of a sturdy vehicle with a driver who was well informed about the routes to the ancient sites and an English-speaking staffer who was to accompany me like a shadow, everywhere and at all times, besides a lot of historical literature too. I thanked Buddha for all the help he was sending.

The flight landed in Almaty at 3 a.m. Thankfully, Assem Seitkalieva and Marat, from the above research organization were there to receive me. We drove to Assem's house on Ablai Khan Street where I spent the next three hours taking a nap and later preparing a small bag with bare essentials for a long journey from Almaty to Alakol.

At 7 a.m., we took the road to the Talgar excavation site. With the discovery of Sanskrit scrolls, sutras written on wooden bars and a rare Buddha image, it is certain that a Buddhist shrine existed here at Talgar. Here lived monks who worshipped not only the Buddha but also female Buddhist deities like Tara. During excavations, a carved image of the Buddha on ivory was found at the ancient settlement.[1] Ivory, obtained from the tusks of elephants, was not available in Central Asia but was found only in India and other African and South Asian countries. Talgar craftsmen obtained ivory from India through trade caravans on the Silk Routes passing through the Semirechiye or the 'Seven Rivers' region of south and south-east Kazakhstan on their way to China.

This was one of the most favoured routes for caravans going to China. Itinerant monks and Buddhist scholars, too, travelled on the routes passing through Talgar. Monks, believers and preachers halted at Talgar. Many of them lived in cave dwellings, several of which are yet to be explored. Archaeological excavations were carried on in Talkhiz and a fortification belonging to the head of a Turkic tribe was found on the site of the Talgar settlement, which was an important post on the Silk Road passing along the foot of the Zailisky Alatau. By the 10th century, during the rule of the Karakhanid dynasty, it became the capital of the territory.

The Semirechiye route was also the Buddhist pilgrimage route that ran along one of the branches of the Silk Road from Navaket through the Kastek Pass and reached the northern slope of the Zailisky Alatau. Through Kastek and Kaskelen, it reached Alma Ata (Almaty) and approached Talgar, a town in the Almaty province of south-eastern Kazakhstan. The route ran across the Ili river valley and through Almaliq, crossed into Xinjiang and China.[2]

On the Road to Talgar

The road was bumpy and I had to wear a support belt tightly around my waist to prevent a backache. Being early, there was not much traffic on the road. At the Ak Bulak village, the white snow peaks of the Tien Shan turned a golden colour with the rising sun. Women with big milk cans were peeping from their roadside yurts, waiting for buyers. In the village, dairy farming and cattle-breeding are the chief occupation and many men and women stood by the road holding cans of milk. Others had laid out baskets of cheese balls and bottles of kumys for sale in front of their yurts. At Kyzyl Kairat, women sat under plastic sheets selling freshly picked cherries and strawberries from their gardens. Soon, we came upon a market from where we turned right towards Talgar Culture House and headed to the excavation site in Talgar. The ancient settlement lay just on the outskirts of the village. Zailisky Alatau's magnificent peaks were close to the town and in full sight. We walked through the cobblestone path of what must once have been a monastic settlement situated in the peaceful surroundings of the valley and set amid flowing streams and redolent with the scent of wildflowers.

You might locate Talgar on the map of Kazakhstan with some difficulty, but hundreds of years ago this was the place where caravans from faraway places like India, Iran, China and Syria came to collect the best quality iron weapons and other household items. The skilled craftsmen could forge the special quality non-rusting iron that involved a rare technique of forging the strong Damascus iron from which household tools and weapons were made. It was a difficult art mastered by the smiths of Talgar with the knowledge being brought by caravans and travellers along the Silk Road, perhaps from Syria.

It is said that Talgar was one of the largest cities of the Ili Valley, situated just 25 kilometres from Almaty. According to archaeologist and director of the Margulan Institute of Archaeology, Professor K.M. Baipakov, an ivory figure of the Buddha was found in the layer dating to the 13th century, when there was a revival of Buddhism in Central Asia. The figure was badly damaged, with a broken head and arms. Two figures stood beside the Buddha. One was presumably a drummer and the other was a figure holding a shaft,[3] perhaps a chhatri or an umbrella. Significantly, murals of royal or religious processions painted on the walls of the Ajanta caves too depict drummers and chhatri-holders leading the march and the image appears to have been carved keeping this ritual in sight.

That the Buddha idol was carved on ivory bespeaks of the ivory trade between Kazakhstan and India through Semirechye and the southern Kazakhstan route. Ivory was not found anywhere close by and India is recorded as the provider of the best ivories from its centres on the western coast at Barygaza, Muziris and Nelcynda, and from the eastern parts of India that is, Orissa, and traded as far as Persepolis.[4] The ivory-carvers of India, too, were famous throughout the world. The trade of ivory was by both the land and the sea route. Indian trading stations along the Silk Road are believed to have traded in elephant tusks.

India's major centres for ivory-carving were located in Mysore, West Bengal, Tamil Nadu, Uttar Pradesh and Rajasthan. The hardness of ivory suited intricate carvings and expert carvers, just like painters, were travelling on the Silk Road to various parts of Central Asia and West Asia to decorate monumental complexes and temples.[5]

The Ivory Buddha seems to have no parallel in the Buddhist centres of Central Asia. Apart from the intricate ivory carvings found at the Begram site in Afghanistan, Buddha images made of ivory were a rarity in Central Asia.

Recent excavations in Talgar led by Professor Karl Baipakov have also brought to light Sanskrit scrolls written in the Tibetan script that appear to have been offered as an invocation to Goddess Tara. The findings highlighted by Dr Gulnara Kapekova, rector of the Zhetisu University (whom I met in Almaty around October 2013) strengthens the possibility of the presence of a Buddhist temple in Talgar, where passing monks offered written mantras on paper, wood and silk to invoke the benevolence of the Buddhist deities, including Tara.

Life in Talgar: The excavated ruins of Talgar revealed the lives of those who lived on the foothills of the Zaili sky Alatau. Here, the rolling streams brought in boulders and pebbles. Flat stone was quarried from the mountains, plenty of wood was available from the forested hills, and clay from beyond the hills. The forests were particularly large and dense enough to be able to provide wood needed for smelting iron and forging it into weapons and tools.

The streams brought down plenty of water for irrigation and people cultivated grain and oilseeds. They stored the produce in large khums (clay jars) and ground them in stone grinders to make flour. They used lamps to light up their houses from the oil pressed out of the seeds. They burned incense wood in beautiful burners to please their gods and also to fumigate/perfume their houses. Water from the mountains was stored in jars. Fowling birds, horses, cows, goats, and sheep were reared for meat, milk and clothing too. Even today, there is a horse station where horses are reared adjacent to the excavation site. A number of horses had been released for grazing on the rich pastureland of the foothills. I climbed on the broad embankment of the ruined city and watched the horses go about their daily training.

At the excavation site, there were remains of the massive gates of the ancient Talgar that once welcomed the travellers of the Silk Road who passed through the city. I later learnt that these were not gates but the ruined towers of the city walls. Below this high and broad wall was a moat, perhaps to save the city from intruders, from flooding by seasonal streams that ran down the mountains in torrents when the snow melted, from wild animals that strolled down the hills in search of prey, and also from nomads who constantly troubled the settled population inside walled cities.

Inside the walls was a vast open area, said to measure over nine hectares criss-crossed by numerous streams flowing down the mountain slopes into the grassy meadows covered with a profusion of wild yellow flowers and tall feather grass. We walked along a cobbled pathway, perhaps the ancient street dividing the city. Along this pebbled street made of boulders lay the ruins of a row of rooms. There was a separate area for the city's craft centre that produced pottery, iron implements, weapons and household items that were found by excavators and now kept in museums and at the Talgar archaeological base station. There were excellent bone-carvers who produced images of gods on bones which could be used as amulets to be worn around the neck or on the arms or perhaps carried by traders and monks on the Silk Routes. The excavators found the bone carving with the image of Buddha from the site. It is estimated that along with such a high-end crafts centre, the town occupied an area of at least 30 hectares.

According to archaeologists, the emergence of Talgar dates back to the 8th century and the city became a flourishing centre due to its skilled smiths, craftsmen and pottery-makers whose renown reached far and wide. Blacksmiths, potters, glass-makers, bone-carvers, metal processors and all kinds of handicrafts developed in the city craft centres. Caravans travelling to the Zhetisu region on its forward journey to China from the west stopped at Talgar or specially came here to buy quality weapons and household tools. In return, they traded their own wares of ivory from India, bronze mirrors from Persia and jewellery from China.[6]

Due to its position on the junction of the caravan routes, Talgar was connected both with the West and the East. It exchanged goods with West Asia, the Middle East and the eastern Mediterranean and with the countries of India and China. It is said to have flourished in the 10th–13th centuries. But life in Talgar declined after the attack by Mongol-Tartars in the 13th century.[7]

Base station: From the excavation site, we left for the base station set up in a rented house in the village. Here, large stone mortars found at the excavation site were preserved in the front courtyard. Various artefacts from Iran, India, Japan and China were found by archaeologists working on the sites. Among the antiquities were bronze mirrors from Iran, ivory chess pieces from India, and jewellery from Japan and China. Parts of plough, hoes, pitchers, serving dishes, lamps, khums, bone-carved pieces, and beautiful incense burners were also found.

Next was the nearby excavation site of Esik. On the way, I got down at the church of Talgar where a crowd had gathered for the Sunday Mass. I spotted a beggar sitting at the church gate begging for alms. People were throwing coins in his begging bowl. I was sure that going about with a begging bowl, could be a tradition from the old monastic days of the village when travelling monks went about with their alms bowls.

In the new town, there were beautiful brick houses surrounded with gardens. There was also a primary school on the way to the main road. Among the luminaries who studied here is Professor Karl Baipakov, the great archaeologist of Kazakhstan, who is now heading the A.K. Margulan Institute of Archaeology. He was born in Talgar and went to study in this school.

The Talgar river flows near the village—clear, white, milky and at great speed, bringing with it large boulders. From the bridge on the river, I watched the villagers of Talgar enjoying the luxury of bathing in the river or just sitting on boulders watching the river go by.

Monk's Cave near Talgar River

From Talgar village, we moved on to the Ile Alatau reserve forest where we halted by the side of the Talgar river in a grove of karagach, a common tree of Kazakhstan. The banks of the Talgar river and the high mountain ranges had been set aflame by the forest which was a riot of colours—from brown to deep red to a bright yellow. Autumn is the best time to be in Kazakhstan. The river running deep below in the ravines flowed swiftly, making a soft hissing sound and its water took on the blue colour of the skies, adding another hue to the forest on fire.

Inside the reserved forest, several barriers had been erected to prevent illegal poaching and felling of forest trees. It was a kind of resort where small wooden houses had come up amid the groves of wild apples for tourists. The biggest attraction was the Buddhist Cave inside the mountains of Talgar.

Gulnar Kapekova, of the Academy of Sciences, Kazakhstan, suggested that I must see the Monk's Cave of Talgar. She thought it wise to request Mariashev, archaeologist and mountaineer, to accompany us to the remote cave in the National Park. Mariashev kindly agreed. Farhat, our friend, drove us to the Ile Alatau and parked under the groves of wild apples. Mariashev, who had climbed several peaks in India and Nepal, was happy to show us the way up the river valley and into the mysterious Buddhist cave. We walked through an unbridled path strewn with wild apples. I picked up a few to taste and found them extremely sweet. We started to climb the mountains. There were no paths, only huge boulders resting precariously on top of each other and the river gushing forth in torrents. We hopped over the river several times—jumping over boulders in search of some route that may take us up the caves. Further up the mountains, we could climb only by means of a pole that we had lopped off from an old tree trunk. Mariashev held a large pole that he stretched out to us in case we floundered while climbing the steep rocks.

The last lap of the climb was very treacherous as both Gulnar and I were wearing heeled shoes. We had to be literally pulled up by old Mariashev and sturdy Farhat further up the mountains. Several times we slipped into the shallow river while climbing onto huge logs kept across the river to cut its force. The rocks were slippery as lichen and moss covered them completely. When we reached the top of the gorge, we were aghast at the deep, dark cave perched at an angle of 70 degrees on the mountain peak. It was impossible to climb into the cave as a huge load of sand flowing from its mouth had constricted the entry, leaving only a small passage.

I was shocked to find Mariashev standing at the mouth of the cave. How he reached there is still a mystery to me! He held out the long pole to support us. Gulnar managed to catch the pole. I, too, began to negotiate the wet and slippery incline. It was like one step forward and two steps downwards. We reached the top after much wriggling and prostrating on the sandy ramp. Finally, we were inside the cave.

The cave was so wide that a dozen monks could have happily fitted into it. It was pitch dark and with our hands we felt the cavern going deep inside the mountains. I guessed there might be an opening leading to the other side of the mountain which had been shut after the monks fled. Perhaps, some important documents lay there. Perhaps there was some beautiful painting on the cave walls. But the walls were dripping with ice cold water and we could easily have collected a pot in a few minutes. The monks certainly did not have to climb down to the river for water.

It was so dark inside that I felt blinded. Farhat lit a cigarette lighter while Gulnar switched on her mobile. We searched for some inscriptions which might have been carved on the rocks. Unfortunately, nothing was visible. We did not climb down immediately but sat inside the cave, thinking about the monks from Talgar who lived there.

Golden Man from Esik

Around the 5th century BC, southern Kazakhstan was inhabited by the Sakas (Scythians), a nomadic people who are considered part of the vast network of Scythian cultures that stretched across the steppes from the Altay to Ukraine. The Saka left many burial mounds inside some of which fabulous relics were found by excavators.

We drove 20 kilometres on the main road from Talgar to see the kurgans (burial sites) at Esik. Protuberances, to mark the locations of kurgans, were scattered all over the fields and along the road running eastwards. Wildflowers spread a carpet of blue and yellow over the kurgans. Several travellers had stopped their cars by the roadside to pluck the beautiful wildflowers growing all along the foothills of Almaty.

Turning off the main highway, a dirt road towards the village Berel brought us to the royal kurgan at Esik from where the Golden Man was excavated. Several families were having a picnic by the side of the kurgan; others were just relaxing in the cool mountain breeze that blows over the tombs. While some kurgans have been excavated, many lie unopened to let the dead sleep peacefully along with their belongings in the other world.

We walked to the opened burial sites where the excavators had dug out antiquities which are now kept at the Esik Museum. The site itself is like a half dugout well. From this same burial site was unearthed the famous Saka prince in 'golden attire' (belonging to the 5th–4th centuries BC) along with treasures of gold that forms the main gold collection of the National Museum at Almaty.[8] What makes them remarkable is the highly artistic craftsmanship of the jewellery that includes a magnificent headdress, a signet ring bearing the image of God Mitra, finger ring, dagger sheath with images of animals, buckles, golden bangles in the form of spiral tubes and earrings. Many of these antiquities now lie in safe vaults of the museum but are displayed during exhibitions. I did not miss an opportunity to visit such an exhibition held at the museum in the summer of 2007. The outstanding craftsmanship of the Sakas was known as the art of 'animal style'.[9] There were buckles in the form of a horse and snow leopards, brooches in the form of ibex and pins on which golden birds fluttered.

In order to see what lay inside the burial site, we retraced the dirt road to the Esik Museum where the 'golden prince' stood in full royal attire. His clothes were covered with gold plates and his high-peaked cap was decorated with the images of winged horses. Here, as luck would have it, I had a chance meeting with Betov Bekh, the archaeologist who dug the royal kurgan and revealed the Golden Man, in 1970, now the national symbol of Kazakhstan.

Betov Bekh Mohammad is now 77, the oldest archaeologist in Kazakhstan. In his 53 years with the archaeological department, he has excavated about 3000 burial sites. Betov Bekh is still working and says that he will never retire. He loves his work. It is his life and soul. He still excavates and carries his family along to all excavation sites. He has excavated the classical Buddhist temple of Kayalik and says that all artefacts found at the site are Buddhist. About the Talgar site, he is convinced that it lay on the Silk Road and someone must have brought the Buddha image carved on bone to Talgar.

I accompanied him on a round of the museum. I asked him about the inscription on the bowl of the Golden Man. He opined that there are three interpretations of the inscription: in Aramaic, Ancient Iranian, and Ancient Turkic. It means 'Blessings on the Royal Man and his children.' I returned to his room where he prepared tea. That cup of tea offered by Betov Bekh was not only invigorating but also inspiring. It was like a potion that energized my body and mind. After drinking several cups of the black tea, I stepped outside the site museum, bade Betov Bekh goodbye and sped away on the road back to Almaty.

From Almaty we had to trace Route 3, the highway northwards in the direction of the great Lake Capshagai, the new Las Vegas of Kazakhstan with its chain of casinos, resorts and luxury yachts bobbing in blue marinas. Even Las Vegas would pale in the light of the new Capshagai which I was yet to step into. I made a promise to myself: I won't gamble in the casinos. But for Buddha, I was ready to play poker.

References

1. Baipakov, K.M. 'New Data on Buddhism in Semirechye and Southern Kazakhstan'. Rtveladze, E. (chief coordinator). *India and Central Asia Pre-Islamic* (Tashkent: Academy of Arts and Academy of Sciences of the Republic of Uzbekistan, 2000), p. 96-97
2. Buryakov, Y.F., Baipakov, K.M., Tashbaeva, K.H., Yakubov, Y. *The Cities and Routes of the Great Silk Road* (Tashkent: Sharg, 1999), p. 117
3. Baipakov, K.M. 'New Data on Buddhism in Semirechye and Southern Kazakhstan'. Rtveladze, E. (chief coordinator). *India and Central Asia Pre-Islamic* (Tashkent: Academy of Arts and Academy of Sciences of the Republic of Uzbekistan, 2000), p. 96-97
4. Warmington, E.H. *The Commerce between Roman Empire and India* (New Delhi: Munshiram Manoharlal, 1995), p. 162-165
5. Thapar, Romila. *The Penguin History of Early India: From the Origins to AD 1300* (New Delhi: Penguin Books, 2003), p. 222, 299, 238-243
   Manfredi, V.M. and Halliday, Iian (trans.). *Alexander: The Ends of the Earth*, Volume 3 (London: Pan Macmillan Books, 2002), p. 180-184
6. Mamraimov, Anwar. *Sacred Places on the Great Silk Road* (Almaty

Kitap Baspasy, Almaty Ltd., 2009), p. 63-64
7. *Ibid.*, p. 63-64
   Buryakov, Y.F., Baipakov, K.M., Tashbaeva, K.H., Yakubov, Y. *The Cities and Routes of the Great Silk Road* (Tashkent: Sharg, 1999), p. 117
8. Baipakov, Karl and Bektureeva, Rosa. *Ancient Gold Collection* (Almaty: Didar Publishing Co., 1998)
9. For the Esik gold collection and other articles of antiquity see: Baipakov, Karl and Bektureeva, Rosa. *Ancient Gold Collection* (Almaty: Didar Publishing Co., 1998)

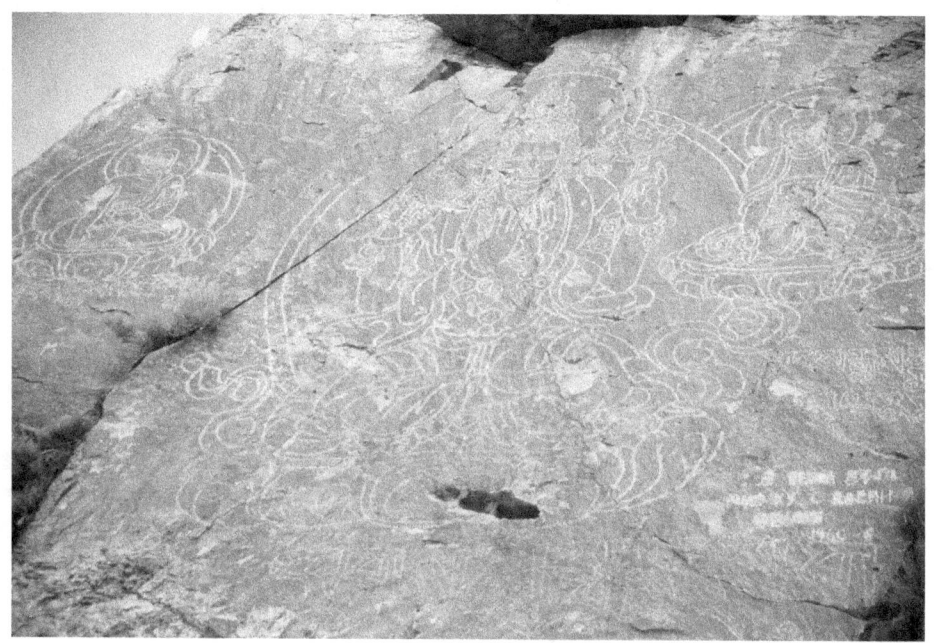

Buddhist deities carved on high rocks at Tamgaly Tas (16th-17th century AD).

Ruins of the excavated Buddhist site of Talgar (8th-9th century AD).

Image of the famous Ivory Buddha of Talgar (13th century AD).

Courtesy: A.K. Margulan Institute of Archaeology, Almaty

Stupa of Tekeli at Kara Gorge, near Taldykorgan (13th century AD).

Remains of a palatial structure found during excavations at Otrar site (9th-10th century AD).

To Kayalik in the Footsteps of Rubruk

Legend has it that in the summer of AD 1253, Rubruk (Friar William de Rubruquis) was sent as an envoy of King Louis IX of France to the Mongol court at Karakoram. Rubruk travelled through Kayalik and gave a vivid description of the 'idol-temples' in the town.[1] I was curious about the Silk Road through Kazakhstan and I did what Rubruk did—journeyed to the ancient Silk Road city of Kayalik.

Rubruk's journey took him on the road through the south of Kazakhstan—the most favoured route for Europeans travelling eastwards to China. He continued along the Chuy through Talas, crossed the Ili and went north in the direction of the town of Equius. The following day, he entered a beautiful plain fed by streams running from the high mountains and falling into a lake. He found the great city of Kayalik 'wherein was a mart and a great store of merchants frequenting it'. Rubruk stayed in Kayalik for a fortnight and mentions three 'idol temples'.

Although I was a bit confused by the names of some towns, mountains and rivers that Rubruk mentioned in his travelogue, I assumed that the modern route via Taldykorgan would approximate the ancient route which the monk might have taken. I began my journey to Kayalik from Almaty via Taldykorgan.

On the way to Taldykorgan, a long stream running alongside the road suddenly metamorphosed into a beautiful lake—the Besgash. Countless eateries had mushroomed by the lake—smoked kebabs and roasted fish seemed to be on everyone's platter. Being a vegetarian, I ignored the fish and kebabs, impatient to get to my destination. But several kilometres before we arrived at Lake Kapchagai, a stream of casinos began to dot the landscape. When I crossed this stretch four years ago, there was not even a single casino. Now, they are everywhere. I read the neon-lit names: The Flamingo, Prince, Ritz Palace, Alladin, Princess, Zodiac... The stretch seemed like a mile straight out of Las Vegas. The serene beauty of the Kapchagai that I had visited in 2007 had been marred by the paraphernalia of a modern world. I preferred the old, quiet, sleepy Kapchagai.

Near the lake, the road branched off to Baqanas, the eastern arm going to Taldykorgan that was 177 kilometres away. At Sarigozek village, the steppes had borrowed the red and purple tinge of the wild flowers. I was distracted by the Genghis Khan mountains, where, it is said, the Khan gathered his troops and strategized the battle at Otrar with his generals. The Khan is dead. The soldiers are no more. Now, thousands of sheep and goats occupy the land that once resonated with war cries.

Near Ainabulak village there was a cemetery with tombs covered under beautiful domed houses. Near Terekty village, we crossed the Balykbi river and turned right towards Taldykorgan, barely 14 kilometres away. A little further we came to the bridge over the fast-flowing, wide Koksu river. On the other side of the Koksu, big arched gateways announced the town of Taldykorgan.

At Taldykorgan, Gulnara Kapekova was waiting for me at a restaurant. We chose to sit in the open colonnaded verandah amid a lovely rose garden for an evening meal and to discuss our plans for the next two days. She proposed that the following day, when we returned from Kayalik, we must go to the forest near Taldykorgan to gather mushrooms. That was exciting! I was full of glee at the prospect of gathering mushrooms and exploring the dense forests. I immediately agreed to this plan scarcely realizing that after a hectic journey to and from Kayalik, I would be too fatigued for mushroom-picking. Alas, I had a long, long journey before me. I had to forget all about mushroom picking.

Buddhist Monastery

After dinner, I was on the road again. Kayalik was 250 kilometres further away from Taldykorgan and I expected to reach the village after midnight. Since there was hardly any traffic on the road going to Alakol, we could gather speed on the highway. The night was moonless and pitch-dark as we drove at breakneck speed. At Sarkent, we stopped only for fuel and drove on the seemingly unending road to the village of Kayalik, where we arrived at 2 a.m. I wondered how Marat could steer through the narrow winding village road to get to the destination. I do not know how, but I slumped on the seat and fell asleep. I woke up when Marat honked at Vladimir's gate. I was not hungry. I only wanted to hit the sack, so Vladimir's wife took me to a cosy room. I slept like a log, waking up only when the hens in Vladimir's backyard created a ruckus at the break of dawn. It was barely 5 a.m.

We sat down for breakfast in the dining room that lay adjacent to the kitchen in a separate building in the campus of the base station for the excavating team. Vladimir's wife had prepared a sweet porridge of rice and milk. There were eggs, bread and homemade apricot jam along with some apple juice. Soon, we left for the excavation site with Vladimir. Since he worked with the excavation team, he knew every bit of the place. After winding through the village, we stopped our vehicle near a wheat field and waded through wheat grass to the Buddhist Temple of Kayalik.

According to Professor K.M. Baipakov, head of the A.K. Margulan Institute of Archaeology, and Dr D.A. Voyakin, head of the Archaeological Expedition Scientific Committee, conducting the excavations at Kayalik, the remnants of a Buddhist temple were excavated during the archaeological researches, conducted in the Antonovka old site (a locality named Kayalik lying in the valley of the Lepsi river).[2] The temple was built of adobe bricks; its floor made from kiln-brick. On the corners were massive half towers that are still visible. At the centre of the temple was found a square hall—a sanctuary surrounded on all sides by corridors which was blocked on its south-eastern part where it was separated by a wall. Probably the chest or an altar that G. Rubruk saw in one of the temples must have been inside such a central hall or sanctuary. Behind the chest, Rubruk informs us, was an image with wings.

The entrance to the temple must have been a grand structure as it is said to have been decorated with two broad pylons placed onto stone blocks. Although there is no trace of the pylons, we still have the account of Rubruk who mentions a practice by the priests of pitching a long pole in the portals to announce that herein lay a temple.

Describing the rites and ceremonies of the idol temples, Rubruk says that the priests 'worship towards the north and clasping their hands together, and prostrating themselves upon their knees upon the earth and holding also their forehead in their hands. The priests of the idol temples have their heads and beard shaven and were clad in saffron-coloured garments. Once shaven, they practised celibacy. About 100 to 200 of them lived together in a convent. They read softly from books and also carry in their hands strings with 100–200 nutshells upon it like the rosary and utter the words "Ou mam Hactani" (Om mani pade hum).'[3]

Rubruk's description of the heathen temple, beyond question, point to its Buddhist character and this is confirmed by the description of the celebration provided by G. Rubruk, says Baipakov. Rubruk writes: 'When I entered the heathen temple, I found the idolaters' priest there. It happened on the first day of the month, when priests put on their vestments, arrange incense, raise lamps and accept the offerings from the people, consisting of bread and fruits.'[4]

During the excavations, big khums, fragments of a jug with a beak shaped like a bull's head, were found on the floors of the central hall and corridors. The ceramics found there date back to the 12th–13th centuries. Among other findings were a metal dagger, metal details of a door and small bronze items.

A Church and a Dacha

From the Buddhist temple, we ventured down to the main road going to Alakol and again turned left into a narrow road near a graveyard a little ahead of a large stele on which the name of the village was written in Russian. It was a part of village Kayalik. This place was probably occupied by the church of Kayalik and visited by Rubruk. But the area was thickly populated with large trees and shrubs that prevented entry from any side. Excavations to look for the ruins of the church mentioned and visited by Rubruk in 1253 could not be made without large-scale deforestation of the area.

We went past the church area along a pebbled road and arrived at the ancient gates of an old habitation. The ruins of the gates appeared like two big mounds. Inside, we came upon an old Russian cottage, also called a dacha, where some decades ago a Russian family had been living. The area surrounding the dacha was an orchard. We know this from the apricot and peach trees that still remain at the back of the house.

The dacha, the horse stable and the cow pen in front were in a shambles. I was tempted to enter the dacha. The floor was wooden and the roof was low and thatched. There were three rooms inside and in a corner of the front room lay a mud oven full of grey ash as if the dacha owners had just left. I touched the ash and felt its warmth. The walls made of reed were peeping from behind its plaster of mud and lime. The wooden beams of the roof were lying exposed. The water tank that once conveyed a steady stream of water could still be seen sitting on a mound of mud. The dacha was dead.

From the dacha, we went down to the Lepsi river and stopped at the old bridge. After taking a few photos of the sweeping river from this vantage point we drove to the Lepsi hydroelectric project that supplies continuous power to Kayalik and the surrounding villages.

The wide expanse of the river had been dammed and the water falls at a great height, becoming almost white with speed.

In winter, the river is frozen but the power generation does not stop as the water freezes only at the surface. Underneath, it still flows at great speed.

By the time we returned to the base station at Kayalik after visiting the excavation site, it was noon. Vladimir's wife had prepared a special kind of stuffed momos for us. Called varenic, it was triangular in shape and stuffed with boiled potatoes. We prepared to leave for Taldykorgan and Vladimir presented a small piece of pottery found at Kayalik as a parting gift.

A Bollywood Dance

By 2 p.m., we finally left for Sarkant, the district headquarters of Taldykorgan, which is 50 kilometres from Kayalik. This time we walked down to the river. I chose a big piece of rock to sit on while Assem dipped her hands in the river and sprinkled some water on her face. The river comes from the melting glaciers of the mountains and there is no sand on its bank; only black debris from the mountain rocks.

Thereafter, we drove non-stop to Taldykorgan and arrived at the Kabanbai Square at about 7 p.m. where we waited for Gulnar at the Independence Park. She arrived in her SUV driven by Farhad, her secretary. She announced that the evening dinner was at the house of Farhad's brother where his niece, a college-going young girl would perform a dance number from Bollywood. We drove to Farhad's house which was like a palace. Here, his brothers and their children, sister and sister's children, father and friends and his beautiful niece Firoza were eagerly waiting to receive us.

The lively gathering soon turned musical. The grandfather picked up his dutar and played a song. Firoza followed with a dance sequence from a Hindi film. Food followed in courses. There were heaps of watermelon, grapes and delicious apples on the table. Farhad's brother had heard of the superb Indian handmade silk that acted like a medicine on the body. I told him about the famous handmade non-mulberry silk of Sualkuchi village in Assam and the Bhagalpuri silk of Bihar.

After dinner, we left with Gulnar to Taldykorgan and spent the night at her house. It had been four days since I had a bath and my chance finally came in Gulnar's bathroom with its hot shower. As I sat under the water, my eyes drooped with sleep. Soon, I was lying half dead on Gulnara's plush bed. Early next morning, we had to leave for Tekeli to see the mysterious stupa which is said to have appeared on the river Karatal from nowhere.

To the Stupa of Tekeli

From Taldykorgan, the drive to Tekeli is barely an hour. It sits at the foot of the Dzhungarsky Alatau mountains straddling the Chinese border and home to the famous Tian Shan brown bear. Three rapid rivers meet at Tekeli—the Kora, Shizhe and Tekeli—that together form the Karatal which is one of the 'Seven Rivers' of the Semirechiye/Zhetysu region and only second to the Ili. It flows through Taldykorgan and empties into Lake Balkash.

The road goes along the Karatal river which was on our left. The journey along the river was awe-inspiring. The small village, whose inhabitants are mostly Russians, has mostly wooden houses with courtyards. The climate is suitable for fruit cultivation as plenty of fruit orchards could be seen along the road. It is also a mining town and most of the settlers were miners extracting zinc, lead and iron-ore from the earth. Tekelinka, a small river, flows close to the village. It is one of the three rivers that flow into Karatal; the other two being Kara and Chidze.

There is only one street in Tekeli which winds its way through the river valley and turns into a pebbled track along the river as it travels through the gorge. A wooden bridge made of wood planks helps pilgrims, travellers and motorists to cross to the other bank of the river in order to reach the stupa. The mountains are populated with wild animals and Gulnar herself once shot a bear who attached her, while those accompanying her tried to hide themselves behind bushes.

Snow-covered peaks, thick spruce forests, fast-flowing streams and emerald meadows welcomed us as we drove through a narrow path along the Karatal and in the midst of high mountain slopes. We crossed the wooden bridge and reached the other side of the Karatal where a winding road took us right to the Buddhist stupa built on a massive piece of rock. No one knows where and when this stupa came from. Gulnar believes it must have fallen from the towering mountains amid which a village lies. For several kilometres, all around the stupa, there was no other structure of which the stupa could have been a part. Gulnar belonged to the mountains of Tekeli and lived near the Kara Gorge. She was an expert on Tekeli and so I believed her. I hazarded a guess, though. Maybe some passing pilgrim or Buddhist Mongols settled in the area, carved out the stupa from the massive piece of rock that had fallen off the mountains in some remote antiquity because no one had seen any temple or monastery on the other side of the high mountains.

There is an inscription in Sanskrit immediately above the engravings which is said to date from the 18th century.

At the back of the stupa, a hollow in the rock is filled to the brim with reddish water which is said to have never dried up. It is the holy water of the stupa. I guess the red colour of the water comes from the iron deposit of the rock itself. We climbed from the backside of the rock on the steps in-built or cut into it and reached the hollow. The climb was steep and I needed help all the way to the top. I recited a mute chant and sprinkled some water on myself. We descended from our perch after praying to the blue sky, the earth and the river that flowed close by. Farhad collected some firewood and lit a fire while Gulnar began a mysterious chant, replete with blessings, I was sure. After straining my ears, I could make out a few words: 'san sia oi nakh pan na pai tun dou...' We repeated after her. The chant reached a crescendo, the fire burnt brightly, the tip of the flames flowed into a thick smoke that reached up the stupa. Gulnar grabbed my hand and all of us joined to circumambulate the fire amid chants. Finally the chant ended and Gulnar explained that the 'sky and the earth are one whole and we are a part of this whole'. She said it was a Sanskrit mantra. I decided to find out about it when I returned to India.

Trek to the Kara Gorge

Our trek to the Kara Gorge, the source of the river, was full of adventure. On the way I saw a large spotted snake warming itself on a rock. It did not move even when I approached it. I wanted to photograph the reptile but discovered through the lens that it was dead and lying motionless on the rock. All around the high mountains grew wild apples, apricot and cherry bushes bursting out of crevices in the rocks. Here and there, wiry streams dripped down the rocks and a variety of wild flowers were blooming in glorious profusion. I photographed over a dozen sweet-smelling, aromatic plants and a variety of wildflowers.

The climb became steeper and the path to the gorge became narrower, made up of sharp pebbles. Gulnar informed me that during World War II, the Japanese had built a tarred road along the gorge, perhaps to surprise the Chinese on the border which is quite close by.

A few kilometres later, we halted our trek and retreated to the bottom of the gorge where the forest guard Gazeez was waiting with a bunch of the aromatic bushes 'birioza' tied up like a broom for Gulnar. It was a medicinal plant that helps maintain proper circulation of the blood and clear out toxins if rubbed into the body. Gulnar was quite enthusiastic about it. Gazeez, Ak Mohd's son, who was our guide had also collected some papyrus wood. Ak Mohd invited us to his forest hut to have some tea and sweet buns. We were hungry and readily accepted his offer. His hut had all the modern facilities: a water filter, electricity, an oven and a warmer, when it snowed.

He had one bedroom and a large hall to entertain travellers. In his backyard was a vegetable garden and hatchery for a daily supply of eggs and vegetables. His hut overlooked the entire Karatal Valley and the stupa. The Kara made a deafening noise and rushed like a white milky river. The water of the Kara was not muddy but clear and bluish green with splendid white streaks where the speed was obstructed by some boulders.

Ak Mohd had planted new trees of birioza in his garden and I guessed there was a demand for the medicinal plant. The apple orchards in his terraced garden were laden with green fruits. I knew he was the happiest old man with the river, the mountains and the stupa as his companions. His children and wife stayed in Taldykorgan and seldom came here. Yet, Ak Mohd looked a happy old man in the company of wild nature.

Worshipping a Tree

It was 11 a.m. when we returned from our trek to the source of Karatal river—the gorge from where the melting glaciers flowed down at maddening speed. At the Tekeli stupa, Assem and I had hopped into Gulnar's splendid SUV with cushioned seats. Farhad drove fast to the full blast of English music. We had to reach Almaty by 2 p.m. A distance of 200 kilometres in three hours! Gulnar appeared a little serious, not her usual self. A little less cheerful, a bit sombre. I thought I knew the reason. Her plans of collecting mushrooms in some forest near Taldykorgan had been cancelled. Though I would have loved such an adventure in the jungle, there was hardly any time to squeeze such a programme.

I thought of Aalia who had prepared a nice vegetarian lunch for me and I was dying to fly into Almaty for lunch. But Gulnar, was not one to be serious for long. She had other plans for us. Near Taldykorgan, the car slowed down and stopped near a huge karagach tree. Here, a crowd had gathered to worship at the base of the famous karagach tree popular for its magical qualities. Many travellers had stopped here and were drawing water from a nearby stream. Gulnar led me to the stream. We dipped our hands in the icy waters and drew some of it to moisten our eyes and face. Then, both of us wrapped a coin into a piece of cloth and tied it to a branch of the tree. We mumbled a prayer and expressed our secret wishes.

Even in Buddhist times certain trees were worshipped as they are now. It is said that holy spirits reside in them and fulfil the wishes of all those who pray there. After praying at the base of the tree, we all started feeling sleepy. Gulnar turned to one side on her front seat and put her feet on the dashboard near the gear box and started snoring. I thought this would cause inconvenience to Farhad but he was driving merrily with huge black goggles over his eyes. I was unable to read his expression. We all had munched too many melon seeds and its relaxant oil was causing drowsiness. All of us could hardly open our eyes. Gulnar slept throughout the journey to Almaty. I was awake and had eaten away all her melon seeds which she had bought at Taldykorgan. Many villages sped by and I recorded the names of most of them. The road was good and there was not too much traffic. We did not stop at Almaty but drove on straight to Medeu.

We skirted the skating rink and turned into a narrow lane shaped like a snake and stopped before a palatial house. This was Aalia's house, a palace with a massive front mosaic and marble courtyard and steps leading to a porch. We drove straight into her front yard, parked the car and reached the reception lobby where Aalia waited for us. Lunch was already late and we were led straight to the dining table. We asked Aalia about the Buddhist Monastery at Medeu mentioned in the Berzin Archives. She knew nothing about it. Alisher, whom we had earlier met in Almaty, had heard about it but had never seen it. We gave up the idea of searching for the monastery and instead, chose to see the statue of Mahatma Gandhi at the National Park in Almaty. The Mahatma, in black marble, was holding a long walking stick. I sat near the statue and explained to Assem and others the essence of the teachings of the great saint and how with non-violence he had managed to save the country from British colonialism. Farhad went to buy ice cream for all of us and we sauntered in the park licking the ice cream sticks and watching children riding remote-controlled cars and their mothers running after them.

At a Yurt in Kaskelen

It was 7 p.m. when we left Almaty for Kaskelen, about an hour's drive towards the west. The snow-laden Zailisky Alatau gave us company. The traffic was heavy and we arrived late. Gulnar (whom I named G-2), the beautiful Kazakh film actress and a friend of Gulnara (G-1, my friend) was waiting for us in her huge white yurt—a restaurant that was set up in a real nomad's camp. It seemed Gulnara was a loved name in Central Asia as during my sojourn I had come across, in my close association, at least four Gulnaras.

A swing rocked by the side of the yurt. A big oven had been set up at the entrance that was glowing red with burning charcoal. Beside it lay a pile of neatly cut and spiced meat ready to be roasted into delicious shashik. A young man was piercing a skewer into the meat and spraying some oil over it.

A pleasant air blew into our face and the atmosphere became very pleasant. We had been travelling since morning from Taldykorgan and the cool breeze was like a balm. Words were sent to Gulnara that her guests had arrived. She came out, her arms outstretched to receive us. We were like long-lost friends meeting after a long time.

Her profession as an actress had not nurtured any arrogance or pride in her. She appeared humble and soft-spoken. She led us all into her yurt where a dozen tables had been laid out for evening guests as her restaurant had become a hot favourite among the city's elite. The drink of the evening was kumys (fermented mare's milk). And the special dish was beshbarmak—sheep's head, cooked for special guests. We toasted with kumys and danced to Bollywood songs. Gulnar and Gulnara gyrated. I followed their footsteps.

From above, the skies stared inside the yurt; the moon and the stars shone upon us as music played and we gyrated to the rhythm of nature and Bollywood. The kumys made us tipsy; there was a revival of energy, much depleted through long journeys on the Silk Route. Kumys is the drink of the Central Asian Silk Route.

It has nourished and revived many a travellers over the centuries. It brought memories of the princesses from the Chinese kingdom who married a Turk kaghan and drank kumys and ate sour meat, perhaps cooked under the seat of a horse-riding nomad. But the meat served on this table was hot, cooked well and garnished beautifully with coloured vegetables. There was *boursac, beshbarmak, qazy* and *karta*, all traditional Kazakh cuisine.

I being a vegetarian had vowed never to touch meat. But the sheep's tongue snatching and eating was a national tradition and I thought I should go by it. Gulnar, the actress, was on diet and had to lose some weight for her next film. She did not put a morsel of food in her mouth but accepted some kumys and salad. At 45, she was astonishingly beautiful and young. She had never married. She showed me the large posters of her recent films.

Gulnar opened the sheep's mouth, found its tongue and sliced it. I had to grab it from her hands and throw it in my mouth at one go. I managed to do all this with great speed. After this, we drank kumys and ate all kinds of meat, vegetables and rice dishes. It was a great evening as all of us sang our own songs and walked a little unsteadily.

It was midnight when Gulnar dropped Assem and me in Almaty and sped away after a tearful goodbye and a promise to meet in Dushanbe next October. Early morning, we had to catch a train to Shymkent. Instead of falling on the bed, I sat on the wooden floor of Assem's room, packing a bag for another long journey on the Shymkent–kyzylorda section of the western Silk Road.

The territory occupied by the modern city of Kyzylorda in the south-west of Kazakhstan, once formed the branch of the east-west corridor from China to the Mediterranean that skirted the Aral Sea after passing through the city and joined the Caspian route to Astrakhan. All river traffic on the Syr Darya, flowing from the Tian Shan mountains to the Aral Sea, crossed the city of Kyzylorda.

I was to scratch this Route 4 from Shymkent and travel up to the city of Sauran located just south-east of Kyzylorda.

References

1. Hakluyt, Richard, Raymond, Charles, Giovanni, Beazley, Van Ruysbroeck, Willem. *The Texts and Versions of John de Plano Carpini and William De Rubruquis: As Printed for the First Time by Hakluyt in 1598, Together with Some Short Pieces* (London: Cambridge University Press, 1903), p. 228-229
2. Baipakov, K.M. and Voyakin, D.A. *Medieval Town Kayalyk* (Almaty: Ministry of Education and Science of the Republic of Kazakhstan, A.K. Margulan Institute of Archaeology, 2007)
3. Hakluyt, Richard, Raymond, Charles, Giovanni, Beazley, Van Ruysbroeck, Willem. *The Texts and Versions of John de Plano Carpini and William De Rubruquis: As Printed for the First Time by Hakluyt in 1598, Together with Some Short Pieces* (London: Cambridge University Press, 1903), p. 228-229
4. Baipakov, K.M. 'New Data on Buddhism in Semirechye and Southern Kazakhstan'. Rtveladze, E., (chief coordinator). *India and Central Asia Pre-Islamic* (Tashkent: Academy of Arts and Academy of Sciences of the Republic of Uzbekistan, 2000), p. 95

Journey to Sauran, Turkistan and Otrar

On the last leg of my Silk Road journey, I was to take the Shymkent–Otrar–Turkistan–Sauran route in south-western Kazakhstan. For hundreds of years this had been a popular route for Westerners going east towards China. For Europeans travelling to the Zhetysu region of Kazakhstan, to the Chu Valley of Kyrgyzstan or to the Karakoram region of present Mongolia, this was the most favoured route running through the valleys of the lower Syr Darya, Chu and the Ili rivers. Even in modern times, the land route from Russia to Kazakhstan, Kyrgyzstan and China and railway lines in the east–west corridor approximate to the caravan path of the ancient Silk Road.

Whether or not there were Buddhist settlements on this popular Shymkent–Sauran route is difficult to say as no concrete evidences have been found so far. But we do learn of the Buddhist site of Sairam, near Shymkent. Sairam was visited by Hiuen Tsang on his way to India and was mentioned in his memoirs, the *Si Yu Ki: Buddhist Records of the Western World*.

In Search of a Buddhist Complex at Sairam

The Buddhist ruins near Sairam, also called Ispijab, lay at a distance of some 30 kilometres from the Khorlug village near Shymkent. This was a popular route along the northern Silk Road on the Shymkent–Tashkent road. *The Cities and Routes of the Great Silk*

Road, mentions that the road from Tashkent went through Turbat and Ispijab to Taraz in the Talas river valley. Northwest, a branch road from Sairam ran to Otrar, joining the route along the lower Syr Darya river to the Aral Sea.

The Ispijab–Taraz route was known to travellers since the time of the Turkic rulers in the 6th century. It was in 568 AD when Turkic Khagan Dizabul received a diplomatic embassy of Justin II from Byzantine headed by Zemarkh who arrived in Taraz in order to make a war alliance with the Turks against Persia.[1]

Ispijab was also known as the 'town on the white river' by the Chinese and identified with Sairam. It was one of the largest trade centres on the Silk Road, drawing merchants from all over Asia. Many merchants had set up their permanent trade houses and caravanserais in Ispijab from where they exported slaves, arms, fabric, metals like copper and iron and swords.[2]

We have records of Hiuen Tsang's route to Sairam on his way from Suyab in the Chu river valley. While coming to India, the Chinese monk Hiuen Tsang entered the town of 'Peh-shwui'/Ispijab/White Water. This, he says, is six or seven li (a Chinese unit of distance, approximately half a kilometre) in circuit and the agriculture and climate are both superior to Taraz.[3]

After reaching Shymkent by the Almaty–Shymkent Express train, I drove along the Aksu river and crossed several villages before reaching Sairam in search of the Buddhist monastery. I thought it would be easy to find the ruined monastery but everyone I met was utterly ignorant about any such ruins. The search proved to be a long one as I stopped at a dozen places to enquire about the temple and retraced the road going left and right into the hills but still found no sign of the monastery.

Although the Buddhist temple had been mentioned by archaeologists who excavated the site, few people seemed to have seen the site or knew about the Buddhist temple along the Aksu. Once, I even stumbled upon the mausoleum of Saint Ibrahim Ata. Not finding it anywhere nearby, I offered a short prayer at the mausoleum and returned to the main road to trace the ruins again. Finally, I thought of enquiring about the site from the Sairam Museum. But it had been closed for the day just half an hour ago. Only the guard was there. He, too, was oblivious about the monastery.

In October 2011, I again visited the site of Sairam village on the way from Otrar to Shymkent to catch a train to Almaty. I was informed by my colleagues at the Otrar Conference that the excavated temple site belonging to the 6th or 7th century lay somewhere near the Ibrahim Ata mausoleum on the high hill adjacent to it. This time I was accompanied by my colleague Nurseit of the Otrar Museum and we reached the Ibrahim Ata site straightaway. At many places, we found heaps of old brick work on the high hills and on the low ground, at the back of the mausoleum amid thick, bushy growth. We later visited the Sairam Museum to check the antiquities that were excavated from the Saiyram site. These included huge pottery khums which must have been used for storage of grains, carved stone pillars, stone bath tubs and mortars that were probably used by the inhabitants of the town.

Much later, I met Professor Baipakov in Almaty and asked him about the Buddhist ruins in Sairam which he had mentioned in his article. He informed me that the structure collapsed long ago and nothing remained of the ruins.

Professor Baipakov in *New Data on Buddhism in Semirechye and Southern Kazakhstan, India and Central Asia-Pre-Islamic* had mentioned a monument belonging to the 7th–8th centuries, that may probably be connected with Buddhism found at Sairam village on the terrace of a hill, on the banks of Kzyl-Su river. A long narrow corridor led through a circular or a drum-like structure (tambour) to a room with vaulted ceiling. A cluster of rooms were also found lying adjacent to the corridor. Fragments of pottery, including pieces of pots and khum, and bronze items were excavated from the temple site.[4] Much of the antiquities found have been preserved at the Sairam Museum. To me, the Buddhist temple still remains a mystery.

Indian Workers at Sauran

We also learn of the close connection between south-western Kazakhstan region and India, especially at Sauran where Indian labour is recorded to have been employed by rich landowners. While writing about the existence of karez (underground water channels) near Sauran, the 15th-century Tajik historian Makhmud Zainaddin Wasifi mentioned, in his *Amazing Events*, two wonderful karez at Sauran, built with the help of 200 Indian slaves employed by one Muslim Sheikh Mir Arab. They were so amazing that people had not seen anything similar to it in the entire world.[5] This is not surprising as along with bulky goods, agricultural products and cotton textiles, thousands of Indian slaves were sent every year to Central Asia, especially during the Mughal rule in India.[6]

The Sauran oasis lay at a distance of about 250 kilometres by road from Shymkent. On the way to Sauran, I passed dozens of villages along the highway going west to Kyzlorda. Dark clouds were gathering over the horizon and it seemed it would rain. I clutched my camera and wondered how I would shoot the ancient cities of the Silk Road. Already the light was insufficient for photography. My worries were forgotten when I saw herders on the steppes. Wearing long hats and heavy boots they were out on their horses accompanied by ferocious watch dogs. Behind them ran a long trail of sheep and goats being put out to graze on the shrub-covered steppes.

The Arys flowed past Temirlan village and all along the river bank lay forests of poplar and an unending belt of fruit orchards, long elephant grass and wild trees and shrubs. Massive road construction work was going on at Temirlan to widen the Shymkent–Kyzlorda Road into a four-lane drive. Heavy rollers were parked in fields and hundreds of labourers had been pressed into road repair. The highway going north-west is an important route and connects with the Aral Sea and the road into Russia.

Near Tortkol village, the road branched left towards Otrar. However, we took the road going straight towards the grape farming town of Iskan towards Koktal where the Karatau mountains suddenly came into view. There the wide expanse of the steppe lands and the dark mountains was enlivened by the train running to Atyrau on the Caspian. As we approached Shaga and Baltakol on the Karachik, we came face-to-face with the 'train of the steppes'.

Sauran fortress was not far from there and after a short distance we took a left turn through a rough shrubby path. The dry river bed of the Ashalgat river (or was it some canal from the Arys?) was the only evidence that once a water source flowed near the fortress. Railways ran close and by the time we came to the Sauran bridge, two kilometres away, two trains had already passed.

At the fortress, massive excavation work was going on. Loaders were pushing trolleys of mud from the ditch around the fortress. Huge ancient gates had been revealed in the digging. A wooden ramp had been built over the deep, wide moat to cross into the fortress.

Sauran was known as one of the strongest fortresses in Turkestan. Besides being a large farming district, it was reputed for its 'incalculable wealth' and was a major centre of trade and ceramic production.[7] Early travellers described it as a city with seven walls.[8] However, it is believed to have been taken by the Mongols without a fight. The neighbouring Otrar was badly ravaged and turned into a ghost town by the Mongol armies. Sauran became one of the principal cities of the White Horde of the Juchi Ulus inherited from his father Genghis Khan. The central city of the White Horde was originally on Lake Balkash but later moved to Sygnaq, which later came under the control of the Shaybanids. It is here that one of the rulers of the White Horde and the grandson and descendents of Genghis Khan named Sasibuka was buried (1309–1315).[9]

The magnificent six-metre high, massive walls of the Sauran fortress tell a tale of its glorious past. It encloses a vast area (roughly 40 hectares); on the top of the wall runs a broad pathway along which guarding soldiers could walk. Built from the special clay of Sauran they are still in a particularly good condition and appear sturdy.[10]

A team of Kazkh archaeologists led by Professor K.M. Baipakov have, during their excavations at the site, revealed the structures of a madrassa and a mosque connected by a cobbled path. Baked bricks, remains of a tandyr (oven), heating systems, patterned ceramics and dishes were unearthed during the excavations.

It is said that Sauran competed with Turkestan and Otrar, the biggest cities on the Syr Darya, but suffered destruction from rival rulers of neighbouring states. It suffered irreparable damage and the mosque and madrassa were completely destroyed during the Djungar conquest of the Syr Darya region in the 17th century and was reduced to a small settlement, and by the 18th century disappeared completely.[11]

A walk inside the fortress led me to a flat area and a terraced incline reaching up to the high walls. This terrace enabled soldiers, in an emergency, to run up the wall within seconds. A pleasant air blew from the Black Hills although it was the hot month of June. I tried to visualize the kind of life that existed inside the city, the kind of trade that went on or the goods that passed through the town.

I climbed up the high peripheral wall of the fortress to have a bird's-eye view of the entire landscape of the oasis and the ruins that lay inside the walls. There were cobbled pathways and massive columns of bricks from which it seemed that there might have been several gateways for entry into the city. A heavy populace was once living inside the walled fortress —the Khan, the warriors, the slaves and the traders. Perhaps an entire city lived within the walls!

The view outside was dull and drab. The steppes appeared parched and devoid of any greenery. No water body existed close by. I was therefore amazed at the flocks of fattened sheep, so big that they looked like cows, scattered all over the landscape, nibbling at dry shrubs. Perhaps, hidden from my eyes, a small stream or a canal flowed nearby and contrary to what I had seen; there was no shortage of fodder for the animals. Sauran must have profited by the trade in wool from its special breed of sheep.

It was at Sauran that I happened to find another connection

with India. This link was Ilgysar. I was fascinated by his love for Rishikesh and the Himalayas. Ilgysar had even rented an apartment on the banks of the Ganga river and lived in Rishikesh for a year as a disciple of Swami Gyan Sagar. At the ashram, Ilgysar practised yoga and lived the life of an ascetic. He grew his hair and tied a bun. Did he attain peace and salvation? I asked him. Yes, said Ilgysar. I wondered why he left that peace and returned to a mundane existence in the steppe lands of Kazakhstan.

'Second Mecca' for Muslims

Sixty kilometres flit past in a jiffy and I had to take a U-turn from Sauran to Turkestan and head to the splendid mausoleum of the 11th-century Sufi saint Khoja Akhmed Yassavi, a dervish, founder of the ascetic brotherhood of Yasavia. The 40-metre-high mausoleum, which is now on the UNESCO list, had intricate blue geometrical patterned tile work. Set amid orchards and rose gardens, the ribbed central dome built of turquoise tiles hanging right over the mausoleum's central hall is said to be the largest in Central Asia.

The town came to be known as the 'second Mecca' for Muslims. Legend has it that at age 63, the Sufi saint Akhmed Yassavi took 'samadhi' like the Indian sadhus and retired to an underground cell, never to see the light of day. Some say that he had no wish to remain alive longer than Prophet Mohammad who, too, died at age 63.[12]

After circumambulating the outer periphery of the mausoleum and spending some time at the brick sardoba in the vast courtyard outside, I entered through the front door. Here, I picked up a head scarf from a basket, removed my shoes and entered the Central Hall. The lofty interiors of the hall or the jamaat khana rose up in a huge column on which the central dome rested. Under the dome lay a huge metal cauldron weighing two tonnes. An alloy of seven metals, it was made on the instructions of Amir Timur. The inscription on the 3000-litre cauldron identified the name of the craftsman who created it: Abdulgazi ibn Sharafuddin. Other inscriptions informed us that the kazan/cauldron for water was a gift of Timur and the year of creation as 1399.[13] It was learnt that the first mausoleum over the saint's grave was very modest and became dilapidated with time. A new one was constructed by Timur after over two centuries.

A corridor led visitors to the tomb of the great saint where a maulvi sat behind a stone screen chanting verses from the Holy Koran. It was very cool and peaceful near the tomb as a pleasant, fragrant breeze blew through the corridors. In the mausoleum complex there were two other mausoleums—one of the Kazakh leader Esim Khan and the other of Rabi Sultan Begum, daughter of Ulugh Bek and wife of Uzbek leader Abul Khair Khan. There were other interesting structures in the complex like the domed bath house and a Juma Mosque on a high ground near the ancient walls of the citadel.

Gods and Goddesses of Otrar

I wanted to sit longer at the great saint's feet, but another destination awaited me—Otrar, 75 kilometres from Turkistan, an oasis spread along the confluence of the Arys and the Syr Darya. It was part of a 'natural corridor' between the Karatau mountain ranges and the Kyzlkum desert through which the ancient Silk Road passed. Today, the highway from Shymkent to Kyzlorda and beyond to the Aral Sea approximates to this corridor.

Otrar is believed to have emerged as early as the 1st century BC and was one of the largest centres of trade, agriculture, science and education in the middle Syr Darya region of Central Asia. The great philosopher and scientist of the Islamic world, al Farabi, was born in the village of Vasij in AD 872.[14] The museum at Shauldar village preserving the excavated antiquities of the Silk Road towns of the oasis, has been named after the scientist and his statue adorns the front gardens of the museum.

Nearly 2000 years ago, numerous settlements emerged in this

fertile oasis of the present city of Otrar, of which only mounds now remain. The largest and the most important settlement is said to have been the high mound of Otrar-tobe, once a grand town comprising a fortress on the hilltop.[15] There were trade centres and craft industries which together with the residential district covered a vast area of about 200 hectares.

Walking to the back of the excavated site, I climbed a high mound that appeared like a hill and approached the ancient structure where several rooms of a palace-like building and open courtyards had been revealed. Some underground structures could also be seen through gaps inside the floor, proving that the revealed structure was multi-storeyed or at least a double-storey.[16] Excavations led by eminent archaeologist, Professor Karl Baipakov were carried out at the sites of Kok Mardan, Mardan Kuik, Pshuk Mardan and Kostobe and important antiquities that were unearthed have been preserved at the Al-Farabi Museum at Shauldar village.

Soon, I was in Kuiryktobe-town Keder where a temple had been excavated. This had been identified as Keder, which was the main town of the Otrar oasis, perhaps its capital. Excavations at Keder led to the unearthing of a palace structure made of paksa (clay mixed with straw and horse hair) and raw bricks that dated between the 7th and 9th centuries. The citadel was gutted in a fire. Ceramics, terracotta figures of 'fravashis' (protector of souls), having 'hooked noses and almond-shaped eyes' were also recovered.[17]

In the 'Parade Hall' of the citadel were found carved wooden panels (now displayed at the Otrar Museum) that decorated the walls of a temple and featured magnificent images of the gods and goddesses, the royal couple, sirens on wooden beams and fantastic animals. According to Baipakov, the image of sirens was widespread in ancient and medieval art. The Kuiryktobe sirens, he found, were similar to images of sirens depicted on the stupas of Sanchi and Bharut, in the grottoes of Bamyan and on the carved ivory items of Begram. These mythical creatures represented the 'Kynara and Kynari' in Hindu and Buddhist texts, says Baipakov.[18]

On one of the boards were the images in a frieze of a couple of idols sitting on 'zoomorphic' thrones and worshippers at the foot of the thrones; the image holds the sun and the moon in raised hands. As auspicious symbols depicted frequently on the top of Buddhist tantric paintings, the sun and moon signify the protective function of the deity.

The wooden frieze is evidence that the sun and moon deities were worshipped in Central Asia. The Maheshvara (a form of Lord Siva) is sometimes depicted as holding the sun and the moon discs. In Buddhist art, the Avalokitesvara is depicted as holding the sun and the moon discs. The attribute is also believed by scholars to be a reference to a deity's association with tantric meditation. Emperors in India also drew their lineage from the solar and the lunar race—the Suryavanshi and the Chandravanshi rajas. The carved wooden sculpture of the above mentioned gods and goddesses of Keder town appears burnt but the image is clearly visible.

The Royal Couple

A scene decorating the surface of another board portrays a royal couple who appear to be involved in some kind of ceremony—perhaps a marriage. The royal lady wears a cloak. A bejewelled diadem crowns her head and her long, plaited hair falls on her shoulders. Her ears are adorned with earrings from which hang oval droplets. Her neck is decorated with a necklace. The face of the man is badly charred. His headdress is in the form of a band. He wears a loose gown wrapped around his shoulders. The couple are in an embracing posture as they grasp each other's hands. They are flanked by persons offering them trays of fruits or other eatables.

'Crawling Snake' on Vessels

One of the khums from the Kokmardan settlement displayed at the museum was eye-catching. It had a snake crawling on its surface. It reminded me of the serpents on the Annau (Dragonite) mosque near Ashgabat in Turkmenistan. Banu, a museum official, informed me that many mud vessels for storage called 'khum', excavated from Kokmardan village, had the motif of the 'crawling snake' pressed on their surface. This was intriguing. The serpent seemed to have some kind of protective role in the life of the inhabitants, that it was the custodian of the wealth of the vessel and of the family. It could also be an incarnation of some deity as it symbolized abundance and protection from evil forces.

The museum also displayed a 'rare orange bead' from India, providing evidence of the Indian trade with the south Kazakhstan–Otrar region.

At Otrar, I wanted to pay obeisance to Arslan Bab, the great saint and guru of Khoja Akhmed Yassavi and whose 12th-century mausoleum lies in Otrar, close to the excavation site at Otrar-tobe. Beautiful trees had been planted along the entrance path to the mausoleum. Painted white with intricate work on the façade, the mausoleum was also a bird house where hundreds of swallows had made their home of mud and straw. The small museum inside the mausoleum had ancient, handwritten copies of the Holy Koran belonging to the saint. Two pillars in the museum hall were from the days of Arslan Bab. In the adjoining prayer hall was an ancient carved wooden canopy resting on pillars. This pillared hall was where pilgrims could find a place to rest for a few moments.

Genghis Khan and Timur at Otrar

In the 13th century, the marauding army of Genghis Khan shattered the peace of this magnificent and prosperous oasis. A trade delegation dispatched by Genghis and headed by an Indian was 'mistaken' for spies and massacred at this frontier town of Otrar by the governor, Inalchuq of the Khorezmian ruler Sultan Mohammad II.[19]

The oasis recovered quickly when Timur made it his base. On his way to China, Timur camped in Otrar in 1405 somewhere on the land that is now covered by the village Temir/Temirlan. Here, death overtook him and snatched away his dream of conquering China. This famous camp station of Emperor Timur was also the place where Nurseit, my friend, lived. The village was only five kilometres from Shauldar and I took the main road going to Shymkent, and turned right just five kilometres before Shauldar. A road sign on the highway announced the village of Temir. At the entrance was a modern senior school for children. The branch road that passed through the village terminated at the Temir railway station.

At the back of the railway station were old houses and a huge water tank more than a century old. I took a round of the small railway station and spent some time inside the cosy waiting hall to have a feel of the village and wondered what it was like in the days of Timur. Surely, there was no village here. Only a vast camp of warriors living in thousands of yurts camped along the Arys river while Timur himself must have camped in one of the numerous citadels of the Otrar oasis.

On the River Arys

It was lunchtime and I had to reach the archaeological base station located on the Arys river for a meal. While driving to the village I spotted wild, single-humped camels running along the road. Some were resting in the open steppes, munching on the thorns and wild bushes. Soon, we turned towards the river at village Shauldar and stopped on the river banks in front of an old house that had been turned into the archaeological base station. There were several rooms around a big courtyard.

The beauty of the Arys river, the sweetness of the village and the pretty little cottages covered with vine creepers and red roses blooming in the courtyard had all turned the base station into a picture-perfect site. Here, Yule and Julie, members of the archaeological team came out to welcome me. Jamila, an employee of the base station had cooked a steaming hot lunch. The dining hall was a huge place with long tables and a running kitchen where food was served round the clock for the excavating staff and scientists, diggers and geologists. We were led to the dining hall where food had already been laid. Delicious fresh and roasted fish from the Arys river, the main dish, was on the table. There was homemade apricot jam and peach marmalade to be had with bread and chai.

In the mornings, Jamila would cook a lovely steaming shorpa served with homemade bread and sunflower sweets. She smiled as I took her photos while cooking inside the kitchen which she strove to keep very clean. In the evenings, I walked along the river bank watching the Arys changing colour from bluish green to a glowing orange from the last rays of the setting sun. A cold wind swept over the banks and the wild vegetation swayed as I sat shivering on the low stairs of the verandah that ran along the outer walls of the ancient house. The backyard led through a pathway amid an orchard and tall poplars to the main museum building.

My room at the Shauldar village base station was cosy with a small bed and clean linen. Jamila had taken care of everything. The nights were extremely cold and windy. At night, wind howled at my windows and whistled through branches of the apricots in the courtyard. It played with the leaves which danced and fluttered and were scattered all over the house. Only the small rose bushes stuck to the colonnaded verandah and stayed still. I would switch on the heater. Now and then, Jamila would peep in and ask in Russian if I felt cold. Even before I could answer, she would hand me a cup of hot tea from her ever-burning samovar or give me an extra-thick quilt.

At Kokmardan Village

At Otrar I accompanied my friends Banu and Gulfam to the nearby village of Kokmardan to enjoy the bounties of Gulfam's rich farm and to have a peep inside a Kazakh village market. The small weekly bazaar of Kokmardan was overflowing with grains, poultry, fish, fruits and vegetables from the nearby Arys. There were multi-coloured bell peppers, brinjals, carrots, onions and potatoes. Canisters of sunflower oil were also brought for sale. Across the road was the animal market. Several truckloads of fodder grass and cattle-feed had been off-loaded here. Buyers were dragging and pulling out stout animals from their enclosures as they refused to leave their masters, making a lot of hue and cry. I bought nothing from the market, yet returned with lots of fruits that the women had given as gifts to a sister from India.

Before I left Otrar, I went to the base station with a heavy heart to say goodbye to Jamila. She was packing some boiled eggs, toast with apricot jam and sweet buns for my long journey. I bid her farewell and planted a last goodbye kiss on her cheeks. Chengizi was waiting with a taxi at the adjacent museum and I left with Nurseit for Shymkent to catch an early morning train to Almaty. It was the last time I ever took a walk along the Arys river. For the last time I saw the beautiful flowers blooming on the banks and the purple feathers of the wild grass growing there. Otrar haunted me always.

Excavations at Khorlug Village

I drove back to Shymkent, 130 kilometres away to spend a night at Khorlug village, at half an hour distance from the station. Here excavations were in progress on the periphery of the village to unearth an ancient city. The sun was still lingering over the harvested fields near the site. I climbed on to the elevated ramp-like structure which I guess could have been the walls of the rooms unearthed during diggings. What I got to see below the walls was really amazing. There was a set of rooms with terracotta and stone floors in which were embedded decorated jars set at a 30-40 degree angle. Surprisingly, they were plain from outside but beautifully designed on the inside. I had never seen a jar like that. The corrugated, wavy, lined and ribbed inner surface meant that the design was not for decoration but for a practical purpose.

What could it be? Were they used for crushing something? Juice of fruits, plants or leaves? The gradient floor of the rooms on which the huge jars or khums were embedded lead through an opening or gully to another place, probably a storage tank. This meant that the ingredients from the jars were carried through the sloping gullies to a tank. It must have been some kind of liquid residue from crushable fruits or leaves. Interesting! Several such designed jars were lying embedded in the floor of the revealed structure.

Last Night in Kazakh Village

It was 8 p.m. when I returned to Khorlug village from a trip to Sairam with Miram, an archaeologist working with the Archaeological Expertise Scientific Committee, headed by Dr D. Voyakin. The sun was still an orange ball, still setting. The day's journey had been long and tiring. Nevertheless, I was happy that I had covered the part of the Silk Road going west towards the Aral Sea—the western route of Kazakhstan. I had covered nearly 600 kilometres on a round trip from Shymkent to Sauran, Turkistan, Otrar and Sairam and was now back at Khorlug village, near Shymkent.

The base station for excavations in Khorlug had been rented in a private village house. A huge amount of pottery discovered at the site had been stored in special yards. The house was quite large with a massive courtyard in the centre of which was a high mound that covered the source of underground water. The wooden floor was covered with thick woollen carpets woven by the women of the family. The old lady, grandmother of the family, handed me a small rug and a pillow. I spread it next to her and lay down. What a comfort after a tiring journey! I thanked the lady and flopped down on the thick rug.

The staff of the excavating unit was spread out all over the courtyard and verandah, sitting in groups, going about their chores and discussing the activities of the day. All were in the mood to relax after a hard day's digging at the site. After dinner, compiling and collation of data would be done in the computer room set up in one part of the house.

It was still not quite dark after dinner was over. I did not wish to go to the women's dormitory to sleep. I set out on a walk through the lovely village for my picture book. The main street of the village was a broad pebbled road. Flocks of sheep were returning home. Their long ears swinging along their neck, their body heavy with curly hair, brown, white and black, they raised a lot of dust as they hurried to their pen.

As the evening progressed, it became pleasantly cool. A soothing breeze from the Aksu blew over the village. After loitering aimlessly for over an hour through the village, I finally went to the dormitory to sleep with the women staff. I had to reach the Shymkent station at 5 a.m. to catch the early morning train to Almaty. I lay down on a makeshift bed on the wooden floor of the dormitory where six more beds had been arranged in a row.

I closed my eyes for a quiet accounting of the day's events. I thought about the great saint Yassavi and his times when Islamic preachers spread the faith through love and education. Of Timur, who built the splendid mausoleum and wondered why it was left unfinished.

In my dream, I found the ruins of the Buddhist monastery at Sairam that had eluded me so far. Suddenly there was a glimpse of the Buddha in a 'bhumisparsh' mudra seated beneath a huge tree—the Bodhi tree. Beside the ruins flowed a river, probably the Aksu. I was elated at finding the Buddha at last after a long, long search. He was smiling at my perseverance. No one from my group was around me. Assem and Hamit were still climbing the small hilly tract in Sairam. I called out to Assem to hurry up to the ruins. She was happy to find the Buddha sitting peacefully beneath the giant tree. Suddenly, someone was shaking me by the arm. The alarm was ringing. It was 4.30 a.m.

It was still dark outside. Even the early birds were dozing. With the help of a small torch I opened the main door of the dormitory and went to the backyard to use the toilet. The black dogs were sleeping below the mound on a heap of grass. I tiptoed to the water pipe to fill a kettle, scared to wake them up. The lady of the house had lit a wooden fire and was already preparing breakfast for the excavating team which left at 5 a.m. every morning to the Khorlug site.

Miram dropped me to Shymkent. I felt choked saying goodbye to the beautiful villages in the land of Kazakhstan. And to the historic Silk Road snaking through the enchanting landscape of the Kazakh steppes along the Syr Darya. While the train slowly chugged along eastwards back to Almaty, I thought of the hundreds of Indians who had travelled along this road to their destination in Sauran where they laboured in the subterranean wells to bring water from the Syr or mountain springs to irrigate the king's vineyards. How they came so far on the road leading to the Aral Sea is intriguing. Did they come of their own volition? Were they slaves or labourers sent by their rulers to their kith and kin living in the territory of what is now southern Kazakhstan? One thing is certain. That in the days gone by, Kazakhstan and India were not places that were poles apart. And that Indian traders and workers could travel anywhere in the world to sell their wares and labour. While many returned to their native places, many settled in foreign lands, married the locals and raised families. It was heartening to note that many Kazakhs whom I met on the Silk Road might actually be Indians settled long, long ago in Kazakh lands.

The night slowly melted away. The darkness of the skies merged into a hint of a glowing morning. The train was still chugging along somewhere in the suburbs of Almaty. Within a few hours, I would catch a flight to Delhi with the Silk Road of Central Asia behind me.

References

1. Buryakov, Y.F., Baipakov, K.M., Tashbaeva, K.H., Yakubov, Y. *The Cities and Routes of the Great Silk Road* (Tashkent: Sharg, 1999), p. 100

2. *Ibid.*, p. 100
3. Tsiang, Hiuen and Beal, Samuel (trans.). *Si Yu Ki: Buddhist Records of the Western Country*, Book II (Delhi: D.K. Publisher Distributors Pvt. Ltd., 1995), p. 29
4. Baipakov, K. 'New Data on Buddhism in Semirechye and Southern Kazakhstan'. Rtveladze, E., (chief coordinator). *India and Central Asia Pre-Islamic* (Tashkent: Academy of Arts and Academy of Sciences of the Republic of Uzbekistan, 2000), p. 93, 95
5. Sala, Renato. *Underground Water Galleries in Middle East and Central Asia* (Kazakhastan: Institute of Geology, Academy of Sciences of Kazakhstan), p. 9
   Mamraimov, Anwar. *Sacred Places on the Great Silk Road* (Almaty Kitap Baspasy, Almaty Ltd., 2009), p.218
6. Levi, Scott (ed.). 'Indian Merchants in Central Asia: The Debate'. *India and Central Asia: Commerce and Culture (1500-1800)* (New Delhi: Oxford University Press, 2007), p. 126
7. Raina, Radha. *Echoes of a Distant Past India and Kazakhstan*. Public Diplomacy Initiative by the Government of India (New Delhi: RHI Printographics, 2010), p. 46
8. Mamraimov, Anwar. *Sacred Places on the Great Silk Road* (Almaty Kitap Baspasy, Almaty Ltd., 2009), p. 209
9. *Ibid.*, p. 219
10. *Ibid.*, p. 212, 216
11. Baipakovs, K., Zheleznykov. *Nomad: Kazakhstan*. No. 6-06-2005
12. Mamraimov, Anwar. *Sacred Places on the Great Silk Road* (Almaty Kitap Baspasy, Almaty Ltd., 2009), p. 196-197
13. *Ibid.*, p. 199
14. Buryakov, Y.F., Baipakov, K.M., Tashbaeva, K.H., Yakubov, Y. *The Cities and Routes of the Great Silk Road* (Tashkent: Sharg, 1999), p. 109
    Baipakov, K.M. *The Site of Kuiryktobe-Town Keder* (Kazakhastan: Almaty Ltd., 2005), p. 79
15. Baipakov, K.M. *The Site of Kuiryktobe-Town Keder* (Kazakhastan: Almaty Ltd., 2005), p. 80
16. *Ibid.*, p. 87

17. *Ibid.*, p. 82
18. Baipakov, K. 'New Data on Buddhism in Semirechye and Southern Kazakhstan'. Rtveladze, E. (chief coordinator). *India and Central Asia Pre-Islamic* (Tashkent: Academy of Arts and Academy of Sciences of the Republic of Uzbekistan, 2000), p. 95
19. Weatherford, Jack. *Genghis Khan and the Making of the Modern World* (New York: Three Rivers Press, 2004), p. 106-107
   Hartog, Leo De. *Genghis Khan: Conqueror of the World* (New York: I.B. Tauris Publishers, 1999), p. 103-104

Epilogue

Largest Buddha Sleeps in Afghanistan!

Afghanistan's sensational search and exploration of the Bamyan caves for the world's largest Sleeping Buddha, measuring 1000 feet, has caused much excitement in the Buddhist world.

If we go by the words of the Chinese pilgrim Hiuen Tsang, who was present at the congregational ceremony held by the Buddhist king of Bamyan, the Buddha colossi is not a figment of imagination. The pilgrim visited Bamyan in the 7th century AD, and mentioned in his memoirs that he saw the amazing Buddha sleeping in the mountains of the Hindukush.

Both *Si Yu Ki—Buddhist Records of the Western World* and *The Life of Hieun-Tsiang by the Shaman Hwui Li* (Trans. Samuel Beal), recorded that in Bamyan:

'To the north-east of the royal city there is a mountain, on the declivity of which is placed a stone figure of the Buddha, erect, in height 140 or 150 feet....To the east of this spot there is a convent....To the east of this convent there is a standing figure of the Sakya Buddha made of metallic stone, in height 100 feet....To the east of the city 12 or 13 li there is a convent in which there is the figure of the Buddha lying in a sleeping position, as when he attained Nirvana. The figure is in length about 1000 feet or so.'

If the description by Hiuen Tsang of the two Standing Buddha colossi is accurate, then even the 1000-feet Reclining Buddha must exist somewhere in the rubble of the Bamyan mountains.

Such a massive image of the Sleeping Buddha could not have been transported to any temple unless it was built block by block like the 100-feet Standing Buddha mentioned in the records of the pilgrim (*Si Yu Ki*). And no shrine hall or courtyard could accommodate such a gigantic image. The Buddha was perhaps carved out of a big mountain just as the gigantic Kailash temple (Cave 16) of Ellora, 30 kilometres from Aurangabad (India), was carved out of the rocks. This astonishingly beautiful masterpiece of rock-carving today dominates the landscape of Ellora much in the manner that the giant Reclining Buddha of Bamyan did during the 7th century. So far, the Kailash cave is believed to be the largest monolithic structure in the world hewn from the rocks by 7000 stone masons over a period of 150 years.

Professor Zemaryalai Tarzi, renowned Afghan archaeologist and an expert on the giant Buddhas, continues his search for the colossus Buddha as he is convinced of the accuracy of Hiuen Tsang's memoirs.

Earlier, Professor Zemaryalai Tarzi and his team is said to have discovered the remains of a 19-metre 'Sleeping Buddha' along with other relics in the mountains of Bamyan.

If found, the 1000-feet image will be much larger than the Sleeping Buddhas anywhere in the world. Today, the largest Reclining Buddha, measuring 34.5 metres, lies in the great hall of the Dafosi temple in China. At Kushinagar (India), the image of the Reclining Buddha measures only six metres. At Ajanta Cave 26, the Buddha measures roughly five metres (20 feet). In Kyrgyzstan, the image found at Krasnaya Rechka, measuring about 8 metres, was taken away to The Hermitage at St Petersburg. The only intact Reclining Buddha now existing in Central Asia lies at the National Museum of Antiquities at Dushanbe. The 12-metre-long image was found in a corridor of the Ajina Tepa monastery in the Vakhsh region of Tajikistan.

Waiting to hear from Afghanistan!

Acknowledgements

In Afghanistan

Dr Omarakhan Massoudi, director general of the National Museum, Kabul, for permitting me to photograph the Buddhist objects recovered during excavations and their publication in this book. Chief curator, Fahim Rahimi for providing a detailed history of the exhibits.

Dr Nicolos Engel, vice-president of the DAFA, for information about the Mes Aynak site.

Doctorsahib Gen. Musa Wardak, Mrs Fauzia Wardak and Ehsanullah who provided food, shelter, and a home to me.

Vivek Katju, without whose help I could not have ventured into Afghanistan.

Gautam Mukhopadhyaya, Indian Ambassador at Kabul and the officials and staff of the Embassy for facilitating my tour to the Buddhist sites.

In Tajikistan

Professor R. Massov, director, Institute of History, Archaeology and Ethnography of the Academy of Sciences and Dr S. Bobomulloev, director, National Museum of Antiquities, for permitting me to photograph the Buddhist objects at the museum in Dushanbe and their publication in this book.

To Zarina Khasanova of Pamir Travels and Gafurov Mirshohid, who planned my journey to the Buddhist sites.

Army Headquarter Shahrituz for permitting my journey to Ushtur Muller and Takht-i-Sangin.

In Turkmenistan

The Institute of History, Academy of Sciences, Ashgabat, for inviting me to attend the 2011 conference on 'Ancient Material Culture of Turkmenistan'.

To Professor Muhammat Mammedow, chairman of the Department of Protection, Research and Restoration of Historical and Cultural Sites, Ashgabat, for permitting me to photograph the Buddhist antiquities and ivory rhytons displayed in the halls of the National Museum at Ashgabat and the State Museum at Mary and their publication in this book.

In Uzbekistan

Dr Ismailova Jannnat Khamidovna, director, State Museum of History, and Dr Vasila S. Fayzieva, director, State Fine Arts Museum, for permitting the use of photos of Buddhist objects in the present book.

Zakirjon Mashrabov, director, Babur Foundation, for inviting me to Tashkent and Andijan in 2007 and 2013.

Shukrat Usmanov of Advantour for helping in organizing my Silk Road journey in 2007.

In Kyrgyzstan

Professor Bakyt Amanbaeva, head of the Sector for Study of Cultural Heritage of Kyrgyzstan, Academy of Sciences, and Dr Elena Poppova, for making available important museum photos from the Chuy Valley.

To Professor Baumer Christopher for permitting me to use the report on excavations at the Novopokrovkaby Society for the Exploration of Eurasia and photos of Buddhist objects found there.

Bhargav Mitra of the Indian Embassy for providing important photos from the Chuy Valley.

In Kazakhstan

Professor Karl M. Baipakov, member of the Academy of Sciences and director, A.K. Margulan Institute of Archaeology, and Dr Dmitry Voyakin, head of the Archaeological Expertise Scientific Committee, for providing all logistical support for my long journey along the Silk Road through Kazakhstan in the summer of 2011.

Professor Gulnara Kopekova, rector, the International Jetysu Institute and State Institute of Archaeology, for providing me shelter in Taldykorgan and accompanying me to the stupa of Tekeli.

Assem Seitkalieva and Marat, who drove hundreds of kilometres with me to the remote Buddhist sites of the Almaty region.

Nurseit of Otrar Museum, who accompanied me on a search of the Buddhist site at Sairam, and which we failed to find. Banu and Gulfam from the museum at Otrar, who provided me a home in their village Kokmardan.

Archaeologist Alisher Akishev, who accompanied me on a tour from Almaty to Zharkent in 2007. Shepherd Feroze who guided me to Taygak gorge to see Buddhist inscriptions.

In India

The India–Central Asia Foundation for including me in the Central Asian Motor Rally, 2013.

Kapish Mehra, managing director, Rupa, for publishing my three consecutive historical travelogues on the Buddhist sites.

Ritu Vajpei-Mohan, commissioning director, Rupa, for accepting my manuscript and her valuable guidance

Rakesh Dwivedi for accompanying me on a rough journey

through difficult terrain in Central Asia.

Sneha Gusain for her work on the book. Preeti Verma Lal for a first critical reading of the manuscript and K. Renu Rao for pointing out blunders.

Ritu Topa of Arrt Creations for designing the map and making my travel route through Central Asia.

B.B. Kumar for advising to keep the text as simple as possible.

www.ingramcontent.com/pod-product-compliance
Lightning Source LLC
Chambersburg PA
CBHW051622230426
43669CB00013B/2154